THE INTERNATIONAL SOCIETY FOR METAPHYSICS
STUDIES IN METAPHYSICS, VOLUME III

PERSON AND GOD

Edited by

George F. McLean
Hugo Meynell

UNIVERSITY
PRESS OF
AMERICA

Lanham • New York • London

INTERNATIONAL
SOCIETY FOR
METAPHYSICS

Library of Congress Cataloging-in-Publication Data

Person and God.

(Studies in metaphysics / the International Society
for Metaphysics ; v. 3)
Includes index.
1. God. 2. Religion—Philosophy. I. McLean,
George F. II. Meynell, Hugo Anthony. III. Series.
Studies in metaphysics ; v. 3.
BL473.P47   1988   211   88–161
ISBN 0–8191–6937–4 (alk. paper)
ISBN 0–8191–6938–2 (pbk. : alk. paper)

All University Press of America books are produced on acid-free
paper which exceeds the minimum standards set by the National
Historical Publications and Records Commission.

THE INTERNATIONAL SOCIETY FOR

METAPHYSICS

DEDICATION

This volume is dedicated to the memory of Prof. Richard M. Martin whose life of work in the field of logic showed the highest genius and creativity. As can be seen from his chapter in this volume, "On Some Theological Languages," the broader concern of his work was life itself, up to its highest realization in life divine. Like Descartes, he felt that logic can now make possible significant advances in Metaphysics and even theology.

The presentation of this paper in Jerusalem, which Prof. Martin considered in some ways the culmination of his service in philosophy, occasioned intensive debate with Prof. John Findlay. That interchange was reflected by Richard Martin in his "On Philosophical Ecumenism: A Dialogue," which has been added as a fitting appendix to the present volume.

Prof. Martin has pointed the way. He presents an inviting challenge to a younger generation of philosophers to develop the similar combination of professional perfection and personal peace required to follow the pathways he pioneered.

ACKNOWLEDGEMENT

Grateful acknowledgement is made to The State University of New York Press at Albany for permission to reprint R.M. Martin, "On Philosophical Ecumenism: A Dialogue," Chap. VIII of *Primordiality, Science, and Value* (Albany, New York: State Univ. of New York Press, 1980), pp. 120-136.

INTRODUCTION

Classically, human understanding of oneself and of one's relation to nature has been founded upon an awareness of one's relation to the divine. Though diversely understood, this has constituted the source, the goal and the deepest meaning of Being. As such, it has provided the basis of personal dignity and the inspiration to strive for a life of harmony with others in justice and peace.

Many developments, in philosophy and beyond, have opened new possibilities for understanding the implications of this for all facets of human life. Often, however, they have implied an emphasis upon either the immanence or the transcendence of the divine in a manner difficult to conciliate one with the other. Further, issues implied in the resultant notion of progress have raised anew questions concerning the nature of God. In turn, in the West this has implied a renewed concern for the meaning found in earlier Eastern and Western religious philosophies. In developing, as will as technologically advanced, societies this has raised the question of the presence of God in all dimensions of human life.

The present volume presents a study of these issues by The International Society for Metaphysics (ISM), hosted by Dr. Nathan Rotenstreich at the Israel Academy of Sciences and Humanities in Jerusalem. It begins by situating the study of God in relation to metaphysics, religious experience and logic. This is followed by a search of the great religious and metaphysical traditions for their sense of the divine. In this light God is studied as the source and goal of all, and consequently as the context for human freedom in time and eternity.

This is the last volume in the ISM series on the person. It follows other works on *Person and Nature*,[1] and *Person and God*[2]. Upon completion of these studies the ISM undertook an intensive series of investigations regarding society, and its issues of unity, truth and justice, and the good. It extended these two series on person and society to the field of culture and cultural heritage understood as personal creativity in community and in history. Together, they constitute an effort to promote the development of metaphysics as a living discipline in our day.

NOTES

1. George F. McLean, ed. (Washington: University Press of America and The International Society for Metaphysics, 1988).

2. George F. McLean and Hugo Meynell, eds. (Washington: University Press of America and The International Society for Metaphysics, 1988).

TABLE OF CONTENTS

Introduction

PART I

METAPHYSICS AND GOD

CHAPTER I

GOD AND THE PROBLEM OF BEING

IVOR LECLERC

INTRODUCTORY: THE ISSUES

We today have arrived at a juncture of thought at which both the question of God and the question of being require basic reconsideration. Contemporary scientific development has necessitated the latter, and this has inevitable implications for the question of God.

Besides that, in our time it has become easier to see that in respect of God the ontological issue runs up against peculiar features and also singular aporiae. For example, the question can significantly be raised, whether God exists--by contrast with other areas of inquiry, in which it would not be significant to ask whether man, or nature, or society exists. In these areas the pertinent questions would be, what is man? what is nature? what is society?; that is, the issue is concerning the ontological status of man, etc., the kind of being which is to be accorded to man, etc. Earlier ages raised the question of the proof of the existence of God, but not whether God exists. That the later question has become common in our time makes it more readily appreciable not only that there is a singular significance about the question, namely that it can significantly be raised, but that the question itself is singularly problematical.

What exactly does the question entail? What does "exist" mean respecting God? Historically the verb "exist" and the abstract noun "existence" arose from a need terminologically to distinguish "*that* it is" in contrast to "*what* it is." So to ask whether it is or exists entailed that the "it" in question be something able to stand out or forth, appears manifest itself. This implied, primarily, that the "it" be a "being" which is the "subject" of "what," i.e., of properties or attributes--the latter "existing" only in a derivative sense of the properties *of* the being as subject. The question facing us is whether the terms "exist" and "being" can consistently and coherently be used in the same sense with respect to God as to natural beings. This is an old issue in the history of philosophy, but it is facing us today with renewed urgency and puzzlement.

This issue has a twofold aspect: one is ontological and the other is categoreal. These are, however, closely interconnected, and neither can be tackled in disjunction from the other, nor can one be taken as unquestionably prior to the other; on the contrary, they intrinsically involve each other. The recognition of this is especially crucial in regard to the question of God. This point needs special emphasis, for not only is there a long and powerful tradition that the fundamental category is "being" --that is, what is ontologically primary is "being," and that it is this which is categorially the subject in thought, so that whatever is the subject is categoreally "a being"--but with regard to God this tradition has in this century received an interesting and emphatic reaffirmation by Whitehead in his *Process and Reality* with his proclamation that: "God is not to be treated as an exception to all metaphysical principles, invoked to save their collapse. He is their chief exemplification."[1] Accordingly Whitehead explicitly maintained that God is to be conceived as an "actual entity" or *res vera*, categoreally no different from any other actual entity or being.[2] This tradition, however, cannot today be simply accepted as a presupposition; it has to be critically examined and justified. For to accept it as an unexamined presupposition constitutes begging the issue which we have seen to be crucial today.

The question now is how we are to proceed with regard to this ontological and categoreal issue. It is evident that fundamental in this is "being," and accordingly that the prime requisite is clarification with respect to "being." The requisite clarification is not simply one of the meanings of the word, for as we are concerned with it the word occurs only as a term in philosophical thought; so what we are up against is "being" as a philosophical *problem*, and one of singular profundity, difficulty, and complexity. In tackling this problem it will not suffice to take, or to seek to clarify, the conception of being in any contemporary philosophical theory of system. For, in the first place, it is precisely every such conception which it is necessary to subject to critical scrutiny. Secondly, every such conception stands in the inheritance of some two millennia of ontological thought, involving different theories and thus divergent meanings of "being," much of which has come in the course of time to acquire the status of tacit presuppositions; consequently the adequate clarification of contemporary conceptions of being necessitates that these presuppositions be brought fully to light and scrutinized. In this we have one of the greatest difficulties involved in the inquiry into the problem of being.

In view of this difficulty it seems to me that the best, most satisfactory, and perhaps the only effective way to tackle the problem of being is by an historical inquiry. For, by examining theories of being in their origin and development we can most readily become clear as to what is included in them and thus what has come to be inherited in subsequent generations of thought. The historical procedure is, however, fraught with a crucial difficulty. It is all too easy, as the history of philosophy amply testifies, to interpret earlier thought in terms of current conceptions and presuppositions, and to do so involves completely frustrating a main purpose in adopting the historical approach, viz., to bring to light current presuppositions. It is accordingly highly important for the inquirer to be specially on guard against such insidious anachronisms. Of course the difficulty will not thereby necessarily be eliminated; but it can be significantly diminished and, in the course of critical scholarship, overcome.

The historical inquiry into being is unquestionably a considerable and complicated task, to be fittingly undertaken in a lengthy monograph and not in a brief paper. All that is possible here is the presentation of some conclusions which are the outcome of such an inquiry.[3]

ORIGIN AND DEVELOPMENT OF THE CONCEPT OF "BEING"

For the origin of the concept of "being" we have to go back to Parmenides. It is true that *to on* and *ta onta*, as Jaeger has said, were used from the very beginning of Greek natural philosophy in the sense of things immediately and tangibly present.[4] But it was Parmenides who for the first time became aware of the philosophical import and implications of the words. The question of how and why he was brought to that awareness, highly relevant as it is, cannot be entered into here. For us now the point is that he discovered the singular significance of saying: *esti*, "it is"--not, "it is something-or-other," i.e., using the verb in its usual copulative function, but in a distinctly new sense; and that he went on to bring out the implications entailed in that new sense. These implications, Parmenides saw, were entailed in the Greek verb "be" *per se*.

This becomes clear by an examination of the verb. Fundamentally relevant here is that the Greek verb *einai*, "to be," stands in contrast to, and excludes, "becoming"--which is expressed in Greek by an entirely different and unrelated verb *gignomai*, having the primary meaning of "to be born." In a recent highly important and detailed study of *The Verb 'Be' in Ancient Greek*,[5] Charles H. Kahn has shown that in this 'is exemplified a basic feature of the Indo-European verb **es-*, namely, that it functions to express "the stative aspect, by which it contrasts with verbs meaning *to become, arrive at, get,* and the like."[6] This stative value is especially strong in Greek, for in this, as Kahn points out,[7] "almost alone among European languages, the stem **es-* has remained rigorously durative, admitting no aorist or perfect forms like *fui* and *been* in the conjugation of *eimi*." His investigation reveals "that the typical or primordial use of the verb is for a living creature or more especially a person as subject (as is always the case in the first- and second-person forms); and that the verb itself indicates a station or position of that person's body at a given moment or over a certain stretch of time."[8] Thus the verb "indicates the extrinsic position or presence of the person in a given place. If no place is specified, the verb alone may indicate simply that the person *is present* somewhere or other, i.e., *is alive* (at a given time)."[9] From this analysis it becomes clear why the Greek verb "be," in addition to its primarily copulative function, also has locative, vital, and veridical uses,[10] and that it has the fundamental sense of "presence."[11]

This fundamental sense is what Parmenides clearly saw: what is, is *now present*. Therefore what is not there, present (e.g., the Pythagorean void) simply "is not" at all. Further, since the verb "be" excludes "becoming," what is must be all complete, what it is, now in the present. Parmenides having brought to philosophical consciousness what basically is entailed in the Greek verb "be"--viz., that what is, *to eon*, "a being," implies its immediate presence and its exclusion of all becoming--this determined subsequent ontological thought till Plato, and beyond.

Advancing from the new philosophical approach of Socrates, Plato concluded that it was necessary to admit *duo eide ton onton*, "two kinds of things,"[12] but he was then faced with the problem of what was entailed in saying that both are "*onta*." Evidently they both were *onta* in the sense of "things present"; but when account was taken of what is entailed in the verb "be" as established by Parmenides, it became clear that only that kind which is *eidos*, "form," since it alone was without becoming, could be regarded as *on alethes*, "true being," as *to ontos on*, "beingly being."

Plato was responsible for a further, most important advance in respect of the concept of being. For this he adopted and adapted the word *ousia* to a new philosophical meaning. The ordinary meaning of *ousia* was that of "property, possession, what is one's own."[13] The argument in the early Dialogues establishing the *eide* (forms) sometimes required Socrates to make the point that things have each their individual form, whereby they are distinguished as each that particular thing, and that this meant that the individual form is *idios*, "its own," pertaining to that individual itself, and he began using the word *ousia* to express this, thereby generalizing the meaning of property, possession, as what is "one's own," "proper to," "exclusively individual to," beyond what is ordinarily considered "property."[14] In this context *ousia* is usually, but not quite adequately, translated as "essence" - *essentia* was a coinage from the Latin infinitive, *esse*, to render the Greek term *ousia* in its later, fully developed sense.

In these early Dialogues it is quickly argued that each "form-itself" also has its *ousia*, in the sense of what is its own, of what properly belongs to it.[15] Then from the *Republic* onward it is evident that Plato had become increasingly aware of the implications of the fact of the word *ousia* having derived from the verb "be," more particularly that it entailed a fundamental connection between what in a thing is "its own" and the "to be" (*to einai*) or "being" (*to on*) of the thing. In the *Republic, ousia* mostly continues primarily to express "what is its own" (essence), but at 479 c and in most instances of its use in the *Theaetetus, ousia* has the meaning of "being," but in a new sense. In this the word *ousia* is not merely an alternative to the participial action noun *to on*, "the being" (analogously to "the thinking," "the running"), but expands that meaning of "being" to include the sense of "what is its own."

This new compound sense of *ousia* is that which is prevalent throughout the later Dialogues. Moreover in these, this compound meaning comes to be extended also to *to on*, so that in these late works *to on* is, in the crucial instances, not adequately rendered by *esse*, "das Sein," "l'etre," or "Being" (the gerund in English replacing the infinitive), or by "existence," for these catch only part of the new sense.

It is this new fully developed sense of *ousia* and *to on* which is taken over by Aristotle, as is clear from his analysis in Book VII of the *Metaphysics*. The appreciation of this, however, tends to be blocked by the traditional translation of *ousia* in Aristotle by "substance," a word which most inadequately renders the meaning of the Greek term. In Ch. 1 Aristotle makes clear that the question, *ti to on* ("what is being"), is the question *tis he ousia* ("what is *ousia*").[16] That is, he was acknowledging the full connotation of *to on* ("being") as developed by Plato and expressed by the term *ousia*. Starting the chapter with the reminder that *to on* has many senses, Aristotle points out that first it indicates *to ti esti* ("what it is") or *tode ti* (a "this" or "individuality"), which means that which is primarily (*touton proton on*) is the "what" (*to ti estin*), and that this is the very thing which is indicated by *ousia* (*hoper semainei ten ousian*).[17] In other words, the "what" is that which Plato had argued is "its own," which is "individual to it" and to indicate which he had used the word *ousia*. The fundamental connection of the "what" which is "its own" (entailed in the word *ousia*) with "being" Aristotle brings out more fully in a phrase (which became for him a technical term) viz., *to ti en einai*, "the what it is to be." That is, this phrase denotes the "what" which is peculiar to it, its "own," whereby it *is*.

BEING AND THE CATEGOREAL ISSUE

But Aristotle was aware of an important incongruity in Plato's doctrine of *ousia*, in which *ousia*, what is "its own," is ascribed to both physical things and the forms. Aristotle argued that while a physical *on* is manifestly a singular individual, its *to ti en einai* or *ousia* thus appropriately indicating it as *tode ti* (a "this"), a "form-itself" (*eidos auto kath auto*) is not thus singular, for it is that which is "participated in," which entails that it is fundamentally *universal*. But a universal indicates "a such" (*to toionde*) and not "a this" (*tode ti*), and therefore a universal could not be *ousia*.[18]

Aristotle was thereby brought to a most important conclusion in respect of "being." Plato's theory of the forms per se as "being" had to be rejected; on the contrary, it was the other kind of *onta*, which Plato had denied the status of *to ontos on*, that had to be regarded as *to proton on*, "being" in the primary sense, for *ousia* properly pertained to it alone. This meant that for Aristotle it was the *physei on*, the physical or natural being, that which is in "becoming," which strictly is *to on* and *ousia*. That is, Aristotle found it necessary to reject the conception of "being" deriving from Parmenides and which was grounded in the verb "be" as excluding "becoming." He had arrived at a new conception of that which is a "being" in the primary sense as essentially "in becoming," and which had therefore to be conceived as in a process of change (*kinesis*) from *dynamis* (potentiality) to *energeia* (actuality).

What did this entail in respect of the status of form? He agreed with Plato that in a physical being *eidos* (form) is to be identified with *to ti en einai* (essence), and thus the *ousia*, of the being. Categoreally considered, this meant that form constituted the predicates of the being as subject. That is, a form "is" only as a quality, quantity, etc., of "the being" which is its subject.

But Aristotle saw that the categoreal issue was quite crucially raised in another respect. Since a physical being is in becoming, in *kinesis*, this entails a substratum, not only as the recipient of the forms, but as underlying the supersession of forms, without which one could not think or speak of "it" as changing. This meant that a physical being had necessarily to be "composite" (*synolos*) of *hyle* (matter) as the substratum and *eidos* (form). Now *hyle* and *eidos* could not be "constituents" or "parts" in the sense in which elements are constituents of a compound whole, for the "elements" (by the very meaning of the word)[19] of a natural being would themselves have to be natural beings.[20] Therefore *hyle* cannot have the status of "a being" (*to on*); it is "that which in itself is neither a particular thing nor of a certain quantity nor assigned to any of the categories by which being (*to on*) is determined."[21] As itself not "a being" it is therefore not known as beings are known, viz., in terms of the categories; it can be "known" only analogically and relatively.[22] The other component of natural being, viz., *eidos*, likewise has to be accorded the status of an *arche* (source) of being--that *eidos* cannot have the status of "a being" is amply evident from his critique of Plato. Further, analogously to *hyle*, there is also a peculiarity in regard to the "knowledge" of *eidos*; since the forms are that in terms of which there is knowledge, they themselves cannot be known in the way the physical things are: *eidos* is the *arche* (source) of knowledge as well as of *to on* (being). In thus distinguishing between *to on* (being) and the *archai* (sources) of being, Aristotle had attained a formulation of a categoreal insight of the utmost importance, which Plato had been able to state only in terms of *mythos* or simile.[23]

This insight was inherited by Plotinus. In common with the new movement of thought of that era he had accepted a single, divine, *arche* (source) of all things, in place of the three *archai* of Plato and Aristotle, and maintained that this One, as the *arche* (source) of being and of the forms (in terms of which there is knowledge) accordingly cannot itself be known and transcends being (*ou me logos, mede episteme, o de kai epekeina legetai einai ousias*).[24] For Plotinus "being" (*to on, to einai*, and *ousia*) is identified with the first emanation, *nous*,[25] the enaction (*energeia*) of whose *ousia* is the second emanation, *psyche*, which is *to ontos on*.[26]

Augustine took an importantly different position on this, one which has been determinative of most subsequent thought. Plato had identified form as *to ontos on*, because only form was in itself changeless, immutable; Augustine held that only God was supremely immutable and perfect, so that only God deserved the title of *Vere Esse*.[27] For Augustine God is "the being" which most completely "is," whose *essentia* signifies perfection.

GOD, BEING, AND THE CATEGOREAL PROBLEM

This Augustinian ontological position, which became the accepted doctrine of most Christian theology, namely that the source of being is "a being," was found to involve many aporiae with which thinkers struggled for a millennium. Central and basic to these is the issue of "being." Augustine had followed in the ontological tradition of Parmenides and Plato. In this the approach is from the meaning of *to on* ("being") to the identification of that which accords with that meaning. Plato, following

Parmenides in holding that the fundamental connotation of "being" is immutability (since the Greek verb "be" excludes "becoming"), identified the forms as "beings" in the basic sense. This
connotation of "being" as immutability was inherited by Neoplatonism and accepted by Augustine, who identified God as "being"
in that sense. The Augustinian position therefore maintains "a
being" as the single source of all other "beings."
   Important difficulties in this position soon emerged. If
"being" fundamentally connotes immutability, how can physical
things, which are manifestly in "becoming," be regarded as "beings" at all? God could not then be the source of being, since
God alone is "being"; God could only be the source of "becoming." But if "being" and "becoming" stand in mutually exclusive
contrast, this entails the absolute transcendence of God, with no
relation to "becoming." The Neoplatonic solution to this difficulty was to identify "to be" (*to einai, esse*, "das Sein," "l'etre")
with form as *ousia, essentia*. Then a natural thing in becoming
"is" by virtue of its form, its "essence." But this involved further difficulties. First the Arab and then Western thinkers saw
that this deprived "being" of the feature of its meaning which
had been basic in Greek philosophy, namely "presence." In other
words, a separation of "existence" from "essence" had occurred.
Accordingly, if "being" means "essence," there is no way to
account for "existence," and for the "individuality" (*tode ti*)
which "to be there, present," "to exist," primarily entails, as
Aristotle had correctly insisted. Aquinas sought to remedy this
by emphasizing the features of act" (which Neoplatonism had
originally identified with "form," but which had, analogously to
"existence," became lost to "essence") and identified "act" with
"*esse*," "to be." But with this new conception of "being" the
original difficulty still remains, for "being" still retains the
fundamental connotation of immutability, standing in exclusive
contrast to "becoming," and thus the problem is not resolved of
how "being" can be the source of "becoming."
   Another most important aspect of these difficulties emerges
in the categoreal issue. With the conception of God as "a being,"
the source of all other "beings," it was entailed that, categoreally considered, the same mode of thinking pertained in respect
of God and the other beings: each is "a being" of which attributes are predicated. Early however it became evident that
attributes could not be univocally predicated of God and creatures, and from the Pseudo-Dionysius, with his "superlative
theology," to Thomas Aquinas, with his doctrine of analogy, a
way out of this categoreal problem was sought. Though both
were thought of as "beings," a fundamental difference between
them as "beings" had to be acknowledged, and to meet this

situation Aquinas, Duns Scotus, and Occam developed the theory of transcendentals as predicates pertaining solely to God.

But in this we are up against a singularly difficult issue, namely, whether the "source" of being can at all validly be thought in terms of the categories, which manifestly pertain to physical things, i.e., in terms of "a being" of which attributes are predicated. Aristotle was more profoundly aware of this issue than was anyone, not only before but also since. He saw that the fallacy basic to the thought of the physical philosophers was that they had conceived the *arche* (source) of physical things as itself a physical thing (e.g., water, etc.). He saw that the same error vitiated the Platonic doctrine, which maintained *eidos* (form) as the *arche* of the changing physical *onta*, beings, but conceived form as itself *to on*, "a being." Plato himself was indeed aware of the fallacy of the "third man" involved in this and, it seems to me, made an important attempt to overcome this difficulty in the *Timaeus* through depicting the forms, along with the *demiourgos* and the receptacle, as the *archai* of the physical world. Aristotle was clear that not only *hyle*, but also *eidos* was not to be understood in terms of the categories, for *eidos* is the *arche* of the categories; for him the *gnosis* of the forms could only be *meta noeseos*,[28] by direct intuition.

It seems to me necessary today to face the question whether the aporiae involved in the dominant doctrine of God as "a being" which is the source of all other beings, are not grounded in the same basic mistake which Aristotle saw in Platonism. I would suggest that this is the case.

The alternative is that we conceive God as "*source* of being." In our conception of God we have therefore to proceed from "being," and thus how "being" is conceived is crucial. The "being" in question is evidently that of the entities validly understood in terms of the categories. It is to be noted that the word "being" here is the participial action noun; I shall distinguish[29] it typographically as "be*ing*." This "be*ing*" entails "presence"; but it entails more than simply "presence" ("existence," *Dasein*). Primarily, the "be*ing*" must be that of "a be*ing*." This means that "be*ing*" entails "individuality," in the double sense of *an* individual and of *what* is individual to it, i.e., "essence" in the sense of its own peculiar definiteness. It is to be emphasized that "be*ing*" does not connote *only* "essence," and that essence does not *constitute* "be*ing*," for "be*ing*" entails "acting." Also, this "be*ing*" cannot exclude "becoming," but rather includes it.

Now this "be*ing*" necessarily entails "source," in a threefold respect. There is required a source of its "definiteness," and equally so of its "acting." Further, since "acting" entails "end," also required is a teleological source. The question then is whether these three "sources" can validly and coherently be combined into one. It seems to me that this cannot be done without falling back into the error to be avoided. Also involved in this is that while "source" of be*ing* entails *transcendence* of be*ing*, "transcendence" here cannot validly entail temporal precedence, for this would imply "a being" as precedent. "Source" has to be transcendent and immanent. The Divine, I would say, is more particularly to be identified with the teleological source, but we should not fall into the error of completely separating the three sources from each other.

Emory University

   Atlanta, Georgia

NOTES

1. A. N. Whitehead, *Process and Reality* (New York: Macmillan, 1929), p. 521.

2. *Ibid.*, p. 28.

3. Ivor Leclerc, *The Theory of Being, An Inquiry into Ontology.* (In preparation).

4. Werner Jaeger, *The Theology of the Early Greek Philosophers* (London: Oxford University Press, 1947), p. 197, note 2.

5. Charles H. Kahn, *The Verb 'Be' in Ancient Greek*, Part 6 of *The Verb 'Be' and its Synonyms*, ed. W. M. Verhaar (Dordrecht/Holland: D. Reidel Publishing Co., 1973).

6. *Ibid.*, p. 217.

7. *Ibid.*, p. 219.

8. *Ibid.*, p. 224.

9. *Ibid.*, p. 224.

10. *Ibid.*, pp. 156ff; 233-35; 330-70.

11. Cf. Jaeger, *The Theology of the Early Greek Philosophers*, p. 197, note 2: "Homer and Hesiod speak of *ta eonta* as that which exists at present and contrast it with *ta essomena* and *ta proeonta*, things as they will be in the future and as they were in the past. This very opposition proves that the word originally pointed to the immediate and tangible presence of things."

12. Plato, *Phaedo*, 79 A.

13. Cf. R. Hirzel, "*Ousia*," *Philologus* 72, 1913, pp. 42-52.

14. Especially interesting as illustrative of this is *Gorgias* 471 B, in which Socrates says: *ekballein me ek tes ousias kai tou alethous* (to drive me out of my property, the truth).

15. Cf. *Protagoras* 349 B; *Euthyphro* 11 A; *Cratylus* 423 A,

424 B; *Phaedo* 65 C., 76 D - 77 A.

16. Aristotle, *Metaphysics*, VII, 1028 b 4.

17. *Ibid.*, 1028 a 14-15.

18. *Ibid.*, 1038 b 34 - 1039 a 2.

19. Aristotle, *De Caelo* 302 a 16-18.

20. Aristotle, *Metaphysics* 1028 b 8-13.

21. *Ibid.*, 1029 a 20-21 (Ross tr.).

22. Aristotle, *Physics* 191 a 8-12, 194 b 9.

23. Plato, *Timaeus* 29 D; *Republic* 308.

24. Plotinus, *Ennead*, V, 4, 1.

25. Cf. *Ennead*, III, 8, 8: *all ousia kai to tauton to einai kai to noein einai.*

26. Cf. Plotinus, *Ennead*, IV, 7, 85.

27. Cf. Augustine, *Confesiones*, Bk. VII, ch. 11: "For it is only that which remains in being without change that truly is."

28. Cf. Aristotle, *Metaphysics* 1036 a 5-6.

29. It is important to distinguish "be*ing*" as a nominalized participle from "being" as a gerund substituting for the nominalized infinitive, and thus from *des Sein* and *l'etre*.

COMMENT

On Ivor Leclerc,

"God and the Problem of Being"

SALVINO BIOLO

The thought-provoking report of Professor Leclerc about the fundamental problem of being, that invited us to a "basic reconsideration," convincingly emphasizes from the start the close relationship of the two metaphysical aspects of the central topic: the ontological aspect that considers being as such, and the theological aspect with its consideration of God.

1. In regard to his introductory remarks, it seems essential to propose some preliminary questions closely connected with the fundamental problem of the existence of God.

Prof. Leclerc points out that contemporary scientific development gives a rather negative meaning to the question: "whether God exists." This seems to be the predominant attitude also of most modern philosophy. Is possible to see in the traditional distinction proposed by Leclerc between "that it is" and "what it is," the implicit transcendental opposition between, and mutual relationship of, essence and existence?

I feel rather perplexed in observing how Leclerc, who seems strongly influenced by the thought of Whitehead, states the basic question as follows: "whether the term 'exists' and 'being' can consistently and coherently be used in the same sense with respect to God as to the natural beings." The term *same* means "identical" rather than "similar but different," and could insinuate at the beginning an attitude suggesting a univocal knowledge of being that would lead in turn to a pantheistic conception of God.

Another crucial point is the twofold aspect of being: ontological and categorial. Why are these two terms so closely interconnected, when the term "categorial" seems to imply a deviation from the correct transcendental and analogical notion of being? I doubt that it is philosophically justified to use the term "categorial" in referring to being, particularly in the usage of Whitehead quoted by Leclerc. In this quotation referring to God he says: ". . . *res vera* categorically not different from any other entity or being." I would like to specify my difficulty in this way: being as such *transcends* everything, that is, it penetrates and supercedes all reality since it involves and is involved in all being, in every aspect and mode of being. Thus it embraces and overflows every category. Being is immanent in all its determinations and may not be confused with any determination whatever: "it is neither a thing nor an idea, it constitutes the profundity of things and the objectivity of ideas."[1]

2. Concerning his interpretation of Greek philosophy, Prof. Leclerc quite correctly emphasizes the enduring stability of being as found in Parmenides, but neglects the differences found in later thinkers.

Considering the explicit ontological and theological nature of the topic, it would have been helpful to consider more deeply the metaphysical aspects of God as supreme Beauty found within the *Symposium* of Plato. This work reaches heights of sublime transcendence in the field of Greek philosophy, which embraces not only aspects of absoluteness and uniqueness but also multiplicity and becoming, as in Heraclitus. Both aspects are reconsidered by Plato and explicitly developed by Aristotle. Although Leclerc gave the two great masters special consideration, he might have more clearly focused their thought to allow an interpretation closer to the traditional one.

Referring to Plato he provides an initial orientation to the analogy of being when he reveals his fundamental distinction between *the identical* and *the different* in both things and ideas. Does Plato exclude completely the real and true nature of being in the things of this world, even if they appear like shadows in comparison with the reality of ideas? If so, what do the typical Platonic insights of *mimesis* (imitation) and of *metexis* (participation) imply, considering the terms of their operations? These basic insights, because they imply a doctrine of analogy, should not be neglected; they include both a certain similarity and a greater dissimilarity in regard to the respective reality of things and ideas. This holds to a much greater extent when we consider the supreme ideas of the Good and of the Beautiful?

I agree with Prof. Leclerc's acknowledgement of Aristotle's fundamental contribution to our central problems. As one who is in agreement with the "perennial philosophy," I would like to suggest that the metaphysical principles of Aristotle should be developed in a different and more coherent direction. For example, his solution of the classic dilemma of Parmenides (being either is or is not) rests upon the basic distinction of potency and act, that suggests an ontological difference between beings as they are this or that, but an ontological similarity between beings as they simply are. This opens a pathway to the future development of the logical and ontological aspects of intrinsic analogy.[2] It is true that every material thing in this world is a "composite" *sunodos* of matter and form. But "matter and form" are the principles of *intrinsic* causes within the natural constitution of material being. The "composite" also demands, as Aristotle explains, the *extrinsic* "efficient and final" causes of that composition.

Considering further Aristotle's interpretation of the knowledge of being, Prof. Leclerc makes a fundamental point: "*eidos* is the *arche* (source) of knowledge as well as of *to on*" (p. 9). Certainly in answer to the question: what is being? Aristotle replies that the cause of being is its immanent form (Met. Z, 17). But allowing that such an interpretation is possible and coherent, I would like to suggest a development in the line of Thomas Aquinas' thought and founded upon an Aristotelian insight. Let me explain further: the *eidos* is a proximate *formal* principle of the knowledge of being and not *an agent*. It is of being as known, but not of being as made to be.

3. Regarding his brief consideration of both St. Thomas and St. Augustine, his brief mention of St. Augustine is correct but is too partial, both for what it says and what it does not say. Augustine has not only provoked struggles among thinkers, but both as a theologian and a philosopher he suggested a radical solution to the problem of the origin of being from God.

The passage from the *Confessions* quoted partially by Leclerc, in its completeness certainly affirms the absolute being of God, but also attributes being, that is relative by participation, to other things:

> Also I considered all the other things that are of a lower order than yourself, and I saw that they have not absolute being in themselves, nor are they entirely without being. They are *real* in so far as they have their being from you, but *unreal* in the sense that they are not what you are. For it is only that which remains in being without change that truly is."[3]

The relationship of beings to God is one of dependency in their common reality, but opposition in their similar yet different being. Some lines earlier Augustine, in one of his most brilliant insights, had explained this very similar idea about the dependency of created things, including the mind itself:

> What I saw was something, quite different from any light we know on earth. It shone above my mind, but not in the way that oil floats above water or the sky hangs over the earth. It was above me because it was itself *the Light that made me*, and I was below because *I was made by it*.[4]

Augustine accepts the transcendence of God from Platonic philosophy but develops it differently in order to accommodate

God as Creator according to the Jewish-Christian revelation. It is metaphysically important for our common problem to emphasize that this Doctor of the Church also uses the term 'source' (*fons*) about God to explain that he is the Principle of all: . . . these knowing God, found that in Him was both *the cause* of the whole creation, *the light* of all true learning, and the *source* of all felicity."[5] "Source" is here clearly used in a metaphorical way to express the metaphysical category of first cause, that is the Creator.

Considering Prof. Leclerc's treatment of St. Thomas, whose conception of analogy is very different from that of Duns Scotus and Ockam, I would like to stress that he further explains the doctrine of creation systematically with an explicit distinction betweem--but not by separating--essence and existence. Therefore being is not only identified with "to be" but also implies "it." Thus Thomas both sought and found a mode of expression that would resolve the supposedly rigorous contrast between the being and becoming of creatures. He could say that the Creator is "a being," but such a singular being that He is the Pure Act of being, who freely makes beings that are capable of, and contain the reality of becoming. In a similar way there is no reason to be frightened of the "same mode of thinking" being used in regard to God and other beings. The correct way of thinking about, and predicating value of, God and creatures is analogous not univocal. Nor is it equivocal but similar and different, although the difference is a major one because He is the *cause propria* of all things.

> What is such through the essence is the proper cause of what is such by participation. But only God is being through his essence, while all other things are beings through participation, because only in God 'esse est sua essentia'. Consequently the 'to be' of every existing reality is a proper effect of God, in such a way that every thing that produces some existing thing does so insofar as it acts in the power of God."[6]

Therefore, strictly speaking, God is not "Wholly other" but "simply different." Total difference is repugnant because it would create an abyss between God and creatures who are related to Him.

4. Regarding the principal conclusions to be reached and the final problems that need to be resolved, it seems that when Prof. Leclerc affirms that: "there are *aporiae* involved in the dominant doctrine of God as 'a being' which is the source of other things," he multiplies rather than resolves the problems. It

is not clear to what dominant doctrine he is referring. He form-
ulates the question by focusing on the problem of the origin of
beings from God, beginning from a conception of being.

In order to clarify my interpretation and to discover some
solution for the main problem, I would like to propose two
questions and two possible solutions.

My *first* question in the form of dilemma regards the origin of beings from God: Is it by emanation or creation? My
dilemma is proposed both in reference to the missing solution in
Aristotle, whose fundamental principles I can accept, and also in
order to seek a further clarification from Prof. Leclerc about
the term "source" in reference to God. "Source" more strongly
suggests a *metaphor* than a technical philosophical category.
Only if that word means "active cause," and in this context
creative cause, is it acceptable. Otherwise I cannot see any way
of overcoming almost impossible difficulties. It is precisely here
that we have need of the doctrine of analogy where we try to
use the fundamental and universal category of "cause."

Leclerc finally asks about individual being which includes
becoming: "Now this 'being' necessarily entails 'source' in a
threefold respect."

The first aspect: "there is required a source of its definiteness." The word "source" here is overburdened with too much
meaning, considering the delicacy and importance of the fundamental question of the origin of being. I therefore think that in
this context "source" may be (a) the *substantial form* which is
the intrinsic principle determining and specifying being as this
or that substance or essence; (b) an *accidental form* which is a
further actual determination of the substance; or (c) the extrinsic efficient Principle, which is the first Cause of singular
beings.

It is essential that we do not confuse the constitutive
intrinsic principles with the extrinsic transcendent first Principle
who is God. Here is the crucial aspect of the entire question. If
by "source" Leclerc means the creative Cause of being, then I
am in agreement with him. However, if by "source" he means
something less as immanent in this world, then I cannot agree
with his vague use of the word. This is not to deny that the
transcendent first Principle is also immanent, but actively and
creatively immanent. Such a first Principle is not to be identified with beings who are relative in their dependence.

The second aspect: "and equally so of its acting." Because
"to act is the consequence of to be" (*operari sequitur esse*) it is
necessary to make some further distinctions that are a logical
application of those we have already made.

First of all: If "source" means the first Cause that makes

every being exist and consequently act, then the expression is acceptable. However, if by "source" he means an intrinsic principle like substance or accident, then the logical consequence must be a type of pantheism.

The third aspect: "Further since 'acting' entails 'end', (there is) also required *a teleological source.*" Because "every agent works for an end" (*Omne agens agit propter finem*) in a determined manner, and this indicates the ultimate existence of an intellect, we must still distinguish: (a) if "teleological source" means *final*, extrinsic *Cause* as an ultimate end to which all is oriented and ordered, it is acceptable. In this instance this final cause must therefore be identified with the first Principle from which every thing originates. This first Cause or Principle makes the teleological order residing in every contingent being, and must be both the first Intelligence and Will that thinks and wills the existence of beings. However this does not appear to be what Leclerc means. (b) On the contrary, if "teleological source" means some principle internal to beings as a constitutive element of their very natures, then it must simply be denied, because it inevitably leads to pantheism.

Finally it seems to me that the crucial point we must always emphasize is that God is both *transcendent* and *immanent.* He is transcendent because, insofar as He gives being to all creatures, He is superior to all relative beings. But by this very same fact of creation He is also immanent, in that He is intimately present causing what is most intimate in beings to be: "Yet you were deeper (*intimior*) than my deepest self and higher (*superior*) than the topmost height that I could reach."[7]

In regard to his final statement: "The Divine is more particularly to be identified with the *teleological source*," I prefer finally to explicitly call that "source" God, insofar as He is the creative "source" which makes the teleological order of the universe including man. But let us not call God "source" if by this we mean an internal principle that is identified with the nature of created things. This seems to be the error that should be avoided at all costs because of the danger of pantheism.

As far as the *second* question is concerned I would like to refer briefly to the general conception of God and being and to the presuppositions related to these questions. What fundamental conception do we have of man as far as he conceives and knows being, and finally God? Only if we are grounded in a sound epistemology and methodology of the knowing and conscious subject can we be capable of both certainty and truth. Unless we are intellectually open to the notion of being and consequently to self-transcendence, and to the absolute transcendence of the *Ipsum Esse*, we cannot have any answer to the problem of being and the mystery of God.

Gregorian University

   Rome, Italy

NOTES

1. "L'etre apparait comme le sens des phenomenes, ce qui le pose et permet de les affirmer. Il n'est ni chose ni idee; il fait la profondeur des choses et l'objectivite des idees." Joseph De Finance. *La connaissance de l'etre.* (Paris: Desclee de Brower, 1966), p. 36.

2. "The notion of being penetrates all other contents, and so it is present in the formulation of every concept. It cannot result from an insight into being, for such an insight would be an understanding we have not attained. It is, as has been said, the orientation of intelligent and rational consciousness towards an unrestricted objective." Bernard J.F. Lonergan, S.J., *Insight* (London: Longemans, Green and Co., 1957), p. 360.

3. *Confessions*, VII, x, 17.

4. *Ibid.* VII, x, 16. It is very significant: " . . . sed superior quia ipsa (=lux) fecit me, et ego inferior quia factus ab ea."

5. *The City of God*, VIII, 10.

6. St. Thomas, III C.G., 66, 6.

7. St. Augustine, *Confessions*, III, vi, 11. "Tu autem eras intimior intimo meo et superior summo meo." It belongs to the brilliant genius of Augustine to have recognized the intimate relationship existing between the immanence and transcendence of God.

CHAPTER II

RELIGIOUS EXPERIENCE

H.D. LEWIS

The notion of religious experience appears to me central to all discussions of major religious issues today. It is however a notion about which there appears to be a great deal of confusion and misunderstanding. There are terms like 'Nature', and 'Freedom', which admit of such a wide variety of interpretation (some of them sharply contradictory) that their use tends to become almost pointless. 'Religious experience' is apt to fall into this class. It is sometimes used to refer to any religious activity or practice whatsoever, and thus to become quite otiose. This is the use that some have in mind when they say that they have never had a religious experience; they just mean that they are agnostics. For others 'religious experience' means some very peculiar type of experience, like having visions or hearing voices, or having a distinctively mystical experience. For some the term is associated, with some but only very limited justification, with an excessively emotional religious indulgence. In its main use, and in the profound importance ascribed to it by devout persons in all ages, the term stands for none of these things. It is important therefore to indicate just what we should normally understand by 'religious experience'. I shall attempt to do this as fairly as I can within a limited space, and I shall also try to give a brief indication of how this relates to other major concerns.

I shall waste no time over those who think of religious experience primarily, and perhaps exclusively, in terms of paranormal phenomena. Such occurrences need not in fact be properly religious at all. To what extent they may be I have discussed in Chapters XIV and XV of my *Our Experience of God*.[1] Those who have had paranormal experiences in the context of their religious life, ascribe importance to them only in relation to other aspects of their faith; usually they minimize their importance and treat them as quite peripheral to their essential commitment. This is why it seemed to me so unreasonable for a critic of the standing of Alasdair MacIntyre, in a well known book[2] some years ago, to make such heavy weather over claims to have had visions of the Virgin Mary, etc. Did she 'speak Aramaic', did she 'remember Galilee'? Questions of this kind seem to me to show a total, indeed obtuse, insensitivity to what religion is essentially like, even in the contexts where visions and voices and other forms of 'the marvelous' are in fact invoked.

But we must be equally careful not to think of religious experience merely in terms of some features of human experience as a whole or some generalizations or deductions from what our situation as human beings is like. Religious experience, in essentials, is not incipient metaphysics, however important it may be for metaphysical reflection. Its peculiar significance derives from its being a distinctive experience which people undergo, as they may have a moral or an aesthetic experience. This does not mean that it is always easy to recognize or delimit, as in the case for example, of some forms of pain. But it would be quite wrong to identify it with features of experience which all can recognize, or with natural occurrences to which some further religious significance may be ascribed. Religious experience is essentially religious, a distinct ingredient, to my mind a vital one, in an essentially religious awareness, and identifiable as such.

I go out of my way to stress this because of a prevailing tendency, in current philosophy of religion, to think that so much of religion is initially neutral, even the sense of the numinous according to some. In my view, we cannot produce any proper form of religion out of non-religious elements. There is indeed a place for the interpretation of experience; perception for example looks very different as the philosopher considers some of its extraordinary features. The last thing I wish to do is to discourage reflection on religious awareness, or to present it as a raw datum which some may accept, others not, and no more. We need in fact to think more carefully about it than anything else in religious commitment at present. But we must not, in the process, so dilute it that it is nothing recognizable in and for itself.

The same goes for some fashionable views which equate religious experience with an alleged contentless relation with God sometimes known as an 'I-Thou relation'. I have a very great regard for Martin Buber, and I wish more heed were paid by those who refer to him to my fairly close discussion, in Chapter XIII of *The Elusive Mind*, of what emerges in a positive way from all that he had to say on this theme. But I make no sense whatsoever, in human or in divine relationships, of a mere relation to which no kind of a distinctive precise significance can be attached. The nearest we get to this is the insight or intuition into the inevitability of there being God, and of this I shall say more shortly. But an encounter which is no particular kind of encounter, a 'meeting' which cannot be characterized in any way, appears to me to be just nothing. To make the invocation of it a way of by-passing all the hard epistemological problems is just an escape from our intellectual responsibility, it plays into the hands of contemptuous agnostics.

For related reasons I dismiss all accounts of religious experience in exclusively emotional terms. Emotion plays its part, but the core of religious experience, I submit, is essentially cognitive. How then should we understand it?

At the centre, it seems to me, is the enlivened sense of the being of God or, if that at this stage is too theistic a term, of some supreme transcendent reality - as involved in the being of anything at all. This is what lies behind the traditional arguments. We all know their inadequacy as arguments, notwithstanding all the refinements attempted in recent times. But they still haunt us, and this seems to me to be because they reflect in different ways the conviction that there can be no ultimate fortuitousness in the being of things. We seek explanations of the way things are, not as a mere psychological compulsion but as rational beings. We do not give up when no sort of explanation is possible, we insist that it must be available somewhere; but no finite explanation is fully adequate, each proceeds in terms of the way we actually find that things cohere, but there remains the question why they should be this way at all, or why anything at all should exist. We can, at least without sheer inconsistency, say that it all just happened, that somehow things began to *be* out of a total void and took the remarkable course which enables us to manipulate and understand our environment, in terms of perfect concomitant variation even to the astonishing vastness and complexities of macroscopic and microscopic science of today. We may not contradict ourselves if we say that all this just came into being out of nothing, but is it credible? Why should anything start up at all, much less take the remarkable intelligible shape they have out of just nothing? On the other hand it is equally unintelligible to suppose that the world has always been, that in no sense has there been any sort of origination. 'Always' in this sense becomes meaningless. Aeons beyond all computation, and certainly beyond imaginative realization, we can at least comprehend, but a strictly infinite past is just not intelligible.

It is these radical antinomies that compel us to recognize some more ultimate reality in which all that we can, in principle, comprehend is rooted, but which is not itself comprehensible beyond the recognition of its inevitability, a mystery, not partial but total, in which everything there is is invested, but not the mystery of mere bewilderment, the mystery of real transcendent being.

Philosophers put this in fairly sophisticated terms. But the sense of it, however imperfectly expressed, does not require great sophistication. It is elicited in various ways, not least by what Jaspers has called 'limit situations', and I have ventured myself elsewhere to indicate in more detail how the sense of the transcendent is awakened in the minds of the most naive as well as of sophisticated persons and societies. It can be traced back as far as recorded history goes. Art and practice as well as intellectual reflection involve it. But granted some intimation in this way of a supreme or transcendent reality, how do we go from there?

It is at *this* point that I would wish to invoke the idea of religious experience. I wish to stress very much that I do not appeal to the notion of religious experience as such to establish the existence of God, least of all in the naive form of insisting that there must be God because we experience him. That would clearly not do without indication of the sort of experience this is and how it is warranted. It could be a gigantic begging of the question. Religious experience properly comes in at the point where we ask, how we go further than the sense of some ultimate all-encompassing mystery involved in all that we are or find.

There are of course some who do not seek to go further. They stay at the sense of profound wonderment at the essentially incomprehensible source of all there is, sometimes almost to the point of the repudiation of finite being. In practice actual religion has rarely been able to remain at this rarefied level. Present existence claims its rights and our attention. Finite existence cannot be denied any more than the infinite, even if it finds no better place than some mode or articulation of the infinite. At some level there appear, from the remotest times to our own, particular practices, attitudes, obligations, varied and suggestive symbolism, all intimating that the sacred which, in one sense, we cannot approach and whose essential mystery we cannot fathom, is nonetheless peculiarly present, 'in thy mouth and in thy heart', as one scripture puts it, that it involves a way of life for us, a purpose, a formative influence in personal and social history, a meaning and a presence articulating itself in all manner of ways and leading, in some instances, to highly refined formulations of belief, even to the curiously presumptuous intimacy of petitionary prayer. Men speak of meeting God, of 'walking' with him, of hearing his voice, of turning away from him, of encountering his wrath and, in the same awareness almost, finding him a seeking, reconciling God who draws all men to their ultimate fulfilment 'in him'. They even speak of God incarnate as a living, limited finite creature who died in a scandalously shameful way. How is any of this to be warranted, affirmed or rejected? What meaning can it have?

It is here, in my view, that religious experience is the seminal and vital consideration. I do not, of course, wish to deny, that the 'insight' into there having to be God, along the lines indicated, is itself an experience. But it is so in the sense that all cognition is experience. To apprehend that twice two is four, or that the angles of a triangle add up to 180 degrees, is experience. But no one would claim, in these cases, that we know from experience, on the basis of what we find or observe, that these things are so, as we know that grass is green and fire is hot. 'The appeal to religious experience', as it is sometimes called, is not a strictly empirical one, in the sense of empiricism which confines it to presentations of sense, but it has more in common with it than strictly a priori knowledge.' Certain things are claimed on the basis of certain things that have happened.

The one qualification of this, and it is a vital one, is the point already noted, namely that at the core of religious experience, is the enlivened insight into the being of God. We do not know this because things happen in any particular way, but, essentially, because they happen at all. The insight involved is peculiar but certainly not quasi-empirical. On the other hand, the enlivening of this insight in peculiar conditions, and the repercussions of it on other crucial aspects of particular experiences, seem to me to be the raw material out of which all other genuine religious awareness is built - and by which it is tested.

At this point there is a very close analogy between the way we know one another and the way we know God. We do not know the existence of other persons generally in any a priori or in any intuitive way, though some philosophers do make that strange claim. We know all we know about other persons, I submit, in some mediated way, however close and intimate this may be. Without some evidence we would not know the existence of anyone. But the being of God we know quite differently, as indicated. It is in no sense a matter of evidence as this usually goes. But *all the rest is*, and it is along these lines that I, at least, react to the familiar challenge of empiricist critics - what would count for or against your belief? For the existence of God I answer 'nothing'. It is not that kind of awareness, it is a quite peculiar insight about which nonetheless much may be said, again along the lines indicated. But for all other affirmations, the live particularization of profound devotion, we turn to specific evidence, to what counts for or against, to what can, in some respects at least, be analyzed and set forth, though by no means in exclusively sensible terms.

I make a special point of stressing this, as so many who are concerned about religion, at highpowered professional levels or more simply, fall back before the fashionable challenge on either blind appeals to authority or some vague noncognitive

attitude or commitment for which there is no rational justification. Interest in religion may be revived today, in fleeting and
transitory ways, by simple-minded appeals to emotion or hysteria
or palliatives to those who hunger for spiritual sustenance - or
we may make do for a while with attenuations which but thinly
disguise the essential secularity of our attitudes. But this will
not last. Religion needs justification, most of all in a sophisticated age like out own. No great religion can survive without it.

It is this justification of what is distinctive in the claims
of the great religions, and the means of assessment and the
basis of dialogue, that is to be found essentially, in my view, in
religious experience, rightly understood. The points of convergence as well as the differences can be much better understood
in these terms and a means made possible of maintaining our
distinctive stances while entering with genuine empathy and
appreciation into the religious devotion of others. It will also be
a very great gain indeed, in all religions, to show that we are
fully equipped to confront the demand for justification and fully
take the point of empiricist critics, though by no means entirely
on their own terms.

Let us return, then, now to the question what a religious
experience involves besides the enlivened sense of the being and
mystery of God. I want first to add here that, if the transcendent is to function adequately as the ultimate answer to our
'why questions', or as explanation in the very special elusive
sense indicated, it must be deemed to be complete and adequate
in all respects in itself, in other words perfect in the evaluational sense as well as self-sustaining. I do not see how anything less than supreme perfection could meet the case, and in
this context I would like to refer you to a quite admirable, but
not I suspect sufficiently regarded, book by Professor Sontag
entitled *Divine Perfection* (Student Movement Press). The sense
of the holy is essentially evaluational, and does not become so,
as is implied in some readings of Otto, by further schematiza-
tion. This point I must leave as it is for our purpose.

The main point to be stressed now is that the sense of
ultimate being, mysterious beyond any fathoming in what it must
be in itself other than ultimate perfection, has a distinctive
impact on other formative features of the total experience in
which it occurs. It corrects the perspective in which we view
the world around us, it highlights what is of greatest import for
us, it makes us see the familiar anew, as in art and poetry; and
it does this under the insistent sense of transcendent being
unavoidably having its place in our thought. The transcendent
claims what it stimulates for its own; and God, whom no man
hath seen, the impenetrably Holy, removed and remote as infi-

nite being from finite, becomes a closely intimate articulate presence in the very core of our own essentially finite awareness.

The substance of what we come to learn about God in this way is finite. It may present difficulties but no difficulties beyond our understanding and resolving in the normal exercise of finite intelligence. *What* we learn is finite and has no irresolvable mystery in it, much is indeed very simple, however astonishing on occasion. The peculiarly divine factor comes in when these exceptional insights into our own situation and its requirements are seen to be induced in a very sharp way, deepened and refined, under the impact of the movingly enlivened sense of the Holy and the transcendent. As I have put it elsewhere, God puts his own imprimatur on certain insights and sensitivities, he underlines, as it were, certain things in our experience and writes his own mind into them. They come to carry his authority additional to their own. They are what he specifically wants us to note. The devout acquire the art of listening and heeding what is communicated thus within our own sensitivity and concentration.

One feature of exceptional importance in this process whereby our understanding is extended in the enlivened sense of the involvement of our lives in a supreme and transcendent reality is the refinement and deepening of moral awareness. The view has often been advanced that we cannot ascribe genuine objectivity to ethical principles unless they are considered to be expressly dependent on some religious reality. This seems to me to be dangerous doctrine. It is plain that persons with no religious awareness or commitment can have profound appreciation of moral ideals and splendid devotion to them. There is no inconsistency or logical impropriety in their being so. The objectivity of morals is autonomous, as I have stressed myself on many occasions, and some of the most notable and persuasive defenders of moral objectivity have been prominent agnostic philosophers such as G. E. Moore and C. D. Broad. Their case, a very convincing one to me, does not rest at all on religion. Ethics has no more direct dependence on religion than mathematics or science. But this does not preclude morality from being, as most persons would take it to be, at the very heart of reliion.

It is so not just because the ultimate is also supreme perfection, and commitment to it is also therefore commitment to what is surpassingly good, but also because it is in the refinement of ethical understanding, in the sharpening of conscience as it may more popularly be put, that the peculiar disclosure of divine intention for us takes place. It is in the voice of our own conscience that the voice of God is most distinctly and significantly heard. This does not make conscience an essentially religious faculty, but it does make it the pre-eminent medium within which the articulation of the mind of God to us takes place. It is here above all that we find our exceptional clue to what God is like and what is our own involvement and special relation to him.

None of this means that devout people are morally infallible or have a monopoly of all good sense and advance in ethical understanding. There are perversions of religion and profound misunderstandings about its nature that have been very gravely detrimental to ethical good sense and which have from time to time brought religion itself into serious discredit. The refinement of moral understanding involves moreover a great deal besides the sharpening of ethical insight as such; it requires sound appreciation of the facts and circumstances in various situations and the over-all consequences of various policies. On these matters the devout may not always be the best authorities, and religion certainly confers no immunity from error on matters of fact. Nor does it always carry with it the guarantee of the finest ethical insight as such. The agnostic may sometimes excel in both regards.

What we can say however is that, other things being equal, the enlivened sense of the transcendent carries with it essentially a refinement of moral sensitivity and that it is moreover to this source that the most impressive advances in ethical principles over the years have been due. This is not the place to justify the latter submission in detail. My concern at the moment is more with the general contention that, while it is inherently impossible for us to rise beyond our finite nature and comprehend the being and mind of God as it is for him, we find the incursion of the divine into specific human experience, and thereby a preeminent clue into what our relation to it should be, in the peculiarly religious toning and refining of moral experience.

This is not the only example, far from it. We may speak in similar terms of our appreciation of the world around us and its significance, and of the impetus this has given, among other things, to the advance of science. The artistic attitude is in the same way close to religion here, and each has immensely fructified the other for that reason. But it is not primarily a matter of general affinity as of moments of profound religious awareness in which the deepening of religious insight as such takes its course in the blending of itself with perceptions and sensitivity in other secular regards which thereby afford distinctive matter, apprehensible in the normal secular way by us, out of which the fullness and the richness and the intimacy of genuine religious existence is shaped, and by which it is also corrected and criticized.

Correction and criticism are indeed of very great importance here. For the distinctively religious factor, in a total religious experience, operates upon and within the other secular features of our situation. These often have faults of their own, and this is how it comes about that we sometimes sincerely ascribe to the voice of God items which are only too grievously marked by our own limitations and failings. It would be fine in some ways if the mind of God were disclosed to us in some indelible and wholly unmistakable way, written in the sky or on tablets of stone or of gold in some inscription which is indisputably divine. Dispute, and presumably doubt, would be at an end. But it does not happen that way. Short of being God ourselves what sanction could we invoke, what are the credentials of a message so conveyed? There is indeed no such way for the voice of God to be heard by finite beings. He speaks in the ways we can understand in his peculiar obtrusion into the normal exercise of the faculties with which he has endowed us. But it is not the mere exercise of finite powers that is involved. There is the peculiar transformation of them which we have the reasons indicated for ascribing to divine intervention in the enlivened sense of the transcendent already described.

A genuine prophet can, for these reasons, be sincerely mistaken, and devout persons have always to be searching out their own minds and hearts to be as sure as they can that what they take to be the voice of god is not the voice of their own errors and failings, or at least tinged by these. That does not preclude firmness of conviction and deliverance. The prophet may speak with authority, but he must be mindful also that he is but a medium, a vessel that is often cracked and broken.

One particular feature of the fallibility of genuine prophetic awareness is the involvement of all of us in the particular circumstances of our age and society. When, as in societies at a relatively low level of moral development, the sense of the divine impinges upon their attitudes, the progress they make will be correspondingly limited and sometimes distorted. If the ethical understanding of a community has not advanced beyond the level of crude retribution and collective guilt, there may well be a genuinely religious ingredient in the perpetuation of ideas which a more enlightened age would find morally abhorrent. What we have to be constantly heeding is the intertwining of genuine religious disclosure and insight with other all too fallible aptitudes and interests of finite creatures. Much in the sacred scriptures of various religions will become more intelligible to us and can be viewed judiciously in their proper setting if we think, as indicated, of divine disclosure as a leaven in the totality of our own aptitudes and aspirations. At the same time the distinctiveness of the transcendent influence must not be lost or wholly merged in the finite media on which it operates.

The precise moment of genuine religious awareness, operating within the functions it claims for its own operation, may not always be easily delimited. It may be sharp as in sudden conversion, but even in these cases there is often a period of subtle maturing in which truly religious elements come to their open and more explicit formulation. More commonly, although religious awareness and sensitivity may be clear and explicit, it has its own ebb and flow, it merges itself in other concentrations of attention, it may be gentle and unobtrusive, in acts of worship or meditation, much as aesthetic awareness is not always easily delimited and isolated from the observations and attentiveness which it takes up into itself. It is for these reasons that some may even fail to detect the moment of live religious awareness or allow it in retrospection to be lost in the media which it embraces. This, in particular is where very careful thought is needed in our times to detect and uphold the element of genuine religious awareness against crude and bogus travesties of it.

This is all the more the case because the live religious awareness lives on in other experiences and practices and also perpetuates itself dispositionally in our way of living as a whole. Its occurrence may be known obliquely and indirectly, and this in notable cases is no mean assurance of its presence. It may well become apparent by its fruits. But we can never rely on that alone. The enlivened individual awareness is the indispensable religious factor, and it is out of it preeminently that the distinctively religious shape of any faith is formed.

In my fuller discussion of these matters, in my book *Our Experience of God*, I also ascribed particular importance to what I described as the patterning of religious experience. There are significant recurrences and variations which I sought to describe. It has often been found, for example, that the enlivened awareness of transcendent being often comes about in situations where we have least justification for expecting it, for example in states of an overwhelming sense of guilt. The latter, especially a sense of grievous wrong-doing, comes between us and one another and between us and God, it drives us on our own inner resources which dry up without the sustaining sense of the world around us and of other persons. It is in this debility that we find the real penalty of sin. But, surprisingly, it is often in just this situation of despair and desperation that men have found the onset of the renewed awareness, sometimes gentle, sometimes disturbing, of infinite being as the end and sustainer of their own existence; and life as a whole becomes renewed again and transformed. The recurrence of this, its variations and the extension of it into the religious consciousness of various societies, builds itself up over the ages into the sense of God, not as mere remote sustainer or 'Unmoved Mover', but as a seeking reconciling God peculiarly involved in what we are and in our relationship with him. This is, to my mind, a very important aspect of the emergence of the more theistic forms of religion.

The same may be said of other situations of desperation, whether we bring them on ourselves or not. It does not follow that distressing circumstances and evil are straightaway resolved. Appalling evil is still with us and presents the severest tension and strain for religious commitment. It is not a problem I can lightly deviate into now. But in these situations also men have found the sustaining and recurring sense of God invading their attitudes as a whole and giving them renewal of strength. God comes to be known as 'an ever present help in trouble'.

My submission, without pursuing any of these illustrations in further detail here, is that it is in the substance and the patterning, which I would also much stress, of the moulding and refining of otherwise neutral sensitivities and attitudes by the insistent impact of the transcendent rather than in *a priori* and essentially empty attempts to determine abstract properties of God, that we find the vindication and shaping, as well as the appropriate critique, of the more particular affirmations and practices of actual living religions. The parallel with 'other minds' is here very close. We do not, as I have persistently maintained elsewhere, know the minds of other persons as we know our own; however close our relationships may be, however intimate, there is an essential element of mediation. The relation we have with God is no less intimate and close because it comes in the mediation of the peculiar modification of our own experience, it is as close as finite-infinite relationships can be, and to those who experience it profoundly there is no barrier that matters.

For many who persist in an agnostic or skeptical view of religion I suspect that a major determinant of their attitude is the expectation that religion must vindicate itself for them, if at all, in some form of supernatural experience of which finite beings are not capable at all. This is the sophisticated version of the expectation that the astronauts may discover God for us. What we need is to know better where and how to look, and to persevere more in the demanding discipline of looking in the right way. Far too often we take it all to be a matter of a few formal considerations one way or the other when in fact it is a matter of living committed lives in the closest association with the witness of profound experience over the ages.

Closely related to the same mistake is the supposition that religious experience is essentially and wholly a private matter. It has to be initially and in itself private, but what matters most is not the intimations of God that we may chance to have in our more exclusively private existence, but rather the absorption into our individual awareness of the wealth and significance of the sustained and developing religious awareness of men down the ages. It is not in a void that we encounter God but in all the rich diversities of our cultures and the formative part of religion within them. This is what must come alive for us in our individual experience.

This is what is sustained for us in various ritual and symbolic practices. How these function, and where they are genuine and healthy, is a subject in itself. There can clearly be perversions and parasitic imitations, just as there can be over-intellectualized treatments of practices where the true significance is closely bound up with the figurative and symbolic expression. Symbolism is not a thing apart, a decorative superimposition, it is a major, and often indispensable way of articulating what is profoundly perceived and felt and finds its appropriate depth in the fertilization and sustaining of one another's experience within a continuing social unit. At the same time the symbol is not final, and the ritual must not become an end in itself, much less be exploited for purposes extrinsic to its proper motivation, indeed as has sometimes happened evil purposes.

All the same, in the last resort, the symbol is not final and it does not exist for itself. It derives its proper power from the continuity of the experience it expresses. The same is true in art. Poetry, or other forms of art, which depend entirely on lively image or emotional overtones, is not the finest. It palls unless it high-lights or exhibits something distinctive and notable, however impossible it may be to distil the meaning from its figurative expression. The symbol must not, in religion, take wing on its own, it must be anchored in experience.

The same is true of the more formally credal expressions of religious truth. There is a place for sophisticated formulation, acutely difficult though it is and full of pitfalls, but it is not, alas as has too often been assumed, an a priori intellectual exercise. It proceeds on the basis of what is taken to be conveyed in the medium of live experiences enriching and extending one another in a variety of social contexts. This means that the theologian has a peculiarly difficult task and requires a greater variety of skills and aptitudes than is usually realized, least of all by the practitioners themselves--a point which I much stressed elsewhere.[3] It is particularly hard because one has to be responsive to the symbolism, and the appropriate artistry, and also to the critical assessment of all which these convey.

A very serious pitfall, most of all for Western theologians and religious thinkers, is to take some striking religious symbol or story out of its context in the total themes of the scriptures in which it appears. This has happened, for example, when juristic metaphors in the New Testament have been made the basis of doctrines of retributive punishment and vicarious suffering in ways appalling to any moral or intellectual sensitivity. Credal affirmations do have their important place, most of all in religions in which the historical factor is important. They help to concentrate attention in the right way. But they must proceed on the basis of what is initially made evident in the formative disclosures in experience.

In Semitic religion there is usually accorded an exceptionally important place to a distinctive form which divine disclosure in human experience is alleged to have taken in a particular stretch of history. This is not the place to assess that claim or the even more astounding claim that the one transcendent reality was able, in some way which baffles all comprehension, to so limit itself as to enter into a fully human limited form in the culmination of the process which had been taking shape in Hebrew history. This remains the central Christian affirmation and I myself make very little sense of recent attempts to retain the formulae and ritual practices of the Christian faith if these central themes, as they seem to me, of the New Testament and traditional Christian understanding are so eroded as to bear little relation to the sources from which they came and the meaning they would normally be given. Far better, it would seem to me to abandon them altogether, though that is far from what I myself commend.

At the moment the question is not the soundness of the distinctive claims of the Christian faith or any other. But there is one point I do want to stress, namely that the assessment of these and like affirmations must, in the last analysis, go back to the profoundest appreciation of the subtle interlacing of normal sensitivity with divine intimation. If this adds up, in the available evidence about Jesus and his background, to the central affirmations of the New Testament and traditional Christian thought, so be it - it is what I myself think. But if the central claims are not to be sustained along those lines I know of no way in which they can be so sustained that can stand in the light of open reflection and criticism today.

It remains most important, however, to recognize that, which ever way the evidence points in respect to the distinctive stances of various religious, this is no bar to the profound recognition of one another's insights and achievements. We have learnt much better today how much of mutual enrichment of one another's experience and insight is possible in this way. The differences, where they remain, must not be blurred, any more than they must be hardened by misunderstanding. We can reach across to one another's practices and histories to the great deepening and enlivening of our own experience, and the gain in this way to the West today is much too evident for me to need to underline it now. We have learnt enormously from varieties of experience that were new to us, and the range of our sensitivity has been much extended. Meditation has acquired a new depth for us, and flights of religious imagination opened up that were little known before. My contention is that the major clue for understanding and assessment, when expertise and scholarship has done its work, is the religious toning and directing of religious experience along the lines indicated.

There is one point of considerable substance which I would like to add. It refers to what I was saying at the beginning about the initial awareness of the transcendent. In my understanding, the transcendent is altogether beyond and other than finite being. Creaturely existence, though wholly dependent, is not any part or mode of ultimate being. This is however much in dispute, not only in extensive features of Eastern thought but in Western philosophies from Plotinus to Hegel and contemporary mystical philosophers like W. T. Stace. This again is a vast issue in itself and the opposition of view varies a great deal in its sharpness. I maintain, however, that this is the crucial issue for today in religious thought. It is not an easy one, and we all have our attachments to entrenched positions which we find hard to surrender. My own allegiance has been made plain in one publication after another. I strongly insist on the distinct reality of finite existences and especially on the peculiar distinctness of persons. On the line we take on this issue will turn, more than on anything else at present, the ultimate understanding we have, and even the sensitivity to genuine religious reality as such. It is an issue we must firmly face, though the last thing we must fall into is the temptation to settle the question lightly out of hand to ensure easy accommodation and good will. The right sort of good will does not call for that sort of price, and is contaminated by it. But we must have this central issue steadily before us, and it is on our success in coping with it, I maintain, that the best eventual progress will be made with all our other major problems and our power to share the wealth of one another's insights and experience.

I have spoken mainly of communication and assessment of truth. No space is left to consider the part which our own responsiveness plays in the process as a whole. The wind may blow 'where it listeth' but 'prayer and fasting' has its place too. An age committed to exclusively secular pursuits, and those not always the most elevated, can hardly expect to be well appraised of things that have to be 'spiritually discerned'. What Simone Weil and others have brought to mind for us about heeding and 'waiting on God' is immensely relevant, and this means more than being religiously attentive in a general way, it means also the continual response, in practice as in thought, of individuals in the ebb and flow of the illumination they have in their own religious experience and what they assimilate from the religious life of their community. It is in these terms, in the exchanges of genuine response, in the part we play ourselves in the formulation of our own religious awareness, that we come again, if I may further reflect my personal allegiance, to our understanding of the more theistic approach to religion and our proper participation in it.

Religious experience, so conceived, is not passive, and it does not under-rate the essential mutuality of living, personal relationship as involved centrally in it. The language of prayer and devotion, of struggle and surrender, as well as the essential serenity, bring us to the vitally personal character of religious existence which we are also apt to overlook, even though some like myself may be inclined to over-stress it. The 'God of the living', even of the wayward and rebellious, the relentlessly seeking God, is the God I have encountered in my own experience.

I hope such an element of personal testimony is not out of place. What matters for us here is that, in discussion and amity, we should enter into one another's views and sensitivity with as much imaginative insight and empathy as we can. Where the gaps can be closed let us hasten to do so, but our main concern is with the truth and 'the wind of the argument withersoever it takes us'. We must understand as much as we can across the boundaries, with humility as much as with firmness. There is no place in true religion for confrontation or rancour, there is all the place in the world for empathy and humility.

King's College

University of London

NOTES

1. See also Chap. 3 of my *Persons and Life After Death*

(London: Macmillan, 1978).
   2. *New Essays in Philosophical Theology*, Chap. XI.
   3. "What is Theology?" *Freedom and History*, Chap. XVII.

CHAPTER III

CRITIQUE AND HERMENEUTIC
IN PHILOSOPHY OF RELIGION

BENOIT GARCEAU

When called to reflect on religion, as on other works of man, the philosopher seeks to understand it. But there are many ways to understand a phenomenon, firstly, to grasp its meaning and to express it in clear and distinct concepts; secondly, to explain it or to sort out the conditions which make it possible; finally, to judge its value. Any search to understand a phenomenon must attempt to answer three questions: What is it; Why is it thus; and Is it as it ought to be? These three questions call upon three different yet indissociable functions of the intellect: its hermeneutic, explanatory, and critical functions.

The philosopher who has decided to try to understand religion soon discovers that he is entering a domain dominated by a separation of the methods of understanding and a fragmentation of religious language. This discretely respected division of labor reserves for the theologian the hermeneutic of religion, for the psychologist and the sociologist its explanation, and for the philosopher its critique. This fragmentation of language arises not only from the fact that each of these disciplines employs a particular mode of understanding, but also from the fact that within each of these languages there are numerous and varied concepts of religion.

It is necessary for philosophers to confront this situation with courage and lucidity, recognizing that their principal task by which they have something valid to contribute to the understanding of religion is to seek to overcome this fragmentation in the human understanding of religion. Guided by this fundamental intent, the only way open is to redo on one's own each of the three questions which religion raises for the intellect--to carry out a *repetition* of the three, hermeneutic, explanatory and critical functions of the understanding in relation to the religious fact. This implies that the philosopher of religion begins to listen to the theologies, the religious sciences, and the critiques of religion in order to be sure how religion is understood. Above all one must examine closely the presuppositions and consequences of each of these groups of disciplines and thus prepare the elaboration of a theory of religious practice.

What is thus sketched out is nothing less than a new type

of philosophy of religion which has become necessary by reason of a break-up of religious language. It is new in contrast to the two principal ways in which, in the western tradition, philosophers have studied religion by using either hermeneutic or critique. Whereas the former was a reflection from within the faith and aimed at understanding its content, the latter dealt with religion as a given which did not escape the rule of reason. It submitted religion to a model of rationality with the more or less explicit goal of guaranteeing the autonomy and freedom of reason in relation to religion. This is not the occasion to write at length on the difficulties raised by each of these approaches to a philosophical study of religion. It is sufficient to note that each employs a particular function of the intellect--either hermeneutic or critical. The hermeneutic of religion only partially answers the questions asked of the intellect by the religious fact. The critique of religion, when separated from a hermeneutic, risks being satisfied with generalities which reduce the religious given to a pre-established rational framework. Both lead to a very impoverished language--a kind of *Logos* without *Praxis*.

In this initial sketch of a "repetition" of one mode of discourse on religion, I propose to reflect on a particular type of critique of religion in order to show how it is impossible for the critique to isolate itself from the hermeneutic: how it is necessary at a certain stage for a critique to appeal to a hermeneutic. I have chosen the critique developed in these times especially in the Anglo-Saxon context of empirical philosophy. In order to situate this, I shall begin by comparing it to other existing types; then I will show the manner in which this critique, which is entirely taken up with judging the value of religion, finds itself driven, despite itself, to restate a presupposed question regarding the nature of religious faith.

THE EMPIRICIST CRITIQUE OF THE LANGUAGE OF FAITH

The empiricist critique of religion took the form of a critique of the validity of religious language, that is to say, it disputed the right of such language to be a candidate for truth or falsity. That questioning was carried out in two different manners; first, in the name of a theory of meaning which stipulates the criteria to which all language must conform in order to be considered as a possible candidate for truth, and second in the name of a theory of knowledge or of a general epistemology. The critique of the meaning of the expressions of faith is a relatively recent enterprise developed by analytic philosophy of religion. It questions something prior to the truth of the expressions of faith, namely, their aptitude for being held to be sensed--the only type of expressions concerning which one can ask if they be true or false. The skepticism that inspires this is not a theological one, questioning in the name of historical data or of a philosophical worldview the truth of religious faith. Rather, it is a "meta-theological" skepticism which questions the validity of the language of faith uniquely in the name of a logical analysis of language. Only with difficulty can this critique of meaning, though it depends ultimately upon a theory of meaning, be isolated from a general theory of knowledge, in particular from a model of knowledge borrowed from the practice of science and rationally justified only on the basis of the fruitfulness of science.

In contrast, the critique of the validity of theological language or discourse based upon a theory of knowledge manifests greater sincerity and clarity regarding its presuppositions, and is practiced today by some followers of the critical rationalism of K. Popper. It does not stop at the language of faith, nor is it preoccupied with judging whether or not it has meaning. Rather it sees in religious faith a transgression of the essential function of reason, namely, to submit to criticism all hypotheses, to try to refute all conjectures without ever pretending to have ethical certitude and without any other manner of approaching truth than through its passing the test of falsification.

I would like to attend to the first form of the critique of the validity of the language of faith, that which is based upon a theory of meaning. According to this theory, which has been reformulated several times since the heydey of logical positivism, a statement can be held as declarative or having a referential value--and therefore being a candidate for truth--only if in principle it is able to be controlled, or subject to verification or falsification, on the basis of empirical evidence. The critique itself consists in judging that statements made by a believer regarding God have only the appearance of declarative statements, since the believer is incapable of showing the manner in which these statements could be verified or falsified. Hence they should be eliminated from all language which claims truth.

One could think that this critique of the validity of language regarding faith presents the believer with a much less serious challenge than the critique of the genesis of religion[1] introduced in our culture by the three masters of suspicion, Marx, Freud and Nietzsche, which seem to create a much more profound crisis for religious faith. This consists in holding the language of faith to be that of a consciousness which is false or not really as it appears; that it is language which has been elaborated with the aim of concealing and justifying the unrecognized interests of one's consciousness. The Marxist theory of ideology, the Freudian analysis of illusion, the Nietzschean genealogy of morals do not consist in questioning that its statements are true or that they are possible candidates for the truth. More radically, they consider them to be residues of the unconscious, whose origin must be reconstructed, even in its material conditions, in order to explain them and to allow consciousness to become independent of them. The radical character of this critique is clear for, as S. Breton has shown, it is the critique not only of a principle, but of *all* principles. Any discussion on the truth or falsity of a theological statement is prohibited when from the outset it is held to be ideological or illusory, and explicable by illogical individual or social factors.

What gives the critique of the validity of religion its importance is that without it the critique of its origin is not justified, for it is the critique of validity as a necessary presupposition for the critique of origin. When the critic of ideology or of illusion undertakes to retrace the origin of a thought in order to explain it, he is convinced that this research has interest and promises useful results. But this research can be of interest only if he is convinced that religious thought, which he wants to explain by the material conditions of its possibility, does not have the right to be held as true and that despite this it nonetheless persists in being cultivated by many. From the beginning among critics of ideology or of illusion there is always an implicit value judgment on that which one attempts to explain as being an anomaly or a symptom of a sickness which must be explained by him in order to free the patient. This value judgment, unless it be only a prejudice, rests upon a critique of the validity of the language of religious faith.

In Marx, one finds one of the most significant examples of this necessary dependence of the critique of the origin of religion upon a critique of its validity. He is convinced that religion is both a false substitute for true happiness and a form of protest against human misery, and hence that it will disappear when man takes into his own hands the direction of his existence. But this conviction depends upon another which is less explicit in Marx's work, but constantly necessary to justify the first. This is the conviction common to all rational atheists that religion has its source in ignorance of the powers of nature and of society, and that it would disappear with the progress of science, just as did alchemy and astrology with the progress of chemistry and astronomy.[2] Only this rationalist postulate--which, it is necessary to insist, deals with the validity of a language of faith--explains that among the products of consciousness enumerated in the *German Ideology*--religion, morality, art, philosophy--only religion must completely disappear. Morals, philosophy and art can be transformed and become moments of human praxis; only religion cannot be retained, precisely because it is presupposed to be irreconcilable with scientific progress. This means that the Marxist critique of the origin of religion is based upon a prior critique which the Enlightenment proposed as its program and which the meta-theological skeptic of our era takes up once again in order to assure its success, namely, the critique of the validity of the language of faith.[3]

A CRITIQUE OF THE EMPIRICIST CRITIQUE OF RELIGIOUS LANGUAGE

Therefore, let us examine more closely this critique of the validity of religion which is carried out in the name of a theory of meaning. This is not the place to present a history of the debates provoked by this critique since it first was formulated in a precise manner by A. Flew.[4] Nor is it the place to examine all the strategies employed to demonstrate, either against this critique the validity of the language of faith, or in agreement with this critique that its result has been to purify religious faith from unsuitable language. I prefer to focus instead on an answer to this critique which I consider most satisfactory because it comes from analytic philosophy itself in which the critique is rooted, and because it submits each of its two principle theses to scrupulously careful examination. This is R.S. Heimbeck's reply in his work *Theology and Meaning*.[5] For reasons I do not understand this has received little attention by analytic philosophers of religion, though it offers the most convincing criticism of the empiricist critique of the validity of the language of faith.

The first thesis of meta-theological skepticism, according to Heimbeck, cannot withstand criticism. It is not true that an expression must be verifiable or falsifiable in order for it to have a referential value or to be used to express a proposition. To believe so is to fail to note the difference between the criterion of *meaning* of a statement and *evidence* of the senses. The criterion of meaning designates the conditions which must be fulfilled in order that a statement may serve to express a true or false proposition, while evidence of the senses designates the sensible conditions which must be satisfied in order that we might know or have the right to believe that this proposition is true or false.[6] Now, the sufficient and necessary condition in order that a statement might express a true or false proposition is not that it be controlled by verification or falsification: its verifiability and its falsifiability only constitute sufficient, but not necessary conditions for its referential value.

The fact that a statement is verifiable or falsifiable, that is, controllable, suffices for one to suppose that it says something about what is real, but it is not necessary that it be controllable in order for it to have such meaning. The sufficient and necessary condition of its referential value consists rather in the fact that it has with other propositions relations of implication or incompatibility.[7] Applied to theological language, this criterion allows one to recognize among the statements used by the believer those which are declarative propositions and hence candidates for truth or falsity. The statement "God is love," for example, has referential value if it is used by the believer in such a way that it entails relations of implication or incompatibility with other propositions. That is to say, if the believer, in making this statement, implies that "God knows all men, wants their well-being and in order to realize it is prepared to give himself," and if it excludes that "God wants the eternal misery of all men."[8]

Having shown that the requirements of verifiability or falsifiability imposed on theological expressions so that they may have meaning result from an unfortunate confusion between verification and semantic entailment, between falsification and semantic incompatibility, between sensible evidence and criterion of meaning, Heimbeck attempts to prove that the second thesis of meta-theological skepticism is equally untenable, and that theological statements are as a matter of fact verifiable and falsifiable in a decisive manner on the basis of empirical givens. Let us note immediately that this task is not strictly necessary in order to refute the empiricist critique of the validity of theological statements; this refutation was already accomplished when it was shown that these expressions do not have to be controllable by verification or falsification in order to be held as valid. If they maintain relations of implication or incompatibility with other propositions these statements have a referential value; they serve to express propositions and are candidates for truth. But Heimbeck wants to do more.

For the skeptic who is steadfast in claiming that a statement has cognitive value only if there exists in principle a way of controlling it empirically, he takes up the task of showing that in theological language there are propositions (and precisely those which provide the foundation of this language) which are not withdrawn from the requirements of falsifiability and verifiability. If his argument succeeds in convincing the reader, then one can see what it promises: to justify one's recognizing objective value for statements of faith which serve as principles for all theological discourse. In this sense, such discourse, far from being reduced to what Wisdom and Flew called a "picture preference,"[9] would have the value of propositions susceptible to being empirically controlled.

A theological system, according to Heimbeck, is formed from two different kinds of propositions: those which admit of no relation of implication or incompatibility with empirically verifiable or falsifiable propositions (for example, "God exists," "God is triune," "God is omnipotent"), and those which maintain such a bond (for example, "God raised Jesus of Nazareth from the dead, near Jerusalem, at $time_2$" which implies the truth of the following two propositions: "Jesus of Nazareth died near Jerusalem, at $time_1$," and "Jesus of Nazareth was alive in the vicinity of Jerusalem, at $time_3$").[10] In traditional Christian theism, propositions of the second kind, grounded on empirical data, serve as the foundation for the first. Heimbeck finds it strange that in recent meta-theological debate one is exclusively occupied with the first.[11] An abstraction has been performed upon the language of faith, retaining for submission to logical analysis only the propositions not having any relation of implication or of incompatibility with empirically controllable propositions. However, when he asserts "God loves all men"--a proposition without empirical incidence--the believer bases the assertion on this other: "God sent His own Son in order to offer his life for the sins of the world," and this on still another: "The Word was made flesh in the person of Jesus Christ," and this finally on this other which implies empirically verifiable propositions and excludes others: "God raised Jesus of Nazareth from the dead, near Jerusalem, at $time_2$"[12] It is necessary therefore, holds Heimbeck, to reverse the flow and apply logical analysis on those propositions anchored in statements of observable facts which serve as principles procuring for all others their positive legitimation.

Heimbeck has no trouble showing the falsifiability of these empirical theological propositions. If a theological proposition has a purely empirical consequence and if this consequence is falsifiable in a conclusive way on the sole basis of empirical data, then the antecedent proposition (by analogy with *modus tollens*) is *ipso facto* falsifiable in a conclusive manner on the sole basis of empirical data. If there is some purely empirical factor which is incompatible with a theological proposition and if this incompatible is verifiable in a conclusive manner solely on the basis of empirical data, then the antecedent proposition (by analogy to *modus pomendo ponens*) is *ipso facto* falsifiable in a decisive way on the sole basis of empirical data.[13] For example, the proposition "God raised Jesus of Nazareth near Jerusalem, at $time_2$" is falsifiable in a decisive way on the basis of empirical data from the fact that it implies "Jesus of Nazareth died, in the vicinity of Jerusalem, at time$_1$", and "Jesus of Nazareth was living, in the vicinity of Jerusalem, at time$_3$". These are falsifiable propositions on the basis of empirical givens, or on the basis that they exclude that "Jesus of Nazareth was dead at moment$_3$", which is itself verifiable in a conclusive manner on the basis of empirical data.

Are such theological propositions having consequents or empirical incompatibles equally verifiable in a conclusive manner? Are they controllable to the extent of being able to be verified by empirical evidence? Yes, maintains Heimbeck, on condition that one acknowledge the originality of the reasoning employed by the believer in order to adhere to this kind of proposition. It is no longer a question of a reasoning by implication or incompatibility, but by inference proceeding from an agglomeration of the signs of that which is found signified therein.[14] To exclude this type of reasoning, under the pretext that it is never conclusive, is, in his opinion, to hold a monolithic conception of reason, to acknowledge only one method, and to be obliged not to recognize the validity of a process which is used not only by clinical psychology and history, but also by the physical sciences.[15] Certainly, this reasoning from signs to the thing signified implies an *a priori*. The choice of empirical data serving as signs signifying the truth of a theological proposition is itself determined by the context to which belongs the theological proposition which empirical data are able to verify. But this circle in which reasoning by signs moves is not unique to the believer; even the scholar cannot avoid selecting empirical data on the basis of a theoretical proposition which the same date serve to control or justify.

The effort made by Heimbeck to show that theological language is empirically controllable led him to defend three closely related theses: 1. In theological language, everything depends upon an aggregation of empirical propositions joined to propositions which are conclusively controllable on the basis of empirical evidence; 2. These propositions, which give all the others their positive justification, are falsifiable and then empirical incompatibles are verifiable; 3. Finally, these propositions are verifiable to the degree that they are the result of an inference from signs to what is signified. Of these three theses, the second is unassailable if the two others are true. In effect, if there are empirical propositions at the source of theological language, which are obtained by inference from an agglomeration of signs and which are verifiable by those signs, there is no difficulty in allowing that in this language there are propositions which are falsifiable in a conclusive manner on the basis of the evidence of the senses.

HERMENEUTIC AND RELIGIOUS FAITH

But does theological language truly rest upon an aggregate of empirical propositions, and are these obtained by inferences based upon an agglomeration of signs? This question is raised by Heimbeck's reply to the critique of the validity of the language of faith. Evidently, this is a question to be resolved by research on the nature of theology and faith, which is a matter for theology. This means that at this stage in its development, the critique of the validity of theological language calls upon an hermeneutic of religious faith, and that the philosopher must therefore suspend his critique and question the theologian in order to learn how religious faith understands itself and how it judges its own language.

M.L. Diamond's[16] recent reaction gives important evidence that the question raised by Heimbeck's work concerns the nature of theology. One of the rare representatives of analytical philosophy of religion to take *Theology and Meaning* into account, Diamond's brief commentaries help to understand the silence which surrounds this book. In Diamond's view, Heimbeck's position rests on an extremely naive conception of theology, that of the "fundamentalist" who presupposes that everything in Scripture is to be taken according to the letter and that Scripture has unquestionable authority. With such a conception of theology, Heimbeck excludes himself from the debate on the verification of statements of faith and condemns himself to not being heard by the participants involved in this debate. Though they recognize that "fundamentalists" have no difficulty in verifying the statements of their faith, fundamentalists remain of no interest because their criteria of credibility are irrevocably outdated by the development of science and have been abandoned by more enlightened theologians.[17]

This reaction is very significant. Heimbeck's answer to the critique of the validity of theological language is criticized and rejected in the name of what theology ought to be. Because it employs a conception of theology which one judges no longer to be in agreement with the criteria of rationality developed by scientific thought, Heimbeck's thesis does not have the right to be heard in discussions on the validity of theology. This reaction reveals a more or less conscious decision at all costs to keep the debate on grounds of validity. This concerns no longer, however, the validity of the expressions of faith, but that of a conception of theology which is to be kept or done away with according as it is or is not in conformity with the criteria imposed by scientific reason.

However, Heimbeck's thesis raises a question of truth-- more precisely, a double question of truth: (a) Is it true that theological language depends upon an aggregate of empirical propositions obtained by inference from an agglomeration of signs? and (b) Is this language itself true? The first question calls, as we have underlined, for a hermeneutic of theology and of faith; the second calls for a critique of the language of faith, no longer as to its origin or validity, but as regards its truth.

What does a philosopher engaged in the debate on theology and verification learn from a hermeneutic of religious faith? One learns two elementary truths without which this debate will be poorly oriented from the outset. One learns, in the first place, that religious faith cannot be reduced to the inevitable outcome of a challenge which would be imposed from without, as would be the case of just any fact. If the Jewish faith is never separable from the experience of the Exodus, if the Christian faith always refers to witnessing the resurrection of Christ, they are, for all that, not understood by those who live them as inferences proceeding from empirical data, similar to the adherence of an historian or psychoanalyst to an hypothesis suggested by reading documents. To liken it to the attitude of a scholar who concerns himself with a theory which can be abandoned and replaced as soon as it no longer succeeds in giving an account of all the facts would be to misunderstand faith. To acknowledge in theological language, as Heimbeck does with good reason, the utilization of the criteria of falsifiability and of verifiability in a manner which is not very different from that which one finds in scientific language, does not necessarily imply that faith itself is inferred from empirical data and is able to be certified or controlled by such date.

Though its certitude is always without evidence, faith never does without signs. This is the second elementary truth which a hermeneutic of faith would bring to light. The presence of signs is necessary for the birth and maturation of faith in another person. In this, faith in God does not have a different status. Whether furnished by the sensible universe, by Scripture, or by the intimate life of the believer, signs are necessary mediators of religious faith. Understood by the believer as an invitation from God who is taking the initiative to address himself to his creature and as communion with him--and not only as an adherence to a discourse on God--faith, like any other communion between subjects, is possible only if based upon communication by signs. It is therefore not altogether wrong to conceive the language of faith as resting on elementary propositions which, in turn, are based upon a reading of signs by one who is disposed to believe signs.[18]

Is this reading of signs by the believer shielded from criticism? No, no more than it escapes the question of truth. But the type of critique that it calls for is not primarily the critique of its origin or that of the validity of its language. It needs a critique of its truth. This is more exigent than the other two for it does not restrict itself to evaluating the language of faith on the basis of an aggregate of objective criteria of validity, nor to judging faith on the basis of the material conditions which seem to explain it. Anticipating in a way both of these critiques, it seeks overall to judge the language of faith on the basis of what is ultimately intended by faith, and to judge faith itself on the basis of the signs by which it is nourished.

This certainly is a critique immanent to the life of faith, and carried out by the faith and for the faith. That the first critique of religion comes from faith itself, is a fact too often ignored by many analysts of religion. Religion is poorly described if its originality is not taken into account. One considers one's faith to be an absolute and exclusive certitude: *absolute* because it is the result neither of a system of thought nor of social or psychological factors, but of a conversion based upon God's initiative; *exclusive* because it does not present itself as the establishment of one meaning among others, but as the sole affirmation of the ultimate sense of the universe. Much more, one is convinced that only one's faith is apt for critiquing its own expression, for deciding on the value of all that one can imagine, conceive, or say of the God envisaged by one's faith.

Moreover, not only do enlightened believers claim the critique of the language of their faith as a task for which they alone are fitted, but they see in it an indispensible task for the health and development of their faith. Without it faith soon succumbs before one or another of the two crises through which it will inevitably pass: (a) that which is produced by the transcendence of its object, that is, of God who must never be assimilated to a being of the world nor thought of as if he were a being among others; or (b) that which is produced by the refusal of the non-believer to admit that what the believer holds as true, with absolute certitude, has meaning and can be true.

If a philosopher judges the truth of the language of faith, they can do so only in the name of the first principle of his philosophy which they consider evident. Any philosophy worthy of the name founds itself, in the last analysis, on a particular answer to the question: "what is the real?", an answer which is commonly called one's "ontology." It is clear that not all ontologies are equally hospitable to the affirmation of God. One who holds a materialist ontology, for example, cannot avoid judging to be false any statement of faith affirming the existence of a God that is the creator of the universe. He will make it seem that he is appealing to a logical analysis of faith language to show that it is unintelligible or incoherent, but he will already have decided, by the type of philosophy he has decided to employ, that the language of faith is an error. Other ontologies could come to a more nuanced judgment--e.g., certain idealist ontologies--and lead to the decision simply that, though the language of the faith is not true, it symbolizes at the level of representation what philosophy knows to be true.

There is, however, a way in which the philosopher and the believer can share the critique of the truth of theology. If they agree to admit that theological language rests on a believing reading of signs, they both are faced with the crucial question: based upon what conditions does the interpretation of signs become possible? This reflection aimed at explicating the *a priori* of communication by signs is an urgent task for philosophy of religion, preliminary in all cases to the apparently more rigorous, but less decisive, disputes on the validity of the language of faith.

University of Ottawa

Ottawa, Canada

NOTES

1. For a further study of the relations between a "critique of the validity" and a "critique of the genesis" of a language of faith, see Stanislas Breton, *Du Principe* (Paris: Aubier, 1971), 289ff. Also see, by the same author, "Critique des ideologies et crise de la foi," in *Foi et épistemologie contemporaines* (Collection "Philosophica," 7; Ottawa: Editions de l'Université, 1977), 71-89.

2. This aspect of the Marxist critique of religion has been brought to light by N. Lobkowicz, "La critique de la religion chez Marx," *Les Etudes Philosophiques*, 3 (1976), 317-330.

3. A good example of the critique of the validity of religion aimed at establishing its falsity and assuring the truth of the skepticism of the Enlightenment *before* undertaking the critique of its genesis, is to be found in Kai Nielsen's *Contemporary Critiques of Religion* (London: Macmillan, 1971), p. 1. See my work on this subject, "La philosophie analytique de la religion: contribution canadienne 1970-1975," *Philosophiques*, 2 (1975), 307-308.

4. "Theology and Falsification," *New Essays in Philosophical Theology*, ed. by A. Flew and A. MacIntyre (London: SCM Press, 1955), pp. 96ff.

5. R.S. Heimbeck, *Theology and Meaning: A Critique of*

Metatheological Scepticism (London: G. Allen and Unwin, 1969). I know of only two brief commentaries by analytical philosophers of religion on Heimbeck's book: A. Flew's "Theology and Falsification in Retrospect," in *The Logic of God: Theology and Verification*, edited by M.L. Diamond and T.V. Litzenburg (Indianapolis: Bobbs-Merrill Company, 1975), pp. 275-79, and M.L. Diamond's, "The Challenge of Contemporary Empiricism," *Ibid.*, p. 45. Note also the excellent article of Jacques Poulain, "Proble mes logiques du langage theologique," in *Les quartre fleuves*, 6 (1976), pp. 54ff, which sees in the work of Heimbeck "one of the most convincing" responses to the empirical critique of theological language.

6. Heimbeck, *Theology and Meaning*, p. 48.

7. *Ibid.*, p. 56.

8. *Ibid.*, p. 91.

9. See Flew, "Theology and Falsification," p. 97.

10. Heimbeck, *Theology and Meaning*, pp. 172-73.

11. *Ibid.*, p. 174.

12. *Ibid.*, pp. 175-76.

13. *Ibid.*, p. 167.

14. *Ibid.*

15. *Ibid.*, pp. 245-46.

16. Diamond, "The Challenge of Contemporary Empiricism" (cited in fn. 5), p. 45.

17. ". . . they [contemporary empiricists] regard fundamentalism as so hopelessly outmoded by the development of scientific standards of believability, that they do not even bother to challenge the thrust of its factually meaningful statements" (*ibid.*).

18. Note that Thomas Aquinas, who saw a triple sense to the word *religio* (i.e., *religare, reeligere,* and *relegere*), conceived of religion as an attitude by which man joins himself with God by choosing him as his supreme end and by ceaselessly rereading, as in a book, that which God expects of him. See *Summa Theologica*, II-IIae, q. 81, a. 1.

CHAPTER IV

ON SOME THEOLOGICAL LANGUAGES

RICHARD M. MARTIN

Nasyami aham bhu nasyati loka:

Sruyatam dharma, Bhagawat.

I

Important steps in the study of linguistic structure have taken place in recent years. By 'linguistic structure' is meant here deep structure, logical structure or logical form, semantic structure, "source" form, or whatever. The deep form is usually contrasted somehow with so-called surface form, but just what the difference is supposed to be is far from clear. In any case, the exact study of logical form has recently come to the fore and now occupies a very central role in contemporary linguistics. On the more philosophical side, there has been sufficient progress to provide genuine guidance in the analysis and reformulation of the metaphysico-theological aspects of our language. Because of the obvious alternatives in the terminology and in the semantics involved, let us speak of theological languages in the plural, each of which may be regarded as a specialization of some one basic linguistic format or "source" system.[1]

It would be unwise and not conducive to conceptual progress ("progress in clarification") to disregard in metaphysics and theology these recent achievements in the exact study of language. As we enter the last decades of the twentieth century, not to take account of them would be to remain *retardataire* and to rest content with outmoded procedures and concepts in a day of highly sophisticated methodologies. In taking these achievements into account, indeed in embracing them as our best guide in the formulation of theories, we must not think that the great traditional views are threatened thereby or are to be abandoned. On the contrary, they are threatened only when we *fail* to bring them into harmony with contemporary knowledge. Here lies a great shortcoming in recent theology. There had been all manner of talk about God's being dead and then found again, about the emotive need but cognitive unacceptability of talk of God in general, of God's revelation in the historicity of man's experience, of the demythologization of process, of the hermeneutics of theological language, of the "peculiar" or "odd" character of much of it, and so on and on. No doubt valuable points have been raised in such discussion, of which account should be taken.

Unfortunately, however, there has been little really deep study directed at harmonizing theological discussion with the *methods* of mathematics, logic, and the empirical sciences, but with what *results*? There have been countless attempts, but most of them rather, it is to be feared, have been rather spurious. What is urgently needed, it would seem, is a profound methodological seriousness in theological discussion, to bring it to the high level of logical sophistication from which it should never have been allowed to decline in the first place. The subject is of infinitely greater seriousness in human life than those in which scientific techniques have won the day hands down. Modern science has, after all, been a tremendous theoretical as well as practical success, whereas theology has had a great fall, at least in the popular view. Let us never forget, however, that success is a kind of goddess to be pursued and ravished only at one's peril.

What is God?--jesting and unhappy humanity has been asking for several millenia and has not sufficiently tarried for the answer. Of course, all manner of attempts have been made to approach this most fundamental metaphysical question, but most of them have been but partial, emphasizing this or that feature at the expense of others. Volumes have been written on these partial answers, as the history of philosophical theology and metaphysics amply attests. Much that is precious from these volumes must be retained. We should not reject the valuable insight and the dearly won progress, however slow, which constitutes the history of these subjects. But, at the same time, we should not be slavish imitators of it, paying no heed to newer and vital developments of relevance. Unfortunately, much of the philosophical theology of our time, as already in effect suggested, has been written as though no progress had been made in the logical analysis of language since the time of St. Thomas, or even Aristotle. Such study is dismissed as irrelevant, or in any case not helpful. Still more unfortunately, where such study has been taken into account, it is not the real thing that is used but some illicit surrogate. The real thing is not easy to come by, and hence it is no wonder that so little recent progress has been made in the use of serious logico-linguistic theory in philosophical theology.

Form to most is a secret, Goethe has told us. Yet without it--without order, system, structure, logical connection, rationality--we can do no discursive thinking whatsoever. We could perhaps do all manner of mental things--perceive, feel, believe, rejoice--but nothing that could be dignified as *thinking* in any ordinary sense of the word. So we should pay some attention to logical form right at the start of our discourse, and to the curious fact that the more attention we pay to it, the less we seem to know about it. Form is all fine and tidy only to those who inquire little concerning it.

The comments here in Part I are merely introductory. In Part II items needed in the logical machinery are enumerated. Part III looks at some recent analytic work on *Plotinus*. Part IV comments concerning the language needed for *St. Anselm's ontological proof*. Attention is called in Part V to important work on the *ex motu* argument of *St. Thomas*. Part VI turns to *Whitehead* and the seminal notion of a *primordial valuation*.

A discussion of the logical foundations of metaphysical *idealism* occupies the remainder of the paper. The comments in Part VII are introductory. Part VIII lays down a few *fundamental principles*. These are generalized somewhat in Part IX. Part X discusses the problem of harmonizing the language of *modern science*, including the mathematical *theory of sets*, with that of idealism. St. Thomas's *five signs of will* are introduced in Part XI, and it is shown how an adaptation of their theory may be accommodated upon an idealist basis. The theory of the *divine will* is made somewhat more exact in Part XII. Part XIII is a few somewhat general comparative comments, and Part XIV looks ahead concerning science, faith, and aesthetic feeling, the theories of which cry out for further development on the basis of what has preceded.

II

For the necessary logical background throughout, let us use the crisp, standard *first-order* theory of *quantification* with *identity*, with *virtual classes* and *relations* added as merely notational conveniences. (Virtual classes, remember, are almost as good as real ones, but, of course, we can never quantify over them directly, although sometimes we can do so with suitable technical artifice.[2] To this framework it is useful to add the theory of the *part-whole relation* as between individuals (Lesniewski's *mereology* or calculus of individuals). And, of course, it would be foolish to try to do without the resources of logical *syntax* and *semantics* developed in recent years. For these let us assume first-order formulations, with the semantics based on suitable relations (especially *denotation*) taken as primitive. To this a method of handling *intensionality* must be added, as well as a method for accommodating entities such as *events, states, acts,* and *processes*. To handle intensionality, let us adapt Frege's notion of taking entities under a given linguistic mode of description or *Art des Gegeberseins*. We can then distinguish between the individual x and x taken under some mode of describing it. (This latter might even be taken as the *ordered couple* of the entity and some one-place predicate applicable to it). And for the characterization of events, states, etc., it is undoubtedly best to introduce a new style of variables, and then squarely face up to the need for new kinds of predicates, the *event-descriptive* predicates, and for general logical principles governing them. But all this is readily available, to some extent anyhow.[3] (If notions of higher-order logic or set theory are needed here or there, attention will be called to them *in situ*).

III

By way of a preliminary, let us note very briefly how logico-linguistics has been helpful in enabling us to clarify some of the historically great theological views. And let us consider, first, the system of Plotinus (which has had so profound an effect on the Islamic world). It may well be contended that Plotinus is the first really *systematic* theologian in the West.

The fundamental relation in the Plotinic system is that of *emanation*, so that we may let

$$\text{`}x \text{ Em } y\text{'}$$

express that x emanates into y. Em is presumably a totally irreflexive, asymmetric, and transitive relation. In addition, let 'One' be a proper name for the Plotinic *One* or *Unity*, and 'All Soul' for the *Psyche* or *All-Soul*. And let 'Int' be a one-place predicate so that 'Int x ' expresses that x is a *Form* or that it is a member of the Intelligible Realm, of *Nous*. And let 'Obj x' express that x is an *object* of the lower cosmos, of the lower world of Nature or of the Sensibles, among which are included human bodies. Roughly, then, we have these four expressions for the four Plotinic levels; two of them, note, are proper names, and two of them are predicates. The proper names are for the multiplicities, which, however, also have a kind of unity, a secondary unity or *fusion*, let us say.

Clearly these four realms are mutually exclusive in appropriate senses, and jointly exhaustive of the whole cosmos. Concerning the One, there are some special principles as follows.

$\vdash(x)(\sim x = \text{One} \supset \text{One Em } x)$,

$\vdash\sim(Ex)(\sim x = \text{One} . (y)(\sim y = \text{One} \supset x \text{ Em } y))$,

$\vdash(x)(\text{Int } x \supset \text{One Em } x)$,

$\vdash\text{One Em AllSoul}$,

$\vdash(x)(\text{Obj } x \supset \text{One Em } x)$.

And also

$\vdash(x)(\text{Int } x \supset x \text{ Em AllSoul}).$
$\vdash(x)(\text{Obj } x \supset \text{ AllSoul Em } x),$

and

$\vdash(x) (\text{Obj } x \supset \sim(\text{E}y) \ x \text{ Em } y).$

Concerning the One, very little can be truly said/not-said in terms of 'Em.' Thus also

$\vdash \sim F \text{ One},$

for most precidates F not containing 'Em.'

The converse $\cup$ Em of the relation Em enables us to handle the "return to the One," which plays so central a role in Plotinus' ethics and theology. (Recall that x bears the converse of R, $\cup R$, to y if and only y bears R itself to x, for all x and y.) We can read '$\cup$ Em' as 'aspires to the condition of', 'desires to return to the purity of', and the like. The Plotinic theology is implicit in the theory concerning Em and $\cup$ Em as regards the One.

A very fundamental problem in Plotinus is to provide for the multiplicity of individual souls in terms of the unity of the All Soul. Roughly this is done in terms of the "Couplement" of the All Soul with individual bodies. The individual souls are thus handled as intensional constructs of a certain sort.[4]

IV

Let us reflect next for a moment upon the celebrated argument of St. Anselm, concerning the existence of God regarded as *id, quo maius cogitari non potest*. Note what must be provided even to formulate this definition in an exact way: a Russellian singular description for some unique entity, a theory concerning the relation of being greater than, a theory of knowledge concerning *concepts* or conceiving, a theory concerning ability or *capability*, and then of course some doctrine as to how all these are interrelated.[5] Think how complicated all this is when we look at it *from close up,* certainly much more complicated than ordinarily thought. It is failure to come to terms with the complications involved that has vitiated most recent discussions of the subject. And until we have looked at the subject closely we cannot be said to understand it in any very deep sense. *Gott wohnt im Detail*, as an old German adage has it, whether we like it or not.

Let 'Per x' express that x as a human person, and 'x Able e, "F"' express that x is *able* (capable) of doing e as (intensionally) described by the one-place predicate 'F'. And let 'x Cncv e, "G"' express that x *conceives* of e under the predicate 'G', and 'e_1 Gr e_2' that e is *greater than* e_2. Also 'a Des e' (or 'a Des x') expresses that a *designates* e (or x). We may then let

'Uns e' abbreviate '~(Ee') (Ex) (Ea) (Eb) (a Des x . b Des e . Per x. x Able e',$\ulcorner$<a, Cncv, b, '{e_1 ∋ (Ee_2) e_2 Gr e_1} '>$\urcorner$)'.

Here the cormers are used in the sense of Quine's quasi-quotesand '{e_1∋ --e_1 ---}' stands for the virtual class of all e_1's such that --e_1--. And '<---->' is a suitable event-descriptive predicate. The definiendum may read, following Hartshorne, 'e is an unsurpassable entity'.

In any steady gaze at Anselm's view, certain principles must be assumed, some of them to be gotten out of the actual text of the text of the *Proslogium* or elsewhere, and some of them to be supplied as necessary addenda. These latter perhaps are too obvious to have been written down, or perhaps are to be presumed as taken for granted, or perhaps are principles the need for which has not been recogmized heretofore. And so it is with all of the historically great philosophical views. Considerable latitude must be allowed to make the reconstructed theory fit the text. The fit is not given automatically and considerable ingenuity is often needed to make it even approximative. The fact, a sad one perhaps, is that we always have to be content with approximations; and, even more annoyingly, there are always alternative approximations that assert themselves with perhaps equal cogency. Thus, we should never claim very much victory even if the fit we achieve seems fairly close. The same is true, incidentally, whether we use methods of modern logical analysis and reformulation or not. The best that we can ever say, it would seem, is that a given historical view is merely the disjunction of the most likely alternative readings of it, howsoever formulated.

In order to prove that God exists uniquely, i.e., that there is one and only one unsurpassable entity, it must hold that soeone ("even the fool") conceives of something under the predicate 'Uns', that every unsurpassable entity (if there are any) exists, that there are no two unsurpassable entities, and that anything conceived as unsurpassable is in fact unsurpassable. With these principles provable fro prior principles governing 'Able', 'Cncv', and 'Gr', it may be proved that

$$\vdash E! \, (\jmath e \, . \, \text{Uns } e),$$

where 'E!' is construed essentially as a *Principia Mathematica*, *14.02. Whether such prior principles are acceptable, and whether the primitives here are suitable for the intended purposes, are of course questions that remain open -- here as for any theological, or indeed even scientific, theory.

V

Important logico-linguistic work on the *ex motu* argument of St. Thomas has been carried out by J. Salamucha.[6] Very briefly and somewhat simplified, his work may be described as follows. Let 'Mx' express that x is one of the *entia realia* in local physical *motion*, and let 'x M y' express that x *moves* y or is the cause of motion in y. Concerning these notions some assumptions are made, that

(Ex) Mx,
(x) $(Mx \supset (Ey)$ y M $x)$,
(Ey) $(y \in C'M . (x)$ $((x \in C'M . {\sim}x = y) \supset y$ M $x))$,
(x) (y) $(x$ M $y \supset {\sim} y$ M $x)$,
(x) (y) (z) $((x$ M $y . y$ M $z) \supset x$ M $z)$,
(x) (y) $((x \in C'M . y \in C'M . {\sim}x = y) \supset (x$ M y v y M $x))$.

Here $C'M$ is the campus or field of the relation M, i.e., the class of entities that bear M to or are borne M by some entity or other. These assumptions then state that there is an entity in motion, that every moving entity is moved by some entity, that there is a "first" entity in the campus of M that moves every other entity in the campus of M, and that M is an asymmetric, transitive, and connected relation. From these assumptions--not all of them are actually needed--it is provable that

(Ey) $({\sim}My . (x)$ $((x \in C'M . {\sim}x=y) \supset y$ M $x))$.

Salamucha discusses in some detail the justification of the assumptions here on the basis of Aquinas' text, especially as in the *Summa contra Gentiles*, I.c. 13. He also considers proofs of some of the assumptions, and a number of alternative approaches to the proof as a whole. His concern is primarily with the validity of the argument given the premises. This indeed was the primary concern also in the remarks above about Anselm. In both cases, of course, a deeper discussion is needed to determine the acceptability of the assumptions, and indeed of the entire linguistic frameworks, in the light of modern scientific knowledge. In the case of Anslem, it is doubtful that appropriate scientific meanings of 'greater than' and 'conceivable' can be found. In the case of the *ex motu* argument, the theory of motion involved is probably at best naive in the light of modern physics. However, such judgements are by no means final, and the essential contents of these proofs may well be forthcoming in other ways.

VI

From St. Thomas to Whitehead is a leap of several centuries in time but a natural next step for systematic theology. Much that in St. Thomas is obscure becomes clarified on a Whiteheadian basis.[7] And it may well be that the notion of a *primordial valuation* is the greatest single contribution to theology in all the years from St. Thomas to the present. Unfortunately, however, Whitehead does not characterize the notion explicitly, scarcely if ever gives an example, and says nothing concerning the structure of the language in which the primordial valuations may be expressed. Nor does he subdivide them in any way but treats them rather isocephalically, gaining therewith a rather unpliable theory. Later on we shall try to broaden it somewhat in order to gain more flexible notions, with which to characterize the divine will. But for the present, let us consider only primordial valuations as they occur in Whitehead.

The primordial nature of God, it will be recalled, is "the unconditioned conceptual valuation of the entire multiplicity of eternal objects" with respect to their "ingression" into, or applicability to, each and every "actual occasion."[8] Thus where a is an n-place predicate standing for an n-adic eternal object, the "proposition" $\ulcorner a\ e_1...e_n \urcorner$ is "valuated" in the primordial nature, perhaps even to just such and such a degreee, where $e_1,...,e_n$ are any actual occasions. To express this we may write (with the numerical superscript 'i')

$$\ulcorner a\ \mathrm{PrimVal}^1,...,e_n \urcorner.$$

The primordial naute then is just the totality of all (acts or states of) primordial valuating. Where Fu 'F is the fusion of the virtual class F, we may let

'*png*' abbreviate 'Fu '$\{e \ni (Ea)\ (Ee_1)...(Ee_k)(Ei)\ (O \leqq i \leqq 1$. $((\mathrm{PredCon}_1\ a\ .\ <a,\ \mathrm{PrimVal},\ e_1>e)$ v $(\mathrm{PredCon}_2\ a\ .\ <a,\ \mathrm{PrimVal}^i,$ $e_1,\ e_2>\ e)$ v ... v $(\mathrm{PredCon}_k\ a\ .\ <a,\ \mathrm{PrimVal}^i,\ e_1,\ ...,e_k>e)))$ '.

Here '$\mathrm{PredCon}_j a$' expresses that a is a j-place predicate standing for a j-adic eternal object. Here j is said to be the *degree* of the eternal object. We need not assume that there are eternal objects of degree greater than some pre-assigned 'k'. So k here is the degree of the eternal object of highest degree admitted, in the sense of having a name for it as a primitive.

Note the really stupendous all-inclusiveness of *the png*. Every hair of one's head is primordially "valuated" with respect to every eternal object, and this to just such and such a degree. The fundamental meaning of 'ought' is presumably provided for here. Every actual occasion ought to have just the properties, to speak loosely, ascribed it in the primordial valuatings. The *png* is thus more the source of value, however, than of fact or of scientific law. It might be thought then that the definition is too restricted, not providing the *png* with sufficient breadth or power. It is all-inclusive with respect to value, but that is all. In a moment we shall broaden the notion considerably, in connection with the discussion of absolute idealism. In terms primarily of 'Primvali' essentially the whole of Whitehead's theology may be formulated, so that little more concerning it need be said here.

In the articulation of these various historical views emphasis has been placed upon the primitive vocabulary needed. It is the choice of this that is crucial, and differences here of course may result in radically different theological systems. Some modicum of clarity concerning the primitive vocabulary must be achieved before we can frame fundamental principles or axioms. Strictly, of course, the two must go hand-in-hand, but in practice the choice of primitive notions usually comes first. But this is only the beginning, the foundation, and should not of course be mistaken for the full edifice.

VII

The foregoing comments, about Plotinus, Anselm, St. Thomas, and Whitehead--chosen in part because of the availability of technical studies concerning the language-structures implicitly employed--are merely preliminary to the main intent of this paper. Let us try now, in what follows, to do what is commonly thought impossible, namely, to reconcile--nay, to bring into indissoluble union--the basic insights of *philosophia perennis* with logico-linguistics. The latter, as we have already seen, is "subject-matter neutral," and hence metaphysically so; it should be as useful for the articulation of any one theological view as well as any other. In any case, this reconciliation is the theme to be explored. If we succeed, at least to some extent, we shall be close to a conception of God, suitably characterized formally and rationally, embracing all fact and value in its "real internal constitution," and of such grandeur and majesty that we would all do well faithfully to surrender our whole lives to comprehend it, and "above all things," in the words of Peirce in a related context, "to shape the whole conduct of [our] life, and all the springs of [our] action into conformity . . . " with it.[9] In this way we should be well on the road to a meeting not only of east and west, but also to characterizing in a most intimate way the union of religion and science, on the other. An overambitious goal, perhaps, but at least one for which it will be worthwhile to help prepare the way, in this ecumenical metaphysical congress devoted in part to the notion of God.

"What is that, knowing which, we shall know everything"? It is not easy to know the real, internal constitution of God's nature, and perhaps no one has ever known it fully. Perhaps no one has ever known it even partially, although this is doubtful. Beliefs, intimations, surmizes, and the like, have often sufficed. No matter, the notion of God should be characterized, it would seem, in so grand a fashion as to contain, in some specific sense, all knowledge of all beings and happenings, here, there, and everywhere, past, present, and future. In particular God's nature should contain, in a most intimate way, all scientific law, both causal and stochastic, as well as all boundary conditions. Hence implicitly it should contain all factually true statements. But God is not merely the repository of truth, but of value, of beauty, and goodness, as well. Science and value, whatever the shortcomings or defects of our knowledge about them, should be properly fused, it would seem, in any satisfactory characterization of the real internal constitution of God's nature. Failure to attain this fusion is to rest content with only a partial and hence inadequate characterization.

The perennial theme "that being is one and identical with God the creator," as Richard Taylor puts it, ". . . is rediscovered in every age and in every corner of the world. It is at once terrifying and completely fulfilling. It will never perish and nothing will ever replace it. Nothing possibly can; its endurance is that of the stars."[10] But even the stars may come and go and still be terrifying. Only if we add the insight of *philosophia perennis*, that being is in its real nature akin to *mind* or *spirit*, in some sense, do we have the basis for a view of the kind described. Whatever spirit is, being is "identical" with it, and being *one*, so also is spirit. "There is only one river, which here and there assumes new forms or is modified in this way and that, either briefly or more lastingly. Here it assumes the form of a ripple, there of a waterfall, and numberless other forms in other places." Being here and now is a material object, but there and then a mental act perhaps. No matter what forms or shapes it assumes or however it is modified, it still may be regarded as identical in character with God the creator, "that from which the origin, subsistence, and dissolution of this world proceed."

VIII

Let 'AS' be a primitive individual constant designating Absolute Spirit or Mind. Immediately we note, as a first metaphysical principle, that AS exists.

Pr 1.   ⊢E!AS.

The existence of individuals is handled here predicatively, where

'E!x' is short for '$^\neg x$ = N'.

N being the null undividual.[11]

It is interesting that Hegel, at the very beginning of his *Phänomenologie des Geistes*, differentiates "Subjective" and "Objective" Spirit from the AS.[12] The one is a "manifestation" of AS, the other, we might say, is an "embodiment" of it. The various objects of nture are embodiments of AS, those of the mental realm, manifestations. Accordingly, two new primitives are needed for these notions. Let us symbolize them by 'Manif' and 'Emb'. Clearly the following principles should obtain concerning these notions.

Pr 2. $\vdash$(x) (y) ((x Manif y v x Emb y) $\supset$ x = AS).

Pr 3. $\vdash$~(Ex) (x Manif AS v x Emb AS).

Thus AS alone manifests or embodies enything, and nothing whatsoever manifests or embodies it. Also nothing is both manifested and embodied by anything.

Pr 4. $\vdash$~(Ex) (Ey) (x Manif y . x Emb y).

We may now define

'SubjSp' as 'Fu '{x ∍AS Manif x}'

and

'ObjSp' as 'Fu'{x∍AS Emb x}'.

Thus the realm of subjective spirit is the fusion of (the virtual class of) everything manifested by AS, and objective spirit is the fusion of (the virtual class of) everything embodied by AS. These definitions give a very natural way of providing for the two Hegelian realms. Should they be regarded as mutually exclusive? If so, we need to postulate that every *part* of a manifested or embodied individual is also manifested or embodied, respectively. Thus, where P is the part-whole relation, we have also that

Pr 5. $\vdash$(x) (y) (z)((x manif y . z P y) $\supset$ x Manif z)

and

Pr 6. $\vdash$(x) (y) (z) ((x Emb y . z P y)$\supset x$ Emb z).

Also it should then obtain that

$\vdash$~(Ex) (~ x = N. x P SubjSp . x P ObjSp),

that SubjSp and ObjSp have no non-null part in common.

If these two spheres are taken to exhaust the cosmos, we have also a *Principle of Completeness*, that

Pr 7. $\vdash (x)$ $(\sim x = AS \supset (AS \text{ Manif } x \vee AS \text{ Emb } x))$.

IX

But perhaps there are realms of derivative being other than these two, or even altogether different. Perhaps the two Hegelian ones are themselves unjustifiable on the basis of modern science, and constitute an illicit dichotomy. These difficult questions we need not attempt to answer for the moment, but we should note that the foregoing material may easily be extended to allow for any number of derivative realms of being--or even for none at all. But let us assume at lease one. And let us speak of manifestation in a wider sense for the moment, so as to include embodiment, as well as whatever further kinds of process are appropriate for generating the given kinds of entities. Thus we let 'Manif$_1$', 'Manif$_2$', and so on, be primitives, and we let

'U$_1$' abbreviate 'Fu $\ulcorner \{x \ni AS \text{ Manif}_i x$ '.

Thus the universe of entities $\cup_i$ is merely the fusion of the entities to which AS bears Manif$_i$, for each i. For each relation Manif$_i$ we then have principles analogous to *Pr 2* and *Pr 3*, and an appropriate extension of *Pr 4*.

If $i = O$, absolute monism results. AS is the only reality and there is nothing else except *māyā*. Even the name 'AS', the very inscriptions of *Pr 1-Pr 4*, and so on, would be dropped. They would all be items of *māyā* and thus presumably not worthy of rational discourse. But even if $i > O$, we could still hold to a form of the doctrine of *māyā* in regarding the entities of U$_1$, U$_2$, and so on, as *māya*-items but allow rational discourse about them. However, if the discourse is to be in accord with modern logic and science, it will quickly be seen to be so important for our human life, and so insistently objective and compelling--and indeed so difficult to come anywhere near getting it right--that the point of talk of *māyā* at all is seen lost. Surely the AS is not the less great, the less worthy of our total and all-absorbing effort to grasp it, if we regard the derivative entities to be genuine in some sense, if only as manifestations of it. In fact, the situation is the other way around. Let us embrace the derivative entities as worthy of our love and respect, and make every possible effort to come to see most intimately how they are interrelated one with another. It is in this way, in part, that we can come to know the grandeur and munificence of the AS itself. However, our "knowledge" of it need not be exhausted therewith, but rather enhanced.

The manifested objects of the U$_i$'s are to comprise whatever it is that our cosmos contains. Precisely how we are to populate them is of course an incredibly difficult matter. Surely they must contain the objects needed for the sciences in their most developed stages. We must not rest content with the ontology of centuries back nor even with the "stale" science of yesterday. But to spell out in detail the ontology of even one science, at its present state of development, would be very difficult, and would tax even the greatest practitioners. Nonetheless, we may suppose it to consist of a presumably small number of U_i's in terms of which the desired assertions of that science can be made. And similarly for other sciences. And we must never suppose that any characterization of the U_i's needed for science would ever be final or complete. On the contrary, they would always be *semper reformanda*, and would exhibit enormous variation in the hands of different practitioners in the same field even at the same time.

X

Of particular interest for philosophers of logic and mathematics is the U_i, or the U_i's, needed for both. If logic is taken as standard, first-order logic, as throughout this paper, no assumption concerning the U_i's needed be made. On the monist view, our only individual is AS, plus the null and world individuals. The latter, however, would be identical with AS, and the null individual N has the proper that

$$\sim E!N,$$

that it does not "exist" in the appropriate sense. (Of course N is a value for a variable, but that is something else again). And if $i>0$, the U_i's are merely those of the sciences as already provided.

Logic as such has no ontology. For mathematics, however, the situation is very different. Let us think of it set-theoretically, in terms of the Zermelo-Fraenkel-Skolem system. Here two U_i's are needed, one for individuals or *Urelemente*--Zermelo himself insisted upon their admission, it will be recalled--and one for the realm of sets. No harm need arise from admitting the *Urelemente*, the very entities that may be presumed to populate the cosmos. The admission of a domain of sets, however, postulates entities that do not populate the cosmos in any obvious sense. Even so, this matter need not deter us, for we may use merely our *Urelemente* but allow set-theoretic talk about them in the manner of the "moderate" realism of Duns Scotus.[14] In this way classical mathematics in the set-theoretical sense may be preserved, and used, moreover, as a basis for the other theoretical sciences. For this, of course, a new primitive is needed, and for applications to the sciences, such new primitives as those sciences require.

The question arises as to whether, once the U_i's required for the sciences have been arrived at, any further ones are needed. Do the ontologies of the sciences suffice for all discourse?--other of course than that concerning the AS and its possible manifestations in SubjSP? Well, surely yes, if 'science' is construed widely enough. Note that the question is merely one about *ontologies*, not about the modes of discourse allowed concerning the items admitted in that science. One and the same act, for example, may be said to occupy such and such a place-time in one context, but to be immoral or illegal or prohibited or whatever, in others.

Mental entities are the occupants of the realm of SubjSp, and any interesting metaphysical idealism may be presumed to admit such entities. The basic items here are no doubt individual souls or minds, and mental acts are presumably dependent upon these fundamentally. It is a bit mysterious as to just what an individual mind is and how it is to be individuated. You have one and I have one, and they are alike in both being minds. Let yours be m_1, and mine m_2, and let m_3, m_4, and so on, be those of others. The calculus of individuals allows us to form then the "group" mind

$$(m_1 \cup m_2 \cup m_3 \cup m_4 \cup \text{-----}).$$

Even this group mind does not of course exhaust the AS, the latter being infinitely greater. Is this group mind a *part* of the AS? If so, then each individual mind is also, each being a part of the group sum. Equally difficult is the question as to how the individual souls or selves are related to the mental acts of, or pertaining to, them. And this in turn leads to the problem as to how such acts themselves are to be individuated.

Individual minds result from the AS by one kind of manifestation, bodies by another. Does the human person, a unique complex of mind and body, result by still a third kind of manifestation? Some idealists might well contend so. To bring then a mind, a body, and a person together, we need the Of-relation of possession.[15] It is not clear whether the mind possesses the body, or the body the mind, or the person the mind, or the mind the person, or the body the person, or the person the body. Perhaps there is possession in all of these ways. In any case, if bodies, minds, and persons result from separate kinds of manifestation, a suitable way of bringing a body, a mind, and a person together must be at hand to provide for a concrete human person.

The idealist, of course, regards minds as *par excellence* the real entities, they being like unto the AS itself. Rather than to regard the other types of entities as arising by other kinds of manifestation, perhaps they should be regarded rather as the result of the *concentration* of soul-stuff in some particular way or other. Each material object is merely soul *concentrated* in a certain way. The notion of concentration, the very prototype of mental activity, then would play the role of the relations of manifestation. But concentration is mental in a way in which the relations of manifestation are not. And if "subject" and "object" are alike, both must be mental. Thus the following "principle," where Conc is the relation of concentration, might well hold, namely,

$$\vdash(x) \ (\text{AS Conc } x \supset x \text{ Like AS}).$$

Everything that results from the AS by concentration is itself like or similar to AS. And likewise,

$$\vdash(x) \ (x \text{ Like AS} \supset x \text{ P AS}),$$

that everything like AS is itself a *part* of it. The former principle might well hold without the latter. If the two principles are taken together, a genuine monism, even a pantheism, is achieved. The development of idealism in terms of the theory of concentration would be more Vedantic that Hegelian. Principles akin to *Pr 2-Pr 4* and *Pr 6-Pr 7* would obtain, with 'Conc" in place of 'Emb", no change being required in *Pr 1* and *Pr 5*.

For the purposes of the subsequent discussion, and to simplify, let us presuppose the theory above as developed in terms of the Hegelian 'Manif' and 'Emv'. But whatever modifications of this might be thought desirable can easily be presupposed equally well.

XI

Howsoever the fundamental ontology is arranged, the AS has remarkable tasks to perform and must be given some remarkable properties, akin to those of the Thomistic God and the Whiteheadian primordial nature. To see this let us consider again the primordial valuations constituting this latter, which will be helpful as a heuristic, enabling us to flesh out the theory underlying St. Thomas' "five signs of will."

The five signs of will, it will be recalled, are *operation, permission, precept, counsel,* and *prohibition*, but St. Thomas is not too clear as to precisely how these are to be construed. The words are used analogically. "A man may show that he wills something . . ." by doing it "directly when he works in his own person; in that way the sign of his will is said to be an *operation*. He shows it indirectly, by not hindering the doing of a thing; . . . In this the sign is called *permission*. He declares his will by means of another when he orders another to perform a work, either by insisting upon it as necessary by *precept*, and by *prohibiting* its contrary; or by persuasion, which is a part of *counsel.*"[16] St. Thomas goes on to note that "since the will of man makes itself known in these ways, the same five are sometimes called divine wills, in the sense of being signs of that will. That *precept, counsel,* and *prohibition* are called the will of God is clear from the words of *Matt.* vi. 10: *Thy will be done on earth as it is in heaven.* That *permission* and *operation* are called the will of God is clear from Augustine, who says: *Nothing is done, unless the Almighty will it to be done, either by permitting it, or by actually doing it.*" These very dignificant but difficult comments should be helpful in attempting to characterize the divine will, whether construed Thomistically or not.

Among the operations we should surely include all the manifestations and embodyings. These operations concern only the ontology. In addition, there are the primordially ordained circumstances, laws and so on. Let

$$\text{'AS PrimOp } a, x_1, ..., x_n\text{'}$$

express that the AS *primordially* operates or has it obtain that the *n*-place predicate *a*, standing for a virtual class or relation, apply to or denote x_1, ..., x_n, in this order.

That the AS is the "creator" of all entities (other than himself) is in effect provided by *Pr7* above. But he is also the ordainer of all scientific, moral, and aesthetic law, and this aspect of the divine activity can be stipulated only by bringing in the relation PrinOp. Thus suppose $\ulcorner ax_1...x_n \urcorner$ obtained, for fixed x_1, ..., x_n, and *a*, not just factually but as the result of, or as an instance of, some scientific law. Then it would obtain that

Pr 8. $\vdash$ AS PrimOp $a, x_1, ..., x_n$,

for such *a*, $x_1, ..., x_n$. Nor need *Pr 8* be restricted to just scientific law. It should be extended to instances of whatever laws are thought to obtain in any of the spheres of knowledge. And if one or more of the x_i's are allowed to be numbers, natural, real, or complex, even laws of a probabilistic kind may also be included here. Think what a staggering principle *Pr8* then is, incorporating as it does all the laws governing the cosmos, construed in the most inclusive possible sense. But surely the AS must be conceived as so great as to incorporate no less.[17]

Clearly also it holds that

Pr 9. $\vdash (y) (a) (x_1)...(x_n) (y \text{ PrimOp } a, x_1, ..., x_n \supset y = \text{AS}$,

so that the AS is the *only* entity capable of the primordial operations. And also

Pr 10. $\vdash(a) (x_1)...(x_n) ((AS\ PrimOp\ a,x_1,...,x_n\ .\ a\ Des_{vc}\ F)$ $\supset Fx_1....x_n)$.

Whatever is primordially ordained to obtain does actually obtain. But the converse need not hold. Not all that obtains is primordially ordained to do so. (The 'Des_{vc}' here is the sign for the designation of virtual classes, where '$a\ Des_{vc}\ F$' is short for '$(PredCon_1\ a\ .\ (x) (a\ Den\ x \equiv Fx))$', 'Den' being the primitive for denotation.[18]

The primordial operations need not be confined to just the demands of scientific law, as already noted. Moral and aesthetic laws, if there are such, are included, and even such boundary conditions as might be thought to obtain independently of law. Perhaps even there are miracles in some sense as the direct result of a primordial operation. If so, the stipulation of such is presumed included here.

St. Thomas speaks of prohibition in a somewhat narrow sense, of prohibiting the "contrary" of a precept. Here let us speak rather of prohibiting the contradictory of an operation. Thus we may let

'AS PrimPrhbt$_{Op}$ $a,x_1,...,x_n$' abbreviate 'AS PrimOp $\ulcorner -a \urcorner$, $x_1,...,x_n$'.

where $\ulcorner -a \urcorner$ is the negation of a. There are other kinds of prohibition, which we shall meet with in a moment.

The primordial operations concern all objects whatsoever, including human persons, actions, events, states, processes, and the like. The precepts and counsels, on the other hand, may be thought to concern only human beings and their actions. Let 'p' be a variable for persons and 'e' for actions of the kind humans are capable of performing. And let P be a virtual class of persons satisfying such and such conditions, and A a class of suitable actions. Then we may let

'As PrimPrcpt 'P','$\{p \ni (Ee) (p\ Prfm\ e\ .\ A\ e)\}$''

express that it is a primordial precept that persons of the kind P should be persons who *perform* actions of the kind A, under appropriate circumstances. Precepts alway seem to be general in this way applying to all persons and actions of given kinds. Counsels, on the other hand, may always be regarded as specific, applying to a given person with respect to a given action.

Are all counsels covered by a precept? It is tempting to think so, whether the precept is explicitly known or exhibited or not. If so, we may let

'AS PrimCnsl p,e, 'P','A" abbreveiate '(AS PrimPrcpt 'P', '{q ⱻ(Ee') (q Prfm e' . Ae')}' . Pp . Ae)',

so that p is counseled to do e relative to P and A just where it is precepted that all P's do A's and p is a P and e an A.

More general definitions, with variables in place of the constants, may be given by letting

'AS PrimPrcpt a,⌐{pⱻ (Ee) (p Prfm e . b Den e)}⌐'

be the primitive form and then letting

'AS PrimCnsl p,e,a,b' abbreviate 'AS PrimPrcpt a,   ⌐ {qⱻ (Ee')(q Prfm e' . b Den e)}⌐' . a Den p . b Den e)'.

Note that by means of precept the AS in effect "orders" a persoⁱr "to perform a work" by "insisting upon it as necessary," in some social, moral, or aesthetic sense. And surely some generality must obtain as a condition for the necessity. Hence the use of the class terms 'P' and 'A'. Counsel, however, is always specific and "persuasion is a part of it." Only a person, even a sum of persons, can be persuaded and hence counseled in this sense.

There are relevant kinds of prohibition corresponding with precept and counsel. Thus we let

'AS PrimPrhbt$_{Prct}$ 'P','A" abbreviate 'AS PrimPrcpt 'P', '{pⱻ ~(Ee)(p Prfm e . Ae)}",

so that persons of the kind P are prohibited in this sense from being persons who perform actions of the kind A. And there are also prohibitive counsels, so that

'AS PrimPrhbt$_{Cnsl}$ p,e,'P','A" abbreviates '(AS Prim- Prhbt$_{Prcpt}$ 'P','A' . Pp . Ae)'.

More general forms of these definitions, with variables in place of the constants 'P' and 'A', may also be given.

Clearly, corresponding with *Pr 9*, we should have that

Pr 11. ⊢(x) (a) (b) (x PrimPrcpt a,b⊃(x = AS . (y) (a Den y⊃Per y) . (y)(b Den y ⊃ Per y))),

when 'Per' is the predicate for persons.

Also where

'p Oblg a'

expresses deontically that p is obliged to be a person of the kind denoted by a, we should have that

Pr 12. ⊢(a)(b)(p) (AS PrimPrcpt a,b, . a Den p)⊃p Oblg b).

This principle assumes that whatever is primordially precepted, so to speak, is deontically obliged. This at least should hold, but not the converse. There are surely obligatory acts not determined so primordially.

No doubt much takes place in the cosmos that is primordially neutral, in the sense of being neither the result of an operation not operationally prohibited. Thus, where 'PredCon$_n a$' *express that a* is an n-place predicate constant,

"AS PrimNtrl$_{OP}a,x_1,...,x_n$' may abbreviate '(PredCon$_n$ a . ~AS PrimOp $a,x_1,...,x_n$. ~ *PrimPrhbt*$_{OP}$ $a,x_1,...,x_n$)'.

And similarly for human actions that are neither covered by precept nor presept-wise prohibited. Thus also

'AS PrimNtrl$_{Prcpt}$ 'P','A'' abbreviates '~AS PrimPrcpt'P','A' . ~AS PrimPrhbt$_{Prcpt}$ 'P','A')'.

Here too, a more general definition may easily be given.

Note that in the foregoing only 'PrimOp' and 'PrimPrcpt' have been needed as primitives, in addition of course to 'Manif', 'Emb', and 'AS'. All the other primordial predicates have been defined within the linguistic framework embodying quantification theory, identity, nereology (or the calculus of individuals), and of course some semantics and event theory. The deontic notion 'Oblg' is also presumed available, either primitively or by definition, but it is not a purely primordial notion, being relative always to a given social group and a specific deontic code.

There is also the all-important notion of a primordial *permission*, to which we now turn.

XII

It is clear, if nothing is done other than its being done either by the Almighty or being permitted by him, ⸜that the operations and permissions exhaust the divine will and that the other "signs" are to be handled as subdivisions. The operations and permissions are thus to be mutually exclusive and jointly exhaustive. Under the primordial operations are included the manifestations, embodiments, operations proper, and the operational prohibitions. These operations are all such that their results, so to speak, *must* obtain if our cosmos is to be the way it is. All the other primordial notions are included inthe permissions, whose results *may* be violated in our cosmos. Note the implicit distinction here between the operations and permissions, on the one hand, and their "results," on the other. The results of the one *must* obtain, but those of the other need not. On the other hand, the operations and permissions themselves constittute the necessary activity of the AS, if our cosmos is to be what it is.

The prohibitions include just the three kinds, operational, preceptual, and counsel-wise, the precepts both the proper and prohibitive ones, and similarly for the counsels. The primordially neutral comprise the operationally neutral and the preceptually so. The primordial permissions, as already noted, then comprise all the primordial activities not included in the operations, i.e., the prohibitions, the precepts, the counsels, and the primordially neutral. These comments may all be summarized by means of three additional definitions. We may let

'PrimOp e' abbreviate '$(Ea)(Ex_1)...(Ex_k)$ ($<$AS, Manif,$x_1>e$ v$<$AS, Emb,$x_1>ev<$AS, PrimOp, $a,x_1>e$ v$<$AS, PrimOp,$a,x_1,x_2>e$ v ... v$<$AS, PrimOp, a,x_1, ...,$x_k>e$)',

'PrimPrmsn e'   abbreviate   '$(Ea)(Eb)(Ep)(Ee')(Ex_1)...(Ex_k)$ ($<$AS,   PrimPrhbt$_{Prcpt}$· $a,b>e$ v $<$AS,   PrimPrhbt$_{Cnsl}$, $p,e',a,b>e$ v$<$AS, PrimPrcpt,$a,b>e$ v$<$AS PrimCnsl, $p,e',a,b>e$ v$<$AS, PrimNtrl-$_{Op}$,$a,x_1>e$ v ... v$<$AS, PrimNtrl$_{Op}$, $a_1x_1,...,x_k>e$ v $<$AS, PrinNtrl-$_{prcpt}$'$a,b>e$)', and

'PrimPrhbtn e'   abbreviate   '$(Ea)(Eb)(Ep)(Ee')(Ex_1)...(Ex_k)$ ($<$AS,PrimPrhbt$_{OP}$, $a,x_1>$ e v ... v$<$AS, PrimPrhbt$_{OP}$, $a,x_1,...,x_k>e$ v$<$AS,PrimPrhbt$_{Prcpt}$, $a,b>e$ v$<$AS, PrimPrhbt$_{Cnsl}$, p,e', $a,b>e$).

These definitions introduce the notions of being a primordial operation, permission, or prohibition, respectively.

Note the use of the variable 'e' for an act or state. And recall that the expressions enclosed in the half-diamonds are event-descriptive predicates. Thus '$<$AS, Manif,$x_1>e$', for example, expresses that e is an act or state of x_1's being manifest by AS. Extensive use is made of such predicates within event logic. [19] Recall also the special use of the parameter 'k' for the degree of the primitive predicate of greatest degree needed as a primitive, and where there are assumed to be primitive predicates of each degree n where $1 \leq n \leq k$.

The notion of the divine will may be thought to be fully analyzed in terms of the disjunction of these three. Thus

'DW' may be short for '$\{e \ni$ (Primop e v PrimPrmsn e v PrimPrhbtn e)$\}$'.

The DW is thus merely the virtual class of all primordial operations, permissions, and prohibitions.

A few principles over and above *Pr 1-Pr 12* above that should presumably obtain are as follows.

Pr 13. $\vdash(a)(x_1)...(x_n)(AS$ *PrimOp* $a,x_1,...,x_n \supset$ (PredCon$_n$ a . $\sim x_1 =$ AS. ... .$\sim x_n =$ AS)),

Pr 14. $\vdash (Ea)(Ex_1)...(Ex_n)(AS$ PrimOp $a,x_1,...,x_n$. AS Prim-

$\text{Prhbt}_{\text{Op}}\ a.x_1,...,x_n),$

Pr 15. $\vdash\!\sim\!(Ea)(Eb)(\text{AS PrimPrcpt } a,b\ .\ \text{AS PrimPrhbt}_{\text{Prcpt}}$ $a,b),$

Pr 16. $\vdash\!(a)(b)(x_1)...(x_n)(\text{AS PrimOp } \ulcorner(a \cap b)\urcorner,x_1,...,x_n \equiv$ $(\text{AS PrimOp } a,x_1,...,x_n\ .\ \text{AS PrimOp } b,x_1,...,x_n)),$

Pr 17. $\vdash\!(a)(b)(x_1)...(x_n)((\text{AS PrimOp } a,x_1,...,x_n \vee \text{AS PrimOp }$ $b,x_1,...,x_n)\supset\text{AS PrimOp } \ulcorner(a\cup b)\urcorner, x_1,...,x_n),$[20]

Pr 18. $\vdash\!(a)(b)(x_1)...(x_n)((\text{AS PrimOp } a,x_1,...,x_n\ .\ \text{AS PrimOp }$ $\ulcorner(-a\cup b)\urcorner,x_1,...,x_n) \supset \text{AS PrimOp } b,x_1,...,x_n).$[21]

Some of the various principles given may need some modification in the light of a more thorough presentation. The whole theory of primordiality in fact cries out for further elaboration and development, being still in its infancy.

XIII

The analysis of the primordial valuations and hence of the divine will, given above, agrees with that of St. Thomas to some extent. A few additional parallels are as follows. Thomas notes that "there is no reason why the same thing should not be the subject of precept, operation, counsel, prohibition, or permission." Clearly one and the same human act can be the result of a prohibitional operation as well as a prohibitional counsel, and hence of a prohibitional permission. St. Thomas contends also that "God ordains rational creatures to act voluntarily and of themselves. Other creatures act only as moved by the divine operation; therefore only operation and permission are concerned with these." This contention agrees with the foregoing, permission here being taken in the sense of the primordially neutral.

"All evil of sin," St. Thomas notes also, "though happening in many ways, agrees in being out of harmony with the divine will. Hence, with regard to evil, only one sign [of will] is proposed, that of prohibition." The evil of sin is precisely what is primordially prohibited by precept. (There is no sin as the result of a primordial operation, all such constituting the primordially good). "On the other hand," St. Thomas goes on, "good [the humanly good] stands in various relations to the divine goodness, since there are good deeds without which we cannot attain to the fruition of that goodness, and *these are the subject of precept*" [italics added]. The primordially good is the subject of precept, and counsel above was taken as instantial of precept. But St. Thomas construes counsel here rather differently, "for there are other goods," he says, "by which we attain to it [the fruition] more perfectly, and these are the subject of counsel."

Here counsel seems to be concerned rather with supererogation. But even some precepts might be stipulative of the supererogatorily good, so that even this last remark could be seen to accord with the foregoing.

Any philosophical discussion of God's will must perforce be speculative, as indeed is the foregoing. There would not seem to be much point in discussing it at all, however, without some analysis of what the phrase is supposed to designate. At best we can merely hypothesize what this might be, and thus we never could be said to know it in any more direct sense. Even so, hypothetical constructs are useful in theology just as they are in theoretical science.[22]

Note that the foregoing hypothetical reconstruction of some features of metaphysical idealism has been given in a semantical metalanguage incorporating a theory of acts. It would seem very doubtful that a more restricted kind of logical framework would suffice for this purpose. Note also that the primordial notions have been handled intensionally. These are given by reference to a *predicate* rather than to a (virtual) class or relation the predicate might designate. The reason for this is the familiar one concerning the intensionality of obligation, to which the primordial notions are akin. It would not do to say, in a deontic logic, for example, that one is obliged to be an F, for F might be equivalent with some G, with respect to which one is not obliged. Reference to the predicate 'F' here instead of to the virtual class F prevents any such unwanted consequence. Hence the intensional treatment, within a semantical meta-language, of the primordial notions throughout, in terms essentially of Frege's *Art des Gegebenseins*.

XIV

An alternative, more sophisticated way of handling manifestation and embodiment, and even some of the primordial relations, suggests itself if a numerical measure is introduced. We may think of the AS as manifesting itself in x *to just such and such a degree*. All entities manifested to the same degree would then be of essentially some same kind. The very difference between manifestation and embodiment could then be handled in terms of difference of degree. Embodiment would be low degree of manifestation. Let

'AS Manif^i x'

express that x is a manifestation of AS to just degree i. If $i =$ O, we could let x be the null entity, and if $i = 1$, we could let *x* be AS itself. AS then manifests itself to maximal degree. Physical objects have low degrees attached to them, and highly mental ones have high degrees. And similarly for the primordial precepts, some of which are more binding than others. Here too it might be of interest to introduce a numerical degree. Whitehead speaks of the degree of a primordial valuation, as noted above. No one, it would seem, has ever developed such a theory in any detail, however, for natural theology and the use of numerical measures are not ordinarily thought to go hand in hand. A quite sophisticated view would result if a suitable numerical measure were introduced, and no doubt some interesting notions would be forthcoming in terms of it.

Nothing has been said thus far concerning physical time, space, casuality, and the like. Any attempt to locate the AS with respect to any of these is quite foreign to the foregoing. It is rather the other way around, all objects of the physical world themselves being embodiments of the AS. Hence the foregoing theory is all couched in the Fregean tense of timelessness, so to speak, as in that of spacelessness, causalitylessness, and so on.

Of course, only the barest logical *maquette* of the full theory concerning AS has been given here. Indeed, to flesh out the foregoing in adequate detail would be a formidable task indeed. Nonetheless, certain general features of what the fuller development would be like should be evident. In particular it would comprise foundations for a theory of objective value as contained in the primordial precepts. Thus, as far as this scheme goes, there is no essential dichotomy between fact and value, but each is handled in its separate way. Nor is there any easy reduction of one to the other. Each is given its proper dignity and the way is left open for discriminating all manner of interconnections between the two. Note also that there is here no illicit dichotomy between reason and faith. Again, it is rather that a rational scheme is available in which a theory of faith may be incorporated. Indeed, it may be that faith, in a suitable sense, is our highest rational activity, for it is always reasonable to let one's mind wander to an O altitude! The task of natural theology in fact may be thought to be just this.

But faith is nothing if it does not issue in action, as many writers in the tradition of *philosophia perennis* have eloquently affirmed. And indeed the notion of the AS is of such staggering grandeur and magnitude, that it seems eminently rational that we should "shape the whole conduct of our life . . . into conformity" with it. To do this, in fact, should be our whole aim, everywhere and always, as the great writers of that tradition have been continually affirming across the centuries. "To interpret the absolute we must give all our time to it." The pursuit of science, of beauty, and of goodness are alike here given their proper role in this endeavor.

There is something compelling about human feeling at what we take to be its highest, in the full experience, say, of a great work of art. It is doubtful that such feeling can be suitably and fully explicated on any other basis than one such as the foregoing. We can go a long way in analytic aesthetics without it, but always with a most essential human ingredient left out--the depth and quality of authentic aesthetic feeling at its best.

The positive contribution of the present paper is merely to have made some tentative suggestions towards giving the *philosophia perennis* the logical backbone it is often thought to lack. Usually in discussions of the AS there is too much logically irresponsible misstatement. But so lofty a topic would seem best served by using such clean-cut logical notions and techniques as are now available. Surely we should let idealism, along with other metaphysical views, grow with the advance of knowledge.

Milton, Mass.

NOTES

1. Cf. Zellig Harris, "The Two Systems of Grammar: Report and Paraphrase," in *Papers in Structural and Transformational Linguistics* (Dordrecht: D. Reidel, 1972).

2. Cf. the author's *Belief, Existence, and Meaning* (New York: New York University Press, 1969), Chapter VI.

3. See the author's *Events, Reference, and Logical Form* (Washington: The Catholic University of America Press, 1978) and *Semiotics and Linguistic Structure* (Albany: The State University of New York Press, 1978).

4. For further details, see the author's "On the Logic of the All-Soul in Plotinus," in P. Morewedge, ed., *Islamic Philosophical Theology* (Albany: The State University of New York Press, 1979).

5. See the author's "On the Logical Structure of the Ontological Argument," in *Whitehead's Categoreal Scheme and Other Papers* (The Hague: Martinus Nijhoff, 1974).

6. J. Salamucha, "The Proof 'Ex Motu' for the Existence of God: Logical Analysis of St. Thomas' Arguments," *New Scholasticism*, XXXII (1958), 334-372 (first published in Polish in 1934). Cf. also J. Bediek, "Zur Logischen Struktur der Gottesbeweise," *Franziskanischen Studien,* XXXVIII (1956), 1-25; and L. Larouche, "Examination of the Axiomatic Foundations of a Theory of Change," *Notre Dame Journal of Formal Logic*, IX (1968), 371-384 and X (1969), 277-284 and 385-409.

7. See the author's "Some Thomistic Properties of Primordiality," *The Notre Dame Journal of Formal Logic.*

8. *Process and Reality* (New York: The Macmillan Co., 1936), p. 46. Cf. also *Whitehead's Categoreal Scheme and Other Papers*, Ch. III, "On the Whiteheadian God."

9. C.S. Peirce, *Collected Papers* (Cambridge: Harvard University Press, 1931-1958), Vol. VI, par. 467.

10. Richard Taylor, *With Heart and Mind* (New York: St. Martin's Press, 1973), Proem.

11. On the null individual, see especially the author's "Of Time and the Null Individual," *The Journal of Philosophy* LXII (1965), 723-736. To characterize the null entity we need of course the calculus of individuals.

12. Pars. 385 and 386.

13. For useful expository remarks, see especially H. Wang, *From Mathematics to Philosophy* (New York: Humanities Press, 1974).

14. See the author's "On Common Natures and Mathematical Scotism," *Ratio* and also in *Peirce's Logic of Relations and Other Studies (Studies in Semantics*, Vol. 12, ed. by Thomas Sebeok (Nisse, The Netherlands: Peter de Ridder Press, 1977).

15. Cf. the author's "Of 'Of'" to be presented at the VIIth International Congress at Dusseldorf, 1978.

16. *Summa Theologica*, I, q. 19, a. 12.

17. *PR8* is of course oversimplified, but a more general formulation and discussion is not needed for the present.

18. Cf. the author's *Truth and Denotation* (Chicago: University of Chicago Press, 1958), p. 106.

19. See again *Events, Reference, and Logical Form* and *Semiotics and Linguistic Structure.*

20. The '$\cup$' and '$\dot{\cup}$' are the signs for the union and intersection respectively of virtual classes.

21. Cf. an alternative treatment of the primordial relations in the author's "On God and Primordiality," *The Review of Metaphysics*, 29 (1976), 497-522. See also "Some Thomistic Properties of Primordiality," and "On the Logic of Idealism and Peirce's Neglected Argument," *Idealistic Studies* and also in *Peirce's Logic of Relations and Other Studies (loc. cit.)*

22. Cf. J. Bochenski, *The Logic of Religion* (New York University Press, New York, 1965). See also the discussion in *Whitehead's Categoreal Scheme and Other Papers*, Chapter IX.

COMMENT

On Richard Martin,

"On Some Theological Languages"

JAN Van der VEKEN

The value of Professor Martin's contribution lies especially in his serious and thorough application of current logico-linguistic theory to the study of religious language. What he intends to show is how logico-linguistic theory can help shed more light on the principles and structures of the main philosophical systems. For this purpose, and by way of central paradigm, he attempts a hypothetical reconstruction of at least some characteristics of metaphysical idealism in a semantic metalanguage. An essential feature of metaphysical idealism is that God is identified with being and that being is conceived as absolute Spirit. One can therefore speak of a monism of the Spirit. The wider purpose, however, is to offer a meta-system that can serve to formalize various philosophical and theological systems such as those of Plotinus, Anselm, Aquinas, Hegel and Whitehead. A few critical remarks are in order here.

1. From a theological point of view there arises the question of identifying the metaphysical absolute (Absolute Spirit, hereinafter referred to as AS) with the religious absolute (called God). AS has at least several characteristics of the Thomistic God and Whitehead's "primordial nature." Nevertheless, Thomas employs a different category as the ultimate and all-encompassive notion, namely, being, whereas Whitehead speaks of "creativity." This would appear to be a point worth noting in formalizing metaphysical idealism. What is to be said about God cannot be deduced from the basic category AS.

2. A second question that can be raised concerning the project itself of formalizing religious language is that before any logical analysis one must first decide which type of philosophy is to be developed. This applies also to the project of formalizing religious language. Which language shall be formalized? Clearly, a prior decision has to be taken here.

Popper's distinction between "context of discovery" and "context of justification" can be insightful here. The expression "justification" can be substituted in this case by "articulation." A logico-linguistic method can therefore only be of service on the level of articulation, not that of justification and not from a heuristic viewpoint. But whence come the fundamental insights of the great philosophical systems such as absolute idealism?

First, there are important themes which continually arise in the history of philosophy and which have brought some people

to speak of "philosophia perennis." Thus Martin says: "that being
is one and identical with God the creator . . . is rediscovered in
every age and in every corner of the world." It is in this context, however, that caution should be observed before identifying the problem of God with the problem of being.

Secondly, in a certain sense the religious notion of God
serves as a touchstone for the great philosophical systems. Even
Hegel has said that religion can do without philosophy but philosophy cannot do without religion. Philosophy as the reflective
critical moment presupposes man's pre-reflective understanding
of being as totality (Heidegger speaks of *vorontologisches Seins-
versta*ndnis). There is likewise a precritical notion of God that
is present in religion before it is taken up again and thought in
philosophy.

A third element of the "context of discovery" in connection
with religious language is our actual experience of the universe.
"If our cosmos is to be what it is . . . ." The relation between
facts in the world and a view on the totality is one of implication or incompatibility.

3. With regard to formalizing religious language, it must be
said that a so-called scientific theology has to comply with the
same rules as those which hold good in the formation of scientific theories in other fields.

First, theoretical constructions are useful in theology just
as in other disciplines. It should be noted however: theology
looks for relations of the type ¬p-->¬q and not for the less
complex p-->q   (in other words theology looks for necessary
conditions of possibility and not for conditions of the type p--
>q). In the latter case reasoning from the consequence to the
cause is not justified (the problem of verification and the reasons why falsification is to be preferred to verification in the
formation of theories). In the case of a necessary condition it is
permissible to deduce from the givenness of q the givenness of
p.

Secondly, a theology which intends to speak scientifically
must insist on being as systematic as possible, that is, it must
systematize as many statements as possible with the aid of as
few fundamental principles as possible. Martin indeed succeeds in
formalizing the principles of absolute idealism with the aid of a
few basic concepts (AS, Manif., Emb., Prim. Prcpt.). All the
other primordial predicates are defined within the linguistic
framework with the aid of the theory of quantification, identity,
the calculus of individuals, and ultimately with the aid of some
semantic rules and principles of the "event theory." The question
that now arises is whether this formalizing contributes anything
from a strictly heuristic standpoint. It would seem that such a

tain theological principles, nonetheless actually fails to provide any new insights.

Thirdly, not only logico-linguistic systems but the insights of current theories of science can teach us rather a lot concerning the relation between the data of experience and the paradigms we employ to grasp the data of experience in a coherent and systematic conceptual framework. Paradigms are employed in theology as well as in natural science. Kuhn especially has pointed out that science usually develops with the aid of paradigms. In other sciences, too, Kuhn accepts the presence of irrational, dogmatic components. Lakatos wanted to mitigate Kuhn's "irrationalism," while Feyerabend stands more on Kuhn's side. For Kuhn "normal" science is the cumulative process in which transmitted principles of a scientific community are schematized, articulated and generalized. Martin's project fits into the context of this theory of science. The extensive awareness that there is, in any case, something which transcends man is rooted in experience as interpreted by religious language. The systems of Platinus, Anselm, Aquinas, and Whitehead, as well as that of so-called absolute idealism (Parmenides, Spinoza, and Hegel) can then be seen as so many paradigms to clarify in a conceptual manner what is given in metaphysical and religious experience, taking into account the demands of logical coherence and adequacy to experience. Though we do not consider the strength of the logico-linguistic method to be found on the level of content, it is nevertheless a useful instrument whereby the current achievements of the so-called formal sciences can be integrated into the study of religious language.

PART II

METAPHYSICAL TRADITIONS AND THE DIVINE

CHAPTER V

THE HINDU METAPHYSICAL TRADITION ON THE MEANING OF THE ABSOLUTE

JEHANGIR N. CHUBB

In order to give an adequate exposition of the Hindu metaphysical tradition it is necessary to clarify some important preliminary issues. Of Hinduism, more than of any other religion, it may be said that it is not a monolithic creed. Within Hinduism one has come to expect some variety in ways of thinking and speaking of the Supreme Being and an even greater diversity of theories concerning man's relation to the Supreme Being. Added to the difficulty of this bewildering diversity of creeds is the reminder of one important trend in Hinduism which points beyond all creeds and concepts to that "from which speech falls back and the mind retires baffled, unable to reach it." Hinduism is both credal and non-credal. This itself would present some difficulty in talking about the Hindu religious tradition. The difficulty is aggravated owing to the fact that its many creeds do not, at least at first sight, cohere to form a single, unified body of teachings concerning the ultimate Reality.

This situation naturally raises the problem of identification. How shall we define Hinduism? Is Hinduism in any sense one or is it merely the name of a conglomeration of doctrines, aproaches, spiritual practices, and forms of worship exhibiting a rich diversity or, as some would say, a chaotic multiplicity? Is Hinduism one religion or a miscellaneous group of religions with nothing more than a geographical unity to bring them under a common label?

One of the purposes of this paper is to show that Hinduism is the name of a unified whole, but that in traditional Hinduism this unity is only a potentiality and a promise that has been realized only partially and imperfectly, leaving a number of tensions and conflicts unresolved. The question, what constitutes the unity of Hinduism has come to the fore in recent times and it is my belief that in the massive and luminous writings of Sri Aurobindo the final unity of Hinduism has not merely been indicated but actually accomplished. As I have said in my article: "Sri Aurobindo as the Fulfillment of Hinduism,"[1] "Sri Aurobindo has added a new dimension to Indian philosophy. He has brought to fruition its penetrating but imperfect search for unity and has raised the spirit of Hinduism to a full and liberated consciousness of itself."

I am aware that this view would be contested by many who

could claim to speak with authority on Hinduism and whose views deserve respect. I shall presently consider alternative answers to the question, what constitutes the unity of Hinduism, assuming that it is possible to interpret Hinduism as a system that can comprehend in a coherent unity all its diverse manifestations. But it should be noted that the controversy here is not over the question, what do the different schools of Hinduism teach, but how are these diverse teachings to be correlated and what principle of interpretation or synthesis should we employ to bring order out of apparent chaos? We may say that the question, what is the Hindu metaphysical tradition on the Absolute is at the first order level of reflection.

The difficulties of exposition which I have raised above will carry us to a second order level. This should make it clear that the method to be used for giving an exposition of the Hindu conception of the Ultimate is not purely a historical one, not a matter of correct exegesis alone. I do not mean merely that presentation must include interpretation and critical evaluation. This would still keep the inquiry at the first order level. What is further needed is an explanatory hypothesis, a vision of an emerging unity, in the light of which the materials provided by historical study are to be interpreted and unified. It is similar to the difference between recording facts of history and interpreting them in the light of a philosophy of history. The facts could be correctly presented and yet seen in a new light. Thus in giving an exposition of the Hindu concept of the Ultimate one has to answer not only the question, what is Hinduism but, more importantly, what is Hinduism trying to become?

It is obvious that the answer to this question cannot be found by merely examining "the Hindu metaphysical tradition" understood as an already developed set of doctrines which are accepted by all enlightened Hindus as forming the core of Hinduism. We may, however, understand "Hindu tradition" not only in terms of a tangible body of doctrines but also, more etherially, in terms of a spirit seeking embodiment. The latter refers to the characteristic form which the spiritual quest has taken in India and which may be described as a search for Truth in its fullness, a search that intends to leave no possibility unexplored and is undeterred by the apparent conflicts and contradictions in its many findings. Undoubtedly, Truth in its fullness must also be a self-consistent whole, but there is always the danger that by adopting a rigid and narrow idea of self-consistency, as most religious philosophies have done, including many schools of Hinduism, one may rest satisfied with a vision of Truth that is partial and truncated. The Hindu tradition is nebulous and elusive with respect to its content but more fully articulate with respect to its spirit and inspiring impulse. Its spirit dwells not in one body but in innumerable bodies, but also breaks out of them. It transcends its manifold expressions and remains doctrinally indefinable.

It is with reference to its spirit that we must indicate how the unity of Hinduism is to be understood and how it is to be achieved, for in traditional Hinduism the unity is still submerged in a mass of conflicting claims and counter-claims. The religious mind of Hinduism aspires after a vision of wholeness in which, to use Meister Eckhart's words, "there is no denial except the denial of all denials." But in the history of Hinduism, particularly in the scholastic period, denial, partisan thinking, and the refutation of 'rival' theories was the accepted procedure. It would, however, be a mistake to regard the strongly polemical writings of the great Acaryas and their followers as entirely out of line with the spirit of Hinduism. The ideal of unity is that of a richly diversified oneness. The diversity is no less important than the unity. To achieve this richness of content each element of the diversity must first be allowed to develop along its own lines in isolation from the other elements, and even in opposition to them, in order that it may discover its own potentialities and articulate itself fully. The achievement of unity and harmony is a dialectical process in which tensions and oppositions must be allowed to develop almost to the breaking point before they can be resolved and embraced in a healing oneness.

This perhaps explains why, though in the *Gita* we are presented with an admirable structured, comprehensive synthesis of all the major strands of Hindu spiritual experience, the unity was not preserved but was broken up in the succeeding centuries into several contending schools of thought. The unity of Hinduism in the Gita was in a way too premature, since the nisus within each of its elements to develop along its own lines and find its own specific mode of self-fulfillment, had not yet been appeased.

It is in recent times that the problem of discovering the underlying unity of Hinduism has come to the fore. In conformity with the spirit of Hinduism one should adopt a non-partisan approach to this problem. There are broadly two conceptions of unity or universality, the missionary and the non-missionary. The former, paradoxically, sustains itself through exclusion and offers at best a procrustean type of universality, universal by the very force of its narrowness. Truth is here walled in and cast into a more or less rigid mold and what lies outside it is dismissed as error and darkness or the dim twilight of half-truths. Or, taking a more liberal attitude, what is outside it is regarded as below it, representing a partial or lower truth whose sole value is that it is a preliminary stage to something beyond it, helpful, at best to the individual to rise at last to the highest stage--one's own--where Truth abides in fullness.

Precisely such a move was made by Vivekananda and is, I believe, largely accepted by the monks of the Sri Ramakrishan Order. Hindu theories concerning the Supreme Being are broadly divided into three groups: *dvaita* (dualism), *visistadvaita* (qualified non-dualism) and *advaita* (non-dualism). These include in-between theories like those propounded by the Gaitanya school and the Śaiva and Śakta philosophies. For Vivekananda, dvaita and visistadvaita represent the Truth stepped down to meet the requirements of less developed souls and are to be regarded as stages through which the seeker passes on his way to the highest Truth which is taught in Śamkara's Advaita. A Christian writer, assuming (mistakenly, according to me) that the Vivek⁻anandian approach represents the generally accepted standpoint of the modern Hindu, remarks discerningly, "The Hindu view is not as tolerant and comprehensive as at first sight appears. It represents a particular understanding of the nature of religious truth and this understanding is dogmatically asserted against any other view." Besides, such a paternalistic and patronizing resolution of conflicting truth-claims would be totally unacceptable to the non-Samkarites who are regarded as the "lesser breeds" within Hinduism.

In an approach that is free of any suggestion of partisanship and condescension the ultimate reconciliation of the seemingly opposed viewpoints must be sought in an integral and all-embracing Whole in which all the *positive* contents in the diverse competing elements are held together and harmonized, not by being arranged hierarchically as representing ascending steps to the highest truth contained in one of them, but as concurrent and complementary poises of an indivisible Reality that dwells indivisibly in each and all of them while at the same time remaining transcendent and indeterminable. Hinduism, according to me, is the Spirit of Truth revealing itself through a slow, evolutionary and dialectical process and finally bursting forth fully in the integral vision and experience of Sri Aurobindo.

Before considering the question of how we are to justify the ascriptions of what would seem to be incompatible predicates to the same Reality it will be worthwhile to look into the Hindu metaphysical tradition concerning the Ultimate insofar as this represents concepts and theories shared by all orthodox Hindus. There is first the acceptance of scripture (*śruti*) as infallible. This, however, will help us only to a limited extent in discovering what the Hindu doctrine is. The scriptures are not systematic treatises, but rather the outpourings in the language of poetry of diverse spiritual experiences of the Rsis who were not unduly concerned about their mutual consistency. Therefore, what the scriptures teach is largely a matter of interpretations, as indeed has been the case, leaving us, at least in Hinduism, without any court of appeal which can decide which interpretation is the right one. All we can do, therefore, is to inquire whether there are any doctrines which are, as a matter of fact, shared by all orthodox schools of Indian thought. I think we may safely say that it would be generally agreed that the Supreme Reality, Brahman or Purushottama, is eternal in the sense of being timeless (*kutastha nitya*), self-existent and the source of all that exists. Brahman is the All and inclusive of everything. "All this is verily Brahman." Further, it is agreed that Brahman is *Sat, Cit, Ananda* (or Being, Consciousness, Bliss).[2] There is also general agreement that Brahman is partless or indivisible so that it would not be correct to say that the being of Brahman is partly *cit* and partly *ananda*. *Sat, cit, ananda* are so related that each includes and is included in the other two. I shall show later how this important notion of the indivisibility of Brahman helps us to answer the objection that in attempting to integrate on an equal footing, as it were, divergent views about the nature of Brahman we are guilty of predicating contradictory attributes to the same Reality.

The Indian view of Brahman and of the universe may be called pantheism. Pantheism is an ambiguous term and one must hasten to add that Indian pantheism is a view which is compatible with panentheism which, while recognizing the immanence of Brahman in the universe (which is Brahman itself in self-manifestation), also insists on affirming the transcendence of Brahman. Pantheism as presented in the *Gītā*, for instance, is the view that there is nothing outside the being of Brahman. The Upanisads declare "All this is verily Brahman" and "As from a blazing fire sparks fly forth by the thousands, so also do various beings come forth from the imperishable Brahman and unto Him again return."

It should be pointed out here that Indian dualistic philosophies occupy a position half way between the *Gītā* pantheism and Christian dualism according to which the universe and human souls are not only outside the being of God but are created *ex nihilo*, i.e., individual souls are not eternal since in some sense they have an origin. All schools of Indian philosophy, however, regard individual souls, *jīvas*, as eternal. But in my opinion such a view can be held consistently only within a pantheistic framework, since it is unthinkable that there could be anything outside the being of Brahman which is coeternal with it. Brahman is and must be "One without a second."[3]

In the *Upaniṣads*, what may be called the essential as distinct from the integral nature of Brahman is indicated in the question, "As from the knowledge of one lump of clay all that is made of clay is known, so what is that knowing by which all things become known?" This is consistent with pantheism according to which the Supreme is not only the efficient cause but also the material cause of the universe. But there is no single picture of Brahman that emerges unambiguously from the Upaniṣadic texts. Brahman is referred to as personal, *saguna*, as the Lord of the universe. "Him one must know, the supreme Lord of all lords, the supreme Godhead above all godheads." "From fear of Him both Indra and Wind and Death as fifth do speed along."

Brahman is also spoken of as impersonal, differenceless and relationless, *nirguna*. "There is here no diversity. Death after death is the lot of one who sees in this what seems to be diverse." Activity and dynamism are attributed to the saguna Brahman. "Supreme too is his Śakti and manifold the natural working of her knowledge and her force." The *nirguma* Brahman is naturally spoken of as beyond all action. But there are passages in the *Upaniṣads* which describe Brahman as simultaneously static and dynamic. "Though sitting still It travels far; though lying down It goes everywhere." "One, unmoving, that is swifter than Mind. . . ." "That moves and That moves not." Again Brahman is described as both immanent and transcendent. "He who is dwelling in all things is yet other than all things. . . ." "That is far and the same is near; That is within all this and That is also outside all this."

The concept of Brahman in the *Upaniṣads* and in Indian philosophy generally is basically non-anthropomorphic. By this I mean that Brahman is regarded as the Transcendent Being which differs both in existence and nature from the purely phenomenal or finite being, not merely in degree but essentially in kind. There is a qualitative distance between the purely finite and the Infinite. But here it is important not to overlook a radical difference between Christian dualism and Hindu pantheism. According to the latter the human individual in his true nature belongs to the Transcendent and not to the phenomenal order or the order of created beings. There dwells within "the cave of his heart," to use an Upaniṣadic simile, a hidden divinity or a hidden Self which has connaturality, not with the mundane and the perishable, but with the Divine and the Everlasting. This hidden reality is not something that we have to become or grow into; we are that eternally.

Brahman, however, is transcendent to the finite intellect and its concepts. It is in an important sense incomprehensible.

This raises the difficult problem: how is it possible to think of Brahman at all, as we undoubtedly do in philosophy, and how can we speak intelligibly of that which is beyond speech? Does the recognition of the ineffability of Brahman launch us on a *via negativa* culminating in the position of the Advaitin and the Buddhist for whom That (*Tat*) transcends and ultimately negates all concepts and categories, including the category of personality and the qualities of Creativity and Love and is Empty (Śunya), not in itself but of all that we positively ascribe to it?

Such a view would clearly be one-sided and not compatible with an integral outlook whose maxim is: a place for everything and everything in its place. And yet this very demand for integrality will compel us to find a place for Advaita and Śunyavāda, not as the whole Truth or even the highest Truth, but as an important and inalienable aspect of the integral Truth. But how is this to be reconciled with the statement that Brahman is ineffable?

The notion of ineffability has not been properly understood and has led to much confusion in rational theology. The ineffable is usually identified with the unconceptualizable. That is only one aspect of the ineffable and it is this aspect which lends support to the (partial) truth of Sámkara's non-dualism and of the Buddhist śunyavāda. The ineffability of Brahman is a consequence of the infinite qualitative distance between Brahman and the phenomenal world. This means that the existence and nature of Brahman are in a mode incomprehensible to the intellect, and hence to know Brahman *directly* (*aparokṣa jñāna*), as it is in itself, one must go beyond the level of concepts. But to transcend a concept is not necessarily to negate it. Our concepts of Brahman need be neither false nor inadequate. It is misleading to say that the intellect can know God only inadequately. The real distinction is not between inadequate and adequate knowledge but between conceptual knowledge (*aparā vidyā*) and direct knowledge (*parā vidyā*). *At their own level* our concepts are both true and adequate, but direct knowledge of Brahman belongs to a different dimension altogether. It does not lie in the direction of greater and greater adequacy of conceptual thinking. Each advance in conceptual penetration merely "shuts us off from Heaven with a dome more vast." In the direct knowledge of Brahman the truth of our concepts is simultaneously confirmed and transfigured. Since the mode of transfiguration is beyond the comprehension of the intellect one would be justified in venturing the paradox that Brahman simultaneously confirms and cancels the predicates that we ascribe to it. There is, however, an aspect of Brahman from which all thought-determinations are totally and uncompromisingly rejected. "There sight travels not, nor speech, nor the mind. . . . It is other than the known." It is "*neti, neti,*" "not this, not this."

We may say, therefore, that at the core of the ineffable Brahman there is a point which is *sheerly ineffable*. It may be represented as the center of a circle turned in on itself and totally absorbed within itself; or as the Face of the Supreme that is turned away from the whole sphere of manifestation. It is into this zero of the sheer ineffable that the Śamkarite and the Buddhist enter and mistakenly declare to be the whole truth. But the circle does not collapse and vanish into its own center, though the individual may choose to merge in it without a remainder. We have here, in the words of Sri Aurobindo, a choice:

> Either to fade into the Unknowable
> Or thrill with the luminous seas of the Infinite.

There are insuperable objections to the claim that Advaita represents the sole truth or even the highest truth. If Brahman is multi-faceted there can be no hierarchy of aspects within it, for that would mean that Brahman can be greater or lesser than itself. We must therefore examine the claim made by the Śamkarites that advaita is the whole truth. According to Śamkara Brahman is differenceless and relationless, and the world, including individual souls, is non-different from the non-dual Brahman. This identity, however, is not identity in difference; it totally negates all differences. Plurality as such, therefore, can only be an illusion, *māyā*. As K.C. Bhattacharyya puts it, "Śamkara's doctrine of Māyā is the logical pendant to his doctrine of Brahman as the undifferenced, self-shining truth." This is true provided Brahman is equated with "the undifferenced Brahman"; but if the latter is held to be just one aspect or poise of Brahmam then it would be possible to separate *advaitavāda* from *māyāvāda* and accept the former as true or partial truth and reject the latter as false. Not only Sri Aurobindo, but some other schools of Indian philosophy as well, affirm advaita to be true but deny that the truth of advaita entails the view that the world of manifestation is an illusion.

The first objection to Śamkara's view is that not only is the fact of illusion not explained but, consistently with the doctrine of *adviata-cum-māyā*, it can have no logical explanation. Ramānuja pointed out that it is logically impossible for a Śamkarite for whom the undifferenced Brahman is the only reality to determine the locus of Ignorance (*Avidya*) on which the illusion of plurality is said to depend. The advaita view that *māyā* is *anirvacantya* (inexplicable) must be taken not as an answer to this objection but as a confession that the objection is unanswerable. "The theory of Illusion," says Sri Aurobindo, "cuts the knot of the world problem, it does not disentangle it; it is an escape, not a solution. . . . This eventual outcome satisfied only one element, sublimates only one impulse of our being; it leaves the rest out in the cold to perish in the twilight of the unreal reality of *Māyā*."

The second objection to Śamkara's doctrine arise from the fact that according to him the function of language is not to describe Brahman--for Brahman, being devoid of all qualities, is indescribable--but merely to indicate it. Talking about Brahman is comparable to a finger pointing to the moon. The finger does not describe that to which it points. But how shall we interpret the metaphor of the pointing finger? What corresponds to it in philosophy is a proposition or a set of propositions with Brahman as the subject term. But if Brahman is totally indescribable how is it possible to indicate what we are talking about? What does the term 'Brahman' mean? It is no answer to this difficulty to suggest that 'Brahman' is like a proper name which denotes without connoting anything. A proper name is bestowed on an individual whom we perceive or, at least, whom we can think of through a description. Besides, in the absence of the individual, the use of the proper name does call up some quality or characteristic that belongs to that individual, and it is only through such a descriptive content that the individual can be identified.

In integral Hinduism Brahman must be regarded as both *saguna*, personal, and *nirguna*, impersonal and relationless. For Śamkara Brahman is only the latter, and yet he speaks of two Brahmans, the higher, nirguna Parabrahman and the lower, saguna Brahman (or Iśvara, the Lord of the universe). Taken in conjunction with Śamkara's doctrine of the three *sattās* (orders of being), *prātibhasika* (illusory), *vyavahārika* (practical), and the *paramārthika* (transcendent) one may get the impression that Śam kara does not after all totally deny the world of plurality and change or its omniscient and omnipotent Ruler (Iśvara), but accords them a temporary reality or a reality of a lesser and relative kind. Such an impression would, however, be totally false. The criterion of reality according to Śamkara is "that which cannot be sublated." As the illusory snake is sublated on the perception of the rope so the *vyavahārika sattā*, the world of plurality, is also sublated on the perception of Brahman. As regards Iśvara, the so-called "lower Brahman," this is what Śamkara has to say in his commentary on *Brahma Sutras* ii.i.14. "Belonging to the Self, as it were, of the omniscient Lord, there are name and form, the figments of ignorance. . . . Hence the Lord's being a Lord, his omniscience, his omnipotence, etc., all depend on the limitations due to the adjuncts whose self is ignorance; while in reality none of these qualities belong to the

Self whose true nature is cleared, by right knowledge, from all adjuncts whatever."

Should we then say that the metaphysical statement "Brahman is the Ruler of the universe" is outright false? This would not be an accurate representation of Śamkara's view. It would not explain why he uses the expression "the lower Brahman" or why he thinks that certain descriptive statements about Brahman are (provisionally) permissible and valid. The clue to Samkara's interpretation of metaphysical statements that ascribe personality or qualities to Brahman is in his view that all such statements are *upāsanārtha*, for purpose of worship and meditation. These statements are not to be taken literally as true. They are not true, but they are not false either. They have no truth-value. In fact they are not statements in the straightforward sense. They are intended to be "as if" statements. For example, the "statement" "Brahman is the Ruler of the universe" must be interpreted to mean, "Meditate on Brahman *as if* Brahman were the Ruler of the universe." These statements have pragmatic value. Contemplation of Brahman as the Ruler of the universe is a kind of heuristic device. *Moksa* or liberation is realized through knowledge of the Parabrahman. But the birth of knowledge requires a period of preparation or spiritual practice (*sādhana*) which consists partly in the purification of one's nature. In view of the devotional hymns that Śamkara himself composed it is likely that he regarded the practice of love and adoration (*bhakti*) of the Supreme Being as the most efficacious way of purifying one's nature and destroying ignorance and the illusion of duality. This may well be the case, but it leaves unexplained how an untrue or not-true supposition concerning Brahman on which the practice of *bhakti* is based can be efficacious in acquiring knowledge of Brahman. Another way of stating this objection is to point out that it is totally unintelligible how a descriptive predicate can point to or indicate the parabrahman if the predicate is pure fiction and has no ontological correlate whatever. Further, and this is what the theistic schools of Hinduism emphasize, love of God is its own justification and leads to its own characteristic mode of self-fulfillment, which is in no way inferior to a liberation in which individuality is sponged out and the sweetness of relationship is cast aside and one chooses to "fade into the Unknowable." Sri Caitanya, while not denying the possibility of thus merging into the undifferenced Brahman, regards it as a low form of salvation. The *jīva* (individual soul) according to him is "the eternal slave of Krsna."

What I have called integral Hinduism finds full expression in the *Bhagavad Gita* as far as the nature of the Transcendent Being is concerned. It does not, however, succeed in bringing out the full significance of the immanence of the Divine in the universe and his providence or reveal the secret of his evolutionary self-manifestation. That final dichotomy between the here and the now in the world of time and the Transcendent beyond time is resolved only in the philosophy of Sri Aurobindo. But in the *Gītā* one does find a reconciliation of the meditative Atman-Nirvāna non-dualistic experience, on the one hand, and the devotional experience of the Lord of infinite auspicious qualities, on the other. These two experiences influence and complement each other. A combination of *bhakti* and *jñāna* unveils the Antaryāmin, the immanent Divine seated in the hearts of all beings. When the Lord of the universe is seen through the eyes of an inner self-enlightenment He appears, or rather discloses Himself, as the Absolute, the Purushottama within, above and beyond all manifestation.

This double spirituality, personal-impersonal, devotional-contemplative, is the essential original Indian experience, which throughout the long history of Hinduism, one or another side of it was emphasized. At certain times the fullness reached its conceptual and expressive form in the very foreground. For instance, the *Īśa* Upanisad and the *Gītā* in ancient times and those later schools, particularly Kashmir Śaivism, which emphasize the reality of Śakti, the creative energy of the Supreme, combine in a single but complex experience the sense of essential identity with the Purushottama and the relationship, presupposing distinction, between the human lover and the Supreme Beloved.

I have so far given an exposition of the supreme and timeless ineffable Being, Brahman, in its transcendent poises of personality, impersonality and sheer ineffability, according to the spirit and underlying intent of the unwritten Hindu metaphysical tradition. I shall now consider the relation of Brahman to the cosmos, the world of changing, developing and perishable things.

On the pantheistic view there can be nothing outside of the being of Brahman. But if the being of Brahman is eternal in the sense of being timeless, how can change, coming into being and passing away, which are characteristics of the phenomenal order, be ascribed to Brahman? In Indian philosophy two different and contrary views have been presented to account for the phenomenon of change. They are *vivartavāda* and *parināmavāda*. The former is the doctrine of the Śamkarites who cut the gordian knot by saying that change is an illusory appearance and hence can in no way be predicated of Brahman. This, as we saw earlier, leaves unanswered the question, to whom or what is the phenomenon of an illusory appearance of change to be ascribed? The alternative view, *parināmavāda*, also runs into insuperable difficulties. The timeless and perfect Brahman cannot change. Hence it is said that change (parinama) occurs in Nature (*Prakṛti*) or in the body of God, but not in God himself. This, of course, is no way out of the difficulty because if there is nothing outside the being of Brahman then a change in Nature or the body of Brahman is also a change in the being of Brahman.

Parinΰmavΰda runs into difficulties because of a mistaken assumption which it does not question that there must be a temporal link between the timeless Brahman and the temporal phenomenal order. Sri Aurobindo does not commit this mistake. For him timelessness is only one of the multiple poises of the Infinite. In this connection he mentions two poises of the Transcendent or Eternity, Timeless-Eternity and Time-Eternity. To these we may add the poise of Eternal Duration. Timeless-Eternity is, in the words of Sri Aurobindo, "the non-manifest timeless, utterly eternal and an irreducible absolute self-existence." Timeless-Eternity articulates itself, as it were, as Time-Eternity in preparation for projecting out of itself the field of manifestation and for bringing into being the phenomenal order. The language of time and succession which is used to state the relation between these two poises is only a convenient way of speaking and not to be taken literally. Time-Eternity, says Sri Aurobindo, is "the Infinite deploying itself and organizing all things in time." It is a simultaneous Eternity of time in which past, present and future are forever together.

The Infinite then moves to still another poise of its being --Eternal Duration. The Divine here is fully personal and knows things not in an all-at-once vision, as in his poise of Time-Eternity, but successively, as they unroll themselves in time. He can thus respond with love and compassionate wisdom to man caught on the wheel of birth and death and suffering. The supreme Divine Will, however, is not part of the temporal order. The Will of God, the Śakti of Śiva, is to be understood as the dynamic aspect of God's being which is the same as Eternal-Duration which includes the order of creation. Creation, therefore, is not something brought about by the *antecedent* will of God, but is itself the unfolding of the dynamic aspect of God in manifestation. God's creative will is not at the *origin* of the created order but expresses itself through it. God wills all in the sense that what manifests or is manifesting and will manifest is included in the Time-Eternity of God's being.

On the pantheistic view we do not have a relation between the world and God considered as two different things. The world is God; it is God in the process of self-manifestation. But it should not be forgotten that there is no temporal relation between the three poses of the Transcendent. Timeless-Eternity,

Time-Eternity and Eternal Duration cannot be brought together into a common temporal framework.

It is time to consider a rather obvious objection which the concept of integral Hinduism I have tried to present has to face. Such a view apparently ascribes irreconcilable predicates to the same Reality, such as 'personal', 'impersonal', 'static', 'dynamic', 'ineffable but conceptualizable', 'sheerly ineffable'. It may be said that one in each of these pairs of predicates may be true but not both, for they cancel each other out and their simultaneous affirmation would be in flagrant violation of the law of contradiction.

It would be pertinent to ask what precisely the law of contradiction forbids us to say. I suggest that what it forbids is not a statement of any particular kind but a mode of utterance which uses two sentences both of which are intelligible, but in such a way that in the result nothing whatever has been said. The statements of transcendent metaphysics that ascribe apparently incompatible predicates to the Infinite are not such empty utterances in which something is asserted and denied simultaneously in such a way that in the end result nothing at all is either asserted or denied. They are genuine statements and the problem arises only when we ask *how* the two predicates in each pair are to be accommodated in the same subject.

As a first step towards answering this question it will be necessary to show that the Infinite does, as a matter of fact, accommodate within its being all the apparently incompatible predicates mentioned above. This raises the question, on what principle shall we select predicates which can truly be ascribed to God? The answer is: only those predicates can be considered which are compatible with divine perfection. Thus it would seem plausible to say that God is good but not that God is evil, that he loves us but not that he hates us, that he is self-existent but not that he is dependent for his being on another.

The next question is, how do we make a selection among predicates which are compatible with the divine perfection so as to decide which of these are to be ascribed to God and which are not? The answer to this question is crucial to our understanding the simple or indivisible and yet multi-faceted nature of the Supreme Being. The answer simply is that no selection need or indeed can be made among the possible predicates that can be ascribed to God. This is because in God there are no 'accidental' qualities, nothing that is but may not have been. We can give no meaning to the statement that a predicate is compatible with God's being except that it represents a mode of divine perfection. In the case of a finite subject what is compatible with its nature may or may not be actualized. This is because the actualization of possibilities in the case of finite beings depends partly on conditions and circumstances outside their being and essence. The Infinite in contrast to the finite does not depend on anything outside itself for any quality of its being. Hence whatever is compatible with God is in God and is God.

It will not be difficult to discern in this statement echoes of the ontological argument. But there is an important difference in my argument which enables it to preserve its validity even when the ontological argument is shown to be invalid. My argument does not claim to prove the existence of God but merely to prove that God does possess all those attributes which our intellect sees to be compatible with the divine essence. The passage is not from concept to existence, but from concept to the nature of that whose existence is not being called in question. The argument may be stated in the maxim: in the case of God's nature or being the possible is the actual.

It remains to show that all the predicates in the three pairs mentioned above are compatible with God's being, that each represents a possible mode of divine perfection and that therefore all of them can truly be ascribed to God. Consider first personality and power. There is nothing in the concept of personality or in the concept of dynamism or power which would lead us to say that they are incompatible with divine perfection. More positively, love and omnipotence which are attributes of personality are perfections in which the divine essence (partly) realizes itself. Hence we may say that God is the supreme Person and his being is active and dynamic (Śiva-Śakti). Similarly in the notions of immutability and a mode of being in and for oneself, a universal impersonality (*kaivalya* of the Samkhya-Yoga and the *Aksara purusha* of the *Gītā*) one cannot detect anything that is incompatible with divine perfection. In fact immutability is something that must belong to a being which is eternal and self-existent. The impersonal poise of the Infinite is, I think, a consequence of its total freedom. The Infinite can freely relate itself to individual souls, and indeed it does, but it is not bound by this particular exercise of its freedom; it is also free to remain unrelated to individual souls in an impersonal universality, like an ocean of consciousness without ripples or waves. The Infinite therefore is also impersonal and immutable.

Let us now consider the third pair of predicates or the distinction between the ineffable which is conceptualizable and the sheer ineffable. The truth of the former has already been established in showing that the different poises of the Infinite, static-dynamic, personal-impersonal, are modes of divine perfection. But how shall we show that a poise of the Supreme which is totally inexpressible in concepts, words and images, the Void of the Buddhists, is also a possibility compatible with divine perfection and therefore necessary to the total divine perfection: Such a poise of the Infinite would not be coordinate with its other poises since it is not another determination of the Infinite, but points to the Infinite as the Indeterminable. It would, therefore, be better to call it, as I have done above, the core of the Ineffable; or we may call it the super-essential being of God. Like impersonality, indeterminability may also be explained with reference to the freedom of the Infinite. If the Infinite freely determines itself in a number of ways it is not tied to its own self-determinations. As Sri Aurobindo puts it, "It is perfectly understandable that the Absolute is and must be indeterminable in the sense that it cannot be limited by any determination or any sum of possible determinations, but not in the sense that it is incapable of self-determination."

It would be in conformity with the spirit of Hinduism to point out that the above deliberation on the nature of Brahman does not reply solely on a conceptual analysis or on a theoretical consideration of abstract possibilities. In Hinduism, if logic does not actually follow spiritual experience, its pronouncements are nevertheless not regarded as authoritative or well-established unless they are confirmed by spiritual experience. The conceptual analysis which I have given above gains strength and support from the fact that all the self-determinations which I have ascribed to Brahman, as also the reference to Brahman as the indeterminable, have been directly verified over and over again throughout the history of Hinduism, from the Vedic times to the present.

One last and perhaps the most important step has to be taken for the solution of the problem of the so-called conflicting truth-claim. We have still to show how the diverse and seemingly incompatible affirmations we have made concerning Brahman are to be reconciled. Or, to put it differently, we must indicate how the seemingly incompatible predicates or poises are held together in the being of Brahman. Can the intellect indicate or make intelligible *how* things are held together in the Supreme or throw any light on the intrinsic possibility of the union of modes of perfection in God?

Here we come to the boundary of reason beyond which it cannot penetrate. We saw that because of the qualitative distance between the Infinite and the purely finite we have to acknowledge that the modes of divine existence and nature must remain incomprehensible to the intellect. This is true equally of the mode of union of attributes in the divine Substance. At this stage Logic, without abdicating, opens the door to Mystery, not the Christian-type sheer Mystery which has to be accepted on faith alone, but a Mystery continuous with logic though transcending it, and erected on the pedestal of reason. It is a Mystery not thrust upon the intellect but one that is affirmed by the intellect itself, reflecting autonomously on the nature of the Supreme Being. In short we have here Mystery within the heart of logic.

Let me make this point in a more analytic and less mysterious way. The different poises of the Infinite are unified in its being in a way that is utterly unique and therefore totally incomprehensible to the intellect. But this is something that the intellect itself can understand and endorse. The Mystery is a consequence of a unique characteristic of the Infinite, so unique that it defines its very status and which it, therefore, does not share with any finite existence. This characteristic is postulated by reason and is not received by us through a take-it-or-leave-it supernatural revelation. I am referring here to the fact--and this is recognized by Christian thinkers as well--that God's being is simple and indivisible. 'Simplicity' is itself a rather complex notion, but I shall try to simplify it insofar as it affects the question under discussion.

The Infinite is simple or indivisible in the sense that its being is totally integrated such that it could never be true to say of the Infinite that it is partly something and partly something else. If such a move were possible there would be no 'mystery' and no serious problem of reconciling incompatible predicates. This can always be done by making a distinction within the being of the subject to which the predicates are applied. One could then say that in one aspect the Infinite is personal and, in another aspect, impersonal; dynamic in one aspect and static in another, and so on. Such a differentiation of aspects within a common subject is possible only in the case of a finite, temporal being, since, being finite, he can shift the center or stress of his consciousness from one part of his being to another, while the rest of his being remains subconscient and unattended to.

The Infinite is eternal and hence not concentrated sometimes in one part of itself and sometimes in another, but is always and simultaneously 'all-there'. It is fullness of being and fullness of consciousness and therefore whatever it is it is indivisibly. No distinctions need or can be made in the Infinite subject to accommodate predicates like personal and impersonal. We may here reverse the Berkeleyian maxim, to be is to be perceived, and say that in the case of the Infinite, to perceive is to be. What is eternally in the consciousness of the Infinite, that the Infinite is. The contrast of subject and object disappears and since knowledge here is what Sri Aurobindo calls "knowledge by identity" the knower (*jñata*) and the known (*jñeya*) become indistinguishably one. The Supreme does not know; it is Knowledge (*Jñana*). In all this we are speaking on the authority of reason and not faithfully echoing the voice of revelation.

Logic and Mystery divide between themselves the 'that' and the 'how' of the divine perfection. Though we must remain content to recognize that the 'how' or the actual mode of union of the diverse elements in the divine being is incomprehensible to the intellect, we may perhaps get a distinct and oblique hint of it when we reflect on an analogous situation that obtains in the sphere of the purely finite. Such a situation arises when we make assertions about the world which are not empirical but categorical. Thus we may have two views concerning the way in which the world of our experience is to be described or interpreted. On one view the world consists of a series of events and there are no permanent or even semi-permanent substances (the Process view). The second view holds that the world consists of things undergoing changes and that events are precisely these changes that take place in substances (the Substance view).

The next question would be, which of these two incompatible views is true? My answer is that both these views are true and that they do not contradict each other. This is because the two views, though distinct, are not mutually related with reference to the question of determining their truth-values. They cannot be brought into a common logical framework in which they can be compared with respect of truth or falsity. The reason for this is that each view contains and absorbs the other. In terms of what is empirically verifiable neither view denies anything that the other asserts; or to state this more positively, each accommodates in its perspective all the claims made by the other that can be empirically tested. Hence the two views cannot be coordinated or placed side by side. It would, therefore, not be correct to say that one is true and the other false. They are both true, alternatively, depending on which view we start with. But whichever view we start with the other view is already taken up in it and therefore cannot present itself as a separate and rival view. Each contains and is contained in the other.

Similarly we may say that there is no real distinction between the many poises of the Infinite and they cannot be coordinated or brought together within a common logical framework where they confront each other in mutual and irreconcilable opposition. We may bring this discussion to a close with a quotation from F.H. Bradley who holds that his Absolute is 'somehow' a non-relational unity. We have shown that reason itself points to Mystery and have given an example of an analogous mystery within finite experience. Hence we may conclude in the words of Bradley, "What must be and what in a particular case is shown to be, that certainly is."

Finally, we must raise the question, what, according to Hinduism, is the purpose or explanation of the self-manifestation of Brahman as the seemingly imperfect order of evolutionary Nature? In traditional Hinduism only two answers are given. They are *mayavada*--the whole phenomenal order is a vast illusion--and *lilavada*, the view that the Lord creates the universe without any purpose, as pure sport (*lila*). I have already shown the logical incoherence of *mayavada*. *Lilavada* is true in the limited sense that the Lord, being perfect, can have no unfulfilled purpose which he needs to accomplish through the process of creation. This in itself does not lead to a denial of teleology within the universe. Just as time is not at the origin of creation and yet the created order is temporally structured, so also, though an unfulfilled purpose cannot initiate the self-manifestation of the Divine, a purposive, evolutionary movement towards a divine fulfillment in time may well be the secret and final aim of the Divine's self-manifestation. *Lila* does not contradict telos and may well contain it within itself. Indeed, without an immanent purpose the Divine 'sport' would, in view of the intense and universal suffering which is so strikingly a feature of it, become, in the words of Sri Aurobindo, "a cruel and revolting paradox."

It is in the integral vision of Sri Aurobindo that one finds the full significance of the immanence of the Divine in, and the secret of, cosmic existence. We can here give only a very brief glimpse into his solution of the riddle of human existence. Sri Aurobindo sees the divine manifestation in an evolutionary perspective whose goal is, in part, the transformation of human nature as such, for which *moksa* or union with the Divine is only a first decisive step, leading eventually to the perfection of human society on earth. Man is not the last term of the evolutionary series. The mental being (*manomayapurusa*) will be replaced or himself evolve into the gnostic being (*vijñanamayapurusa*), thus opening the way for a divine life here on earth in a divine body. Sri Aurobindo calls this the "supramental transformation" which will "carry with it a lifting of mind, life and body out of themselves into a greater way of being in which yet their own ways and powers would not be suppressed or abolished, but perfected and fulfilled by the self-exceeding." "The Supramental," says Sri Aurobindo, "is a truth and its advent is in the very nature of things inevitable. . . . I believe the descent of this Truth opening the way to a development of divine consciousness here (on earth) to be the final sense of the earth evolution."

NOTES

1. *International Philosophical Quarterly*, June 1972.

2. Although it is true that Śamkara does characterize Brahman as *saccidānanda*, it is doubtful if, logically, he is entitled to do so since for him Brahman is featureless, *nirguna*, and beyond all descriptions. See below.

3. St. Thomas holds the curious view that one can assert without any conceptual incoherence that God created a world that is eternal. But in what sense could God have created it? Clearly the being of an eternal world would not be dependent on God. At best one could say that the continued existence of the world depends on God but not its original existence. Even this partial dependence would not be intelligible unless God is thought of as a temporal agent, which he is not according to St. Thomas.

COMMENT

On J.N. Chubb,

"The Hindu Metaphysical Tradition on

The Meaning of the Absolute"

MARGARET CHATTERJEE

It might be both disconcerting and necessary to begin by saying that the concept of the Absolute is absent in the majority of the schools of Indian philosophy. The thought of the sub-continent does, however, include three forms of absolutism-spiritualistic or that which derives from the Upanishads, theistic, and nihilistic. Hindu thought shows an interesting pendulum, from an elaborate cosmogony in Vedic times to Upanishadic absolutism, then to various forms of theism, on to reformist types of monotheism in the nineteenth century. All these diversities show that Indian thinkers were always interested in the destiny of man, the metaphysical foundation of human freedom, detachment rather than attachment. Three other things must also be stressed: (1) that it was believed that liberation could be attained by a diversity of paths; (2) that the special experiences of special people were as relevant as logical arguments to the discovery of the supreme Being; and (3) that intellectual exercises must be backed up by yogic practices. The types of locutions used in elucidatory discourse about the Supreme being in the Hindu tradition are threefold: (1) the *neti neti* path or *via negativa* (2) metaphorical language (3) paradox.

Professor Chubb's paper, I suggest, unwittingly faces us with the question whether there is a difference between the metaphysical and religious import of absolutism. Hindu thought sees no difficulty in conflating the two. In the thinking which stems from Greek cum Judeo-Christian origins it has been stressed time and time again that the philosopher's concept of the absolute can by no means provide a focus for religious consciousness. The Advaitin, however, adheres not merely to a particular form of philosophic absolutism, but this constitutes for him a form of "religious belief". However, Professor Chubb regards Advaita as being wanting in some way, otherwise he would not project Sri Aurobindo's philosophy as going beyond Advaita in a desirable manner. He claims both that Aurobindo belongs to the Hindu tradition and that in his philosophy he raises "the spirit of Hinduism to full and liberated consciousness of itself". He thus sees Aurobindo as a kind of apex or terminal point.

This is also referred to by him as a spiritual quest described as a quest for unity. But there seem to be two quests for
unity mentioned by him. There is the "problem of discovering
the underlying unity of Hinduism"--he significantly speaks of
'unity' and 'universality' interchangeably. There is also--again
according to Chubb--the unity which the Hindu is alleged to be
seeking: his search for the Truth, for wholeness. The truth is
said to burst forth, be it noted, not in a system, but in an
"integral vision and experience" of a particular person. Regarding these two senses of unity, Chubb's language at times re-
sembles that of thinkers like Bhagwan Das and Radhakrishnan
who maintained a universalistic thesis about *sanātan dharma*--
the inspiration of which was a pre-independence nationalist
impulse. One of India's most original theologians, P. D. Devanan-
dam, on the other hand, has spoken of Hinduism as a 'family of
religions'. If we take this line we are under no obligation to
produce an essence, a reified something as the alleged unity
underlying the members of the family. We need not even invoke
family resemblance in the style of one of the twentieth century
prophets. I would myself hold the view that the unity of Hinduism (including under this the specific cultural factor of religion)
is found at the level of practice--rituals, pilgrimages, institutions etc.--and not in philosophical content.

As to the second sense of unity to which Chubb refers, the
alleged quest of unity, we need not adhere to this stereotype
any more than we need adhere to the stereotype of 'otherness'
which it is customary to associate with the so-called religions of
transcendence but which has been criticized so ably especially
by Rabbi Abram Heschl, among scholars in recent times.

Chubb is sympathetic to the Advaita form of Vedanta and
speaks of this as pantheistic. Although the point is somewhat a
verbal one, and a matter of definition, it seems difficult to
maintain the pantheistic thesis if we say, as he does, that according to Advaita there is (I quote) "qualitative distance between the purely finite and the Infinite". More tenable is his
point about ineffability. It is notoriously paradoxical to speak of
the ineffability of Brahman and yet maintain the possibility of
aparoksa jnana, to speak of what is *anirbacaniya* or unspeakable
as *Sat-cit-ananda*. Now what Chubb suggests is this. Here we
find not a collision of logic with experience or that experience
takes us beyond logic (and these are two of the possible answers offered by others) but we have he says, and I quote, "a
Mystery continuous with logic though transcending it, and erected on the pedestal of reason". No doubt here we are certainly
aware of the inadequacy of concepts. But how can mystery be
continuous with logic? What Chubb has in mind, I think, is the

notion of a transformed sort of consciousness as advocated by Aurobindo, which would be able to do precisely that - take one, so to say, where reason left off.

We need to know now why Chubb should regard Aurobindo as in some way or other 'fulfilling' the Hindu tradition. His main merit, in Chubb's view, is in accepting Advaita minus the theory of *mayavada*. The Gita, he says, brings out the nature of divine transcendence, a kind of transcendence, I would be inclined to say, not too different from the early conception of Yahweh in Judaic thought. But the full significance of divine immanence in his view is brought out in the divine descending movement - a redemptive process - proclaimed by Aurobindo. Chubb raises the question of God's attributes, saying that these are such as are "compatible with divine perfection". This way of putting it is more in line with Leibniz's phrase "the compossibility of positive predicates" than with anything in the Hindu tradition. Aurobindo's absolutism is open-ended, the openness stemming from human possibilities (something quite compatible with a loose form of *karma* theory) and the possibilities of divine initiative. It is also clearly a form of absolutism, which looks upon the destiny of man with hope, which thinks in terms of an evolutionary perspective which would transform human nature and therefore human society. Aurobindo's goal was no less than the divinization of man upon earth - a plurality of individual ascents with the pilgrims all returning to illumine the cave - that is to say a model with many levels and movement both upwards and downwards.

Let me fasten on six points.

(1) The first is a warning about regarding *Advaita Vedanta* as the crown and summit of the Hindu tradition. The way in which Aurobindo himself draws on many diverse strands of religious thought in the sub-continent is good evidence of the diversity within Hinduism. From Tantra he derives the concept of *shakti* which he puts in place of *cit*. The idea of centres of consciousness is also a Tantric idea. From the Mahayana Buddhist concept of Bodhissatvahood he derives the motion of redeeming humanity. From Sankhya he adopts the idea of an evolutionary process directed towards the liberation of man. From popular religion in Bengal he takes the idea of the Divine Mother. The Hindu tradition encompasses all these and more. This encompassing is expressed by Aurobindo himself in his use of the word 'integral'. Aurobindo departs from the Advaitic tradition in more ways than he conforms to it. There is no time to spell this out now, but one of the key points which illustrates my contention is his treatment of the gap between *sacchidananda* and the phenomenal world. He sees this not so much as a

metaphysical divide but as a *challenge*. The *paramūrthika* and the *vyavahārika* are to be brought closer together by the *sūdhak* who, in the words of another tradition, returns to the cave. If we are to fasten on to the most provocative contribution of Advaita to our theme it will be no doubt the concept of *nirgun Brahman*, the idea that attribute language will always be inappropriate with reference to what is ultimate. The inexhaustibility of the divine is to be experienced and not fitted into the straight-jacket of our human intellectual categories. But here of course we run into the risk of pitching the experience in so high a key, to use a musical metaphor, that not only is it beyond reach, but the very use of the word 'experience' loses its justification.

(2) The second issue concerns *evolution*. Aurobindo understood evolution not in terms of becoming more and more saintly or more and more intelligent but in terms of becoming more and more conscious. What is interesting here is that mind is not regarded as the terminal point. Beyond mind is spirit. The cultivation of inwardness--something which is the mark of the advance toward spirit--enables man to act as the spearhead of the cosmic evolutionary process. Supra-mental rationality is the top rung of a Jacob's ladder which cannot be thrown away. In terms of the Hindu tradition we have also to note another departure on the part of Aurobindo. The new order will arise not from the destruction of the old, from the ashes of great conflagration, from *pralūya*, but from a process of transmutation. Upanishadic tradition had spoken in terms of realizing what one is. Aurobindo states emphatically in *Life Divine*, "It is in his human nature, in all human nature to exceed itself by conscious evolution, to climb beyond what he is."

(3) The third issue concerns *transcendence/immanence*. To my mind what Aurobindo brings into the Hindu tradition is a conception of man as a self-transcending being. Built into the very fabric of things are possibilities between which men can choose, as if there were a divine conspiracy involving man, so that the world could be made nearer to the heart's desire. Man himself is understood as a tool of the immanent power at work in the universe - a power risen to self-conscious awareness. This highlights a new dimension of the transcendence/immanence issue--the dimension that concerns, not the question of cosmic origin and dependence, but the role and destiny of man.

(4) The fourth issue concerns *lila* as a principle apparently vastly different from that of *telos*. Both *lila* and *telos* are anthropomorphic ideas. Each, however, has different resonances. In Aurobindo's thinking, as in the thinking of the *shakta*, divine creativity is understood *not* in terms of antecedent *will* but as

an outpouring of dynamism. Even the word 'emanation' does not put us on the right track. The divine cosmic dance of Shiva is the most potent symbol of this energy in Indian art. The image symbolizes both energy and delight. While Aurobindo had hailed in Heraclitus a fellow-devotee of divine energy he had found the element of *ananda*, of joy, lacking in Heraclitus. *Lila* then should be understood as an outpouring of creativity, not as an arbitrary activity which is antithetical to eschatology. It is significant that Aurobindo abandoned the cyclical analysis of change given by the ancient Hindus, making room not for a linear view of change so much as a spiral where joy and sorrow each have their place. The cross-fertilization between Heraclitus and the Hindu tradition in Aurobindo produces strange results. For example, Aurobindo speaks of the soul as a spark which is not merged in the fire. His conception of the destiny of man is certainly not one of 'merging', but of an order of consciousness where individuality is retained, something consonant with the splendid image used by Professor Findlay at the close of his paper.

(5) A fifth and tough metaphysical problem centres on the place of contradictions. Shankara deals with this by resorting to level language with movement in one direction so to say, the higher cancelling out the lower. It must be stressed that, in facing the problem of contradiction, Hindu thought resorts neither to sublation nor to antinomies of choice. Aurobindo seems to resort to two ways: in terms of philosophical discourse he resorts to poetic language and in terms of religious experience to the inner realization of the *sadhak*. The Hindu religious tradition accommodates surd elements into a view of life conceived of as made up of various states. Tantric thought encourages a deliberate espousal of the grotesque, the unclean, etc. All this of course is not to come to terms with logical contradiction. Hindu religious thought tends less to analogical reasoning than to parable and poetry. The fragmentary view of truth provides sanction for saying not only that each man is partly wrong but that each is partly right. This is the metaphysical basis of nonviolence and perhaps prevents whatever absolutist elements there may be in the Hindu tradition from being tied up with statism. If the verdict of logic and the *sadhak's* experience diverge from each other, the Hindu religious tradition favours the latter rather than the former. It would be generally expected that intellectual exercises cannot take one far once human ignorance, the Hindu counterpart of finitude, is admitted.

(6) Sixth, and finally, I would like to mention some of my own reservations about the concept of 'realization' which provides perhaps the biggest stumbling-block in Hindu religious

thought--a stumbling-block especially if one is used to thinking of the Supreme being in terms of "sum qui sum": the *mahāvākya* of the book of Exodus. There must always be a major divide between those who speak in terms of the quest of a supreme religious *experience* and those who speak in terms of the quest of a supreme *Being*. One might wonder if there is such a thing as a paradox of realization pertaining to the former. Have not yogic practices perhaps been aimed at providing some sort of safeguard against this? My other reservation is whether the concept of realization can admit of *progress* in spiritual life. Can there be a further growth in identity? Aurobindo is able to think in terms of spiritual growth precisely because he avoids the language of merging and draws on the Vaishnava tradition in no small measure. These considerations take us beyond metaphysics. But we have already seen that there is no hard and fast line between metaphysics and religion in some of the thought-systems of Indian origin and in such systems one is adrift in a flooded monsoon territory where it may not be easy to find our bearings.

Delhi University

Delhi, India

METAPHYSICAL TRADITIONS AND THE MEANING OF THE ABSOLUTE: THE LOCUS OF THE DIVINE IN CHINESE THOUGHT

ELLEN M. CHEN

INTRODUCTION:

What, according to the Chinese, is the divine, where is it located, and how does man partake of it? In Western philosophy such questions are treated in metaphysics. But the term metaphysics[1] presents itself as a problem when we apply it to the Chinese terrain. For the Western man knowledge and consciousness are identified with the divine. Plato's divided line (*Republic*, 509-511) shows that the realm of science, taking mathematics as the paradigmatic science, is already removed from the physical realm, being intermediary between the natural world of change and the divine world of changeless forms.[2] In the Western tradition down to the seventeenth century, metaphysics or natural theology meant the study of subject matter beyond and transcending the physical realm.[3]

But the Chinese had a very different notion of what was divine and where the divine was located. In Chinese metaphysics, there was no negation or transcendence of the physical realm as such; the divine was always conceived as in nature or nature itself. In the Western tradition influenced by the Greeks the divine was beyond nature, to be identified with thought or intellect. The Chinese had always identified the divine with life or creativity; it was no other than *tzu-jan*, the self-creative power of nature itself.[4]

This difference in the understanding of the divine is crucial in grasping the cultural and spiritual dimensions of the Chinese. Metaphysics, as the science of the divine, is man's search for the highest values and his effort to embody these in his person and activities. Hence, a different understanding of what constitutes the divine and where it is located results in very different manifestations of realizing the divine in human life. The main purpose of this paper is to show that major religious philosophies in the Chinese tradition--philosophical Taoism, Confucianism, religious Taoism, and sinicized Buddhism--all share in this affirmation and devotion to the physical realm as divine.[5]

PHILOSOPHICAL TAOISM: The Divine as Cosmic Creativity, Immortality Through Universal Change

In the allegory of the cave (*Republic*, 514-520) Plato portrays man as pitifully oblivious of his existential plight. Only through an arduous process of ascent could he manage to leave the dark imprisoning cave, emerge into the light of the day, become acquainted with clear and distinct objects in the real realm, and finally recognize the sun as the Father, generator of life and intelligence of all beings.

Whether Plato propounded a two-world theory is a matter of debate.[6] At least most scholars agree that ontologically, the divine is not to be identified with the physical realm of our sense experience. Things in this world participate in the separate divine exemplars which are never fully embodied in this world of generation and corruption. The physical world into which mortals are born and in which they conduct their lives is not the locus of the divine. To rise up to the divine we must ready our mind's eye for a greater influx of light and vision.

In contrast, for the Chinese, the union with Tao is through a process of descent. The *Chuang Tzu* (6:14) speaks of dropping one's body and limbs, repudiating intelligence, departing from one's physical form and getting rid of consciousness. The divine is Hun-tun, the faceless one; and Hun-tun dies when it is opened to consciousness (7:7); *Complete Works*, p. 97.

The myth of four stages of consciousness in the *Chuang Tzu* (2:15); *Complete Works*, p. 41, serves best to illustrate the Taoist approach to the divine. The best and most blessed state is when consciousness is yet unconscious of itself; this is the undifferentiated continuum, a unity-without-multiplicity. The second is when things come to be, yet interpenetrate; there is consciousness of the existence of things, yet there is no consciousness of the lines of demarcation among them--this is the state of multiplicity-in-unity. The third is when consciousness of the boundaries of things appears. Thus names[7] standing for different entities come to be. However, because there is yet no consciousness of the distinction between good and evil, the world is still without internal strife--this is the state of multiplicity-and-unity. The last state arrives with the awareness of the distinction between good and evil. At this point strife enters the world, thus the unity of the world is irretrievably lost--this is the state of multiplicity-without-unity.

From this myth it is clear that in Taoism consciousness is not the pathway to the divine. Hun-tun,[8] the unconscious state, is the divine state, while consciousness as a movement away from the divine is the cause of alienation, strife, and death.

Thus Taoism also presents a two-world theory: the divine

world of original nature and the superstructure created by human intelligence. Man's return from the conscious human realm to the sacred natural realm is through a relaxing of consciousness, it is a return from the dazzling light of the sun to the soothing dimness of the moon.

In Plato, forms are bits of immutable and immortal beings by virtue of their perfection and self-identity. The immortality of anything consists in either being an imperishable self-identical form or having the capacity to be assimilated to such a form. While the body with its senses grasps only perishable objects and thus is perishable, the intellect is capable of apprehending immutable forms.[9] Man's hope for immortality, therefore, rests with his mind. This is through identifying first man with his soul, then his soul with his mind--taking thinking to be the most excellent activity of the soul--and finally, his mind with the imperishable forms. The conviction is that mind, which has no nature of its own, derives its nature from the object of its knowledge,[10] for the knower becomes what is known. Man's anchorage onto the unchanging, self-identical, immutable forms through his mind guarantees the immortality and permanence of his soul.

In Taoist metaphysics, change alone is immortal. Change means renewal which guarantees continued life and perpetual youth; immortality belongs to what can change continuously without ever exhausting itself.[11] Within this perspective the individual who identifies his life with his own fixed and limited form which circumscribes its change is destined to perish. Immortality consists in shedding one's form, individual or specific, in repudiating the intellect and breaking the shell of individuality which rigidly determines and separates the self from others,[12] in sinking down and expanding the self so that it eventually becomes merged with the universal life force--this matrix which gives rise to all forms and individuals is alone immortal.

The Taoist sage is not an independent form capable of subsisting by itself. His umbilical cord with the All unsevered he "values drawing nourishment from the Mother."[13] The Taoist yogi situates himself at the meeting point of the conscious and the unconscious. His dying is at the same time a resurrection; one moment he is emerging into the being and determination of individual existence, another moment he reverses to the non-being of universal becoming.[14]

In such a metaphysics, forms as specific and individual determinations are passing expressions of the universal process of becoming. Immortality consists not in holding on to these passing expressions, but in becoming one with the all transforming life force itself. Death happens to him who has reached an awareness of the self cut off from the totality.[15] He who can render his life fluid, who can be indifferent to this form or that, who can assume any form any time, passing from one form to another with ease, is capable of long life.[16] The Taoist does not hold on to his self-identity, but rejoices in becoming the butterfly, bird, fish, indeed all forms of life.[17]

The philosophical Taoist concept of immortality is clearly modeled upon the natural world itself. The natural world, devoid of consciousness of self, assumes endless transformations, and thus is long lasting. The *Tao Te Ching* says: "Heaven and earth are long lasting. . . . Because they do not live for self, therefore they live long." (Chap. 7) In Aristotle, divine immortal substances do not have their seat in the sublunary realm[18]--which explains the lowly position assigned to the physical realm in Aristotle's metaphysics. In Taoist metaphysics, Tao as the principle of change underlying all is the life pulse of the physical world itself, thus the affirmation of the physical world as divine in Taoist metaphysics.

CONFUCIANISM: The Divine as Creator of Life, Immortality Through the Species Life

In Confucianism the divine is life and what is creative of life: the *I-ching* speaks of I as a power that 'gives and furthers life without end.'[19] The main difference between the Taoist and the Confucian is this: the Taoist abandons himself to the divine as cosmic life, thus he returns to and blends with the *natura naturans*; the Confucian steps forward to take upon himself the burden of caring for the world of ten thousand beings, thus he devotes himself to the well-being of the *natura naturata*.

In the Teachings of Confucius and Mencius, we witness thought emerging from life, the conscious issuing forth from the unconscious, and man stepping forward from nature.[20] But what happened in Greek philosophy--where intelligence, once emerged from the matrix of life, claimed its independence from life-- never happened in China. Confucius did not exalt reason over life. What was aimed at was the mean in perfection.

> Confucius said: I know why the Way does not shine.[21]
> The intelligent goes beyond it,
> The stupid falls short of it.
> I know why the Way does not operate.[21]
> The capable goes beyond it,
> The incompetent falls short of it.[22]

That the intelligent and capable can go beyond, and thus eclipse the light of the Way and render it inoperative, shows that for Confucius the Way is still the Way of nature. We have seen that Taoism regards intelligence as the unholy element, a useless outgrowth of nature.[23] The Taoist perfect man is in the state of Hun-tun, transcending knowledge and virtue. In Confucianism, if nature is holy, man is also holy--his intelligence and moral insights are genuine endowments from Heaven.[24] In their right measure human thinking and action should not break the boundary of nature; for man to go beyond nature would be as undesirable as if he were to remain in complete ignorance. The goal is the harmony and balance between man and nature, between thought and life.

Thought plays its proper role in Confucianism, but it is not for its own sake; it must always bend back to be in the service of life. In Aristotle thought as divine is its own end: "The excellence of the reason (*nous*) is a thing apart."[25] In the Aristotelian system theoretical sciences take precedence over practical and productive sciences, and contemplation is higher than action.[26] The Confucian vision of the divine, however, does not transcend the practical realm: "Tao is not removed from man, he who in perusing Tao becomes removed from man cannot be said to be in pursuit of Tao."[27] For Confucius words are meant to produce deeds and studies are undertaken only after one's moral duties have been discharged. Learning (*hsüeh*) always means learning how to be a human being, it is never pure intellectual pursuit, but the practical wisdom of how to live a virtuous life.

In Confucianism there is a real unity and continuity between Heaven, earth and man. To a Confucian the entire universe is one holy family, with Heaven and Earth as the great Father and Mother generating all beings in between. Since I am given life and provided with life's sustenance, my response to my existence is one of gratitude to Heaven and Earth, and a deep sense of fellowship and devotion to all beings in the world.

This means that ethics is the most holy concern in man's spiritual union with the divine. The whole conception of Confucian ethics is built upon an affirmation of the goodness and holiness of life, nature and natural inclinations.[28] This is opposed to Kantian and certain strains in Christian ethics according to which virtue, as the autonomy of the moral will, is at war with the inclinations of nature.

In Confucian ethics good and evil are understood to be what furthers or destroys life on earth.[29] A good ruler imitates heaven and earth by acting as father and mother to his people; he has compassion for them, eases their hardships, assists in their planting and harvesting which sustain their lives and livelihood.[30] A reckless ruler prevents growth and destroys life on earth, imposes public works or military duties at harvest time.[31]

Such a ruler loses his 'Mandate of Heaven' (*t' ien-ming*).[32]

If we reflect on the meaning of *ming*, the mandate, we immediately see the connection between *ming* meaning 'command' and *ming* meaning 'life.' The power to command is vested in him who holds the power of life and death: the ruler commands by holding the life and death of his subjects in his hands. But in this capacity he is merely imitating the rule of heaven--the *Li chi*[33] says that the ruler is called 'Son of Heaven' because he is the representative of Heaven on earth. In Confucianism Heaven as the *yang*, the ultimate source of life, holds the power of conferring or withdrawing life from any earthly ruler. Only the ruler who obeys and carries out the commands of Heaven is blessed with continued life and power on earth, while he who displeases Heaven shall have his physical and political life cut short.[34] The political empire is verily a divine vessel which must be borne by the ruler with the utmost care and reverence. Only as long as the earthly ruler submits himself to the will of Heaven does he continue to hold the Mandate of Heaven.[35]

The intrinsic connection between life as divine and virtue as rooted in, and in turn as sustaining nature, determines the Confucian understanding of what is immortal. Since each individual owes his life to his family and society, his immortality is premised on the furtherance of his family and societal life. There is a way of immortality for the public person.

> The best are those who have established virtue, the next best are those who have established deeds, and still the next best are those who have established words. When these accomplishments last through the ages, they may be called immortal.[36]

For the superior man (*chun-tzu*) as a public person, immortality consists in his contribution to the health, expansion and continued life line of his society. One imitates the bright virtue of Heaven if through public actions and policies one brings about peace, harmony, prosperity and culture to his people, like in the figures of Yao, Shun and the Duke of Chou.[37] Or one may secure immortality through deeds by making heroic personal sacrifices in overcoming tribal enemies or natural disasters, as in the case of the Yellow Emperor's defeating Chih-yu, or the great Yu's curbing the Flood. But if one is denied these opportunities, as in the case of Confucius himself,[38] one could still achieve immortality by committing to writing[39] those ancient teachings which shall serve as ideal inspiration for future generations.

Immortality for the private person consists in furthering the life line of his family. The Confucian sense of personal morality revolves around this central obligation. One's parents, having given one life and love and thus participated in the creative and nurturing act of Heaven and Earth, deserve one's special reverence. In the same way one must also participate in this creative act by giving birth to a male heir who will perform the sacrifices and carry on the family line after one's departure. When Mencius says: "There are three unfilial states, the greatest among them is to die without a (male) heir,"[40] he meant that the extension and continuity of the family line on earth is the most sacred duty of a filial son. Such a statement, needless to say, had led to great injustices to women and inflicted mortal sufferings on wives who failed to produce a son. What it showed was the blind Confucian will to live and give life. To a Confucian life flows from Heaven, but the concrete life activities are manifested on earth; thus in a sense everything depends on what happens on earth where the divine drama of life unfolds.[41]

RELIGIOUS TAOISM: The Pursuit of Physical Immortality

Religious Taoists range from those who merely aim at long life to those who fervently affirm their belief in the possibility of physical immortality.[42] The fact that religious Taoism enshrines philosophical Taoist texts among its sacred canon[43] shows that at least scripture-wise there is continuity from philosophical to religious Taoism. Of course, for those religious Taoists who believed that man's *summum bonum* consisted in physical immortality, the same texts must be interpreted to suit their religious needs.[44] Here we shall not expound the techniques involved in internal and external alchemy,[45] but merely try to point out the theoretical presuppositions of the elixir seeker and use as our main text the *Pao P'u Tzu*. In its insistence on physical immortality in this very life and body as the only acceptable mode of man's participation in the divine, religious Taoism presents a theory unique in the history of religions.[46]

The desire for long life and immortality have always been the deepest desire of the Chinese. The *Tao Te Ching* (chap. 59) aspires to "the way of long living and lasting seeing." Yet because it does not see a way to physical immortality as such,[47] its ideal is to live as long a life as nature permits. The *Chuang Tzu* strikes a tragic note in the face of death. Then, rising to the occasion it affirms the marvelous transformations that all things constantly undergo. Intoxicated with this vision of cosmic change, the tragedy of personal death is overcome. The *Chuang Tzu* not only accepts life and death equally, but it identifies them forthrightly and laughs at those who observe various

regimen in hopes of prolonging life.[48] In the thoroughly relativ-
istic universe of the *Chuang Tzu,* in which one starts a journey
today to arrive at one's destiny yesterday and in which to live
one second is considered equal to the life-span of Methuselah,
even the delaying tactics employed in the *Tao Te Ching* are
abandoned.

In Confucianism the divine and creative is identified with
Heaven, the *yang* principle which fertilizes the earth and gives
rise to all beings. Confucianism fixes its gaze upon the living
universe of ten thousand things. The individual's duty is to
further the species life of man, participation in which constitutes his immortality. Religious Taoism also identifies the *yang*
as the divine.[49] But, unlike the Confucian, the religious Taoist
so affirms his individuality that he wants to keep himself alive
indefinitely.

In the *Mencius* (3A:5) we are given the origin of the burial
custom as another example that filial piety, as all other virtues,
is rooted in the feeling component of man. Because humans
could not bear the sight of their parents' bodies being devoured
and mawed by foxes and wild cats, they started the custom of
interring the dead. Now this unbearable feeling is applied to
himself by the religious Taoist when he visualizes himself as
dead. He simply abhors the thought of his own death, with or
without proper burial.

> Now deep underneath the Nine Springs, in a long
> night that never ends--first providing sustenance for
> ants and worms, ultimately fusing into one body with
> dust and the earth--the very thought of this makes
> one burn with restlessness and shiver with anxiety.
> One cannot help but groan and sigh![50]

The religious Taoist identifies himself with the coming out
process. Refusing to be re-absorbed into the ground he must
look for a way to maintain his body permanently separate from
the body of the earth. It is not that he repudiates the physical
universe, but this is the very way he affirms its goodness and
divinity. If life is good and immortality is the desire of all, then
man must find a way to attain immortality. To him the position
of philosophical Taoism is inconsistent and untenable. By accepting the inevitability of perishing it negates its own thesis: this
physical world can be recognized as good and divine only if the
subject-object, ego-world relationship is maintained. Reabsorp-
tion of the ego by the world, which abolishes the ego, also
abolishes the significance of the world for the ego. The *Pao P'u
Tzu* criticizes the *Tao Te Ching* and particularly the *Chuang Tzu*
for identifying life and death.[51] This only shows the loss of

heart on the part of these authors. While the philosophical Taoist accepts fate passively, his religious counterpart, James Ware remarks, "was Confucianist enough to insist upon doing something to achieve personally a share in God's permanency."[52]

Thus religious Taoism comes to fulfill the desideratum of philosophical Taoism. The true man (*chen jen*) is not one to accept the fate of other beings. Universal perishing, which swallows up all others, need not apply to him. Although most things in nature are doomed to perish, man can do ordinary nature one better by finding a way to be exempted from the fate awaiting all others.[53] Indeed, nature is full of exceptions and man, endowed with intelligence by heaven, is already an exception to other beings. Perhaps taking a hint from the *Lieh-Tzu*[54] which says that to enrich oneself by stealing from nature one can get away with impunity, the religious Taoist sets out to steal the secret of immortality from heaven and earth. For those courageous, persevering, rich and fortunate few who are willing to follow through the regimen, immortality or at least extremely long life can be attained. The religious Taoist's priority is shifted to discovering and appropriating the secrets of the universal creative power for the purpose of nurturing and making immortal his own body.

This consists in recognizing that the immortality of the physical universe and the immortality of the physical individual are premised on two different principles. The universe is immortal by virtue of its cyclical movement by which *yin, yang* and all opposites generate each other, thus life leads to death which in turn leads to new life. In contrast, individual life is associated with *yang* alone, *yin* being exactly what leads to death and perishing. Thus in order to maintain himself in existence, the individual must not hold on to the universal Tao which exacts his death, but to the *yang* principle within him which alone guarantees his continued life.

Already, the *Pao P'u Tzu* believes, there are in nature substances such as gold and other precious elements which, due to their predominance of *yang*, can last as long as heaven and earth. Such substances, once extracted from the womb of the earth, are not reabsorbed into the earth. If man can find a way to ingest such substances and make them reconstitute his blood, sinews and organs, he shall so strengthen the *yang* in him that he will be immune from the encroachment of *yin*,[55]

There is no room to explore the interesting question of body-soul relationship in Chinese Taoism and contrast it with Western and Christian views,[56] or to discuss the role of moral and spiritual perfection in the make-up of the Taoist immortal.[57] We do wish to point out that in his search for freedom and immortality the religious Taoist seeks to transcend the limitations of a corruptible body. Yet it is still an immortality not away from, but within the physical universe. There is transcendence of the social order, with its interminable relationships which weigh down the free spirit. But the immortal who can rise above the earth to roam in any part of the vast universe has no inherent objection to making his abode on earth. In the Orphic-Pythagorean tradition immortality was conceived through identifying man with his soul and then through liberating his soul from entanglements with the body and the physical world. Immortality was based on the soul's renunciation of, and liberation from, the body.[58] The religious Taoist, however, identified the seat of his life with his body and believed that only when his body was made strong enough would the spirit it housed not be dispersed and perish for lack of proper dwelling.[59]

SINITIC BUDDHISM: Immortal Land with All Her Creatures

The religious Taoist wants to keep the candle of his life burning without end,[60] the Buddhist *nirvana* is exactly the blowing out of this candle. There is no greater antagonism to the Chinese love for life than Buddhism in its original teaching. Buddhism's overall influence on China has been to produce a negative attitude toward life and the world.[61] It also introduced into the Chinese *psyche* a note of rebellion against the sufferings and evils in life. Though these were experienced by the Chinese, they were neither clearly articulated nor fully confronted within Taoism or Confucianism.[62]

Yet the Chinese over long years had adopted Buddhism and made it a part of their spiritual heritage. We shall ignore the doctrinal differences of various schools of Buddhism that arose and disappeared in China. Instead, we shall mention those elements in Chinese Buddhism which demonstrate the continuity of our theme. In our view the metaphysics of T'sen-t'ai, Hua-yen and especially Ch'an, carrying on the Chinese vision in the unity and harmony of man and nature, were the result of the intellectual assimilation of Buddhism by the Chinese. Pure land, stressing sincerity, filial piety, love, and salvation for all, may be considered the Confucian branch of Chinese Buddhism; it was the result of the emotional assimilation of Buddhism by the Chinese.

The language of Chinese Buddhism remains negative. Yet through a strange kind of logic it turns negation in the service of affirmation. Thus, through a negative language a most positive doctrine emerges.[63] Two points can be mentioned.

In Christianity man's union with God is understood to be a vertical ascent, moving away from creatures and things to rise up to God.[64] In Chinese Buddhism, salvation involves a process of going back to the non-differentiation of man from other beings in nature. If transiency, the root of sorrow and suffering, is the character of all existing beings, living or non-living, sentient, or insentient, rational or irrational--this is the doctrine of dependent origination (*pratityasamutpada*)--man is in the same situation as all other beings. Thus, if man finds salvation, it is *not* his salvation *away* from the rest of nature, but *together* with all nature. The Mahayana Buddhist discovers Buddhahood in himself through discovering Buddhahood in all things. Instead of lifting himself above nature, love for all is premised on the individual's identity with all in the Tathagata-garbha.[65]

The important question for the Mahayana Buddhist is not so much his own salvation as the need to transcend his deluded consciousness.[66] Through the doctrine of no-ego Buddhism enables the believer once for all to comprehend the message of the Buddha, namely, that salvation does not aim at the fulfillment of the self distinct and apart from others--as with the doctrine of substance in Western philosophy--but is mainly an integrative process. There is no such thing as the salvation of the 'I' alone, there is only the salvation of the 'I' in solidarity with the 'all' in the Tathagata-garbha. The buddhisattva must refuse salvation until all is saved, because there can be no entrance of Nirvana for him without the 'all,' this 'all' which includes all sentient and even all non-sentient beings. But if all must enter and none is to be forsaken, then samsara is nirvana and nirvana is samsara.[67] The doctrine of no-ego in Mahayana teaching is the complete antithesis of the doctrine of substance as self-sufficiency and self-identity in Hinayana and Western philosophy.[68] Even the Absolute of the Tathagata is not a substance.[69]

The Chinese Buddhist does not merely sink down and identify himself with all beings which are marked by transitoriness, he sinks down and identifies himself with this very transitoriness which constitutes Buddhism's definition of evil and suffering. True to the Taoist insight,[70] for the Chinese Buddhist the truth and reality of all things is exactly this birth-death, generation-extinction, appearance-disappearance, being-non-being that we find in the world. Salvation does not consist in the separation of one of these correlatives regarded as value from its disvalue, as in Western metaphysics in which the divine is conceived through the severance of form from matter, act from potency, life from death, being from non-being . . . etc. Rather, transcendence is attained by identifying and yielding oneself unconditionally to this dynamic naturalness (*tzu-jan*)[71] which accepts and embraces all opposites, because this dynamic naturalness is no other than the Absolute itself.[72]

Mahayana, by positing a pantheon of Buddhas and Buddhi-sattvas and by affirming the efficacy of grace in salvation, is the negation of Hinayana as a doctrine of self-help. Ch'an is the negation of Mahayana to the extent that it so affirms the samsaric order and everything in it that the need for salvation is completely overcome. Sooner or later one must realize that there can be no true liberation by running away from anything. *Wu* (*satori*) is this very awakening that Buddahood is not anywhere else, but immediately within oneself; thus there is no need to search for anything. Further, if Buddhahood is in everything, everything is as holy and dignified as Buddha himself. This entails that any subordination of one being to another or one value to another is a needless bondage. The Ch'an Buddhist bows to neither the Buddha nor the Patriarch.[73] "Kill the Buddha if you happen to meet him."[74]

On the devotional side, the identity with and compassion for all beings means that the Mahayana Buddhist aims not at transcending physical life as such, but man together with all beings must transcend evil, suffering, and alienation. Thus a new orientation begins. The devotee prays not for the end of rebirth. Instead, he prays that he be reborn in the Pure Land where life without suffering is interminable.[75]

That Nirvana in Pure Land is conceived as entrance to a special land shows the deep-seated Chinese attachment to the land. That the Pure Land is understood to be situated in the west is even a clearer indication of what the Chinese conceive to be divine and immortal. If the sun represents consciousness, value and distinction, the Western Land as the land of sunset belongs to the unconscious. Salvation in Pure Land means reentrance into the primordial womb wherein all things are yet pure and undefiled.[76] In Christianity nature as physical world is always what is yet to be redeemed.[77] For the Chinese, nature, land, and sleep[78] redeem man from sufferings and evils.

The Pure Land of Limitless Life is the answer to the deepest desires of every Chinese. While the Indian is obsessed with ways which will liberate him from rebirth, while the Western man aspires to immortality in a transcendent realm which is the total opposite of this physical order,[79] the Chinese aspires to immortality in a land in which all forms of being, men, animals, even inanimate things, are preserved.[80]

In retrospect Buddhism through its *mahakaruna* teaching[81] supplied a much needed salvation doctrine to the Chinese mass. Both Confuciansim and Taoism are elitist in character. The insight that Buddha nature is in all things has its precedence in the Confucian notion of *jen* as the heaven endowed seed of virtue and sagehood in all men which should never go untended for a single moment.[82] But in practice Confucius' doctrine of rites and rules of propriety did not extend down to the common people.[83] The vision of universal salvation is certainly closer to philosophical Taoism which repudiates the Confucian one-ordered hierarchical universe: we read in the *Chuang Tzu* that Tao is in all those things that humans consider lowly and valueless.[84] Yet the *Chuang Tzu* repudiates love. Since fishes swimming in the ocean forget themselves as well as all other things, love or compassion is quite unnecessary.[85] The religious Taoist is not only an elitist, he is an egotist. Such salvation as he conceives it precludes universal applicability.[86] Indeed, while consigning the vast majority of mankind to perishing, his appeal is to exceptions in nature, even exceptions among men.

Pure Land is more true to the Chinese aspiration because it is a pure faith. Philosophical and religious Taoisms and Confucianism are strictly speaking faiths seeking understanding which had to look for evidence in the face of lived experiences. But faith, unhampered by such considerations, simply declares the heart's desire. The Pure Land vision is the consummation of the Chinese vision of the divine, which, as it was in the earliest consciousness, reaffirms itself throughout successive stages of religious evolutions in China. Today the Chinese are still inspired by this faith in the goodness of land and life, though under a very different ideology and thus through very different expressions.

CONCLUSION:

In this paper we have tried to show that for the Chinese the physical universe is the locus of the divine. In China the opposition between the spirit and the flesh is not couched in the imagery of the opposition between man and nature. Rather, because for the Chinese the natural world is the locus of the divine, all major forms of Chinese thought have taken nature to be the ultimate standard. In that regard we may say that Taoism has served to articulate the Chinese aesthetic ideal, art is man's transcendence of self toward the creativity in nature. Confucianism, as the ethical ideal of the Chinese, takes virtue to be rooted in nature, and the highest ethical ideal being the harmony among humans and nature. Buddhism in China transformed itself into a world-affirming religion and, instead of renunciation of life, the Chinese Buddhist prays for unending life. Even the Chinese notion of science in religious Taoism did not go beyond imitating nature by capturing nature's secrets to immortality, and the Chinese theory of law and government is flatly an effort to imitate the effectiveness of nature which governs by non-action. Unlike the Greek mind, the Chinese mind never declares its independence from nature, but bending back it models itself upon nature, always holding nature up as its norm.

St. John's University

   Jamaica, New York

NOTES

1. The term 'metaphysics' was coined by Andronicus of Rhodes (60 B.C.) who in arranging Aristotle's corpus found a body of treatises without a title. After reading the contents he decided that these treatises pedagogically had to be studied after the study of Aristotle's physical treatises. Thus he called this body of work *Ta meta ta physica*, hence metaphysics.

2. In Pythagoreanism and Plato, the power for abstract thinking as exemplified in mathematics is a requisite in man's ascent to the divine. This is the origin of the division of sciences into physics, mathematics and metaphysics in Aristotle (*Meta.* 1026a16-20), although unlike Plato, Aristotle was not keen on mathematics. This emphasis on the power of abstraction as a liberation from matter colored classical theory of knowledge. The same classification of the hierarchy of the sciences, with obviously less justification, continued into the Middle Ages. See St. Thomas Aquinas, *The Division and Methods of the Sciences*, trans. A. Maurer (Toronto: The Pontifical Institute of Medieval Studies, 1958).

3. Christian Wolff (1679-1754) in his *Philosophia sive Ontologia* (Frankfurt-Leipzig, 1729) divided metaphysics into three special branches: ontology or natural theology, cosmology, and psychology, each with its distinct subject matter.

4. The *Tao Te Ching*, chap. 25: '*Tao fa tzu-jan.*'

5. Neo-Confucianism as both an affirmation and negation of the basic Chinese reverence for the physical order occupies a unique place in the development of the Chinese *psyche*. It deserves a full treatment at a separate time.

6. John N. Findley, *Plato: The Written and Unwritten Doctrines*, (New York: Humanities Press, 1974); Charles P. Bigger *Participation: A Platonic Inquiry*, (Baton Rouge: Louisiana State University Press, 1968); Eduard Zeller, *Outlines of the History of Greek Philosophy*, (New York: The Humanities Press, 1931); and Werner Jaeger, *The Theology of the Early Greek Philosophers* (Oxford, at the Clarendon Press, 1947). The first two affirm while the last two deny the existence of a two-world theory in Plato.

7. In later developments, with the formal arrival of con-

sciousness, naming was no longer regarded, as in Taoism, the last stage of safety. Instead it was considered the first requisite for the peaceful and orderly organization of the world. In the philosophies of Shen Pu-hai, Confucius, Hsun tzu and Han Fei, the conviction was that if only names were properly designated and applied, everything would have its rightful place, thus we may be spared the conflicts and strifes of a chaotic world.

8. I have avoided translating Hun-Tun as Chaos. Chaos in Western philosophy understood as the 'unordered given,' 'an antecedent irrational surd' has a negative content entirely alien to the Taoist term. However, since the publication of two pioneering volumes, David L. Hall's *The Uncertain Phoenix: Adventures Toward a Post-Cultural Sensibility* (New York: Fordham University Press, 1982) and N.J. Girardot's *Myth and Meaning in Early Taoism: The Theme of Chaos (hun-tun)* (Berkeley: University of California Press, 1983), I am ready to drop my reservations.

9. *Phaedo*, 78-80.

10. Aristotle, *De Anima* 429a20-28.

11. The *I-ching*, The Great Appendix, II, chap. 8. See James Legge, trans. *The I Ching* (New York: Dover Publications, 1963), p. 399.

12. In the *Chuang Tzu*, these are called 'sitting forgetfulness' (6:14), 'fasting the mind' (4:2), and 'today I have lost myself' (2:1); Watson's translation, pp. 90-91, 57-58, and 36 respectively.

13. The *Tao Te Ching*, chap. 20.

14. The *Chuang Tzu*, 2:3; Watson's translation, p. 39-40.

15. According to the *Chuang Tzu* (1:3), 'The ultimate man has no self, the spirit man has no accomplishment and the sage has no name;' Watson's translation, p. 32.

16. The *Lieh Tzu*, chap. 1. A.C. Graham's translation, *The Book of Lieh-tzu*, (London: John Murray, 1960), p. 20.

17. The *Chuang Tzu* 1:1, 2:11; Watson's translation, pp. 29, 49.

18. Aristotle discovers three kinds of non-sensible immortal substances: God, the Unmoved Mover (*Meta*. XII, 7), the intelligences which move the planetary spheres (*Meta*. XII, 8) and the human reason which upon death exists apart from the body (*Meta*. XII, 1070a24-26; *De Anima* III, 5).

19. The *I-ching*, The Great Appendix I, chap. 5. Legge's translation, p. 356.

20. *Mencius*, IIIA:4.

21. See Wing-tsit Chan, *A Source Book in Chinese Philosophy* (Princeton: Princeton University Press, 1963), p. 99, note 14 regarding interchanging this line with the fourth line.

22. The *Doctrine of the Mean*, chap. 4.

23. The *Chuang Tzu*, 8:1; Watson's translation, p. 98.

24. *Mencius*, VI.A:15 & 16.

25. *Nicomachean Ethics*, 1178a22-23.

26. In every subject matter of study, whether physics, metaphysics, ethics or politics, solitude or self-sufficiency is finally the highest value for Aristotle. See Whitney J. Oates, *Aristotle and the Problem of Value* (Princeton: Princeton University Press, 1963), p. 316.

27. *The Doctrine of the Mean*, chap. 13. Max Weber's statement in *The Religion of China* (New York: The Free Press, 1951), p. 155, that Confucianism had no metaphysical foundation is misleading. Such a statement is based on the biased view that metaphysics, which is man's search for the divine, must be e- quated with other-worldliness.

28. *Mencius*, IV.B.12 & 26, VI.A.7.

29. See *Mencius*, VI.A.8.

30. *Analects*, I:5.

31. See the *Book of Documents*, trans. Bernhard Karlgren (Stockholm: Reprinted from the Museum of Far Eastern Antiqui- ties, Bulletin 22, 1950), p. 59.

32. See *Analects* 2:4; *Book of Odes*, Ode number 267,

33. See *Li Chi*, trans. James Legge (New York: University Books, 1967), Vol. 1, p. 107.

34. See Karlgren, p. 26.

35. C.K. Yang remarks that "the Confucians fully endorsed the divine character of political power by supporting the con- cept of the Mandate of Heaven. Mencius' (ca. 372-288 B.C.) reinterpretation of the concept of Heaven's will in terms of the people's interest and public opinion resulted in a redefinition of the duties of the ruler, but did not offer a secular theory on the origin of power." *Religion in Chinese Society* (Berkeley: University of California Press, 1967), p. 108. See also Herrlee G. Creel, *The Origins of Statecraft in China*, (Chicago: The Univer- sity of Chicago Press, 1970), vol. 1, pp. 44-45.

36. The *Tso Chuan* (Tso's Commentary on Spring and Au- tumn Annals), Duke Hsiang, 24th year.

37. See *The Book of Documents*, 1:1 'The Canon of Yao'; V:6 'The Metal-Bound Coffer'. See Karlgren, p. 1 ff, 35ff.

38. Unlike the Taoist, the Confucian individual desires name and fame that accrue to the self. See *Analects* 1:1; *The Doctrine of the Mean*, chap. 11.

39. For the Chinese, writings and words possess the numi- nous quality of the holy and the spiritual. Mencius treats speech and spiritual power as belonging to the same category (The *Mencius* 2A:2). Confucius regards the words of sages to be as

awe-inspiring as the Mandate of Heaven (*Analects* 16:8).

40. *Mencius* 4A:26.

41. In Confucianism, the honor of the ancestors comes from their living descendants; the dead is promoted or demoted according to how his posterity is doing on earth. Thus rank or achievement in this world is a deadly serious matter. Filial piety prescribes not only paying respects and procuring comforts for parents while they are alive and observing the proper rites when they have departed, it requires that one be an achiever, inasmuch as a man who is a failure is by definition an unfilial son. See *The Doctrine of the Mean*, chaps. 16, 17, 18.

42. Nathan Sivin in "Chinese Alchemy and the Manipulation of Time" delivered at the Massachusetts Institute of Technology, January 25, 1976. (This is a summary of Joseph Needham, *Science and Civilization in China* [Cambridge, England: At the University Press, 1954-1974], V, Part 4). "The dominant goal of Chinese alchemy was contemplative, and even ecstatic. . . . The alchemists constructed their intricate art, made the cycles of cosmic process accessible, and undertook to contemplate them because they believed that to encompass the Tao with their minds--or, as they put it, with their hearts and minds (comprised in one word, '*hsin*')--would make them one with it."

43. See Ch'en Kuo-fu, *Tao-tsang yua* n-liu k'ao (Peking, 1915, 1963).

44. Ho-shang-kung's commentary on the *Tao Te Ching* is full of these examples. See *Ho-shang-kung's Commentary on Lao-Tse*, trans. Eduard Erkes (Ascona, Switzerland: Artibus Asiae Publishers, 1950), especially chaps. 5 and 6.

45. See Joseph Needham, *Science and Civilization in China* (Cambridge, England: At the University Press), Vol. II, pp. 139-164; Vol. V, Part 2; Nathan Sivin, *Chinese Alchemy: Preliminary Studies* (Cambridge, Mass.: Harvard University Press, 1968).

46. The origins of philosophical and religious Taoisms will be dealt with elsewhere. From a study of the thought sequence it is clear that historically philosophical Taoism as a distinct school of thought arose as a rebellion against the emergent rationalism in Confucianism. Thus it harked back to a mythical past prior to the emergence of consciousness, reason and morals, when man and nature were not yet separate. Religious Taoism, on the other hand, originated from ancient shamanism. Their vision and some of their practices could have been from time immemorial. But shamanism, as Professor Mircea Eliade pointed out in *Shamanism* (Princeton: Princeton University Press, 1964), p. 449, already marked man's emergence from, and his effort to control, nature. Thus to the extent that philosophical Taoism's central insight is the seamless unity of man and nature, whereas

both Confucianism and religious Taoism entered the stage when man became conscious of his distinct existence in nature, religious Taoism is on the same side as Confucianism.

47. See my paper 'Is There A Doctrine of Physical Immortality in the *Tao Te Ching*?', *History of Religions*, Vol. 12, No. 3 (February, 1973), 231-249.

48. The *Chuang Tzu*, 15:1. Watson's translation, pp. 167-68.

49. See Fung Yu-lan, *A History of Chinese Philosophy*, trans. Derk Bodde (Princeton: Princeton University Press, 1953), Vol. II, p. 431.

50. The *Pao P'u Tzu*, 14:3a by James R. Ware, trans. *Alchemy, Medicine, and Religion in the China of A.D. 320*, (Cambridge, Mass.: The M.I.T. Press, 1966), p. 229.

51. The *Pao P'u Tzu*, 8:5a; 14:9b.

52. Ware, p. 2.

53. The *Pao P'u Tzu*, chap. 2.

54. The *Lieh-Tzu*, chap. 1. Graham's translation, pp. 30-31.

55. *Fung Yu-lan*, p. 431.

56. Cf. Needham's *Science and Civilization in China*, Vol. V, Part 2, pp. 71-126, "The drug of deathlessness; macrobiotics and immortality-theory in East and West."

57. In the outer chapters, the *Pao P'u Tzu* addresses itself to these issues. See also Mircea Eliade, *Immortality and Freedom* (Princeton: Princeton University Press, 1958), pp. 284-292.

58. Paul Ricoeur, *The Symbolism of Evil* (Boston: Beacon Press, 1967), p. 287ff.

59. The *Pao P'u Tzu*, 5:1b. Cf. Needham, *Science and Civilization in China*, Vol. V, Part 2, p. 85ff.

60. 'That-which-is' is the palace of 'that-which-is-not.' The body, being the abode of the inner spirits, is like a dike. When the dike crumbles, water is no longer retained. It is also like a candle. When the candle is at its end, fire no longer dwells there." The *Pao P'u Tzu*, 5:1b.

61. See Hu Shih "The Indianization of China" in *Independence, Convergence and Borrowing* (Cambridge, Mass.: Harvard University Press, 1937). To counter Hu Shih's position, Kenneth Ch'en in *The Chinese Transformation of Buddhism* (Princeton: Princeton University Press, 1973) points out those aspects of Chinese culture that have influenced Buddhism in China.

62. Perhaps due to this very affirmation of nature as good, and human nature as but an extension of physical nature, in China there was never a real head-on confrontation with the problem of evil. In this it differed from classical Western philosophy, which by locating the divine beyond the physical realm, readily identified evil with matter, and Christianity, which by taking the soul as ordered to God and the body as ordered to

the soul, distinguished between physical and moral evil, the seat of which was in the soul. In the Neo-Confucianism of Chu Hsi, *ch'i*, translated by Wing-tsit Chan as 'material force', was taken to be the principle of evil. But this position was never consistently worked out.

63. See the *Heart Sutra (Prajna-Paramita-Hrdaya)*, the *Diamond Sutra* (Diamond *Prajna-paramita*), and *The Awakening of Faith (Mahayana sraddhotpada-sastra)*.

64. That the Christian mystical universe is a hierarchical one is evident from the titles of treatises by the mystics. Dionysius the Areopagite, who wrote the very influential "On the Celestial Hierarchy" and "On the Ecclesiastical Hierarchy," was probably the first one to coin the word hierarchy in Christian theology. Walter Hilton, a fourteenth century English mystic, wrote "The Ladder of Perfection" which reaches from earth to heaven. From St. John of the Cross, the mystic's mystic, we have "The Ascent of Mount Carmel." See William Ralph Inge, *Christian Mysticism* (New York: Meridian Books, 1948).

65. See *The Lion's Roar of Queen Srimala*, a Buddhist Scripture on the Tathagatagarbha Theory, trans. Alex & Hideko Wayman (New York: Columbia University Press, 1974).

66. The *Awakening of Faith*, trans. Yoshito S. Hakeda (New York: Columbia University Press, 1967), pp. 32-33.

67. Nagarjuna (2nd Century A.D.) was the first one to enunciate this doctrine in the *Madhyamika-karika*, XXV, 19.

68. Cf. Aristotle's description of God in *Metaphysics*, XII, 7.

69. See D.T. Suzuki, *Studies in the Lankavatara Sutra* (London: Routledge & Kegan Paul Ltd., 1930, 1957), p. 136.

70. Walter Liebenthal says: "The Chinese Buddhist were all Taoists whenever they wrote philosophy." *Chao Lun*, trans. Walter Liebenthal (Hong Kong: Hong Kong University Press, 2nd edition, 1968), Preface, p. xii.

71. See 'The Recorded Conversations of Shen-hui' in Wing-tsit Chan, *A Source Book in Chinese Philosophy*, pp. 443-444.

72. Hui-ssu (514-577) of the Tien-t'ai school says: "Owing to the accomplishment of concentration, one knows that the cycle of life and death is the same as Nirvana, and owing to the attainment of insight, one knows that Nirvana is the same as the cycle of life and death" (*Ibid.*, p. 405). This paved the way for Shen-hui (670-761) of southern Ch'an to declare that enlightenment "means entering Nirvana without renouncing life and death." (*Ibid.*, p. 441).

73. *Original Teachings of Ch'an Buddhism*, trans. Chang Chung-yuan (New York: Vintage Books, 1971), p. 120.

74. Chan, p. 447.

75. The three sutras of the Pure Land sect in China and Japan are the *Larger Sukhavati* (*vyuha*), the *Smaller Sukhavati*, and *Kuan-Fo-ching*.

76. We suggest that the Tathagatagabha performs the same function as Hun-tun in Taoism.

77. In Christianity physical nature as the given has to be purified and exalted to enter the realm of spirit. See a miniature from the 15th-century French Book of Hours, showing Mary with the Holy Trinity, in C.G. Jung, *Man and His Symbols* (New York: Dell, 1964), p. 226. This picture shows that even when Mary, as nature and body purified, is elevated to Heaven, she still sits demurely alone in a corner, subordinated to the Trinity which occupies the center of the painting.

78. *Mencius*, 6A:8.

79. Traditional arguments for the immortality of the soul is premised on its rationality. Thus irrational beings are inadmissible to the divine realm. Even the Christian world with its celestial and terrestrial hierarchies, with saints and angels singing praises to God, pales before the richness of the Pure-Land terrain wherein animals and even stones attain immortality, not as means of enjoyment for gods or men, but on their own account.

80. See P'eng Chi-ch'ing, *Ching-tu sheng-hsien lu* (Records of Saints in Pure Land) (Taipei, 1974).

81. Buddhism teaches that the divine, whether as Buddha, Amitabha or Kuan-yin, is *mahakaruna*, unbounded love which crushes all barriers. See D.T. Suzuki, *The Essentials of Zen Buddhism* (New York: E.P. Dutton, 1962), p. 345.

82. *Mencius*, 6A:8, 11.

83. See Kuan Feng and Lin Yu-shih, "Third Discussion on Confucius," in *Chinese Studies in Philosophy*, 2 (1971), 246-263.

84. The *Chuang Tzu*, 22:6.

85. *Ibid.*, 5:5, 6:3 & 5.

86. Hsiao, T'ien-shih, *Ju shih ho ts'an, Tao-chia yang-sheng-hsueh kai-yao* (Essentials of the Taoist Way of Nurturing Life, Integrated with Confucian and Buddhist Teachings) (Taipei, 1962), argues that the perfection of an immortal requires intellectual, moral and spiritual perfection. Otherwise what is the value of immortality or in what way is an immortal man better than an immortal ass? Well, in the Pure Land, there are immortal asses.

CHINESE GLOSSARY

Chen-jen	真人
Ch'en Kuo-fu	陳國符
Ch'i	氣
Ch'ih-yu	蚩尤
Chün-tzu	君子
Han Fei	韓非
Ho-shang-kung	河上公
Hsin	心
Hsün Tzu	荀子
Hua-yem	華嚴
Hui-ssu	慧思
Hun-tun	混沌
Kuan-fo-ching	觀佛經
Hsiao T'ien-shih	蕭天石
Pao P'u Tzu	抱朴子
P'en Chi-ch'ing	彭際清
Shen-hui	神會
Shen Pu-hui	申不害
Tao fa tzu-jan	道法自然
T'ien-ming	天命
T'ien-t'ai	天台
Tso-chuan	左傳
Tzu-jan	自然
Wu	悟
Yü	禹

CHAPTER VII

GOD - TO WHAT, IF ANYTHING, DOES THE TERM REFER?
AN EASTERN CHRISTIAN PERSPECTIVE

METROPOLITAN PAULOS GREGORIOS

If I were to treat simply "The Christian View of God," I would have more or less to read out the title, go into a fairly large period of silence, and then conclude with "thank you, friends, for sharing with me the Christian view of God." For in your silence, you would also have expressed the Christian view of God. Please do not imagine that the length of the silent period would have been due to my going into a trance or something of that sort. It simply happens to be the case that silence would be the best way to speak about our ignorance of God, and it takes time to give adequate expression to that ignorance.

The ignorance can, however, be of two kinds, one natural, and the other taught. The natural ignorance is not to be regarded as somehow superior to the taught or acquired one. In this particular case, the movement from natural ignorance to taught ignorance (*docta ignorantia*) is itself a process of growth and self-realization which makes the acquisition of the knowledge of the unknowability of God itself a creative process of considerable value.

But religious leaders do a lot of talking about God, not always knowing what is being talked about. In this paper, I shall treat three questions, mainly:

(a) Is God a comprehensible reality? what of God is a legitimate subject for discourse?

(b) To what does the Christian doctrine of the Triune God refer?

(c) What is really meant by speaking about God's transcendence and immanence?

The perspective from which I write is that of an eastern Christian trained in the west. That may in itself lead to contradictions, which my friends may be able to detect and point out to me. But the basic ideas are from a tradition which Eastern Christians regard as the authentic Christian Tradition. This tradition does not follow the thought of an Augustine, of a Thomas Aquinas, or of a Karl Barth. It was shaped through the centuries, and formulated to a fair extent by the three Cappadocian Fathers--St. Basil of Caesarea, (died ca. 379 A.D.), his younger brother St. Gregory of Nyssa, (died ca. 395 A.D.), and their friend and colleague St. Gregory Nazianzen, (died ca. 390 A.D.). They were Asians from what is today the north-eastern part of Turkey. On the foundation which they formulated subsequent eastern Christian thinkers have built-- among the Byzantines Maximus the Confessor and Gregory Palamas, among the Slavs Khomiakov and Soloviev. The foundation still remains adequate to the needs of this modern age, and what I say here owes much to this eastern heritage.

THE COMPREHENSIBILITY OF GOD

St. Gregory Nazianzen, in his second Theological Oration, quotes Plato who had said that it is difficult to conceive God, but that to define him in words is an impossibility.[1] The Christian Father then goes on playfully to say that this is clever of the philosopher in that he gives you the impression that while Plato himself has been able with difficulty to conceive God, he has no responsibility to tell us what he has conceived since in his view it is impossible to define God in words. The Nazianzen then goes on to say: "But in my opinion it is impossible to express Him, but yet more impossible to conceive Him."[2] He continues in the next paragraph: "It is one thing to be persuaded of the existence of a thing, and quite another to know what it is."[3]

It was Gregory of Nyssa who made this point philosophically clear. The Nazianzen was of the view that it was the feebleness of our equipment, the limited nature of our mind, that causes the incapacity to comprehend. He even hoped that some day we will overcome this incapacity and know God, so that we would know him as we are known.[4] His colleague Nyssa went further, and made certain basic clarifications:

a) that God is of a different order of being than anything else, and that his incomprehensibility is related, not so much to the limits of our mind, as to God's nature itself;
b) that there is a difference between God's *ousia* or his is-ness, and his *energeia* or operations in the creation; and
c) that the knowledge of God, when it comes, is never strictly intellectual nor simply mystical, but a form of self-knowledge when that self has become more truly the image or created finite manifestation of God.

Nyssa agrees that we can have faint and scant apprehension of the nature of God through our reasonings about what

God has revealed of Himself, but that this does not amount to any comprehension.[5] However, this unknowability is not a unique characteristic of God alone. The creation itself shares this unknowability. For example, can we claim to know, exhaustively, notions like space or time or even the human mind, Gregory asks. We can have notions about them, but we also know that these notions have to keep changing again and again in the light of experience.

Nyssa insists on the basic distinction and difference between the Self-existent and the Contingent, or the Uncreated and the Created. The Platonic assumption of the co-eternity of Creator and Creation is explicitly rejected by Nyssa as well as by the other Cappadocians. Basil stated that the universe had a beginning, that this beginning is also the beginning of time, and that time and the world as we now know it will also come to an end.[6] Even heaven is not co-existent with God, but was created and therefore has a beginning.

Nyssa made the same distinction between "He who is" and "the things that are" (*ho ontos on* and *ta onta*). The "one whose being is" is not in the same class with "those that merely exist." In fact Gregory has three classes:

1. the Being who has being by His own nature,[7]
2. non-being, which has existence only in appearing to be,[8]

(and in between these two),

3. those things which are capable of moving towards being or non-being.[9]

The latter two are dependent on the negation of, or derived from, the first, i.e., He who is.

The distinction between the Uncreated and the Creation, in Gregory of Nyssa, may be summarized as follows:

Uncreated Being	*Created Existence*
1. Self-derived	Other-derived
2. Self-generating	Other-generated
3. Self-subsistent	Contingent upon the will of the Creator
4. Not subject to non-being	Capable of moving into being or non-being
5. Perfectly good	Capable of good and evil
6. Is what it wills and wills what it is, hence does not move from *arche* to *telos*, nor is in process of becoming	Always has to become what it is, or move into non-being, hence always becoming or perishing.
7. Simple	Compound

The simplicity of God does not, however, preclude either conceptual distinctions or distinction of persons. One of the conceptual distinctions made classical for Eastern thought by Gregory of Nyssa is the distinction between *ousia* and *energeia*. It was not a distinction created by him. Most likely it was created by his adversary, Eunomius of Cyzicus. He used the distinction as a major tool in vanquishing his adversary, the Arian heretic. Eunomius had developed the distinctions among being, operative power, and operated effect, i.e., *ousia, energeia,* and *erga*. The distinction had an epistemological function, namely that human reason could deduce the nature of the operative power from an understanding of the operated effect, and from the understanding of the operative power move to the nature of its being. The *erga* or operated effect can be an object of our understanding, which then becomes the first step to ascend to the second step of understanding of the *energeia* and then ascend to the third step of understanding the *ousia*.

This is what Gregory refuted. He held that there was no clear road from *erga* to *energeia* or from *energeia* to *ousia*. The wind is the *energeia* which creates the *ergon* of a sand-dune. But if you did not know what the wind was, how can you move from the knowledge of a sand-dune to the knowledge of the wind? Or in today's terms would a photograph and a green leaf constitute sufficient ground to understand the nature of light? Can you understand a human being from his excretions and from a ship which are both his *erga*?

Gregory thus denies the assumption that we can move from the knowledge of Creation to the knowledge of the Creator.

He rejects also the principle of *analogia entis* or *analogia fidei*. The only analogy he concedes is the *analogia metousias*, but this does not lead to a knowledge of the *ousia* of God. The *analogia metousias* helps only to compare the degree of participation in the *energeia* of God. The degree of participation is measured by the degree of conformity to the good by the impulsion of the will of each towards the good. The *energeia* thus does not lead to knowledge of God's being. It is only God's *energeia* which we can know or apprehend.

Words about God can serve a useful purpose in so far as they lead to the worship of God, or to greater participation in the good.[11] But they cannot capture or conceive God nor can they adequately express His being. As Gregory of Nyssa says:

> After all, God is not words, neither has He his being in sound and speech. God is in Himself as He is ever believed to be, but he is named by those who invoke Him, the name not being the same as what He is (for the nature is ineffable); but He has names given to

Him in accordance with what is believed to be His operations in relation to our life.[12]

To sum up then, words about God are certainly not descriptive but evocative. Their main purpose is not to provide knowledge, but to lead to worship. His names as well as any descriptions we make about Him are our creations, related to our experience of His operations. His *ousia* or being remains beyond all grasp. For He is not like the things that make up the created order. His being is *sui generis* and no analogy or reasoning can comprehend it. There is no concept adequate for apprehending the Truth of God.

THE DOCTRINE OF THE TRINITY

All doctrines are verbal. This applies also to the Doctrine of the Trinity, a doctrine composed, after all, of words. It is a human creation, developed out of the understanding of the *energeia* of God that reaches out to us.

The central *energeia* that has reached out to us is the person of Christ, Christians believe. The central form in which God's *ousia* impinges upon us through His *energeia* is the form of a man who was born in Palestine 2000 years ago. This is the heart of the Christian faith and experience; it is from this that the doctrine of the Trinity takes shape.

But this doctrine is much misunderstood, not merely by Muslims and Jews with their more strict monotheism, but also by very many Christians. St. Basil makes it clear that one cannot attribute any kind of number to the Godhead, because Divinity is without quantity and number relates to quantity.

> In reply to those who slander us as being Tritheists, let it be said that we confess one God, not in number but in nature (*ou toi arithmoi, alla tei phusei*). For not everything that is called one in number is one in reality nor simple in its nature, but God is universally admitted to be simple and uncompounded. Yet God is therefore not one in number. . . . Number pertains to quantity; now quantity is joined as an attribute to corporeal nature; therefore number is an attribute of corporeal nature.[13]

Here our logic comes to a standstill. The Cappadocians insist that they are not Tritheists, and yet they do not want to ascribe the number One to God without qualification. A heroic effort is made to explain this problem in the famous *Epistle 38* attributed to St. Basil, but which was probably from the pen of his brother, St. Gregory of Nyssa. Yet another vigorous effort is made by St. Gregory in his oration, "On Not Three Gods," to defend himself against the charge of Tritheism. But the result seems to me unsatisfactory. If the Unity of God is in the same genre as the unity of the gold in three gold coins, then we are justified, by the ordinary use of language, to speak of three Gods, as we speak of three coins.

But this certainly is not the intention of the Cappadocians. A more mature point of view is expressed by Nyssa in his first book against Eunomius. He had already made a distinction between the operation of God *ad extra*[14] and the mutual immanent relations within the Godhead. There he also makes clear that enumeration is possible only for circumscribed finite realities. The Divine life has no parts or boundary. The names which we give God, including those of Father, Son and Holy Spirit, have "a human sound, but not a human meaning."[15]

> There is nothing by which we can measure the divine and blessed life. It is not in time, but time flows from it. . . . The Supreme and Blessed Life has no time extension accompanying its course, and therefore no span or measure.[16]

Or again,

> In whom there is neither form (*eidos*) nor place, no size, no measure of time, nor anything else of those things which can be comprehended.[7]

No number, no measure, no duality or non-duality, no monism or non-monism--all our usual categories have to be folded up and laid away. You must forgive me therefore if I fail to give you a satisfactory metaphysical account of the Three-in-One. I do not have any understanding of the mystery, of that mystery I am sure because of my faith. But I have no concepts, analogies or illustrations by which to explain the Holy Trinity. Three things I derive from that doctrine:

> that God is love, and that in the divine being there are three persons or centers which respond to each other in freedom and love; that God is a community of freedom and love; that in this freedom and love is also the good, the true being of all that exists.[18]

The patristic tradition has examined all efforts to explain the Trinity in terms of analogies in creation, and have rejected them as inadequate. Even the Nazianzen who sometimes used the analogy of the human mind and human word to denote the relation between the Father and the Son, had to say:

> I have very carefully considered this matter in my

own mind, and have looked at it from every point of view, in order to find some illustration of this most important subject (the Holy Trinity), but I have been unable to discover anything on earth with which to compare the nature of the Godhead.[19]

He mentions expressly the course, the fountain and the river, the sun, the ray and the light, and then concludes:

Finally then, it seems best to me to let the images and the shadows go, as being deceitful and very far short of the truth.

Gregory Nazianzen, as well as Gregory of Nyssa, who had both a fairly high view of the use of philosophy, would both admit that philosophical language is not at all suited for the discourse about God. It is better to be silent, or if you must give utterance, to use the hymns of praise. And the Nazianzen himself has given us many such hymns, for example, this translation by Bossuet:

Tout demeure en vous, tout court apres vous;
Vous êtes la fin de toutes choses;
Vous êtes un, vous êtes tout;
Vous n'êtes rien; vous n'êtes ni un ni tout;
Comment vous appellerai-je, O Vous,
A qui tout nom peut convenir et le seul qu'on ne peut nommer.[20]

GOD'S TRANSCENDENCE AND IMMANENCE

If God is not a body, then there is already something awkward about speaking about God's transcendence and immanence because these have to do with location, and location for non-spatial entities is inconceivable for us.

Whitehead's effort to find a non-spatial or temporal transcendence has not quite yet succeeded. The kingdom that is always in the future denotes only the transcendence of history itself. Those who speak about the future of God as the future of history commit the double iniquity of identifying God with human history in a manner that is not legitimate and of taking human history to be the whole of the universe.

On the other hand, those who claim that God's being is independent of the being of the universe, shoulder the heavy burden of explaining the state of that independent being in relation to the universe. The difficulty for me is to understand words like 'independent' or 'self-sufficient' in relation to God. Sufficiency and dependence are terms that belong to quantity and relation in a created world; to apply these, even in a negative sense, to the Uncreated Being seems difficult.

In the first place, as Gregory of Nyssa says, to be infinite is to transcend all boundaries, whether of conception or of time and space. The infinite cannot stop at any boundary and must by necessity transcend all--whether the boundaries be intellectual, quantitative or qualitative. Gregory insists that every finite being must of necessity come to the boundaries of its finitude, whether in concept or being, and the infinite always extends beyond. The definition of the infinite being is not that beyond its boundaries there is nothing, but that beyond every boundary, being is.

The transcendence of God is thus not merely conceptual or qualitative or temporal or spatial. It is in transcending every boundary that the infinity of God is manifested.

But let us beware about the false statements: a) that God is beyond the creation, as if God was nonexistent this side of the boundary of creation; or b) that God is "wholly other," so that the creation can exist *along-side of God* as His "other."

Both ideas, to which Professor Boyce Gibson refers in the slender volume of essays edited by Professor John Smith, i.e., the idea of God's self-sufficiency and non-dependence, on the one hand, and his "wholly otherness" with occasional sorties into the universe, on the other hand, are in that form unacceptable to the Eastern tradition. Neither an "immobilist" view nor an "interventionist" view of God is acceptable.[21] Boyce Gibson completely misunderstands the authentic Christian tradition of creation when he asserts:

> It is just not possible to say that creating makes no difference to the creator for the something which is there, and formerly was not there, is in relation to Him; He is related where formerly He was unrelated.[22]

Gibson's mistake is in using the adverb "formerly," for the authentic tradition holds that time has its beginning only from creation, and that there was not, to parody the Arian formula, a "then when the Creation was not," though it has come from non-being into being. Perhaps his bigger mistake is his direct insistence that theology "is committed to getting the analysis straight."[23] What presumption!

The analysis of God's transcendence and immanence cannot be straightened out in such categories as apply to relations within the creation.

Gregory of Nyssa does the trick more dialectically than most modern philosophers. The principles of logic applying to the spatio-temporal creation cannot be applied to the Godhead.

There we can only say that from the side of the Universe, we experience both discontinuity with and participation in God. What it would be like from God's side we cannot conceive.

God's immanence also is understood by Gregory in a fairly sophisticated way. We can only indicate that understanding in fairly quick short-hand. God's operative energy is the ground of the creation. It begins, it moves, and it reaches its appointed destiny, only by virtue of God's will and word. The creation is God's will and word, and that is the principle of immanence. Existence is always by God's will and word, and when the will-and-word is withdrawn, there is only non-existence. Thus the authentic Christian tradition does not regard the cosmos as the body of God, or as something outside of God, for outside God there is only non-being. It is in God's will-and-word that the universe has its existence, and it is by will-and-word that God is immanent in Creation.

THE CONCEPT AND THE REALITY

Reason or *ratio* is always a proportionality between reality and knowledge. The dualism between reality and knowledge is itself grounded in the other dualism of subject and object,- which in turn generates the concepts of the *pour-soi* and the *en-soi*, the object-in-consciousness and the object-in-itself.

All these dualisms cry out to be overcome. But they will not be overcome by reason or *ratio*, which is what generates the dualities. The irrationality of reason, exemplified by the classical antinomies of Kant, cannot be overcome by reason.

The concept as such belongs to the realm of reason and stands in need of overcoming. It is a kind of puerile naivete that drives logicians and philosophers to capture reality in a net of concepts. We are part of that reality, and no equipment we have is capable of subducting reality from our minds. Let us give up that wild-goose chase.

For a thinking person, the word God should not stand for a concept. It is a symbol pointing to many things:

a) an affirmation of the contingent, therefore, un-selfsufficient and dependent character of our own existence as well as of the reality in which we participate--the reality we call the universe;

b) an affirmation that the cause of all causes is of a different genre than the links in the causal chain;

c) an affirmation that all created things have to move towards a goal which is ultimately good.

This is also what the Cappadocian Fathers meant by the term Creator. The Creator, who does not owe his being to someone else, has caused this universe to begin, keeps it going and will lead it to its destined end. The one who does that is personal, i.e., capable of responding in freedom to others. He/she is also love and wisdom. He/she cannot be captured in concepts. But he/she can be loved and united with. There all duality gives place to the union of love.

In fact it is God's freedom which makes him/her beyond the reach of our finite grasp. The human person with a great capacity to understand, has also the great capacity to bring that which he/she understands under his/her control. Every science generates its own technology. If we could comprehend God, we would also devise the technology to control Him and use Him, i.e., to enslave Him. The freedom of practically everything else is such that despite its freedom, it can be subdued by our analytic reason, at least to a certain extent. Even humanity, the highest and most evolved element in creation, we so seek to understand, control and manipulate. Do philosophers expect that God would place him/herself as an object of our comprehension, so that he/she too can be enslaved by us? Ask love for the answer.

Dr. Paulos Mar Gregorios
Metropolitan of Delhi and the North
President, World Council of Churches

NOTES

1. The English Translation of *Timaeus* 28 E, by John Harrington reads: "To discover the maker and father of this universe is indeed a hard task, and having found him it would be impossible to tell every one about him." *Timaeus*, Everyman's Library, 493 (London, New York, 1965), p. 14. See the Greek

τὸν μὲν οὖν ποιητὴν καὶ πατέρα τοῦδε τοῦ παντὸς εὑρεῖν τε ἔργον καὶ εὑρόντα εἰς πάντας ἀδύνατον λέγειν·

2. *Second Theological Oration*: IV.

3. *Idem*: V.

4. *Idem*: XVII.

5. *Contra Eunomium* II: 130, PG 45:953.B.

6. *Hexaemeron* I:3.

7. *To on, ho tei heautou phusei to einai echei.*

8. *To me on, ho en toi dokein einai monon estin.*

9. See *De Vita Moysis*, P.G. 44:333, *Gregori Nysseni Opera* vol. VII:I:40.

10. *Contra Eunomium* I: 274-275. PG 45:333D, GNO I:106-107.

11. *Contra Eunomium* II:136. PG 45:956.

12. *Ibid*. II:149. PG 45:956.

13. *Epist* VIII: Tr. Roy J. Deferrari, *St. Basil, The Letters,*

Loeb. Classical Library, (Cambridge, Mass., Harvard University Press, 1926), vol. I. p. 52.

14. *On Not Three Gods* NPNF. Vol. V, p. 334.

15. *Contra Eunomium* BK I:39 NPNF, p. 93.

16. *Contra Eunomium* I:26 NPNF, p. 69.

17. *C.E.* I:26 NPNF, p. 69.

18. My own formulation.

19. *Oratio Theologica* V: XXXI NPNF. Vol. VII p. 328 A.

20. Cited by J. Plagnieu, *S. Gregoire de Nazianze, Theologian*, p. 333 note. (Paris: Editions Franciscaines, 1951).

21. A Boyce Gibson, "The Two Ideas of God," in John E. Smith (ed.) *Philosophy of Religion* (New York: London, 1965), p. 61 ft.

22. *Ibid.*, p. 65.

23. *Ibid.*, p. 67.

CHAPTER VIII

GOD, PHILOSOPHY AND HALAKHAH IN MAIMONIDES' APPROACH TO JUDAISM

DAVID HARTMAN and ELLIOTT YAGOD

INTRODUCTION

This paper on the absolute in the Jewish metaphysical tradition does not pretend to do justice to the variety of approaches, both mystic and rationalistic, found in the Jewish tradition. Although Judaism has generally revolved around a common normative tradition, there has never been an officially recognized Jewish theological or philosophical approach to God. One finds, then, parallel movements of diversity of views on theological issues, on the one hand, and attempts at gaining consensus of behaviour regarding the legal patterns of Jewish spirituality, on the other. Leibovitch appeals to this important historical fact in order to deny that theology has significance in Judaism and to argue that law alone constitutes the essence of Judaism.[1] While sharing his concern with neutralizing the importance of factual judgments in Judaism, we nevertheless believe that the relationship between empirical and metaphysical assertions, on the one hand, and the Halakhah (Jewish law), on the other, is considerably more complex than the position he expounds. In this paper, we shall attempt to focus on a strand within the Jewish metaphysical tradition, namely that which emerges out of the Maimonidian tradition.

To understand why we chose Maimonides, it must be noted that striving for consensus of practice regarding the law was a vital feature of the Jewish tradition. One may even claim that theology entered the Jewish tradition via its influence on practice. Scholem has argued that the esoterric teachings of the mystics were able to capture the minds of the broad community because this theology offered one a symbolic approach to practice. Mystic theology transmuted the meaning of practice and turned halakhic practice into symbolic mystical experience.[2] In other words, theology entered into Jewish spirituality only if it could transform, in some way, the nature of practice. It is the law which mediates the theological in the Jewish tradition.

Maimonides was a rare figure who was a recognized master in both Halakhah (Jewish law) and philosophy. Maimonides is the great codifier of Jewish law. While his influence on the development of Halakhah was unique and outstanding, he was, also, one of the great teachers of philosophy and metaphysics in the

Jewish tradition. His work, *The Guide of the Perplexed*, influenced the development of Jewish philosophy. There were other serious Jewish philosophers who did not threaten the anti-philosophic strand in the Jewish tradition because they did not command the enormous respect, halakhically speaking, which Maimonides had in the community. Maimonides' great talmudic erudition made him a threat in philosophy. You had to confront Maimonides' philosophic views because you could not ignore his halakhic views.

Secondly, what makes Maimonides important in our study is that as an individual he was an archetype of the halakhic mind who embodied the entire scope of the halakhic discipline. No facet of the law was unknown to him. One can not claim that he was not a legalist; yet, on the other hand, he was seriously engaged in philosophy. Pines claims that, in contrast to many other Jewish philosophers, Maimonides' approach to philosophy was not apologetic. There was a genuine openness and commitment to the philosophic tradition. His concern with philosophy was a concern with truth and not simply with demonstrating the merits of the Jewish tradition.[3]

Professor Efraim Urback in his recent work on rabbinic thought repeatedly emphasizes that in the rabbinic tradition the primary concern was practice.[4] In attempting to formulate theological notions or a metaphysics of history, the rabbinic mind always asks the important question, "How does this theory relate to practice, how does it affect practice?' Urbach states that the rabbis were not interested in a coherent metaphysical tradition *per se.* Their major question was with what view of the universe and God would inspire one to observe the commandments with greater devotion. The emphasis was upon love and fear of God; theoretical speculation was introduced as a way to motivate practice. This view is shared by many rabbinic scholars as well as by students of the biblical tradition. The Jews are anchored to practice. Both the biblical and rabbinic traditions relate man to God, not via a metaphysical philosophic system, but through forms of practice embodied in the life of the committed person: not the mind, but the will; not thought, but action.

This practical tendency in the biblical and the rabbinic traditions led Spinoza to criticize Maimonides' placing philosophy within the biblical tradition.[5] Spinoza was critical of Maimonides' claim that the prophet must necessarily be a philosopher. For Spinoza, Moses had a gifted imagination but did not ground his teachings on universally valid principles. The Bible is a book of laws and Spinoza goes so far as to claim that universal morality is beyond the scope of the Bible. The Bible is shot through with legal particularism so that to maintain that one finds in the Bible a philosophic conception of God is to distort both the spirit and the content of the Bible. The major figure of whom Spinoza was most critical was Maimonides, because if Maimonides were right then philosophy and revealed law could merge. If Spinoza were right then the primacy of law in the Jewish tradition would displace any tendency towards metaphysical speculation.

The Spinozistic criticism of Maimonides was continued by the contemporary historian of philosophy, Isaac Husik, who claimed that Maimonides was unaware of the enormous gap separating the tradition that emerged from Athens and the tradition that emerged from Jerusalem. The Bible was concerned with morality, the Greeks were concerned with theoretical truth. This polarity between theoretical and practical perfections also influenced Leo Strauss' approach to Maimonides.[6] The major critique of Maimonides, then, focuses on his being a master halakhic legalist who maintained that the metaphysical tradition was intrinsically rooted in the Jewish tradition. The task of this paper is to show how Maimonides was able to integrate what appeared to Spinoza, Husik and others to be two incompatible traditions.

Let us now examine some of Maimonides' statements which characterize his approach to the relationship of practice and theory in the Jewish tradition. Maimonides, in the *Guide*, III, 27, states:

> The law as a whole, aims at two things: the welfare of the soul and the welfare of the body. As for the welfare of the soul, it consists in the multitude's acquiring correct opinions corresponding to their respective capacity. . . . The second thing consists in the acquisition by every human individual of moral qualities that are useful for life in society so that the affairs of the city may be ordered. . . . Know that as between these two aims, one is indubitably greater in nobility, namely, the welfare of the soul--I mean the procuring of correct opinions--while the second aim-- I mean the welfare of the body--is prior in nature and time.

To Maimonides, the uniqueness of Torah as distinct from other legal systems is that whereas *nomos* is concerned solely with social well being, Torah is also concerned with knowledge of God, i.e., with imparting correct beliefs.[7] The primacy of metaphysics is mentioned not only in *The Guide of the Perplexed*, but also in his codification of Jewish law, the *Mishneh Torah*. In "The Laws of the Foundations of the Torah" IV, 13,

Maimonides states that the study of the law is "a small thing" and the study of physics and metaphysics is "a great thing":

> Although these last subjects were called by the sages "a small thing" (when they say "A great thing, *Maaseh Mercabah*; a small thing, the discussion of Abaye and Rava"), still they should have the precedence. For the knowledge of these things gives primarily composure to the mind. They are the precious boon bestowed by God, to promote social well-being on earth, and enable men to obtain bliss in the life hereafter. Moreover, the knowledge of them is within the reach of all, young and old, men and women; those gifted with great intellectual capacity as well as those whose intelligence is limited.

Although the study of metaphysics is primary and of greater value (we shall soon indicate in what sense), nevertheless the study of the law is prior in time because practice of the law leads to social well-being and thus creates the social and political conditions necessary for enabling many people to engage in the study of metaphysics.[8] Placing study of metaphysics above study of the law upset the religious sensibilities of many halakhists.[9] They were far more perturbed by this statement in the *Mishneh Torah* than by *The Guide of the Perplexed*. Placing the study of philosophy above the study of talmud was perceived as undermining the very primacy of the legal tradition. Yet, this statement was made by the great master of the legal tradition. The primacy of philosophy is mentioned again in the *Mishneh Torah* at the end of "The Laws of Repentance" as well as in Chapter 2 of "The Laws of the Foundations of the Torah." There the claim is made that only through metaphysical knowledge of God can one arrive at the goal of love of God. Worshipping God out of love is made possible only by philosophy. The law does not create love, it creates social well-being. Metaphysical knowledge of God, i.e., following the path of the study of physics and metaphysics, creates in man the capacity to love God.

In the *Guide*, III, 52, Maimonides repeats the claim which pervades his total philosophic world view: practice creates reverence for God whereas knowledge creates love:

> For these two ends, namely *love* and *fear*, are achieved through two things: *love* through the opinions taught by the Law, which include the apprehension of His being as He, may He be exalted, is in truth; while *fear* is achieved by means of all actions prescribed by the Law, as we have explained.

The critique of Maimonides for having elevated philosophy to so high a level had two features. First, it appeared to be a distortion of the tradition since the tradition emphasized practice. The tradition's concern with study always had as its goal the study of law. Guttman and Scholem, who relate the contemplative tradition in Maimonides to the talmudic emphasis upon study, are only partially correct since when the talmudic tradition spoke of the importance of study it always had in mind the study of the law.[10] It did not refer to metaphysical contemplation of God. Therefore, Maimonides appears to undermine the basic Jewish emphasis on the primacy of practice and on the primacy of the study of the legal tradition. This was typical of medieval critiques of Maimonides.

Secondly, Maimonides seems to be indifferent to the centrality of history. Maimonides' attempt at understanding God in ontological terms, as the perfect necessary being and not as the God who freely reveals Himself in events in history, appears to negate the God of the Jewish tradition. The primacy of an-event-based theology, of open-textured events, and of the spontaneity and the radical freedom of God to reveal Himself in events stand in utter contrast to a theology of the God of metaphysics, the absolute, self-sufficient God who draws man to worship Him in virtue of His perfection. It is in great historical events that one finds the living God of the Bible. In Maimonides' thought, history appears to play a very limited role in mediating the religious passion for God. Maimonides, therefore, is alien to the Jewish tradition because his approach a) undercuts the centrality of legal study and b) neutralizes the centrality of events and of history in one's relationship to the absolute.[11] We shall cite examples of how Maimonides completely turns around certain obvious currents within the Jewish tradition.

1) In the creation story in Genesis the obvious direction of the story is that of days leading up to the creation of man and of the Sabbath. Man's being created last points to an anthropocentric creation. God's creation of nature is meant to serve His unique creation, i.e., man. In fact, one of the most popular classical commentaries on the Bible quotes a midrash which asks why the Bible began with the account of creation since the Bible is essentially a book of law. The answer given is that the creation story has a didactic point, namely, to teach that since God is the creator of the world, He has the right to give the land to whomever He pleases. Therefore, Israel's justification for the land of Canaan comes from the story of the creation of the world. According to the spirit of this midrash, were it not for a moral-practical justification, the account of creation would ap-

pear pointless. Maimonides, however, does not see in the account of the creation of nature (and in reflecting on the God of nature) the centrality of man. He sees rather a theocentric universe in which man is insignificant in comparison with the intelligences and with the richness of the infinite Being, who creates a universe as a consequence of the overflow of His infinite power and perfection.[12]

2) The story of the encounter between Moses and God, where Moses asks for the divine name, also reveals Maimonides metaphysical perspective. The midrashic approach to 'Ehyeh-Asher Ehyeh' (I will be who I will be) [Exodus III, 14] reflects a God who announces to Moses and to the people that He will be present in their struggle. He is a God who can be relied upon to be responsive in history.[15] Buber remarks in his essay, 'The Faith of Judaism':

> Not "I am that I am" as alleged by the metaphysicians --God does not make theological statements--but the answer which his creatures need, and which benefits them: "I shall be there as I there shall be" [Exod. 3:14]. That is: you need not conjure me, for I am here, I am with you; but you cannot conjure me, for I am with you time and again in the form in which I choose to be with you time and again; I myself do not anticipate any of my manifestations; you cannot learn to meet me; you meet me, when *you* meet me: ... [14]

Buber's approach is similar in spirit to that of the midrash. Maimonides, however, in the *Guide*, I, 63, writes:

> Accordingly when God, may He be held sublime and magnified, revealed himself to Moses our Master and ordered him to address a call to people and to convey to them his prophetic mission, [Moses] said: the first thing that they will ask of me is that I should make them acquire true knowledge that there exists a god with reference to the world; after that I shall make the claim that He has sent me. For at that time all the people except a few were not aware of the existence of the deity, and the utmost limits of their speculation did not transcend the sphere, its faculties, and its actions, for they did not separate themselves from things perceived by the senses and had not obtained intellectual perfection. Accordingly God made known to [Moses] the knowledge that he was to convey to them and through which they would acquire a true notion of the existence of God, this knowledge being: *I am that I am*. This is a name deriving from

the verb *to be* [hayah], which signifies existence, for *hayah*, indicates the notion: he was. And in Hebrew, there is no difference between your saying: he was, and he existed. The whole secret consists in the repetition in a predicative position of the very word indicative of existence. For the word *that* [in the phrase "I am that I am"] requires the mention of an attribute immediately connected with it. For it is a deficient word requiring a connection with something else. . . . Accordingly Scripture makes, as it were, a clear statement that the subject is identical with the predicate. This makes it clear that He is existent not through existence. This notion may be summarized and interpreted in the following way: the existent that is the existent, or the necessarily existent. This is what demonstration necessarily leads to: namely, to the view that there is a necessarily existent thing that has never been, or ever will be, non-existent.

To the midrash and to Buber, Israel requires the knowledge that God will be present with them in their suffering. To Maimonides the slave people, who are beginning their pilgrimage to become a holy covenant people, must know that the God of being is a necessary existent and that the predicate, I am, is identical with the subject, I am. What a change in spiritual climate! How could Maimonides take a dramatic statement rooted in history, a promise to be ever present--"I shall be there"--to be a statement of the proposition that God is the necessary existent?[15]

3) In the first commandment, 'I am the Lord thy God who brought Thee out of the land of Egypt', where the central focus is the liberating power of God in history, Maimonides' interpretation is that God is a necessary being not dependent on anything other than Himself. Divine self-sufficiency, perfection, and autonomy, are the content of the first commandment. To Maimonides, the first half of the sentence is intelligible without the second half. One can understand the meaning of 'I am the Lord they God' independent of the description 'who brought thee out of the land of Egypt.' For Yehuda Halevi, as for the *Mekhiltah*, the liberating experience of the exodus from Egypt and reflection on God's power in history confirm the reality of God for Israel.[16]

4) What characterizes Jewish prayer is the feeling of divine presence and responsiveness to man's suffering condition. The Halakhah gives expression to this vital element in the structures of the *amidah* prayer: three blessings of adoration, followed by thirteen petitional requests, concluded by three blessings of

thanksgiving. Fundamental to this experience is the feeling that man can pour out his needs to God, that man can bring his needs to a God who is called Our Father, Our King. The God to whom one prays is the God who is with me in my suffering, the God whose *shekhinah* (indwelling) suffers with Israel during their entire *galut* (exile). In contrast to the profound intimacy and expressiveness felt by the praying Jew before God, one ought to consider the religious atmosphere and the tone of Maimonides' treatment of negative theology (*Guide* I, 50-60), where the fundamental point is that there is no comparison between God and man. In these chapters of the *Guide* one discovers that language is necessarily deficient regarding God. One can never talk about God's essence, one can only talk about God's action. Any statement which aims at asserting anything about God must be transformed into a negative statement. God is existent becomes He is not non-existent. God is alive becomes God is not dead. God knows becomes God is not ignorant. Statements describing God's compassion, feeling, and mercy are but human projections in no way attributing affect to God:

> God, may He be exalted, is said to be merciful, just as it is said, "Like as a father is merciful to his children," and it says, "And I will pity them, as a man pitieth his own son." It is not that He, may He be exalted, is affected and has compassion. But an action similar to that which proceeds from a father in respect to his child and that is attached to compassion, pity, and an absolute passion, proceeds from Him, may He be exalted, in reference to His holy ones, not because of a passion or a change. [*Guide*, I, 54].

The gap between a religious world view coming out of the Bible and the midrash, and Maimonides' world view is obvious in Maimonides' treatment of negative theology, and, above all, in his statement that true prayer consists in silent reflection. Language is a compromise and the ultimate religious ideal is to express adoration not through poetic description of God but through contemplative silence:

> The most apt phrase concerning this subject is the dictum occurring in the Psalms, "Silence is praise to Thee" [Ps. 65:2], which interpreted signifies: Silence with regard to You is praise. This is a most perfectly put phrase regarding the matter. For of whatever we say intending to magnify and exalt, on the one hand we find that it can have some application to Him, may He be exalted, and on the other we perceive in it some deficiency. Accordingly, silence and limiting

oneself to the apprehensions of the intellect are more appropriate--just as the perfect ones have enjoined when they said: "Commune with your own heart upon your bed, and be still. Selah" (Ps. 4:5). [*Guide*, I, 59].[17]

Maimonides, the great master of the Jewish halakhic tradition, was an honest and coherent thinker. How could he have missed so obvious a difference in emphasis and in outlook between the religious experience of the absolute which comes through in his legal and his philosophic writings and that of the Jewish tradition? Our concern is not to discover the historical philosophic influences on Maimonides' world view. This has been done by Professor Pines in his introduction to *The Guide of the Perplexed*. Our concern will be to indicate internal religious concepts emanating from the Jewish tradition which may have influenced Maimonides' philosophic religious outlook.

THE METAPHYSICAL AND THE JEWISH TRADITIONS

The two internal principles which may have led Maimonides to his profound embrace of the metaphysical tradition were a) the principle of idolatry and b) the notion of love of God. These two central categories of the Jewish legal tradition may account for Maimonides' metaphysically oriented descriptions of God, the insistence on negative theology, and his statement that Moses taught the notion of God as necessary existent to the Jewish community immediately after their departure from Egypt.

Maimonides, both in the *Mishneh Torah* and in the *Guide*, claims that "the foundation of the whole of our Law and the pivot around which it turns, consists in the effacement of these opinions from the minds and of these monuments from existence" (*Guide* III, 29). Maimonides has in mind the idolatrous opinions of the Sabians. Likewise, in the *Mishneh Torah*, "Laws of Idolatry," II, 4, Maimonides writes:

The precept relating to idolatry is equal in importance to all the other precepts put together, as it is said, "And when ye shall err and not observe all these commandments" (Num. 15:22). This text has traditionally been interpreted as alluding to idolatry; hence the inference that acceptance of idolatry is tantamount to repudiating the whole Torah, the prophets and everything that they were commanded, from Adam to the end of time. . . . And whoever denies idolatry confesses his faith in the whole Torah, in all the prophets and all that the prophets were commanded, from Adam till the end of time. And this is the fundamental principle of all of the commandments.

Maimonides codifies the halakhah that the prophet has the right to temporarily suspend any norms of Jewish law. There is only one case where suspension, even temporarily, is not permitted and that is with regard to the laws of idolatry.[18] The uncompromising demand to reject idolatry is the central concern of the law. Toleration of anything that may lead, in any way whatsoever, to one's embracing idolatry undermines the essential purpose of the law. Maimonides, therefore, codifies the laws of idolatry in the first book of the *Mishneh Torah*, the *Book of Knowledge*. In his introduction to the *Mishneh Torah* Maimonides explains the purpose of the first book:

> I include in it all the precepts which constitute the very essence and principle of the faith taught by Moses, our teacher and which it is necessary for one to know at the outset; as for example, acceptance of the unity of God and the prohibition of idolatry.

In "The laws of Repentance," III, 15, Maimonides wrote regarding the definition of the heretic:

> Five classes are termed Heretics; he who says that there is no God and the world has no ruler; he who says that there is a ruling power but that it is vested in two or more persons; he who says that there is one ruler, but that He is a body and has form; he who denies that He alone is the First Cause and Rock of the Universe; likewise, he who renders worship to anyone beside Him, to serve as a mediator between the human being and the Lord of the Universe. Whoever belongs to any of these five classes is termed a heretic.

Maimonides classifies together in the same law one who claims that there is no God, one who believes in polytheism, and one who believes that God has a body and a form. This decision evoked the rage of the Rabad:

> Why has he called such a person an heretic? There are many people greater than and superior to him who adhere to such a belief on the basis of what they have seen in verses of Scripture and even more the words of those *aggadot* which corrupt right opinion about religious matters.[19]

The gist of the disagreement is that the Rabad cannot understand Maimonides' insistence on calling an otherwise pious, halakhic person a heretic. How can one who lives sincerely by

the law, who follows all the commandments and who is committed passionately to every detail of the discipline of Halakhah, be
classified together with one who is an idolater? How can the
great enemy of Jewish spirituality, idolatry, be found in the
heart of one who is totally loyal to the Halakhah?

Maimonides was undoubtedly aware of the likelihood of
such objections, yet his opposition to false notions of God was
uncompromising. Essential to understanding Maimonides' metaphysical treatment of God in the sections on negative theology
in the *Guide*, are chapters 35 and 36 in part one. Maimonides
claims there that although he realizes that the study of physics
and metaphysics are esoteric disciplines requiring great preparation and great maturity and are not disciplines capable of being
studied by the masses, nevertheless one should not withhold
from the multitude knowledge of the fact that God is incorpo-
real and that He is not subject to affection. Maimonides writes:

> For just as it behooves to bring up children in the
> belief, and to proclaim to the multitude, that God may
> He be magnified and honored is one and that none
> but He ought to be worshipped, so it behooves that
> they should be made to accept on traditional authority
> the belief that God is not a body; and that there is
> absolutely no likeness in any respect whatever be-
> tween Him and the things created by Him; that His
> existence has no likeness to theirs; nor His life to the
> life of those among them who are alive; nor again His
> knowledge to the knowledge of those among them who
> are endowed with knowledge. They should be made to
> accept the belief that the difference between Him and
> them is not merely a difference of more and less, but
> one concerning the species of existence. I mean to
> say that it should be established in everybody's mind
> that our knowledge of our power does not differ from
> His knowledge or His power in the later being greater
> and stronger, the former less and weaker, or in other
> similar respects, inasmuch as the strong and the weak
> are necessarily alike with respect to their species and
> one definition comprehends both of them. . . . Now
> everything that can be ascribed to God, may He be
> exalted, differs in every respect from our attributes,
> so that no definition can comprehend the one thing
> and the other. (*Guide* I, 35)

A central motif in Maimonides' writings are his repeated arguments for teaching the masses about God's incorporeality. In the same chapter, Maimonides writes:

For there is no profession of unity unless the doctrine of God's corporeality is denied. For a body cannot be one, but is composed of matter and form which by definition are two; it also is divisible, subject to partition.

Maimonides concludes the chapter with the same principle he used in the *Mishneh Torah* to categorize the different forms of heresy:

But it is not meet that belief in the corporeality of God or in His being provided with any concomitant of the bodies should be permitted to establish itself in anyone's mind any more than it is meet that belief should be established in the nonexistence of the deity, in the association of other gods with Him, or in the worship of other than He.

Maimonides was philosophically convinced that false belief regarding the nature of God is idolatry.[20] Hence he had to face the halakhic implication of this claim. Idolatry is not only mistaken forms of worship, but is, as well, a mistaken conception of the object of worship. Idolatry is constituted not only by how I worship but, more importantly, by whom I worship. False belief, e.g., belief in divine corporeality, entails idolatry in that instead of worshipping God, one is worshipping a figment of human imagination. Hence, correct belief (philosophy) is crucial in order to correctly identify and describe God and thus avoid worshipping false gods.[21]

The purpose of the law, however, is to correct mistaken forms of worship:

The essential principle in the precepts concerning idolatry is that we are not to worship any thing created--neither angel, sphere, star, none of the four elements, nor whatever has been formed from them. Even if the worshipper is aware that the Eternal is God, and worships the created thing in the sense in which Enoch and his contemporaries did, he is an idolater. ("Laws of Idolatry," II, 1)

The law protects Israel from the mistake idol worshippers made in developing intermediary worship. The Halakhah provides a correct way of worship which will not lead to removing God from the consciousness of man through mistaken forms. Essential idolatry, however, involves not only mistaken forms of worship but mistaken conceptions of God. This is only corrected by understanding how unity and corporeality are contradictory. Only by understanding physics, the nature of change, the relationship between potentiality and actuality, the structure of nature, etc., can one root out an idolatry based, not upon wrong practice, but upon mistaken belief.[22]

Maimonides considered mistaken practice to be a lesser sin than belief in corporeality. In *Guide* I, 36, Maimonides writes:

> Now the idolaters thought that this prerogative [being worshipped] belonged to that which was other than God; and this led to the disappearance of the belief in His existence. . . . For the multitude grasp only the actions of worship, not their meanings or the true reality of the Being worshipped through them. . . . What then should be the state of him whose infidelity bears upon His essence . . . and consists in believing Him to be different from what He really is? . . . Know accordingly, you who are that man, that when you believe in the doctrine of the corporeality of God or believe that one of the states of the body belongs to Him, you "provoke His jealousy and anger, kindle the fire of His wrath," and are "a hater, an enemy, and an adversary," of God, much more so than "an idolater."

In other words, Maimonides says to the Jewish community, who have a defined way of worshipping God which distinguishes them from pagans, that, if they lack a philosophic understanding of God's otherness, idolatry will reappear in the house of Jewish Halakhah. Paganism will grow in Jewish soil if man does not understand how unity and incorporeality entail one another.

Maimonides then argues that, if you want to excuse Jews of this mistaken notion because the Bible itself may be responsible for teaching men that God has a body and that He is subject to affections, you ought to hold a similar attitude with regard to a gentile idolater, for he worships idols only because of his ignorance and because of his upbringing. Maimonides does not allow a double standard. He does not allow the tradition's rage against idolatry to be turned outward and not inward. The philosophic knowledge that Maimonides gained from the Greek philosophic tradition was of central importance for his understanding of the Jewish belief in the oneness and uniqueness of God. Wolfson correctly points out that the Bible taught only that God was other than the world. The notion of divine simplicity and the notion that corporeality is a negation of the concept of unity are not biblical, but rather philosophic.[23] Maimonides' knowledge of philosophy gave him a new understanding of idolatry.

Maimonides, however, was not only a philosopher. As a

committed halakhic Jew he could not keep this knowledge from the community. He knew that the law did not allow any compromise regarding idolatry. He did not follow the path of many medieval philosophers, like Averroes and those within the Jewish tradition, in allowing the masses to believe that God was corporeal .[24] Were Maimonides only a philosopher and not a halakhist, he would surely have refrained from evoking the wrath of the Jewish community by claiming that pious halakhic Jews with incorrect theological beliefs were idol worshippers. If, as Leo Strauss claims Maimonides only sought a justification for philosophy but not an interpenetration of philosophy and law, he should never have codified the principle that he who believes that God has a body is an idolater and an heretic. His insistence that the whole community accept certain basic truths of metaphysics even if only on the basis of authority is grounded in his "halakhic" commitment to the community and to the halakhic principle of not allowing any compromise regarding idolatry.

Metaphysics, then, for Maimonides is a complement to the law. Philosophy continues the battle of the law to uproot the last vestiges of idolatry in the world. Moses, therefore, had to teach the community about the nature of God in order to uproot idolatry from within the Jewish people. It is not arid philosophical rationalism that inspires Maimonides. The motivation is not that of the esoteric elitist intellectual, but that of the observant Jew committed to the principle that "he who rejects idolatry accepts the entire Torah."[25]

The goal of Torah which makes it unique among legal systems, is its concern with developing love of God. Love of God, according to Maimonides, is nurtured only by philosophical knowledge. Even though Maimonides recognized the limitations of the intellect and restricted the scope and nature of knowledge of God, he still believed that only knowledge, comprised of the intellectual discipline of physics and metaphysics, would lead man to love of God.

> This God, honoured and revered, it is our duty to love and fear; as it is said "Thou shalt love the Lord, thy God" (Deut. 6:35), and it is further said "Thou shalt fear the Lord, thy God" (Deut. 6:13).
> 2. And what is the way that will lead to the love of Him and the fear of Him? When a person contemplates His great and wondrous works and creatures and from them obtains a glimpse of His wisdom which is incomparable and infinite, he will straightway love Him, praise Him, glorify Him, and long with an exceeding longing to know His great Name; even as David said "My soul thirsteth for God, for the living

God" (Ps. 42:3). And when he ponders these matters, he will recoil affrighted, and realize that he is a small creature, lowly and obscure, endowed with slight and slender intelligence, standing in the presence of Him who is perfect in knowledge. And so David said "When I consider Thy heavens, the work of Thy fingers--what is man that Thou art mindful of Him?" (Ps. 8:4-5). In harmony with these sentiments, I shall explain some large, general aspects of the Works of the Sovereign of the Universe, that they may serve the intelligent individual as a door to the love of God, even as our sages have remarked in connection with the theme of the love of God, "Observe the Universe and hence, you will realize Him who spake and the world was." (*M.T., Hilkhot Yesodei ha-Torah*, II, 1-2).

In chapter ten of "The Laws of Repentance," chapter four of *Hilkhot Yesodei ha-Torah*, chapter fifty-two in *The Guide of the Perplexed*, part three and throughout the *Guide*, Maimonides expressed his conviction that theoretical knowledge and opinions make possible the love of God.[26]

Why are the disciplines of physics and metaphysics unique in enabling a person to achieve love of God? Why are the practice and the study of the law only necessary and not sufficient conditions for achieving love of God? In order to comprehend philosophy's unique contribution in producing love of God, one must compare Maimonides' understanding of creation with his approach to revelation. Creation, to Maimonides, reflects the overflow of God's perfection. *Olam hesed yebaneh*, the world is an expression of God's love and power. Central to Maimonides' understanding of God's revelation in nature and of man's relationship to the universe is the realization that man is not the center of God's creation. The world does not exist for man; God's creative power and wisdom were not exclusively focused on the creation of man. Hence, a most important function of metaphysical reflection is to heal man from feelings of grandiosity. Man realizes, when reflecting on the cosmos, that he is insignificant in the light of the hierarchy of beings. Metaphysics and philosophy, then, from a religious perspective, create humanity. Philosophy heals human egocentricity. Philosophy locates man in a theocentric universe where he cannot but realize his modest and humbling place in being.[27]

Maimonides' treatment of Job in the *Guide* III, 22-24, is placed after he established clearly man's place in the hierarchy of being. One can tolerate suffering if one gains a proper understanding of one's significance in being. Reorienting one's place in being is Maimonides' explanation of the conclusion of the book of Job. Job did not receive an answer to the problem of evil; he received a different perception of being and of himself which enabled him to continue living despite his suffering:

> This is the object of the Book of Job as a whole: I refer to the establishing of this foundation for the belief and the drawing attention to the inference to be drawn from natural matters, so that you should not fall into error and seek to affirm in your imagination that His knowledge is like our knowledge or that His purpose and His providence and His governance are like our purpose and our providence and our governance. If man knows this, every misfortune will be borne lightly by him. (*Guide* III, 24)

Maimonides was not referring to theodicy, but, rather, to a way of transcending suffering by gaining another perspective on being. Philosophy's presentation of an objective world independent of man, where man occupies a most modest position in a hierarchy of perfections culminating in the awesome, ineffable perfection of God, transports man from an anthropocentric to a theocentric universe and thereby gives man the strength to cope with human suffering.

This insight is also present in Maimonides' treatment of the *akedah*, the binding of Isaac. Maimonides analyses the story of Abraham only after treating of the human implications of the study of physics and metaphysics (Job). Abraham, the founder of belief in the God of history is asked in the command to sacrifice his only son Isaac (history), to express a relationship to God which, in fact, negates the significance of history:

> As for the story of Abraham at the binding, it contains two great notions that are fundamental principles of the Law. One of these notions consists in our being informed of the limit of love for God, may He be exalted, and fear of Him--that is, up to what limit they must reach. For in this story he was ordered to do something that bears no comparison either with sacrifice of property or with sacrifice of life. In truth it is the most extraordinary thing that could happen in the world, such a thing that one would not imagine that human nature was capable of it. Here there is a sterile man having an exceeding desire for a son, possessed of great property and commanding respect, and having the wish that his progeny should become a religious community. When a son comes to him after his having lost hope, how great will be his attachment

to him and love for him! However, because of his fear
of Him, who should be exalted, and because of his
love to carry out his command, he holds this beloved
son as little, gives up all his hopes regarding him,
and hastens to slaughter him after a journey of days.
(*Guide* III, 24, pp. 500-501)

Abraham's going through the experience of the *akedah*
symbolically demonstrated that the ultimate goal of Torah lies
beyond history. The archetypal act of love of God is constituted
by the ability to abandon history. Maimonides' treatment of
Abraham and of Job reveal his belief in the liberating power of
philosophy to direct man to live in history, after having discovered meaning beyond history.[28] In chapters eight through twen-
ty-four of the third part of the *Guide*, Maimonides elaborates
the practical implications of negative theology. Job and Abraham
dramatically represent the radical implications of divine otherness which is the central notion of the theory of negative theology.

Maimonides attributed a liberating function to philosophy.
For disinterested love to be possible, man's understanding of
himself, the world and the essential purpose and meaning of life
must undergo radical transformations. So long as man is anchored solely in history and is concerned exclusively with human
needs, he cannot recognize and therefore love a God who does
not exist for the sake of man. Philosophy creates the conditions
for love because it enables man to appreciate an objective reality independent of human needs.

As mentioned above with regard to idolatry, a central
biblical motif is God's otherness and difference from the world.
Philosophy, e.g., the analysis of unity, non-corporeality and
negative attributes, offers a more exact and rigorous understanding of God's otherness. This movement to revealing the
implications of divine otherness is the movement of the one
seeking love of God. Love is expressed in the confirmation of
the independent worth of the beloved. It is only philosophy
which gives meaning to man's affirmation of God's independent
existence. In Maimonides' writings, the yearning quality of love
finds expression in knowing how the universe reveals the actions
of God. Love becomes passionate when the universe is perceived
from a theocentric perspective. Knowing what God is not and
how He is radically other than and separate from the world
provides man with the intellectual tools for self-transcending
relational love.[29]

While philosophy points to divine perfection and to divine
manifestations which are indifferent to and independent of human needs, the revelation of the law is substantially different.

In the *Guide* III, 32, Maimonides explains how to interpret the meaning of many laws in the Torah. Reminiscent of Hegel's notion of the cunning of reason, Maimonides argues that God utilizes the given conditions of history to further His purpose. God does not ignore the given context of history. The revealed law is not indifferent to the limited capacities of people. The law reflects the patience of the divine teacher who works with the actual materials of history. Although, logically speaking, God could change the nature of man to accord with the practices of a perfect law, God, argues Maimonides, chose not to. God chose to adopt the role of the teacher patiently seeking to overcome the limitations and shortcomings of the people of Israel.

For example, at the time of the giving of the Torah, animal sacrifices constituted the accepted form of worship. No one, claims Maimonides, thought it reasonable to worship a god other than by offering animal sacrifice. God accepted this pattern of worship, even though this pattern of worship was characteristic of paganism, and He permitted its use in Jewish worship. Because, Maimonides argues, man cannot be expected to change suddenly or to completely give up patterns of behaviour to which he has become accustomed, He restricted animal sacrifices to specific places and to be administered only by certain people, i.e., priests. Prayer, a higher form of worship, was permitted by anyone and in all places.

In other words, there is a hierarchy of forms of worship. While legitimizing sacrifices, the law's intention was that man will eventually transcend this form, and will adopt a higher form of worship. Similarly verbal prayer is a stage meant to be superceded by the highest form of worship, i.e., contemplative silence. Silent prayer reflects man's ability to be moved by God's perfection independent of His responding to human needs. There are, then, three stages of worship in history: 1) the stage of eradication of idolatry by limiting animal sacrifices; 2) worship grounded in God's responsiveness to human needs, i.e., verbal petitional prayer; and 3) silent adoration of God because he is God.

Revelation of God's wisdom in the law, as distinct from His revelation in nature, is a response to an imperfect human condition. Study of the law reveals God's legislative involvement with men. The study of the law reconfirms for historical man his central importance in the divine scheme. "The Torah spoke in the language of man." God is perceived in the law from the perspective of human needs. Maimonides was very comfortable claiming that there are human purposes for the commandments. In contrast to a mystical approach, to Maimonides, commandments reflect what is good for man.[30] They have no meta-historical significance. The cosmic significance that mystics attributed to the commandments is alien to Maimonides' attempt to make the law totally earth bound.[31]

Besides focusing on divine absolute perfection, philosophy leads to love of God by healing of the imagination. To Maimonides, imagination is the great enemy of religious development.[32] Human imagination is both the source of idolatry and of inauthentic love. At the end of the *Guide*, III, 51, Maimonides proclaims that individuals whose knowledge of God is based on imagination, and not on knowledge of objective reality, are outside the palace of the king. Only the philosopher enters into the palace of the king, i.e., is able to love God, because only the philosopher has some grasp of the reality of God independent of human imagination:

> As for someone who thinks and frequently mentions God, without knowledge, following a mere imagining or following a belief adopted because of his reliance on the authority of somebody else, he is to my mind outside the habitation and far away from it and does not in true reality mention or think about God. For that thing which is in his imagination and which he mentions in his speech does not correspond to any being at all and has merely been invented by his imagination, as we have explained in our discourse concerning the attributes. (*Guide* III, 51.)

For love to be real, the object of one's love must be recognized in itself. Imagination creates a narcissistic love, a love of one's own creation and not of an independent reality. Man is liberated to love only when the passion of love emerges in response to an objective reality and not to a subjective projection of what one imagines God to be. One loves another human being only if one can respond to another as another and not as a projection of one's needs and imagination.

PHILOSOPHY, THE HALAKHAH AND DISINTERESTED LOVE OF GOD

The central question which will be dealt with now is whether the disinterested love of God which results from the study of philosophy can be legitimately identified with the highest goal of the Halakhah. Martyrdom was traditionally considered to be the purest expression of love of God.[33] How can disinterested love of the absolute become the paradigm of the most valued achievement of this religious way of life? Is this not simply a hellenization and hence a distortion of Judaism? In the biblical and rabbinic traditions, one confronts the primacy of history and law. God, in the Bible, is fundamentally the lord of history. His autonomy consists in his freedom to break into history miraculously and spontaneously. Scholem correctly observed that Maimonides neutralized the pathos of the messianic yearning, for, in principle, messianism is unnecessary in Maimonides' thought.[34] Contemplative love of God is possible, though rare, without redemption in history. To Maimonides, messianism is merely a shift in political conditions. Human nature remains the same. There is no rupture or new creation in history.[35]

Guttman claims that Maimonides ignored the important difference between contemplative communion and moral communion.[36] Husik says that Maimonides was deceived in not realizing that the Bible is fundamentally practical and not theoretical. Were we to accept the implications of the aforementioned views, we would be compelled to conclude that Maimonides, the great teacher of the law, was unaware of the fact that his profound religious passion to become a lover of God was essentially foreign to and a gross distortion of the Jewish tradition.

Scholars have argued that this is the great puzzle of Maimonides. This, however, is not the only possible orientation to Maimonides. Maimonides' neutralization of the religious significance of history and of divine miraculous interference in the fixed structures of reality, and his emphasis on cultivating a passionate love for a God who draws men in virtue of His perfection, and not in virtue of His ability to satisfy human needs and requests, may have their roots in various features of talmudic Judaism. While Judaism's preoccupation with abolishing idolatry justifies and explains Maimonides' interest in philosophy, this does not imply that the ethos and the religious orientation of philosophy ought to become dominant for the Jew. In identifying the disinterested love of God of philosophy with love of God of the Halakhah, Maimonides was giving expression to certain features of talmudic Judaism which, we believe, both explain and justify his radical move.

Our use of the terms "certain features of talmudic Judaism" is due to the fact that the aspects of talmudic thought chosen for discussion do not constitute *the* dominant orientation of rabbinic Judaism. As Professor Urbach has shown, there are many diverse schools of thought in rabbinic Judaism. In this paper, we present a particular strand that is characteristic of an important aspect of the talmudic tradition. This strand provides the grounds for the development of a spiritual orientation which enables one to live with the gap between the biblical world of divine immediacy and the post-biblical world, which is silent and unresponsive to man's moral condition. Nature becomes neutralized and, so to speak, demythologized, and the biblical passion is reinterpreted so that men's relationship to God is no longer sustained by the visible and public interference of a moral God in the processes of nature and history.

The following passages in the Talmud exemplify this spirit:

Our Rabbis taught: Philosophers asked the elders in Rome, "If your God has no desire for idolatry, why does He not abolish it?" They replied, "If it was something of which the world has no need that it was worshipped, He would abolish it; but people worship the sun, moon, stars and planets; should He destroy the Universe on account of fools! The world pursues its natural course, and as for the fools who act wrongly, they will have to render an account. Another illustration: Suppose a man stole a measure of wheat and went and sowed it in the ground; it is right that it should not grow, but the world pursues its natural course and as for the fools who act wrongly, they will have to render an account. Another illustration: Suppose a man has intercourse with his neighbor's wife; it is right that she should not conceive, but the world pursues its natural course and as for the fools who act wrongly, they will have to render an account." This is similar to what R. Simeon b. Lakish said: The Holy One, blessed be He, declared, not enough that the wicked put My coinage to vulgar use, but they trouble Me and compel Me to set My seal thereon! (*T.B., Abodah Zarah*, 54B)

To fully appreciate the radical shift in sensibility from biblical thought, compare this with several biblical passages:

To Adam He said, "Because you did as your wife
said and ate of the tree about which I commanded
you, 'You shall not eat of it,'
Cursed be the ground because of you;
By toil shall you eat of it
All the days of your life:
Thorns and thistles shall it sprout for you.
But your food shall be the grasses of the field;
By the sweat of your brow
Shall you get bread to eat,
Until you return to the ground--
For from it you were taken.
For dust you are,
And to dust you shall return."
(*Genesis* III, 17-19)

Do not defile yourselves in any of those ways,
for it is by such that the nations which I
am casting out before you defiled themselves.
Thus the land became defiled; and I called it
to account for its iniquity, and the land
spewed out its inhabitants. But you must keep
My laws and My rules, and you must not do
any of those abhorrent things, neither the
citizen nor the stranger who resides
among you; for all those abhorrent things
were done by the people who were in the land
before you, and the land became defiled.
So let not the land spew you out for
defiling it, as it spewed out the nation
that came before you.
(*Lev.* XVIII, 24-28)

If, then, you obey the commandments that
I enjoin upon you this day, loving the
Lord your God and serving Him with all
your heart and soul, I will grant the rain
for your land in season, the early rain
and the late. You shall gather in your
new grain and wine and oil--I will also
provide grass in the fields for your
cattle--and thus you shall eat your fill.
Take care not to be lured away to serve
other gods and bow to them. For the Lord's
anger will flare up against you, and He
will shut up the skies so that there will
be no rain and the ground will not yield
its products; and you will soon perish
from the good land that the Lord is
giving you.
(*Deut.* II, 1-17)

A key expression in the talmudic passage quoted above, is "did hu shelo titzmah" (it is right that it should not grow). Stolen wheat or grain ought not grow; a raped woman ought not become pregnant. Nature ought not respond and give of its strength and bounty to the consequences of evil. In other words, the expectations that nature and morality are organically related, and that the lord of history and the lord of nature are one are legitimate and worthwhile expectations. Yet, although the talmudic author legitimizes this biblical sensibility, he realizes that it does not accord with what in fact happens. This is another form of the generalization, "olam ke-minhago noheg" (the world maintains its natural course). There is a natural *minhag*, literally a custom. (Strauss remarks that the term used is *minhag*, custom, and not *tevah*, nature).[37] One cannot live expecting nature to reflect the moral law. One is trained to have an organic sensibility in the sense of believing that the world should" express moral distinctions, yet, one is taught to accept the nonrealization of this organic relationship. This demythologization, this learning to live in a universe that is strange and unresponsive to my deepest moral yearnings is very definitely a characteristic of talmudic Judaism.

There are other texts which also reveal this sensibility:

Raba said: This latter agrees with R. Jacob,who said: There is no reward for precepts in this world. For it was taught: R. Jacob said: There is not a single precept in the Torah whose reward is (stated) at its side which is not dependent on the resurrection of the dead. (Thus:) in connection with honouring parents it is written, that thy days may be prolonged, and that it may go well with thee. In reference to the dismissal of the nest it is written, that it may be well with thee, and that thou mayest prolong thy days. Now, if one's father said to him,"Ascend to the loft and bring me young birds," and he ascends to the loft, dismisses the dam and takes the young, and on his return falls and is killed--where is this man's happiness and where is this man's prolonging of days? But "in order that it may be well with thee", means on the day that is wholly good; and 'in order that thy days may be long', on the day that is wholly long.

Yet perhaps there was no such happening?--R. Jacob saw an actual occurrence. Then perhaps he was meditating upon a transgression?--The Holy One, blessed be He, does not combine an evil thought with an (evil) act. Yet perhaps he was meditating idolatry, and it is written, that I may take the house of Israel in their own heart?--That too was precisely his point: should you think that precepts are rewarding in this world, why did the (fulfillment of these) precepts not shield him from being led to (such) meditation?" *T.B., Kiddushim,* 39B)

The struggle with acknowledging the discrepancy between the biblical promise and the given reality finds expression in the talmud's asking "Perhaps there was no such happening?" How do we know that a child who listened to his father and sent away the mother bird really died? The text then simply says: "Rabbi

Jacob saw an actual occurrence." The text, however, continues to ask, "Perhaps he sinned?" Perhaps he sinned in his thoughts? How can one ever know if a person is truly righteous? How can one know that the person who died really didn't deserve his death? What we notice, then, is an attempt in the text not to give in too easily to an empirical reality which falsifies religious expectations. Yet, in the end, one cannot ignore the evidence Rabbi Jacob brings which negates biblically-inspired expectations. Rabbi Jacob, however, doesn't conclude that there is no God. Rather than claim there is no reward, he concludes, "sekhar Mitzvah behai aimah lekah" (there is no reward for precepts in this world). While biblical anticipation remains, it is transferred to another time. In the present reality, one must live with the gap between what the bible promises and what one actually experiences:

> In the West (Palestine) they taught it thus: R. Giddal said: (And Ezra praised . . . the) great (God): i.e., he magnified Him by pronouncing the Ineffable Name. R. Mattena said: He said: The great, the mighty, and the awful God. The interpretation of R. Mattena seems to agree with what R. Joshua b. Levi said: For R. Joshua b. Levi said: "Why were they called men of the Great Synod? Because they restored the crown of the divine attributes to its ancient completeness." (For) Moses had come and said: The great God, the mighty, and the awful. Then Jeremiah came and said: Aliens are destroying His Temple. Where are, then, His awful deeds? Hence he omitted (the attribute) the 'awful'. Daniel came and said: Aliens are enslaving his sons. Where are His mighty deeds? Hence, he omitted the word 'mighty'. But they came and said: On the contrary! Therein lie His might deeds that He suppresses His wrath, that He extends long-suffering to the wicked. Therein lie His awful powers: For but for the fear of Him, how could one (single) nation persist among the (many) nations! But how could (the earlier) Rabbis abolish something established by Moses?--R. Eleazar said: Since they knew that the Holy One, blessed be He, insists on truth, they would not ascribe false (things) to Him. (*T.B., Yoma* 69B)

This text also reflects the difference between the historical reality of the talmudic period, i.e., the destruction of the temple and the exile, and the reality depicted in the Bible. In the prayer of Moses, God is great, mighty and awful. This is accepted as a correct description of God. Moses is the highest authority for halakhic jurisprudence. His authority embraces not only normative behaviour but also what is to count as correct descriptions of God. The crisis of religious language begins during the time of Daniel and of Jeremiah. Descriptions of divine power appear at odds with a reality where the children of Israel are enslaved by foreign nations. "God is awesome" does not accord with the Temple being destroyed and pagans fornicating in the holy of holies.

One could have said, "I do not fully understand Moses' prayer because I'm not a Moses. Moses' language is correct and I shall use it even though my own reality offers disconfirming evidence. Who am I to Judge?" There were (and are) those who continued to believe in reward in this world. Perhaps the righteous are "rewarded" by suffering and the wicked "punished" by prosperity so that in the world to come each one will fully receive his due, i.e., the righteous only rewards, the wicked only punishments.[38]

In the above text, however, the author did not negate his own perception of reality, but he did not claim that Moses' language was false. The biblical description as reflected in Moses' prayer is placed in suspension. A new response to the gap between my reality and the authoritative normative reality is adopted, i.e., silence. You continue praying but you do not utilize that language which is disconfirmed by reality. The men of the great assembly widen the range of the meaning of language, by widening the range of experience relevant for confirming this language.[39] The word "mighty" in the biblical context refers to God's victorious power in history. Prophets defeat kings, pharoahs submit to the overwhelming might of God. The reality of the talmudic writers did not confirm a God who was powerful and victorious and, therefore, they were compelled to reconsider the meaning of divine power.[40] The men of the great assembly interpret power to mean the compassion and the long-suffering mercy of God. Self-control in the face of blasphemous provocation constitutes the new meaning of power:

> Vespasian sent Titus who said, Where is their God, the rock in whom they trusted? This was the wicked Titus who blasphemed and insulted Heaven. What did he do? He took a harlot by the hand and entered the Holy of Holies and spread out a scroll of the Law and committed a sin on it. He then took a sword and slashed the curtain. Miraculously blood spurted out, and he thought that he had slain himself, as it says, Thine adversaries have roared in the midst of thine assembly, they have set up their ensigns for signs. Abba Hanan said: Who is a mighty one like unto thee,

> O Jah? Who is like thee, mighty in self-restraint, that
> Thou didst hear the blaspheming and insults of that
> wicked man and kept silent? (*T.B., Gittin*, 56b)

In God's self-control, Israel, in exile, finds a way of continuing
to use biblical language. Biblical divine power continues to be
present, but in a neutralized form.

A most important statement in the text, besides the shift
in meaning of biblical language, is the question how did Daniel
and Jeremiah have the right to remain silent and not submit to
Moses' authoritative and hence correct description of God? The
short and simple answer was that God loves the truth and
therefore they would not lie. Believing that God insists on truth
enabled them to be honest to their own experience, and not to
allow Moses' language to define their altered reality.

The three examples discussed above reveal the tension in
talmudic thought between the organic mythic consciousness of
the Bible and the sober realism of talmudic Judaism. In talmudic
Judaism, one encounters the world of divine responsiveness and
mutuality ("If you will hearken to my command, I will . . . ")
not in everyday reality but in institutionalized memories, e.g.,
the biblical readings and the ambience of the Sabbath and the
festivals.[41] The talmudic Jew inhabits two worlds: one where
history and nature reflect God's power and judgments and another world where violence and corruption yield wealth and
prosperity. Titus enters the holy of holies with a prostitute and
mockingly challenges God to dare strike him down. In response
to this event, the talmud points out that Titus failed to realize
that divine power often takes the form of divine silence.

The talmudic age testified to divine silence and to the
tragic dimension of Jewish approaches to history. A major concern of talmudic Judaism was how to continue as a spiritual
people in a world that does not confirm biblical expectations.
The talmudic sages never give up the biblical organic consciousness. They retained the belief in God's power to reveal Himself
openly in history, but tried to restrict and to confine it to past
memories and to eschatological hopes. The crucial question facing any analyst of talmudic Judaism is how effective was this
attempt at restricting the biblical mythic consciousness? Was it
successfully neutralized? Did it cease being, in Jamesian terms, a
live option? Or did it remain constantly just below the surface
threatening to explode in the face of rabbinic sobriety and
realism? This is a difficult but inescapable problem to resolve.
One must examine currents in Jewish mystical and philosophic
thought to discover the various forms that the interrelationship
of biblical and rabbinic thought assumed in Jewish history.[42]

One thing, however, is clear. One who internalizes talmudic

suppression of biblical consciousness can build a spiritual life in the absence of responsive historical events. The everyday spiritual existence of the talmudic Jew is characterized by loyalty to the law. To rabbinic man, God is present in history because His law is present. Because the Torah and the covenant are eternally binding, God's presence for man is confirmed. The law, and not events in history, mediates divine concern. Instead of seeking instances of God breaking into history, the rabbinic teachers expand and elaborate biblical law to cover enormously wide ranges of experience. As more of reality falls under the authority of the law, God's will and influence become more deeply felt.

The receiving of the Torah was not perceived as an event of the historical past, but as an ever-present challenge. "When you study My words of Torah, they are not to seem antiquated to you, but as fresh as though the Torah were given this day" (*Psikta d'Rab Kahana*, piska 12, sec. 12). The written law was not perceived as a closed system of law. Elaboration and expansion of the Torah made the revelation at Sinai a contemporaneous event for students of Torah.[43] The passion of the encounter with the living God of the Bible is retained but is expressed in uncovering new layers of meaning in Torah.

Though he is silent regarding the tragic dimension of history, talmudic man is extremely articulate and confident about his ability to understand the range of meanings contained in the revelation of the law:

> Rab Judah said in the name of Rab, When Moses ascended on high he found the Holy One, blessed be He, engaged in affixing coronets to the letters. Said Moses, "Lord of the Universe, Who stays Thy hand?" He answered, "There will arise a man, at the end of many generations, Akiba b. Joseph by name, who will expound upon each Tittle heaps and heaps of laws". "Lord of the Universe," said Moses; "permit me to see him." He replied, "Turn thee round". Moses went and sat down behind eight rows (and listened to the discourses upon the law). Not being able to follow their arguments he was ill at ease, but when they came to a certain subject and the disciples said to the master "Whence do you know it?" and the latter replied "It is a law given unto Moses at Sinai" he was comforted. Thereupon he returned to the Holy One, blessed be He, and said, "Lord of the Universe, Thou hast such a man and Thou givest the Torah by me!" He replied, "Be silent, for such is My decree." (*T.B., Menabot* 29b)

The student of Moses, Akiba, uncovers dimensions in Moses' Torah which Moses himself does not understand. Yet it is Moses' Torah that is the basis of Akiba's legal inferences. Akiba is dignified and articulate; he has mastered the complexities of divine speech coming out of the Torah. Nevertheless, though articulate in the realm of the law, halakhic man lapses into utter silence when trying to understand the Lord of history:

> Then said Moses, "Lord of the Universe, Thou hast shown me his Torah, show me his reward." "Turn thee round", said He; and Moses turned, round and saw them weighing out his flesh at the market-stalls. "Lord of the Universe," cried Moses, "such Torah, and such a reward!" He replied, "Be silent, for such is My decree."

To the questions, "Why choose Moses and not Akiba to stand at Sinai?" and "Why does Akiba, the illustrious genius of Halakhah, end his life in so horrifying and shocking a manner?" the answer given is, "Be silent, for such is My decree."

Rabbinic halakhic man, however, feels dignified and confident in the academy of learning:

> We learnt elsewhere: If he cut it into separate tiles, placing sand between each tile: R. Elisezer declared it clean, and the Sages declared it unclean; and this was the oven of 'Aknai. Why (the oven of) 'Aknai?--Said Rab Judah in Samuel's name: (it means) that they encompass it with arguments as a snake, and proved it unclean. It has been taught: On that day R. Eliezer brought forward every imaginable argument, but they did not accept them. Said he to them: "If the halachah agrees with me, let this carob-tree prove it!" Thereupon the carob-tree was torn a hundred cubits out of its place--others affirm, four hundred cubits. "No proof can be brought from a carob-tree," they retorted. Again he said to them: "If the halachah agrees with me, let the stream of water prove it!" Whereupon the stream of water flowed backwards. "No proof can be brought from a stream of water," they rejoined. Again he urged: "If the halachah agrees with me, let the walls of the schoolhouse prove it," whereupon the walls inclined to fall. But R. Joshua rebuked them, saying: "When scholars are engaged in a halachic dispute, what have ye to interfere?" Hence they did not fall, in honour of R. Eliezer; and they are still standing thus inclined. Again he said to them: "If the halachah agrees with me, let it be proved from

Heaven!" Whereupon a Heavenly Voice cried out: "Why do ye dispute with R. Eliezer, seeing that in all matters the halachah agrees with him!" But R. Joshua arose and exclaimed: "It is not in heaven." What did he mean by this?--Said R. Jeremiah: That the Torah had already been given at Mount Sinai; we pay no attention to a Heavenly Voice, because Thou hast long since written in the Torah at Mount Sinai, after the majority must one incline.

R. Nathan met Elijah and asked him: What did the Holy One, Blessed be He, do in that hour?--He laughed (with joy), he replied saying, "My sons have defeated Me. My sons have defeated Me." (*T.B., Baba Mezia* 59 A.B.)

Prophecy may not decide a problem of Jewish law. "Heaven" may not interfere in the development of Torah. In order to sustain the emergence of the halakhic process talmudic man proclaims the priority of human reason before the intrusions of revelation in his use of the biblical phrase "(Torah) is not in heaven." (Deut. XXX, 12) God gave the Torah to man, and man, with the use of reasoning and argumentation, is autonomous in guiding its development.

In a text reminiscent of Spinoza's comparison of the prophet with the philosopher, the midrash compares the scribe, i.e., the scholar of Torah, with the prophets:

They (the scribes and prophets) are like two agents whom a king sent to a province. With regard to one he wrote: If he shows you my signature and seal, trust him, but otherwise do not trust him. With regard to the other he wrote: Even if he does not show you my signature and seal, trust him. So of the words of prophecy it is written, If there arise in the midst of thee a prophet . . . and he gives thee a sign (Deut. XIII, 2), but of the words of the Scribes it is written, According to the law which they shall teach thee (Deut. XVII, 11). (*Midrash Rabbah, The Song of Songs,* I, 2)

In the talmudic development of the law, one does not need prophecy or the intervention of God to confirm the legitimacy of a legal argument. In supplanting the prophet as leader of the community, the scholar presents the credentials of intellectual competence to reason and argues persuasively about the law.[44]

These features of rabbinic Judaism, i.e., the preeminence of human legal reasoning above prophecy, the neutralization of the mythic-organic passion of the Bible, and the attempt at curbing the expectation of divine confirmation in history, create the conditions for the emergence of a spiritual outlook in which one's relationship to God is not spiritually nurtured by the miraculous presence of God in History. The God of the Halakhah is similar, *mutatis mutandis*, to the perfect God of Aristotle. For the Halakhah, God is perfect and his wisdom is reflected in the structure of the law; for Aristotle God is perfect, and His wisdom is reflected in the structures of reality. In the former case, human reason is adequate to uncover divine wisdom in the Torah, in the latter case, human wisdom can understand God's wisdom in nature. One is drawn to God through the development of His Torah without the aid of revelation or other non-rational intrusions in history. The passion of the *talmid hakham* (the talmudic scholar), like the passion of the philosopher, involves a movement from man to God, i.e., the passion of eros. Aristotle's God, who attracts man in virtue of his perfection, can be loved by rabbinic Jews insofar as eros and the neutralization of dramatic historical events have become part of their religious sensibilities. Yehuda Halevy clearly understood the profound difference between a tradition grounded in revelation and one grounded in reason.[45] The battle between philosophy and revealed religion was not only a question of competing truths; it involved, as well, questions of human adequacy and the legitimacy of human reasoning. Eros and agape characterize the poles of the profound conflict between a tradition grounded in revelation and one nurtured by human initiative and creativity. The talmudic tradition that we have isolated is a tradition which neutralized the religious need for grace, for miracles and for the idea of a God who breaks into history. This particular tradition may have influenced Maimonides to assimilate the Greek metaphysical tradition into rabbinic Judaism.[46]

Maimonides did not regard history as being the principal location of the relationship of man and God. As Urbach has shown, Maimonides went very far in banishing the prophet from having any relationship to the development of the law.[47] Maimonides was personally averse to magnifying the place of miracles in the tradition.[48] He did not believe that history will ever offer a permanent solution to the human condition.[49] The law will be present and needed in (his conception of) the messianic world. Human freedom and susceptibility to sin are unchanging features of life. "Olam ke-minhago noheg" (the world maintains its natural course) is the quintessence of Maimonides' theory of history. He rejects the eschatology of a new creation and only insists on belief in creation. Eternity *a parte ante* is rejected in order to introduce a theology of will, which, in turn, makes possible the giving of the Torah.[50] Maimonides did not require a theology of history where history would end supernaturally or otherwise. He, therefore, accepted eternity *a parte post* and rejected eternity *a parte ante*:

> I have already made it clear to you that the belief in the production of the world is necessarily the foundation of the entire law. However, the belief in its passing-away after it has come into being and been generated is not, in our opinion, in any respect, a foundation of the Law and none of our beliefs would be hurt through the belief in its permanent duration. (*Guide* II, 27)

Maimonides' philosophical orientation did not seek to restore God's miraculous interference in history in the messianic world. He required the notion of God's will to justify the authority of Halakhah. Yet, after introducing a theology of will and hence making sense of the revelation of the Torah, Maimonides undermines the prophetic, eschatological passion by accepting eternity *a parte post*. Maimonides, like his talmudic predecessors, sought to cultivate a passion for God grounded in disinterested love of God.

No doubt the above is not the only way to make sense of the rabbinic tradition. Many great masters of the mystic tradition were talmudic scholars. The movement from the talmudic tradition to the Greek metaphysical tradition is certainly not a logically inevitable one. Yet, one ought to be very cautious when analyzing the notion of the absolute in the Jewish tradition. The problematic and interesting nature of this theme results from the fact that the Jewish tradition considered the biblical and the rabbinic traditions to be one tradition. The written Torah (Bible) and the oral Torah (Mishnah, Talmud, etc.) are one. Once the Jewish spirit united both traditions into one-single revelation, it became possible and intelligible to interpret *Ehyeh asher Ehyeh* as ~I am that I am"--I am the necessary being--and not as "I will be with you in your suffering." Because Maimonides was the great master of talmud, he was bold enough to introduce his legal codification, the *Mishneh Torah*, with four chapters dealing with the primacy of the metaphysical tradition and to claim, in *Hilkhot Talmud Torah*, that the discipline of "talmud" included both the study of law and of philosophy.[51] Surprising and unpredictable spiritual orientations and sensibilities emerge in a tradition where one of its respected teachers, R. Johanan, can say:

> God made a covenant with Israel only for the sake of that which was transmitted orally, as it says, "For by the mouth of these words I have made a covenant

with thee and with Israel."⁵² (*T.B., Gittin,* 60B)

Hebrew University and
Shalom Hartman Institute
Jerusalem

NOTES

Quotations from *The Guide of the Perplexed* are from the Shlomo Pines translation (Chicago: Chicago University Press, 1963.

Quotations from the *Mishneh Torah* are from the Hyamson translation (Jerusalem, 1965).

Quotations from the Bible are from *The Torah: The Five Books of Moses* (Philadelphia: J.P.S., 1962).

Quotations from the Talmud are from *The Soncino Talmud.*

1. See Y. Leibowitz, *Yahadut Am Yehudi U'medinat Yisrael* (Tel Aviv: Schocken, 1975), p. 15.
2. Gershom G. Scholem, *On the Kabbalah and Its Symbolism,* trans. by R. Manheim (New York: Schocken, 1965), pp. 94-100, 122-130.
3. Shlomo Pines, "The Philosophic Source of *The Guide of the Perplexed,*" in *The Guide of the Perplexed* (Chicago and London: Univ. of Chicago Press, 1963), pp. CXXXIII-CXXXIV.
4. Emphraim E. Urbach, *The Sages: Their Concepts and Beliefs,* translated by I. Abrahams (Jerusalem: The Magnes Press, 1975), pp. 17, 18, 36, 65, 284-5. See Julius Guttman, *Philosophies of Judaism,* trans. by David Silverman (New York: Anchor, 1966), pp. 30-43.
5. B. Spinoza, *A Theological-Political Treatise,* trans. by R.H.M. Elwes (New York: Dover, 1951), chaps. 1, 2, 7 (pp. 115-119). See S. Pines, "Spinoza's Tractatus Theologico-Politicus, Maimonides, and KanNt," *Scripta Hierosolymitana,* xx (1968), pp. 3-54; Leo StrausNs, *Spinoza's Critique of Religion,* trans. by Elsa M. Sinclair (New York: Schocken, 1965), chap. 6; D. HartmaNn, *Maimonides: Torah and Philosophic Quest* (Philadelphia: J.P.S., 1976), p. 237, n. 6.
6. Leo Strauss, *Persecution and the Art of Writing* (Glencoe, Illinois: The Free Press, 1952), pp. 78-94; D. Hartman, *Maimonides,* introduction and chap. V. '
7. *Guide* II, 40.
8. *Ibid.* III, 27, *Mishneh Torah,* "Laws of Repentance," chap. IX.
9. See comments of the Kesef Mishneh to *Hilkhot Yesodei*

HaTorah, IV, 13; Isadore Twersky, "Some Non-Halakhic Aspects of the *Mishneh Torah"* in *Jewish Medieval and Renaissance Studies,* ed. A. Altmann (Cambridge, Mass.: Harvard Univ. Press, 1967).

10. See D. Hartman, *Maimonides,* pp. 44-45; J. Guttman, *op. cit.,* p. 177; G. Scholem, *The Messianic Idea in Judaism and Other Essays on Jewish Spirituality* (New York: Schocken, 1971), p. 25; *T.B., Kiddushin* 40b, *Baba Kama* 17A.

11. See the passionate yearning for Olam Haba (an ahistorical relationship to God) in Maimonides' introduction to *Helek, M.T.,* "Laws of Repentance," VIII, and in *Guide* III, 51.

12. See Rashi's commentary to Genesis I, 1 and *Midrash Tanhuma,* Berashit II. See *Guide* III, 13-14; Leo Strauss, "Jerusalem and Athens," *The City College Papers,* VI (New York: 1967), pp. 8-10, 20, for an analysis of the differences between the place of man in the hierarchy of being in Greek and in Biblical thought.

13. *"Ehyeh-Asher Ehyeh.* The Holy One, blessed be He, said to Moses: Go and say to Israel: I was with you in this servitude, and I shall be with you in the servitude of (other) kingdoms." *(T.B., Berakhot* 9b). See *Midrash Raba,* Exodus III, 6.

14. Martin Buber, *Israel and the World: Essays in a Time of Crises* (New York: Schocken, 1948), p. 23; see M. Buber, *Moses: The Revelation and the Convenant* (New York: Harper and Brothers, 1958), pp. 39-55; *Kingship of God,* trans. R. Scheimann (New York: Harper and Row, 1967), pp. 103-106; Emil L. Fackenheim, *God's Presence in History* (New York: N.Y.U., 1970), pp. 3-34, for a serious attempt at making sense of God's presence in history in the modern world.

15. See Strauss, "Jerusalem and Athens," p. 17. For earlier interpretations of *Ehyeh Asher Ehyeh* as making a metaphysical and not a historical statement, see H.A. Wolfson, *Philo: Foundations of Religious Philosophy in Judaism, Christianity and Islam* (Cambridge, Mass.: Harvard Univ. Press, 1929), vol. 1, pp. 19, 210: C.H. Dodd, *The Bible and the Greeks* (London: Hodder and Stoughton, 1964), p. 4. For critical textural analysis, see B.S. Childs, *The Book of Exodus: A Critical Theological Commentary* (Philadelphia: The Westminster Press, 1974), pp. 60-77 and Moshe Greenberg, *Understanding Exodus* (New York: Behrman House, 1969), pp. 78-84.

16. "'I am the Lord thy God': (Ex. 20:2), Why were the Ten Commandments not said at the beginning of the Torah? They give a parable. To what may this be compared? To the following: A king who entered a province said to the people: May I be your king? But the people said to him: Have you done anything good for us that you should rule over us? What did he do then?

He built the city wall for them, he brought in the water supply for them, and he fought their battles. Then when he said to them: May I be your king? They said to Him: Yes, yes. Likewise, God. He brought the Israelites out of Egypt, divided the sea for them, sent down the manna for them, brought up the well for them, brought the quails for them. He fought for them the-battle with Amalek. Then He said to them: I am to be your king. And they said to Him: Yes, yes" (*Mekhilta*). Trans. J.Z. Lauterbach (Philadelphia: J.P.S., 1933), tractate Bahodesh, V). See Yehuda Halevi, *Kuzari*, I, 11, 25, 83-89; IV, 3.

17. *Guide* I, 64, p. 157; II, 5, p. 260; III, 32, p. 526, 51, p. 623. See F. Heiler, *Prayer: A Study in the History and Psychology of Religion*, trans. S. McComb (New York: Oxford Univ. Press, 1932), chap. IV.

18. *M.T., Hilkhot Yesodei HaTorah*, IX, 3, 5.

19. Isodore Twersky, *Rabad of Posquieres* (Cambridge, Mass.: Harvard Univ. Press, 1962), pp. 282-6.

20. See Leo Strauss, "How to Begin to Study the Guide of the Perplexed," in *The Guide of the Perplexed*, op. cit., pp. 20-24. Wolfson claims that declaring openly, as opposed to simply accepting "in one's heart," belief in divine corporeality constitutes idolatry. See his interesting discussion in "Maimonides on the Unity and Incorporeality of God," *JQR*, 56 (1965), pp. 112-36.

21. "Hilkhot Abodah Zarah" deals with practices that were prohibited in order to protect the community from pagan and idolatrous influences. The laws of idolatry, therefore, begin with an account of how mistaken forms of worship were responsible for the growth of idolatry and the disappearance of monotheism. In chap. I of "Hilkhot Yesodei HaTorah," Maimonides deals with idolatry based upon a false understanding of the notion of the unity of God.

22. *Guide*, I, 55.

23. H. Wolfson, "Maimonides on the Unity and Incorporeality of God," and *Philo*, II, pp. 94-101.

24. See D. Hartman, *Maimonides*, p. 294, n. 92.

25. See Guttman, *op. cit.*, p. 159.

26. *Guide* I, 39; III, 28; see D. Hartman, *Maimonides*, p. 265, n. 61. See Pines' introduction to *The Guide of the Perplexed*, pp. xcv-xcviii, cxi, cxv; "Spinoza's tractatus Theologico-Politicus, Maimonides and Kant," p. 26, and his forward to D. Hartman, *Maimonides*, for the changes in Pines' approach to Maimonides' understanding of knowledge of God. Pines' present position is that Maimonides seriously doubted the possibility of metaphysical knowledge of God.

27. See *M.T., Hilkhot Yesodei HaTorah*, IV, 12.

28. The description of Abraham of the *akedah* should be

balanced by other texts describing his efforts to establish an historical community dedicated to the belief in the unity of God: *Book of the Commandments*, positive commandment III: *M.T., Laws of Idolatry*, I; and *Guide* III, 51, p. 624.

29. See *Guide*, III, 51, pp. 620-623; I, 59, p. 139.

30. See *Guide*, III, 26, 28, 31.

31. See G. Scholem, *Major Trends in Jewish Mysticism* (New York: Schocken, 1941), pp. 25-37; *On the Kabbalah and Its Symbolism* (New York: Schocken, 1965), pp. 95, 127, 130.

32. *Guide*, I, 52; II, 12.

33. *Mishnah Berakhot* IX, 5. See Urbach, *op. cit.*, chap. XIV, and p. 443.

34. "Toward an Understanding of the Messianic Idea" in *The Messianic Idea in Judaism*, p. 30.

35. *M.T., The Book of Judges*, "Kings and Wars," chaps. XI, XII.

36. Guttman, *op. cit.*, pp. 177-8. See I. Husik, *A History of Medieval Jewish Philosophy* (New York: Meridian and Philadelphia: J.P.S., 1958), p. 300.

37. "Notes on Maimonides' Book of Knowledge," in *Studies in Mysticism and Religion Presented to Gershom G. Scholem* (Jerusalem: The Magnes Press, 1967), p. 273 and *Natural Right and History* (Chicago and London: University of Chicago Press, 1965), pp. 81-3. See Maimonides' *Eight Chapters*, VIII; Notes by Prof. Louis Ginzberg to I. Efros, *Philosophical Terms in the Moreh Nebukim* (New York: Columbia Univ. Press, 1924), pp. 134-5.

38. *T.B., Kiddushin* 39b. See Urback, *op. cit* p. 268-271; 436-444.

39. See different versions of this midrash in *T.J., Megillah*, III, 7. In the Babylonian version, the prophets, Daniel and Jeremiah, initiate the problem. The men of the great assembly offer a solution by reinterpreting the categories. In the Jerusalem version, the prophets themselves indicate the direction of the solution.

40. See *Mekhilta* VIII, for examples of the wide range of uses of notions of divine power. Rather than offering a strict definition of divine power, the *Mekhilta* collects a variety of correct uses of the concept.

41. See G. Scholem, *On the Kabbalah and Its Symbolism*, pp. 95, 120-1, 132-3, 130-135.

42. See G. Scholem, "Toward an Understanding of the Messianic Idea," especially, pp. 17-24.

43. See Gerson D. Cohen, "The Talmudic Age," in *Great Ages and Ideas of the Jewish People*, edited by Leo W. Schwarz (New York: Random House, 1956), pp. 143-212.

44. See D. Hartman, *Maimonides*, pp. 102-126.

45. *Kuzari*, I, 1-13, 98, 99.

46. See Urbach, *op. cit.*, pp. 303-4, for a discussion of the relationship of grace (hesed) and law. Our exposition supports Urbach's interpretation of the bold statement in *T.B.*, Pesahim 118a: "To what do these twenty-six (verses of) "Give thanks" correspond? To the twenty-six generations that the Holy One, blessed be He, created in His world, and did not give them the Torah, but sustained them by His grace." "There was need of grace," comments Urbach, "so long as the Torah had not been given." For a different approach which emphasizes the need for grace in Maimonides' quest for knowledge of God, see Simon Rawidowicz, *Studies in Jewish Thought*, edited by Nahum N. Glatzer, chapter 7, Philadelphia, J.P.S. 1974.

47. E. Urbach, "Halakhah u-Nevuah," *Tarbiz*, 18 (1946), pp. 1-27. See D. Hartman, *Maimonides*, pp. 116-122. In contrast to Maimonides' approach, see Yehudah Halevi III, 41. This difference is not unrelated to differences of their overall philosophic world views.

48. See D. Hartman, *Maimonides*, IV. See Maimonides' "Treatise on Resurrection" and "Eight Chapters," chap. VIII; D. Hartman, *Maimonides*, chap. IV.

49. *M.T.*, "Laws of Repentance," IX, and "Kings and Wars," XII.

50. *Guide*, II, 25.

51. *M.T.*, *Hilkhot Talmud Torah*, I, 11-12. See I. Twersky, "Some Non-Halaklic Aspects of the *Mishneh Torah*," pp. 111-118.

52. Urbach, *The Sages*, chap. XII.

COMMENT

On David Hartman and Elliott Yagod,
"God, Philosophy and Halakhah
in Maimonides' Approach to Judaism"

ISAAC FRANCK

Dr. Hartman devotes a very substantial part of his paper to an exposition of the dialectical tension in the millennial mainstream of Jewish theological and metaphysical thought, between the two ideas of God: on the one hand the Biblical - Halakhic - liturgical - psychosocial - anthropocentric - emotive - personal - mitzvah oriented idea of *the God of human history and of the history of Israel*; and on the other hand the contemplative - speculative - conceptual - theoretical - analytico-logico-philosophical - abstract idea of a "wholly other," distant, imperturbable God, Whom one loves disinterestedly, with a metaphysical and intellectual love akin to Spinoza's *amor dei intellectualis*. Where I would be inclined to question Dr. Hartman is:

First, on his *philosophical claim* that this dialectical tension *can be* resolved and that a disjunction between these two God-ideas can be avoided.

Second, on his *historical claim* that a critical analysis of the post-Biblical Rabbinic, *mitzvah*-oriented tradition shows this tradition to have successfully accommodated within itself the idea of God as the "wholly other"--the purely intellectual, non-anthropocentric idea of the God of the philosophers--and thus to have reduced the tension and eliminated the disjunction between the two.

Third, his claim that Moses Maimonides in particular *believed* that he had succeeded in his own writings, and that *he had in fact succeeded* in resolving that tension completely and in having incorporated the philosophical idea of a non-anthropocentric God into his philosophy of Judaism, for the mainstream of the tradition.

The fact of course is that the tension between these two God-ideas has persevered throughout the centuries, and is very much a dynamic focus in the thought and writings of such 20th century philosophers of Judaism as Franz Rosenzweig, Martin Buber, Abraham J. Heschel, Mordecai M. Kaplan, Emil Fackenheim, Louis Jacobs, and in Israel, Yeshayahu Leibovitz and others. But perhaps the most cogent evidence of the continuing tension is conspicuously discernible (1) in the spirited and ever self-renewing controversies around the philosophical views of

Maimonides that have punctuated without abatement the history of Jewish thought from the 13th century to our own day; and (2) in Maimonides' own assessments of his philosophical idea of God.

It was not only Isaac Husik[1] and Julius Guttman,[2] preeminent historians of medieval Jewish thought, who saw the disjunction between Maimonides *the philosopher* in *The Guide of the Perplexed*, and Maimonides *the Halakhist* in his *Code* (the *Mishneh Torah*) and his other works in *Halakhic* Judaism. Maimonides' contemporaries and those commentators who wrote about his work during the two centuries immediately following him--men like Shem Tov Falaquera,[3] Kaspi,[4] Narboni,[5] Shem Tov,[6] Anatoli,[7] Ephodi,[8] and others--had many ambivalences and evidenced many dialectical tensions about the Maimonidean doctrine of God. They perceived in the idea of a remote, wholly other God--who is totally unaffected by human feelings and conduct, who does not respond with anger or joy to human transgression or worship, and whom the philosopher truly worships only through detached contemplation--a threat to the received idea of the God of Abraham, Isaac, and Jacob, the Jewish people's traditional God of history, Giver of the Commandments, and Dispenser of reward and punishment, and to civil and political tranquility. One of these very early commentators, J. Kaspi, wrote: "If the people were to find out about this doctrine, they would not be able to tolerate this truth, and would grow wild and uncontrollable in their conduct."[9] It is thus not to be wondered that in some Jewish communities the study of *The Guide of the Perplexed* was banned, and in many of the *Yeshivot*, the Talmudic Academies in Eastern Europe, the study of *The Guide* was forbidden.

As for Maimonides himself, it seems clear to me--and in this I follow the interpretation of the late very great scholar, Leo Strauss,[10] and also of a short and neglected work, in Hebrew, by an Israeli scholar, Yaacov Becker[11]--that Maimonides had in mind two distinct, though over lapping, audiences for the *Code* (i.e., the *Mishneh Torah*) and for *The Guide*, respectively. He wrote the *Mishneh Torah* principally for the masses and teachers of the Jewish community with the objective of strengthening, elevating, deepening, enriching their commitment to *Torah* Judaism, their faith in the God of Abraham, Isaac and Jacob, and their dedication to a life of inspired ethical rectitude and nobility, and to a society of justice and mercy. For that audience, the fulfillment of the commandments and a sense of reciprocal personal relationship and involvement with the God who was the source of these commandments were *the* methodologies for the pursuit of these goals.

The Guide was written for a select audience of religiously committed Jews who had been exposed to philosophical and scientific ideas, analyses and speculations. They were struggling with doubts and perplexities which science and philosophy raised in their minds about aspects of their faith, and were in search of a cogent philosophical frame of reference for their Judaism. In *The Guide* Maimonides hoped to provide answers to those troubled by these doubts and perplexities, erect for them a firm philosophical foundation for Judaism, and thus strengthen their commitment to it. He hoped that there could be a steady and even accelerated increase in the overlap of the two groups, facilitated in part by exposing the small number of the philosophically-minded intellectual elite to a searching analysis of "the reasons for the commandments" - *ta'amei hamitzvet* - in relation to the Maimonidean philosophical God-idea.

Contained in *The Guide*, at times explicitly pointed to and at other times hinted by indirection, was what Maimonides preferred to have remain a *secret* doctrine, *not to be revealed to the community*, a doctrine of a distant, totally different, imperturbable God, true worship of Whom takes the form of intellectual love and contemplation. Maimonides distinguishes in several places in *The Guide* between "true belief" and "necessary belief," "*Emunah Amitit*" and "*Emunah Hekhrahit*." *True* belief is the philosopher's belief in the *philosophers' God*, a God Who does not need customary worship, Who is totally unaffected by whether or not the *Halakhah* or the Commandments are fulfilled, Who does not get angry and does not rejoice (these are only anthropomorphic metaphors). On the other hand, belief in the God of traditional *Halakhah*, the God of the Commandments, Maimonides calls *necessary* belief, necessary for the people, for the maintenance of social tranquility, for a civilized social order, and for humane conduct toward each other on the part of humans. The careful reader of *The Guide* will note how often Maimonides refers to the "*Ormah elohit*," i.e., "God's shrewdness" in having ordained the ritual laws and observances, not because God has any need for them, but as a "ruse" (Shlomo Pines' translation), a kind of trick in order to reduce cruelty and injustice and achieve just and humane relationships among humans. For example, the cult of animal sacrifices was ordained in order to wean away the people of Israel from *human* sacrifices, a barbaric cult that was widespread among the pagan idol worshippers who surrounded Israel at that time.[12] Other such "Divine Ruses" are referred to in *The Guide*.

The obvious question that confronts us is, why should this Maimonidean, detached, wholly other, imperturbable God be sufficiently perturbed to have any concern for the justice and tranquility of the social order among humans, or for the fulfill-

ment of Commandments generally? And why should the philosopher, who understands the *true belief* and the passion for the
intellectual contemplation and love of God, be concerned with
fulfilling the Commandments? In the text of *The Guide*, using an
example, the question takes this form: "For God, and for the
philosopher, what difference does it make whether the animal to
be eaten is slaughtered by the prescribed, ritual, humane method, or whether its meat is simply cut from the flank of the
living animal[13]--(again a widespread practice among the pagans
of the time)?" Permit me to defer the answer to this question
while I turn to a very brief consideration of the second theme
in this commentary.

   In characterizing the Philosophical God-Idea of Maimonides,
Dr. Hartman quite properly and vigorously stressed the Anti-
Idolatry motif constantly reiterated throughout Jewish teaching
about God, and especially the forceful and aggressive Anti-Idolatry of Maimonides. One surpassingly important element in the
Philosophical God-Idea developed at length in Maimonides' *Guide*
is the *utter unknowability* of God by the human mind.[14] God's
essence is completely unknown to man; only His *existence* is
known. No affirmative attributes can be attributed to God. God
is completely, utterly unknown and unknowable. "Our knowledge
of God," says Maimonides, "consists in our knowledge that we
are unable to comprehend Him."[15] The *Guide's* theology is a
radical Negative Theology. What is *known to man* is necessarily
known to him in terms of *human knowledge*, as he knows the
world of his existence. Now, God can not be known to man
because essential knowledge of God is available only to God
himself. According to Maimonides, for man to try to know God
is as if man tried *to be God*.[16] This doctrine is summarized in a
sort of precept: "*Ilu y'dativ, he-yitiv*," "If I knew Him, I would
be He," a precept found in Joseph Albo's "*Ikkarim*."[17]

   The doctrine of the utter unknowability of God is ancient
in Jewish Philosophy. It was well developed by Philo,[18] reiterated by Saadia[19] in the 10th century, and by Maimonides, Albo,
and later philosophers of Judaism. But Maimonides espoused a
radical negative theology. He formulated the vigorous warning
that ". . . he who affirms that God has positive attributes . . .
has abandoned his belief in the existence of God without being
aware of it."[20] No wonder then that Maimonides admonished the
reader of *The Guide* that the doctrine of God's unknowability
"Should not be divulged (or revealed) to the masses,"[21] and that
Leo Strauss suggested that this teaching ". . . contradicts the
teaching of the law . . . and is even subversive."[22]

   But this doctrine, though apparently heterodox, is of even
more ancient vintage. The prophet Isaiah is quoted by Maimo-

nides in the course of his exposition of the unknowability of God, and in support of this doctrine. Isaiah declared, in the name of God: "*Lo mahshvotai mahshvoteikhem, v'lo darkeikhem d'rakhai . . . ." "My thoughts are not your thoughts, and your ways are not my ways . . . ."*[23] However, my own interpretation is, though I believe it to be hinted by Maimonides, that this doctrine of God's unknowability dates back even further, to Moses. When Moses inquired of God, "Who shall I say sent me?" the reply Moses heard was the incomprehensible and awesome words, "*Ehyeh asher ehyeh . . . ,*"[24] generally translated as "I am who I am,' or "I will be who I will be," the words confronted him with a double incomprehensibility. First, the meaning of the words, simply as words, was incomprehensible. Second, the Being to Whom the words ostensibly referred was incomprehensible. Moses later pursued the enigma by asking God to show him His (God's) nature. In the reply that Moses received to this later question are provided implicitly the unravelling and separation from each other of the two earlier enigmas. For in hearing God's reply, "*Ki lo yir'ani ha'adam vaha*i . . . ," ". . . for man cannot see me and live . . . ,"[25] Moses learned that the Entity or Being to which "*Ehyeh*" refers is indeed, and must forever remain, incomprehensible. But he also learned that the linguistic problem is resolved, and that the meaning of the words "*ehyeh asher ehyeh*" perhaps ceases to be impenetrable. Though God gives it as the answer to the question about His identity, the locution "*ehyeh*" is not substantival, it is not the equivalent of a noun; *it is not a name of anything; least of all is it a proper name,* like Socrates. *The locution is an admonition,* a directive, which says "Do not inquire into what I am, because I am incomprehensible. I am what I am, ask no further. Man cannot know me, I am wholly different."

This doctrine of God's utter unknowability is the ultimate anti-idolatry. It is possible for us to know only *what God is not,* and *what is not God.* "Only God is God."[26] Anything known or knowable is not God. God is utterly different and unique. To worship anything known or knowable is *idolatry.* To give one's ultimate and absolute allegiance or loyalty to anything but God, to any known or knowable thing, to any person, or aggregate of persons, or to any human institution, is *idolatry.* It is only that wholly other, utterly unknowable God of Philosophy that is worthy of contemplation and of pure, disinterested, intellectual love.

Now, you may ask, isn't this radical Negative Theology barren of consequences, morally vacuous, tantamount to a vague mysticism, and destructive of any Rational Theology? I think not. It is not Mysticism, because it does not itself claim to have, and radically rejects all claims to the possession of, any access to some intuitive mystical insight into the essential nature of God. The fact that God is unknown is a mystery, but this does not make the doctrine of God's unknowability a doctrine of Mysticism. The doctrine is not destructive of Rational Theology, because it is not a *Theology of silence*, akin to the Wittgensteinian precept: "Whereof we cannot speak, thereof we must be silent." On the contrary, this Theology imposes on the theologian who espouses it the duty to do a lot of talking, by way of *"unsaying,"*[27] morning, noon, and night, all the many things that humans have said and will continue to be saying in their talk about God, even when they claim that God is unknowable. It is not an ethically vacuous doctrine. It does have ethical consequences.

Which leads me to my third and final theme, namely the answer to the question I mentioned earlier, as to why the Imperturbable God, and the philosopher who contemplates and disinterestedly loves Him, should be at all concerned about the traditional commandments. Here I complete the circle, and come around to an agreement with one aspect of Professor Hartman's thesis, though I arrive at it from another direction. It is perhaps paradoxical, but in Judaism even the non-anthropocentric, philosophical, idea of an utterly *different* God converges toward the *Halakhic*, socio-ethical, Commandment-oriented traditional mandates for social existence.

1) For Maimonides, the highest, most noble pursuit of the philosophical Jew is *indeed* the contemplative love of God. However, a necessary condition, that may make possible this kind of contemplative life for an increasing number of philosophically minded persons, is a *Torah*-society. Its norms and adherence to Commandments will assure the tranquil, just, and civilized order that maintains the conditions for a philosophical life.

2) If only the *unknowable God of Radical Negative Theology* is worthy of worship--of the highest, ultimate, absolute loyalty and allegiance--this has consequences for social ethics, for norms and prescriptions by which to govern interhuman relationships. In all human societies there is an unavoidable, inescapable need for the exercise of authority, for superordinate and subordinate relationships and positions of humans in the social order. A traffic light system is an exercise of the authority, and a police system enforces this authority. What are the limits of authority of humans and human institutions in a society?

Therefore, in the perspective of Radical Negative Theology, what are the limits of the authority of humans and human institutions when they perform necessary superordinate roles in relation to other human beings? It seems to me immediately and most obviously entailed by this doctrine that no human being(s), no human institution, no human law, may demand or expect or coerce the supreme, ultimate, and total allegiance, loyalty, or obedience on the part of any other human being. No human being(s) or institutions may "play God" toward, or "Lord it over" any other human being. No human(s) may exercise any *absolute* authority over any other person. The exercise of such absolute authority over other humans is self-idolization; it is the "absolutization of the relative;" and it also coerces the victim who accepts such absolute authority to in fact practice *idolatry*: ". . . for unto Me are the children of Israel servants, not servants to servants."[28]

Thus, the *otherness* and *unknowability* of God in the Maimonidean, philosophical God-idea, the *true* God-idea which Maimonides wished to keep secret from the masses, does entail a system of social ethics. But the masses were not prepared to understand and accept the *true beliefs* about God and live by them. Indeed, these true beliefs would be likely to lead the masses to violent and disorderly conduct. *They* need the *necessary beliefs*, e.g., that God is a dispenser of reward and punishment, not because they are true, but rather as a means to an end, in order to maintain a civilized society.

Maimonides does not provide a traditionalist resolution between these two divergent God-ideas, nor does he claim to have done so. The disjunction between these two God-ideas seems to me irresolvable in traditionalist terms, and while the attempt so to resolve it is an interesting exercise, its product strikes me as only an addition to almost 800 years of tension and confusion, rather than as a contribution to clarity. This tension will continue, and, not withstanding the tension, the spiritual and intellectual vocation of Judaism will struggle on as heretofore. Philosophically, what is important is not resolution, but rather clarification, a very modest adumbration of which I have tried to contribute in this brief commentary.

Kennedy Institute of Ethics

Georgetown University

Washington, D.C.

NOTES

1. Isaac Husik, *A History of Medieval Jewish Philosophy* (Philadelphia: The Jewish Publication Society of America, 1941).
2. Julius Guttmann, *Philosohies of Judaism: The History of Jewish Philosophy from Biblical Times to Franz Rosenzweig*

(Philadelphia: The Jewish Publication Society of America, 1964).

3. Shem Tov Falaquera (1225-1290), *Commentary on the Guide of the Perplexed* (Moreh Hamoreh).

4. Joseph Kaspi (1279-ca.1340), *Commentary on the Guide of the Perplexed,* and *Amudei Hakessef Umaskiyot Hakessef.*

5. Moses Narbeni (R. Moses Yosef of Narbonne) (died after 1362), *Commentary on the Guide of the Perplexed,* Goldenthal, ed. (Vienna, 1852) (See Husik, Fn. 1 above, p. 449.)

6. Shem Tov Ben Joseph (ca. 1461-1489), *Commentary on the Guide of the Perplexed.*

7. Joseph Anateli (ca. 1194-1256), *Malmad Hatalmidim.*

8. Ephodi, (a Hebrew acronym for Profiat Duran) (died ca. 1414), *Commentary on the Guide of the Perplexed.*

9. Joseph Kaspi *Amudei Hakessef Umaskiyot Hakessef,* p. 8.

10. Leo Strauss, "The Literary Character of the *Guide for the Perplexed,*" in *Persecution and the Art of Writing* (Glencoe, Illinois: The Free Press, 1952), pp. 38-94.

11. Yaacov Becker, *Mishnato Haphilosophit Shel Rabbenu Moshe Ben Maimon* (Tel Aviv: J. Shimoni Publishing House, 1955).

12. Moses Maimonidos, *Guide of the Perplexed,* Shlomo Pines, (Chicago: University of Chicago Press, 1963), III, 32 (pp. 526, 530-531 in Pines' translation) and III, 47 (p. 593 in Pines' translation). On the "Divine ruse," see e.g., *Guide* III, 32, especially pp. 526-529 in Pines' translation.

13. *Guide,* III, 26, pp. 508-509 in Pines' translation.

14. *Guide,* I, 51-60.

15. *Ibid.,* I, 59, p. 139.

16. *Ibid.,* I, 60, and III, 21, p. 485 in Pines' translation.

17. Joseph Albo, *Sefer Ha-Ikkarim* (The Book of Principles) Isaac Husik, trans. (Philadelphia: The Jewish Publication Society, 1946). Volume II, p. 206.

18. Harry Austryn Wolfson, *Philo: Foundations of Religious Philosophy in Judaism, Christianity, and Islam* (Cambridge, Mass.: Harvard University Press, 1948), Vol. II, Chap. 11, pp. 94-164.

19. Gaon Saadia, *The Book of Beliefs and Opinions,* Samuel Rosenblatt, trans., (New Haven, Conn.: Yale University Press, 1948).

20. *Guide,* I, 60, p. 145 in Pines' translation.

21. *Ibid.,* I, 59, p. 142 in Pines' translation.

22. Leo Strauss, "How to Begin to Study the *Guide of the Perplexed,*" in Moses Maimonides, *Guide of the Perplexed,* Shelmo Pines, trans., pp. xlviii ff.

23. *Isaiah,* LV, 8-9.

24. *Exodus,* III, 14.

25. *Ibid.,* XXXIII, 21.

26. Elliott E. Cohen, in an article in the early 40's.

27. Anton C. Pegis, "*Penitus Manet Ignotum*," in *Mediaeval Studies*, XXVII (1965), pp. 212-226, especially pp. 219 ff.

28. *Babylonian Talmud*, Tractate *Kiddushin*, 22b.

CHAPTER IX

PHILOSOPHY, MAN AND THE ABSOLUTE GOD: AN ISLAMIC PERSPECTIVE

BAHRAM JAMALPUR

It is necessary to clarify the precise meaning of four fundamental concepts: philosophy, independence, man and God.

Philosophy, by its very nature, is the reflection upon reflection; as the reason of all reasons, philosophy is the primordial search for the ultimate horizon of meaning. In intellectual history, there are two fundamental definitions of philosophy:

1. Philosophy as the Love of Wisdom
2. Philosophy as the Possession of Wisdom

What most concerns the Eastern world, and particularly the Islamic tradition, is the philosophy as the possession of wisdom.

No matter which definition of philosophy appeals to us, however, we are talking about human philosophy and not philosophy as such. Whatever the ultimate and the Divine ground of philosophy may be, philosophy as a human phenomenon begins with man and is essentially related to humanity in general.

Philosophy does not belong to any particular man, race, society, nation, language or religion. By the grace of God, it is the outcome of human understanding which calls itself into question and so transcends all conceivable categories. Most certainly and on contrast to what the late Professor M. Heidegger has claimed, philosophy is not Western in its essence, nor is the only proper philosophical language not Greco-German. Philosophy is not the slave of any race, language or religion, because Wisdom in its very essence transcends all traditions. Philosophy begins with the presence of man in the world, encompasses all cultures and hopes for the transcendence of man in order to comprehend the Ultimate Mystery.

Independence is a mystery that unfolds itself throughout man's history but never reveals itself in any perfect form since for man, as a limited being in the world, there can be no Absolute Independence. Note that by independence we do not mean liberation. Independence is above and beyond liberation. One attempts to liberate one's self in order to become independent and yet one may become liberated without achieving true independence. Liberation as a political concept by necessity assumes a prior period of its negation, but independence as a positive ontological phenomenon must itself be independent; thus it is a self-asserting concept.

For men of Wisdom there can be no true independence without an authentic philosophy of independence and there can be no genuine philosophy of independence without the veritable independence of philosophy itself. The ground of independent philosophy is man's self-consciousness in time and in history. Therefore we must unfold the notion of man in the light of self-consciousness and within the mystery of time and the context of history.

What is man? Man is a being in space and time: the former accounts for his material dimension whereas the latter constitutes an essential dimension of his spirituality. Man, in truth, is a temporal being; he is a-being-in-the-world who experiences the process of becoming, which conditions his very being. This conditioning is so fundamental that it manifests itself in his entire system of thought. As an objective being in the world of becoming he experiences a collection of factual events which we call the objective or the quantitative sense of time. However, due to his reflective power of consciousness man, as an internally dynamic being, is able to go beyond the objective perspective and condition his environment through what we may call the subjective or the qualitative sense of time. It is the subjective interpretation of the objective world of temporal events that creates history.

Man is an historical being. In the light of quantitative time, history creates man and, in the light of qualitative time, man creates history. Matter, in the sphere of body, is the symbol of the will to power. Spirit, in the sphere of consciousness, is the symbol of the will to love. The ontological unity of power and love is the symbol of the will to justice which constitutes humanity within society and history.

In substance, "spirit" has two essential dimensions: first, the inner self-identity or "I" which asserts itself from within and by means of reflection upon itself; and second, the qualitative manifestation of the ego in time and through history. Both aspects of the phenomenon of history are truly necessary and complementary for the everlasting search for meaning in the realm of self-consciousness. The first aspect is the ground of self-identity so that the spirit may be identified by human consciousness and retain its ego throughout history. The second aspect is the ground of the temporality of spirit which permits it to unfold through the mystery of time, and to leap beyond factuality in order to comprehend the transcendental aspect of history.

If "spirit" were limited to the ego it would have lacked the necessary "elan vital" for its conscious unfoldingness, and if it were limited to pure manifestations then it would have lost its self-identity. Therefore, spirit by nature must possess both ego or reflection upon itself, and manifestations or the unfolding through time and history.

The ultimate hope of any spirit is to become truly and completely conscious of itself, and this is completely realized only when the implicit unity of the spirit becomes explicit. The ontological assertion of the explicit unity of spirit can be observed when the will to power and justice are united in and through love. In the light of the spirit, the qualitative interpretation of time, which constitutes history, provides us with the possibility of authentic self-consciousness, which in the form of philosophy is the ground of independence.

We must remember that man can become politically free yet remain philosophically dependent. In order to become philosophically free, philosophy itself must experience independence. In truth, it is the destiny of philosophy to experience independence and gain freedom. Philosophy as the possession of Wisdom calls itself into question and for this reason after confrontation with various other disciplines asks about itself in a manner that transcends all limitations. In fact, it is the duty of philosophy, not only to confront other disciplines but also to confront itself and provide us with a critique of its own.

In the beginning religion based on revelation, science based on the study of facts, mysticism based on intuitive illumination, and philosophy based on reason, were all unified in their search for Truth as it revealed itself on the human horizon. But in the course of history, a necessary yet only a temporal separation took place, so that philosophy might have a chance to reflect objectively upon other disciplines while developing its own self-awareness. Despite this fundamental separation, we must never forget that the call for the harmony of religion, science, mysticism and philosophy has been with us from the very beginning. The foundation for such assertion is the belief in the ultimate Unity of Being (*Wahdat al-Wujud*). The ultimate recall of Eastern Wisdom in general and Islamic Philosophy in particular is the awareness of various levels of human understanding despite the unity of the whole. This is the ultimate reason why philosophy, after its early separation, must return to the state of togetherness with religion, science, and mysticism. Philosophy at the level of self-awareness through independence, becomes completely conscious of this primordial duty. According to this line of reasoning, this discussion does not center about a purely exclusive philosophy, but rather is devoted to the spirit of independent philosophy within the Islamic tradition.

There are two basic schools of thought within the Islamic tradition, namely, *Falsafa* and *Irfan*. Unquestionably Ibn Sina (Avicenna) and Malavi (Rumi) are the best representatives of these Islamic movements. Consequently, we will devote the rest of our discussion to a comparison of their notions of the Absolute God.

The most fundamental presupposition of Islamic thought is that God and Man are so essentially related that, for us, the full understanding of one demands the full knowledge of the other. Man cannot know man if he does not know God, and man cannot know God if he does not know man. We must not forget, however, that such assertion does not deny the absolute priority of God's Being and the knowledge of God over man, since such claim is valid only in relationship to man and not in itself. God has created man in His image, which implies that man possesses the image of God. Furthermore, since God does nothing in vain and there is nothing accidental about His divine intentions, God must have great love for man, whom He has created in His image. This love by its very nature encompasses man's being and overflows from his inner being; in the final analysis it must return to its origin. In short, God has a unique love for man and man, as the image of God, has a unique love for God.

According to Islam, God's love for man, which is ontologically prior to the creation of man, is a mystery, even to the angels. The angels ask God why He wants to create man as His own representative on earth rather than angels, since man shall commit sin whereas angels will not. God's answer to such a common sense objection in *The Holy Quran* is that "I know what you do not know."[1] A mystery even in the angels, God's love for man is a mysterious reality, even to man. Whatever the reason behind such a gift, man's love for God, which in the beginning under the grace of God was in harmony with God's love, is ontologically dependent upon God's love for man.

The temporal break of this mysterious relationship, according to The Holy Quran, is based on disobedience which is attributed, first of all to Satan[2] as the personification of evil and second, to man who possesses a weakness for evil as a separation from God.[3] If religion is taken to be what The Holy Quran tells us, namely, "The Way to God," then the purpose of Islam as the universal religion becomes clear. It is to awaken man and restore the temporally interrupted relationship so that, through submission to God's will, man can possess his unity with the whole creation, know himself, and finally, love God for whom he has been created. This is a well-understood objective of Islam which has been accepted by almost all Muslim thinkers. Therefore, the Muslim philosopher has one ultimate purpose in mind,

namely, to make explicit the mystery of the God-man relationship which is expressed so implicitly in the highly symbolic
language of *The Holy Quran*. Performing such a noble task, the
philosopher must know, not only God, but also man. Knowing
that he is inwardly related to himself and existentially so involved in the mysterious relationship to God, the philosopher may
begin with himself, and then in the light of the divine grace,
seek to know God. But the real knowledge of man comes after
the philosopher becomes aware of the divine reality and realizes
the image of God. Only then can he make explicit the implicit
mysterious relationship of God and man which ontologically are
never separate, yet whose relationship is temporally broken.

Let us now begin with the notion of God, which has the
utmost priority in the Islamic world, and focus our analysis on
the comparison of Inb Sina and Molavi's understanding of God in
terms of Being.

The philosophies of the Sina and Molavi both center around
Being, since without Being Ibn Sina's esoteric metaphysics would
not make any sense. Therefore, we may say that there is an
implicit fundamental agreement between Ibn Sina and Molavi
that Being is the mystery of *Hikmat*. Our aim in this section is
to present a view of Being which through synthesis can encompass the essential assertions of both the esoteric approach of
Ibn Sina and the mystical approach of Molavi, and yet point to
the dialectical tension between two Muslim thinkers. Whatever
the mystery of Being may be, both Ibn Sina and Molavi agree on
the following four main points: First of all, Being cannot be
reduced to merely a notion in our mind, since it implies reality
in itself, and reality cannot be reduced to a sheer subjective
notion. Therefore, any philosophical system that reduces the
meaning of Being simply to an abstract term that can exist only
in man's mind stands outside this tradition. Second, man does
not begin his search from non-being but rather from an implicit
awareness of Being, and this is not acquired through abstraction
but is given to man. Third, whatever the implicit meaning of
Being may be, it cannot be defined,[4] since it is most primordial.
Fourth, man must seek to make explicit the notion of Being, not
by sheer conceptualization and abstraction, but through "intuition" and in the light of illumination.[5]

One of the fundamental presuppositions of Ibn Sina is the
implicit assumption of his ontology that there is a correspon-
dence between the transcendent Being in reality and being as
the transcendental concept. On the one had, Being in reality
which transcends all beings is intelligible in itself, since its
origin is Thought Thinking Thought. On the other hand, Being is
the first transcendental concept, which transcends all concepts

and comes into man's intellect as the root of his intelligibility. Being in the objective world of reality is the most real and so the most intelligible, which gives reality and meaning to all other beings. Being, in the subjective world of man, is the most universal and so the most intelligible idea which gives reality and meaning to all other concepts.

Since every true concept corresponds to a real being, the hope of man is to reach an understanding of the transcendental concept of Being which would mirror the real transcendent Being in reality. Man can accomplish this task, only because he is a bridge between the objective world of reality, since he is a being in the world, and the subjective world of intellection, since he is in the possession of his own intellect. Man must seek to make explicit the implicit notion of Being so that he may realize The Pure Being of God, which is Thought Thinking Thought.[6] Although Ibn Sina never loses sight of conceptualization and argumentation, in his more esoteric writings[7] he not only points to the limitations of logic but emphasizes the utmost importance of "intuition" which comes from the Divine Illumination through the Agent Intellect.

According to Ibn Sina, in the light of two fundamental logical notions that man's intellect acquires without any inference, namely, "necessary" and "possible," man realizes the meaning attached to the Necessary Being and the Possible Being.[8] Being, in the fullest sense, refers to the Necessary Being or God. Therefore, once the meaning of God as the Necessary Being in and through itself is understood, then its denial involves a necessary contradiction.[9] Thus, in the fullest sense, Being, the first transcendental concept, refers only to the Necessary Being in itself, which transcends all beings. Now insofar as Being represents the being of a created world, namely, the possible being, whether it be necessary through another or possible in and through itself it points not only to the emanation of God in the possible world, but also the presence of the meaning of Being in every possible concept.

On this level, on which the term Being is applied for ten categories, one substance and nine accidents, Ibn Sina warns us against the view that Being is simply a name which, not on the basis of one meaning, is shared by ten categories. For if this were the case, then the meaning of "substance is" would be the same as "this is a substance," and to assert that "substance is" would be the same as "substance substance," which are absurd consequences. If Being would not be used for ten categories, according to one meaning, then we would have ten meanings of being and then ten meanings of nothing, which is absurd, since we would not be able to say that an entity either is or is not.[10]

Then Ibn Sina tells us that Being is not a genus because, unlike a genus which is applied equally to all of its species, the meaning of Being in the created world refers first to a substance and secondly, to accidents; and in the realm of accidents, first to quality and quantity and secondly, to other more dependent accidents.

Molavi, however, does not quite agree with the parallel hierarchy of beings and concepts in Ibn Sina's ontology, where Being as reality transcends all beings and Being as "Idea" is the first transcendental over all concepts. Molavi has no quarrel with Being as reality. He agrees with Ibn Sina that Being, insofar as it points to Reality in its most primordial sense, refers to God. Being in itself is God, and God in Himself is Being.[11] But Molavi disagrees with Ibn Sina on three accounts: First of all, Molavi denies the possibility of man ever having a concept that may mirror God.[12] Of course, there is no disagreement between the two thinkers as to the impossibility of a finite being such as man ever being able to perceive The Infinity.[13] Molavi opposes Ibn Sina's construction of a positive notion of the Necessary Being in itself, which though, it transcends all of our concepts, yet as the first transcendental, can reflect God. Molavi insists that any true awareness of God, which is mystical in its nature, is by no means bound either to an ordinary or a transcendental concept. Man possesses no concept of God, since God is understood in terms of "The Vision" which provides no ground for an image or a direct rational concept. Man becomes aware of God in terms of what we may call Beyong Being--a Pure Non-Conceptual Vision of Truth--that only "The Great Silence" can communicate.[14] Second, based on the denial of the positive concept of God, Molavi disagrees with Ibn Sina that the discursive philosophy, by its very nature, can gain any Divine Insight. Of course, Molavi takes the discursive philosophy to be nothing but a system of rational construction founded on a limited tool called logic which, in fact, is taken to be a barrier against the true vision.

Molavi's objection at this point, which appears a number of times in *Masnavi*,[15] is quite unfair and misleading since, as we indicated before, Ibn Sina's metaphysics is so related to the esoteric ontology that by no means can it be reduced to a simple logical system. In the theology of *Isharat va Tanbihat*,[16] Ibn Sina claims that there are two different, yet related, channels to truth. One is "The Discursive Method," which provides a system of knowledge, and the other "The Intuitive Method," which provides the vision of Truth. Ibn Sina points to the beginning and the end of human knowledge as the sphere of "intuition," which implies that although logic is used, its application is limited to a sphere between two realms of "intuition." Yet in a rare occasion in *Danishnamah-i 'Ala'i*[17] he asserts that all knowledge is first found by "intuition" and that the discursive method is limited to teaching. Thus, he admits not only the possibility but even the actuality of a mystical knowledge when all is seen through "intuition."[18] Also, the language of *The Recital of Bird* bears witness that when it comes to the vision of Truth, man acquires a different mode of consciousness.[19] On the basis of these remarks, it seems that Molavi has misunderstood Ibn Sina's philosophy by reducing the system to the surface of *Shifa*; yet it is fair to note that the difference between the two thinkers still remains, since Molavi totally denies the value of any discursive thinking and asserts that only Intuition provides us with the vision of God. Third, Molavi, unlike Ibn Sina, applies to the world a paradoxical statement, namely, that on the one hand, the world is real insofar as only God is Real.

It seems that what Ibn Sina conceives about the notion of "Matter" Molavi applies to the created world. "The Prime Matter for Ibn Sina is not nothing but a 'negative potentiality' that possesses no form."[20] This, of course, leads to two basic problems: First of all, how can God create what possesses no form? Second, since creation is understood as the outcome of God's knowledge, how can God know that which has no actuality? Whatever the possible solutions to these unsolvable problems may be, it is clear that "the Prime Matter" is so far removed from the Divine emanation that one may say that it possesses no being.[21] Molavi, who does not believe in the Aristotelian notion of matter,[22] applies a similar paradox to the created world, namely, that when it is taken to be Being, then God is Beyond Being, and when God is seen as true reality, then the world, though it is the manifestation of God, possesses no being of its own; and in truth, the world qua world is Nothing.[23]

In order to grasp Molavi's understanding of God, we must focus our attention on the notion of the Absolute. The Absolute, by definition, is the unconditional reality that conditions all reality since it transcends Being, and so we may call it Beyond Being. In its "ultimateness" it stands above the logical, the epistemological, and the existential dichotomy of subject and object. The unconditional Absolute, by virtue of being the Absolute, can neither be considered an object nor a subject. The Absolute is not an object, since it is not a non-reflective entity. The Absolute is not a subject, since for every subject there is an object that stands outside of its realm, whereas the Absolute is such that none can stand outside of its sphere.

In truth, the Absolute encompasses the subject and the object, Being and non-Being. The Absolute, on the one hand, is above the subject and object dichotomy and, therefore, cannot be approached either as an object or a subject; on the other hand, the Absolute is so close both to the object and the subject that "knows" them qua object and qua subject through "love." This is because, although the Absolute in itself is beyond and beyond, owing to its ultimate desire to be known through love, it manifests Itself, which constitutes the world of subject and object dichotomy. The world is a mirror that reflects God implicitly whereas man in the world is a polished mirror that reflects upon this reflection and becomes the explicit mirror of God.

Since without man the world is nothing but an unpolished mirror; then we may say that without man the world cannot love God. Man then not only completes "the circle of existential manifestation," but by loving God, gives meaning to the world. Because nothing stands outside of the Absolute, man as knowing God through love, is nothing but the highest manifestation of The Absolute Loving The Absolute.[24] Thus, Molavi rightly claims that through love as true union, all are absorbed by and through the Absolute. Therefore, the mystic can "see" that, in truth, there is no other reality but the Absolute.

For the sake of comparison, let us once again reflect on the fundamental notion of God in Molavi's mystical ontology and Ibn Sina's esoteric metaphysics. First of all, both thinkers agree that there is a reality named God who is the Absolute One. God is the Absolute because He stands above the object and subject dichotomy and, therefore, can be considered neither a thing nor a limited consciousness. The Absolute God is One because there is none like God. We must note at this point that although both Ibn Sina and Molavi make use of non-Platonic language concerning God, their notion of God cannot simply be identified with Plotinus. For Plotinus "The One" has no duality, and since knowledge implies the duality of the subject and the object, One is taken to be above thought, so that It cannot know itself or any other being.[25]

As we indicated before, Ibn Sina defines The Absolute as Thought Thinking Thought and Molavi, although he admits to the unmanifested simple Absolute which is totally present to Itself, claims that the Absolute in Its manifestation is thought which seeks to be known through Itself. This brings us to the first seed of disagreement, namely, when Ibn Sina uses the term "One" he means the absolute simplicity of God's unconditional reality, which necessitates that from "One" comes only "one." Molavi, however, has no quarrel with "the unconditional," since he also believes that, with the exception of man, none can condition God. But Molavi cannot admit to the absolute simplicity of God in the sense that Ibn Sina uses this rather complex terminology because, for Molavi, there are two dimensions of the Absolute, the not-manifested and the manifested.

When Molavi applies the term "One" to God, he means a non-composite being who encompasses all and through many reflects His oneness. In short, Molavi is not forced to assert the Greek idea that from One comes only one. Molavi believes that man as the image can condition God except insofar as He relates Himself to Himself through the manifest world. When it comes to the mystery of God's creation, Ibn Sina, based on two doctrines that from the pure One only one can come into being, and that from the pure Thought only thought can appear, asserts that from God the absolute Thought emanates a Separate intellect.[26] Ibn Sina describes the descending line of creative emanation which constitutes the world of many, primarily in terms of the dual aspects of the first intellect that, on the one hand, is aware of God and on the other hand is aware of itself. When the descent arrives at the tenth separate intellect, we are faced with the Agent intellect which, on the one hand, provides "Forms" to the sublunary world and, on the other hand, provides man with the intelligible forms which prepare the image of God for ascension.

Molavi, although through his poetry he points to the first intellect and the Universal Soul, never asserts a systematic model of creation and nowhere does he agree with the emanation of intellects from God. But he finds no difficulty in asserting that the world is nothing but the direct and the indirect manifestation of God and, in truth, that the world is nothing but God Manifested. This brings us to another crucial point of disagreement. Although both thinkers agree that the world is not created out of nothing,[27] Ibn Sina provides a theory of holy emanation that at least accounts for some degree of separateness of beings, whereas Molavi insists totally on the ontological togetherness of all beings. Ibn Sina's theory of holy emanation on the one hand claims that the Being of all beings is in the mind of God, since the first created intellect is nothing but an idea in God's Mind and also in *Isharat va Tanbihat*[28] insists upon "continuous creation," yet on the other hand points to the separateness of possible existential beings. But Molavi claims nothing but a continuous-all-encomassing-manifestation of God which constitutes the world as nothing but God manifested.

Ibn Sina and Molavi both agree that all of reality depends upon God, not only in its Being but also in its intelligibility. It is God the Absolute that must explain the possibility, the existence, and the intelligibility of the world and not the other way around.[29] They both agree that, owing to God's goodness, He loves man and, in turn, it is due to His love for man that He creates the world. Therefore, God is not the world and this is the meaning of Transcendence, which is described as Thought, or Thought Thinking Thought. But God is present in His Act and so He must be present in the world, and this is the meaning of immanence which is described as love, or Love Loving Love, Molavi, however, goes a leap further and claims that the world is nothing but the unity of the manifestation of God or God's unity manifested, which implies that the world has no reality of its own, and there is only One Being, namely, God.

University of Utah

    Salt Lake City, Utah

NOTES

1. *The Holy Quran*, Sura II, Ayat 30.
2. I*bid*., Sura II, Ayat 34.
3. *Ibid*., Sura XIX, Ayat 115.
4. Ibn Sina, *Danishnamah-i 'Ala'i* (Theology), ed. M. Mo'in, pp. 7-11.
5. Molavi, *Masnavi*, Tehran Edition, Bk. V, p. 428.
6. Ibn Sina, *Danishnamah-i 'Ala'i* (Theology), ed. M. Mo'in, p. 108.
7. Ibn Sina, *Danishnamah-i 'Ala'i* (Tabi'yat), ed. S.M. Mishkat, pp. 141-143.
8. Ibn Sina, *Isharat va Tanbihat* (Iranian Translation), p. 181.
9. Ibn Sina, *Najat* (Cairo, 1938), p. 224.
10. Ibn Sina, *Danishnamah-i 'Ala'i* (Theology), ed. M. Mo'in, pp. 36-77,
11. According to Molavi, "The Absolute Unity of Being" is the ground of the unity of vision.
12. When the spirit became lost in contemplation, it said this: "None but God has contemplated the beauty of God." *The Divana Shamsi Tabriz*, tr. R.A. Nicholson, Poem XXIII, p. 91.
13. Ibn Sina, *Risalah dar Haquiqat wa Kaifiyat-i Silsilah-Mawjudat*, pp. 4-6.
14. Molavi, *Masnavi*, Tehran Edition, Bk. IV, p. 377.
15. *Ibid*., Bk. I, p. 56.
16. Ibn Sina, *Isharat va Tanbihat* (Iranian Translation), pp. 247-257.
17. Ibn Sina, *Danishnamah-i 'Ala'i* (Tabi'yat), ed. S. M. Mishkat, pp. 141-143.
18. Ibn Sina, *Isharat va Tanbihat* (Iranian Translation), pp. 254-256.

19. "As God is my witness: it falls to your hidden being to appear, while it falls to your apparent being to disappear." *H. Corbin, Avicenna and the Visionary Recital,* tr. W. Trask, p. 187.

20. Ibn Sina, *Isharat va Tanbihat* (Iranian Translation), p. 101.

21. Ibn Sina, *Khutbat al-Gharra',* tr. K.M.K. Akhtar, "A Tract of Avicenna," *Islamic Culture* (Hyderabad-Daccan, 1935), Vol. 9, pp. 221-222.

22. According to Molavi, the so-called material world is constituted by unlimited particles that in some sense can see the Absolute Truth. "Air, earth, water and fire are worshippers. To us they are dead but to God they are alive." Tehran Edition, Bk. I, p. 23.

23. Q. Ghani, *Tarikh Tasawuf dar Islam,* p. 421.

24. "We are even as shadows, He is all who seek,
      Lo, by Him is spoken every word we speak!"
Molavi, *Divana-i Shams,* Tabriz Edition, p. 137.

25. Plotinus, *The Enneads,* Tr. S. MacKenna, Ennead VI, Tractate 9, Section 3.

26. Ibn Sina, *Danishnamah-i 'Ala'i* (Theology), ed. M. Mo'in, pp. 111-112.

27. In this respect they both have been accused by the orthodox theologians to be infidels. Ibn Sina strongly condemned such an impurtation in the following poem:
      "It is not so easy and trifling to call me a heretic
      No belief in religion is firmer than mine own
      I am the unique person in the whole world and if
            I am a heretic
      Then there is not a single Musulman anywhere in the world."
S.H. Barani, "Ibn Sina and Alberuni," *Avicenna Commemoration Volume,* p. 8.

28. Ibn Sina, *Isharat va Tanbihat* (Iranian Translation), p. 179.

29. *Ibid.,* p. 177.

COMMENT

On Bahram Jamalpur,
"Philosophy, Man and the Absolute God:
An Islamic Perspective"

FRANCIS KENNEDY

Dr. Jamalpur's paper makes a doubly significant contribution. First, he brings the very important element of a specifically Islamic strain of thought. In addition, he has chosen to focus on an area whose clarification is a vital pre-requisite to any discussion of God, the divine nature, our knowledge thereof, etc. The paper suggests to me a developed harmony between non-dualist Hindu concepts of *maya* and the position of Molavi that only God is real. I suspect that there is a rich vein of questions of historical fact and philosophical nuance which merits investigation.

The main point at issue in Dr. Jamalpur's paper is its contrast of two figures. One, Ibn Sina, or Avicenna, is closer to the ideal of the classical philosopher stressing the importance of discursive, rational approaches to human knowledge. He would, however, not deny an important role within his schema for intuition as a (necessary?) means if we are to know God--though that phrase, 'to know God' may be overly naive and misleading. The other figure in the paper, Molavi, would rule out conventional philosophical knowledge in the area of knowing God and rely instead on intuition or on its religious counterpart, mysticism. (For reasons of brevity, "intuition" and "mysticism" are used here with a greater degree of interchangeability than I could theoretically justify).

Each of the main figures in Dr. Jamalpur's paper thus points us to the very delicate question of the relationship between philosophy and mysticism especially when, as in this case, the mysticism is informed and shaped by a specific, well-defined, positive revelation. The question of this relationship is one which underlies much of the paper. Thus we read:

> In the beginning, religion based on revelation, science based on the study of the facts, mysticism based on intuitive illumination, and philosophy based on reason, were all unified in their search for Truth as it revealed itself on the human horizon.

The theory for such a unity is well expressed:

> God and man are so essentially related that, for us, the full understanding of one demands the full know-

ledge of the other. Man cannot know man if he does not know God; and man cannot know God if he does not know man.

The task which is laid before philosophy is almost an integral part of theology. Thus:

> the purpose of Islam . . . is to awaken man . . . so that . . . man can possess his unity with the whole creation, know himself, and finally love God for whom he has been created.
>
> . . . . .
>
> Therefore, the Muslim philosopher has one ultimate purpose in mind, namely to make explicit the mystery of the God-man relationship which is expressed so implicitly in the highly symbolic language of the Holy Quran.
>
> . . . . .
>
> But the real knowledge of man comes after the philosopher becomes aware of the divine reality and realizes the image of God.

What then is the place in philosophy of mysticism--or of intuition--bearing in mind the comment made above about their relationship?

I would like to sharpen this question with a few thoughts from Aquinas. In that tradition, philosophy has an important but limited--indeed, self-limiting--role to play. It can provide knowledge that God exists, offering also some content, however tentative, to the idea 'God'. It can show that God is an essential-- perhaps better, existential--point of reference for us as noted in one of the quotations from the paper. Philosophy would, however, locate the question of mysticism in the theological, i.e., non-philosophical, camp. It would say that mysticism--and revelation - is important, even hypothetically necessary (i.e. if we are to know God, then . . .), but *not* philosophical. Even the Augustinian tradition of Bonaventure, Roger Bacon, Henry of Ghent, even Scotus, while allowing more room for mysticism and revelation, would do so almost at the expense of philosophy. In the present context they might find themselves closer to Molavi than to Ibn Sina. There is, therefore, an a-symmetry present: philosophy needs, demands, a mystical/revealed/intuitional element, without being able to supply that need.

If I may be allowed to jump 800 years, we are essentially 'Hearers of the Word', to quote the title of one of Karl Rahner's early works. Our philosophical structure is such as to make us open to the gift of mysticism, or of revelation - *should that gift be offered.* Further than that philosophy cannot go. There is a void which is able--ought--to be filled by revelation, if revelation exists. Philosophy can at most show that revelation is not a self-contradictory idea. (There is, of course, a place for philosophy not in its own right but as a technique for explaining, elaborating etc. the data of revelation *once such data have been accepted as revealed.* That, however, is a separate question.)

From that position a philosophical position which *does* go further--which *does* seem to have a place for intuition, for mysticism--is of special interest.

The same question might might be posed briefly from a different angle, providing almost by a counter-argument an indication of the fundamental importance to Western thought of the philosophy/mysticism, philosophy/revelation separation. Is Heidegger right to claim that Western philosophy has forgotten Being? Is it the case that Western philosophy has shunted Being, or the knowledge of Being, off to the area of mysticism and theology, as opposed to the area of philosophy? If so, is the undoubtedly mystical atmosphere of at least his later writings a sign that his proposed de-struction of Western metaphysics is having more positive results than some of his critics allow?

St. Peter's College

Glasgow, Scotland

PART III

ORIGIN AND THEOPHANY

CHAPTER X

ORIGIN: CREATION AND EMANATION

RICHARD V. DeSMET

THE NOTION OF ORIGIN

For the scientist the notion of origin designates the state of affairs which conditions the arising of a new phenomenon. It implies not only the general disposition of the universe and its material energy at the initial moment of this arising, but more properly the immediate antecedents, conditions, factors and the decisive instant of the change which initiates that phenomenon. The arising of the latter is an event--*eventus*--an observable novelty, but within a basic continuity of matter and time and becoming generally considered as evolutionary. Such an origination is specific, not universal; and relative, not absolute. Even if the scientist seeks the origin of the whole universe, he can only seek it through a mental journey backwards toward a primary state of matter--as extremely condensed energy, for instance--beyond which he can, nevertheless, assume a prior, though undeterminable, state of the same matter.

The metaphysician, on the contrary, undertakes a more radical investigation concerning the very being of the universe and all its components, including matter itself in any of its states. How is it that there exists a universe rather than no universe? This question is forced upon him by the general contingency of all the existents which through their connections make up the universe. Whether our universe has a first instant or is beginningless in its duration--alternatives which both boggle our imagination--it ever appears unable to account for its existence. Hence, we are presented with the question, not of its temporal, but of its ontological origin. This question is not to be answered through a backward journey in time but through an ecstasis in the etymological sense of the term, a reaching of the mind beyond itself and the whole universe towards a Reality which cannot be less than Being itself (*Esse, Sat*), Self-existent and Self-communicative. This is generally designated as God or the Absolute--the *Brahman* of Vedanta. My purpose here is not to prove its existence but to speak as correctly as possible of the origination of our universe from this Absolute.

THE NEED FOR LAKSHANA OR ANALOGY

In all matters regarding the Absolute, language must be adapted and appropriated to a difficult task. Our everyday language is shaped by our experience of the relative which it normally endeavours to express. But besides its power of expressing, it possesses various capacities of evoking, alluding to, indicating, conveying or even signifying indirectly, yet correctly enough, what it does not or cannot express directly. In India, its power of indirect signification or indication is called *lakshgnaâ* (distinct from *lakshana*: definition or characteristic mark). Of the three chief types of *lakshanâ* the one directly useful to the metaphysician is the *jahad-ajahal-lakshanâ* which corresponds closely to the *intrinsic analogy* of the Christian Schoolmen which itself originates in Aristotle and Pseudo-Dionysius. It permits making sense of theological language or God-talk.

For instance, when Shankara or some of his disciples explain that "*Satyam jñânam-anantam*" (*Taittirîya Upaniṣad*, 2,1) is a valid definition of Brahman, they use that *lakshanâ* and display its process. The sentence means that the Absolute is Reality-Knowledge-Infinite. The pupil who naively understands the first term *Satyam* (Reality) in its primary and expressive meaning as 'concrete material substance' such as solid earth is told that he must correct this misleading superimposition (*adhyâsa*) since the second term *Jñânam* (Knowledge) immediately negates it. Similarly his primary understanding of *Jñânam* (Knowledge) as a contingent activity or quality of the knower is to be corrected because the third term *Anantam* (Infinite) debars such an understanding. *Jñânam*, says Shankara, must be infinitised on the basis of the pure root *jña* (know), not of any of its derivatives The Absolute is not infinite Knowledge, Know-ing or Know-er, but pure Know in the most elevated sense. And it is similarly *paramârthatah Sat*, i.e., Being in the supreme sense of the term. Here he uses the participle *sat* (be-ing) instead of the verbal root *as* because of an exigency of his Sanskrit language, but his intention is similar to that of St. Thomas Aquinas when the latter says that God is eminently *Esse* (Be). Although two terms are used, their infinitisation implies that they merge in identity without, however, losing their *svârtha*, the positive meaning of their roots, as Shankara is careful to point out. Thus their *lakshanâ* is intrinsic analogy and the divine Absolute which they define as infinite Be and Know is yet simple (*akhanda*, undivided, incomplex). This example shows how in all theological topics our mind must and can transcend the anthropomorphism innate to language through a processing in three steps: *adhyâsa*, superimposition; *apavâda*, negation, removal of all limitations; and *paramârthâpatti*, assumption of the supreme sense which alone is consistent with Absoluteness.

APPLICATION TO THE NOTION OF CREATION

Let us now start from an 'adhyâsic' assertion of divine

creation, such as we find in the *Upanishads* or elsewhere. 'Brahman is the Root of the world' or 'Brahman is that omniscient, omnipotent Cause from which proceed the origin, subsistence and dissolution of this world' or 'God is the Creator of all things, visible and invisible' or 'Consider the heaven and the earth and all that they contain; know that God has made all that from nothing and that the race of men is born in the same manner.' All such formulations affirm that the one God, the Absolute, is the unique intelligent Source or Cause of the totality and entirety of all other beings. But the terms they are made of are liable to many misinterpretations and a decantation of their anthropomorphism is to be effected by the metaphysician.

Hence, we come to a negative definition of creation, such as the classical one formulated by Aquinas: Creation means a production of reality out of nothing of itself or of any matter (*productio rei ex nihilo sui et materiae*). This will be elaborated and completed presently.

Provided this purification is complete, the mind is ready to climb up to the level of eminence (the Dioysian *Hyperochê* or Shankarian *paramârthâpatti*) and to say, for instance, with Aquinas: Creation is the emanation of the whole universe by and from the universal Cause (*emanatio totius universi a causa universali*).

THE STEP OF PURIFICATION THROUGH NEGATIONS (APAVĀDA)

All models of production fail to give us an adequate support of representation for the idea of creation. Creation is unique and transcends them all. Like God himself, it pertains to no genus. Hence, we have to ascend to it by way of negations (*apophasis, apavâda*). In order to reconcile the two ideas of 'divine' and 'production' we have to eliminate the ordinary connections of 'production' with either pre-existing object or pre-existing matter or pre-existing time, with necessity or want, with transformation and instruments of transformation, with mutability of the creator or his self-improvement, and with relationship that would be a reality in the Creator.

No Independent Pre-existence of the Created

Let us, first, eliminate the weak sense of 'production' as 'mere manifestation'. It does not arise from a state of latency, dormancy or concealedness, but from its own antecedent absence (*prâg-abhâvât*), for it has no independent pre-existence; it never exists except as divinely produced.

Virtually, however, or, to use Shankara's terminology, as still undifferentiated, it pre-exists in the power of its Cause, just as it is eternally known by it independently of its production. "And so," writes St. Thomas, "a creature as pre-existing in God is the divine Essence itself" (Et sic creatura in Deo est ipsa Essentia divina." *De Potentia*, III, 16, 24). This is an important application of the theory which the Indians call *sat-kârya-vâda*, namely, of the virtual pre-existence of an effect in the being of its cause. The statement of *Bhagavadgîtâ*, ii, 16: *Nâsate vidyate bhâvah* (out of nothing, no thing can arise) is true for an Aquinas or a Bergson as much as for the Indian schoolmen.

No Pre-existence of the Matter of the Created

Unlike any production of nature or man, creation neither needs nor presupposes any pre-existing matter or other constitutive element. This is due to its character of total origination. Neither is there a pool of pre-existing forms from which the creator would draw. What is created is the universe of existents in which and with which their matter is co-created as well as any other possible constituent. Whether matter is energy or something else should not concern us here. What counts is the realization that the totality of the universe derives immediately from the Creator.

This ontological origination of all finite existents *qua* beings does not preclude the temporal originations that take place within the becoming of the universe. Matter is the permanent stuff of all transformations and generations. This prime matter is an ubiquitous component of the beings of the material universe and never a distinct and complete existent apart from them. As a component it is not the term of any special creation, but shares in the ontological origination of the material existents of the universe.

A question raised in Vedânta philosophy is whether the Absolute itself is not the material cause of the universe. The term used is *upâdâna* which may be rendered etymologically as 'subdatum' (*upa+a+dâna*). It is indicated by the ablative case '*yatah*' and is thus the 'whence' of the effect, that 'from which' the effect derives its substantial reality. On the level of material transformations, that 'whence' is a material stuff, for instance, clay in jars or steel in scissors, etc. On the basis of such examples, some Indian systems have assumed the existence of an eternal stuff, the *Pradhâna* or *Prakrti* of the Sâmkhya system or the primordial atoms (*paramânu*) of Vaiśeṣika, as the *upâdâna* of the universe. Nevertheless, the denotation of the word *upâdâna* transcends such specific meanings. That which provides the substantial reality of effects need not be a material cause. In Vedanta, it is the Brahman-Âtman which is said to be the *upâdâna* of the universe and this Brahman is surely not material since it is Spirit (*Cit*) or pure 'Know' (*Jña*) as we have seen earlier. If it were the material cause or stuff of the universe, it would have to produce it through self-mutation (*parinâna*) or atomic vibration, but any such process is excluded from the Absolute. Yet, as its total Source, it is its immanent and reality-giving Cause, i.e., its *Upâdâna*.

Some quotations from Shankara will throw further light on this problem. The causation of the world presupposes "no independent matter, unreducible to the Âtman, such as the Pradhâna of the Sâmkhyas or the primordial atoms of Kanâda" (*Aitareya Upaniṣad Bhâsya*, 1,1,1). "What the *Shruti* calls *ajâ*, i.e., the causal matter of the four classes of beings, has itself sprung from the highest Lord" (*Vedânta Sûtra Bhâsya*, i,4,9). Brahman alone is "that from whence these beings are born," i.e., their *upâdâna*, as denoted by the ablative *yatah*; "there is no other substance from which the world could originate" (*Ibid.*, 1,4,23). But how can this divine *Upâdâna* provide the reality of the universe? Because, "in the beginning, before creation, when the differences of names-and-forms (*nâma-rûpa*, the specific essences) were not yet manifested, this world was but the one Âtman" (*Ait.Up.Bh.*, 1,1,1.). These *nâma-rûpas* pre-existed only "in the manner of something future" *bhâvisyena rûpena*), i.e., virtually, as effects to be pre-exist in the actual power of their cause. "These *nâma-rûpas*, which are identical with the Âtman in their unmanifested state, can become the causal elements (*upâdâna-bhûte*) of the manifested universe. Hence, it is not incongruous to say that the omniscient (Âtman) creates the universe by virtue of his oneness with causal elements, namely, names-and-forms, which are identical with himself" (*Ibid.*, 1,1,2). Their manifestation, however, does not mean that the partless Âtman undergoes a process of diversification: "the case is rather like that of a clever magician who, independent of any materials, transforms himself, as it were (*iva*), into a second man seemingly climbing into space" (*Ibid.*).

No Need of Instruments or Demiurge

Considering that the creative Power need not be applied upon a pre-existing material which it would have to shape, St. Thomas concludes that it needs no instruments. Similarly, Shankara asserts that "the absolutely complete power of Brahman does not require to be supplemented by any extraneous help" (*Ved.S.Bh.*, 2,1,24).

The same reason rules out any demiurge. A demiurge might be required for the function of shaping up, structuring, ordaining and governing the universe according to an intelligible pattern, in the same way as man in his works generally imposes his own plan upon the materials he uses. The Nyâya system which assumes the independent existence of the materials of the world posits a divine Lord to fulfill universally this role of patterning agent or *nimitta-kârana*. It is thus a dualism (*dvaita*) which accepts two distinct causes of the world, a material *upâdâna* and a lordly *nimitta-kârana*. But Shankara, who upholds a strict non-dualism (*advaita*), holds that the one Brahman which is the non-material *upâdâna* of the world "is at the same time its *mimitta-kârana* because outside Brahman as substantial Cause there is no other ruling principle for the *Shruti* says that prior to creation Brahman was one only without a second" (*Ibid.*, 1,4, 23.). It can pattern the world intelligently, being Intelligence itself; indeed "its high Power is revealed as manifold, as inherent, acting as force *and knowledge*" (*Ibid.*, 2,1,24).

No Need of a Temporal Beginning of Creation

Creation-talk is spontaneously mixed up with the notion of a first instant of the universe. But 'ontological origination' does not by itself imply 'temporal beginning' even if the reverse is true. Duration is a property of being; it denotes the 'unity of active existence' of a being. In God, it is eternity which is the strict unity of his perfect active existence. In mutable beings, it is time which is the relaxed unity of their imperfect and developing existence; every such being has its own concrete time or duration. Universal time is rather an abstraction which serves the mathematical purpose of measuring the concrete durations of mutable beings and the concrete duration of the universe itself as the interrelated totality of such existents. It is this abstraction which seems to reign over and above creation and even to precede it. But concrete time is co-created with the universe since, being a property of its being, it does not precede it but rather follows from its essential mobility and evolving changeability. Whether it starts from a first instant or is beginningless depends entirely on the Creator's free decision and cannot be settle by any deductive process. This is the conclusion of St. Thomas in *Summa Theologica*, I, 46, 1.

The End of Creation Implies No Need or Desire in the Creator

Is it anthropomorphic to say that creation has an end, a purpose? Men's works are purposeful. Even a madman, Shankara remarks, does not act without some purpose. But can the Absolute have purposes? Would this not imply that it has desires and, hence, wants? But then it would no longer be the perfect Brahman, which is Bliss (*Ânanda*) and Peace (*Shânti*) because "all its desires are eternally realized."

An Indian distinction comes here to our help. That between

artha, goal, purpose, and *kāma-phala*, the fruit that accrues to the doer according to his desire (*kāma*) to satisfy a need which he feels. Creation is a *niskāma-karma*, a work prompted by no desire to satisfy a need of the Creator. But, being an intelligent work, it is not devoid of *artha* or purpose. Obviously, this purpose can only be the good of the creatures. It is *loka-samgraha*, the maintenance of the cohesion of the world, and more precisely the welfare and the final salvation of man (*Bh.Gîtâ Bh.*, iii, 24).

This assertion raises a problem. For Shankara, man's uppermost desire is to know the Brahman (*Brahma-jijñāsā*) not, however, through any inferior kind of knowledge for it is *avagati-paryanta*, i.e., it aspires after a knowledge which "culminates in comprehension." And this most blissful intuition can only be obtained by the grace of the Lord since this is asserted by the infallible *Shruti*. In the same way, a Christian like St. Thomas affirms that the deepest desire of man is for a blissful intuition of the divine essence itself and that this stands beyond the grasp of the natural power of his intellect though well within the reach of his desire and of his receptive capacity. It is at this point that St. Thomas articulates his teaching on divine grace and the possibility of a supernatural complementing of nature. His thesis of the natural desire of man's intellect for a beatific vision of God's very essence shows that the highest end of creation depends on the merciful liberality of the Creator. This gratuitous end will, even more than the lower but sufficient end which consists in *loka-samgraha*, bring about an extrinsic glory of God as the author of the final goodness of creation. But this, being extrinsic, will not accrue to him as an accidental adornment or self-accomplishment. Nothing,indeed, can be added to the eternal perfection of the Absolute.

As Participated Being, the Creature is Non-Being

Creation is the production of finite existents in the whole measure in which they are be-ings. Obviously, the Absolute cannot produce other Absolutes but only finite participations of itself. But what is the ontological weight and positivity of such be-ings? There are interpretations of Shankara's Vedanta which view it as an acosmism and attribute only illusory being to all effects. What is the verdict of Shankara himself?

Shankara uses the terms 'being' and 'non-being' on different levels which we may clarify with a judicious use of capital and small letters. On the level of ordinary language, creaturely effects and their Cause are beings (*sat*), are imbued with existence (*sattâ*). "Should any effect originate from nothing, then, even though perceived, it would be imbued with unreality; but this is not the case, hence, Brahman exists" (*Taittirī ya Up. Bh*, 2,6,1). Yet Brahman transcends so immensely its effects that compared to them it must be said to be non-being (*a-sat*). This consideration is the root of apophatism. But Brahman is not absolute Non-being (*atyanta Asat*) for it is non-being simply because it is absolute Being (*atyanta Sat*), i.e., Being is the supreme sense of the term (*paramā rthatah Sat*). And now we have to say that compared to it creatures are non-Being (*a-Sat*) although they are not absolute Non-being (*Asat*). They are, he says *Sad-Asad-vilaksana*, unable to be denoted by either *Sat* (Being) or *Asat* (Non-being) if those terms are taken in their supreme sense. This is the level of language on which Shankara's teaching moves generally because his centre of reference is the Absolute rather than the relative existent. He is a radical valuationist who measures everything to the absolute Value, the Brahman, and declares its unequality to it rather than the degree of its participation of it. This manner of thinking and speaking is legitimate but it has misled many into acosmistic interpretations of his doctrine.

In the West, a St. Thomas generally prefers the language of participation. A participated being is in its own deficient way what the absolute *Esse* is without any restrictions. This *Esse* or Being is not a logical genus but the ontological Reality of God. And its participations are not parts of that partless Reality, nor accidents, complements, explicitations or developments of it, nor in any way additive to it.

Shankara too considers the effects of creation as mere *upâdhis* (external affixes) of Brahman. An *upâdhi* is an external adjunct, like the mask of an actor or the clothes of a man which only seem to characterize them; it has only the appearance of a *vishesana*, i.e., of a real attribute. Thus all names-and-forms (*nâma-rûpa*) are but *upâdhis* and in no way affections of their Cause. But like any *upâdhi* they need the constant support of this total Cause which pervades (*vyâpin*) them most intimately without any loss of its unalterable transcendence. This is why they are comparable to magical illusions which do not affect the magician but depend entirely on his power, while the appearance of their independent subsistence is due to the spectator's ignorance. This comparison together with the concept of *upâdhi* do away with pantheism and preserve nevertheless the central notion of the creatures' total dependence on their Creator.

Creative Activity Is Not Additive to the Divine Essence

When man produces something he does it not only with the help of materials, instruments and so forth but also through an operation which is distinct from, and additive to, his substantial essence. This, however, is not due to the essential nature of causation, but only to the weakness of his power which prevents him from ever being the total cause of his effects. Causing as such only demands to be an ontological communication of the cause to the effect so that what makes us say that this is an effect, whether it be its external form, its internal structure or its substantial reality, derives from the being of its cause. It does not demand necessarily that the cause lose what it gives or that its causing be an operation additive to its own being. The higher the cause, the more independent and immune to change it is in the exercise of its power. The highest power is the power of intelligent volition which in its utmost degree can posit its term freely and without any self-alteration. Thus no other novelty is consequent upon divine volition but the ontological novelty of its effect.

The supreme Âtman, says Shankara, due to his "absolutely complete power" creates "like gods, etc., who, without availing themselves of any extraneous means, produce palaces, etc., *by their mere intention* which is effective in consequence of those beings' peculiar power" (*Ved. Sût. Bh.* 2,1,25). His creative volitions are not additive to, but identical with, his essence. Indeed, "how are they found in Brahman? As essentially Reality-Knowledge, and as pure in virtue of being their own âtman" (*Taitt. Up. Bh.*, 2,6,1). The distinction between creative volition and divine essence is not ontological but logical: it is by 'upâdhic', extrinsic, relation to its created term that this essence is to be thought of as creative volition.

THE POSITIVE AND ADEQUATE DEFINITION OF CREATION

After refining the gross notion of creation with the help of negations meant to clear away all anthropomorphic misconceptions, we can now with St. Thomas define creation adequately and eminently (*paramârthatah*) as the intelligent and free emanation of the whole reality or positivity of the universe from the pure *Esse* (cf. *Summa Theol.*, I, 45, 1).

The term 'emanation' comes from the Indo-European root *mad-*, to bubble, to flow; thus it means the flowing out as from a source. It is in this etymological sense that it is used here by St. Thomas. From the time of Leibniz, however, 'emanation' became associated with the diverse brands of pantheism to express a *necessary* flowing of the universe from an Absolute governed by an inner necessity of self-explication, self-development or self-realization. Whether this necessity is conceived as physical, 'vital,' or moral, pantheism destroys the simplicity of fullness and perfection of the subsistent Esse which it posits but

anthropomorphically; its divine Principle lacks the perfect transcendence of the Brahman-Âtman or the absolute God; and its
emanations lack the radical contingency of true creatures. It is,
therefore, in no pantheistic sense that the term 'emanation' is
to be understood in the above definition.

What emanates from the Creator is the whole reality or
positivity of the universe. This includes the existence and essence of each of its beings, their preservation, their activities
even of free-will, their finalistic gropings and development, the
evolution from inorganic matter unto life and from living species
unto man, the achievements of his cultures, etc. It includes
cosmic matter and spirits, time--whether beginningless or not--
space--whether limited or unlimited--the necessary and the contingent, the regularities of law and the coincidences of hazard.
Thus creation does not concern only the origins of finite existents, but as universal emanation it is also conservation, motion
and activation (by the *pravrtti-rahito pravartaka*, the Mover devoid of motion of *Ved.Sût.Bh.*, 2,2,2), providential governing and
finalisation.

But what about the negativities in the universe? These
cannot be the proper effects of the power of the one who is
pure Positivity, but arise only consequentially from the natures
of creatures: finiteness from their contingency; liability to physical evil such as harmful accidents, diseases, destruction or
death from the competitiveness of the immense plurality of
material existents within the one realm of matter where chance
encounters predominate; error from the imperfection of finite
intellects; and moral evils such as vices and sins from the imperfection of created free-wills. All these are tolerated rather
than willed by the Creator who can nevertheless accomplish the
end of creation and thus overcome its inherent deficiencies.

From the side of the creatures, creation is total ontological
dependence. This is a relation inherent in them and whose
ground is their very positive reality as emanating from God. According to St. Thomas's refined theory of relationship, this
relation is not logical only but real because its ground is intrinsic to the related; its reality is co-created with the creature. As
to Creatorship, its correlation, it is but a logical relation because it is not grounded in anything pertaining to the Creator
but is the same reality of his creatures which is extrinsic to
him. Thus these paired relationships are unreciprocal.

The name given by Shankara to the relation of the universe to Brahman is *tâdâtmya*, often translated as 'identity' but
rendered more correctly as 'having that *(tat)* as one's *âtman*'.
The term *âtman*, which is the reflexive pronoun, does not denote
here what we normally call the self but the substantial cause

(*upâdâna*) as internal to the effect, as in the expression 'the jar is *mr̥d-âtmaka*, i.e., is internally constituted of mud or clay.' In this expression, *âtman* does not connote intelligence but it generally does. The *tâdâtmya* of creatures is thus their ontological dependence on That (Brahman) as on their innermost and transcendent Cause. "It is an accepted principle, even in the world, that an effect is intimately dependent (*anuvidhâyin*) on its (substantial) cause" (*Br̥hadâranyaka Up. Bh.*, 1,5,14). This dependence imparts no reality to the cause but only to its effects for "as long as an effect subsists, it is impossible to assume the dissolution of its (substantial) cause, since on the dissolution of the latter the effect also cannot subsist. On the other hand, we may assume the continued existence of the cause although the effect is destroyed; for that is actually observed in the case of clay" (*Ved.Sû t.Bh.*, 2,3,14). Hence, that relation is not real in both terms. It is not reciprocal: "names-and-forms in all their states have Brahman alone as their Atman, but Brahman has not its Atman in them (i.e., *tâdâtmya* is not mutual). Since without this (Brahman) they simply do not exist, they are said to have their Atman in it (*tad-âtmaka*). And it is because of these two *upâdhis* or external adjuncts, (names-and-forms), that Brahman is related to all mundane activities" (*Taitt.Up.Bh.*, 2,6,1). This is another way of saying that the ground of 'creatorship' is found exclusively on the side of the creatures. This theory of *tâdâtmya* "does away with the independent (*svabhâvika*) existence of the embodied self . . . and of the world" (*Ved.Sût.Bh.*, 2,1,14). These are not simply different (*anyat*) from the Absolute since in their whole being they depend on it. "The creature," says St. Thomas, "is no part of the essence but its essence is from God" (*"non est ex essentia Dei sed est ex Deo essentia" Summ.Theol.*, I,41,3, 2). And Shankara: "the effect is non-different (*an-anyat*) from the Cause, i.e., is essenceless and absent apart from it" (*Ved. Sût.Bh.*, 2,1,14). Thus explained, the non-difference supplied by *tâdâtmya* does not eliminate distinction but stresses the ontological character of the creature's dependence as well as the Creature's transcendence. "If absolute equality were insisted on, the relation of cause and effect would be annihilated . . . , (a relation) which is based on the presence in the cause of an excellence (which is absent in the effect") (*Ibid.*, 2,1,6).

All these clarifications do not suppress the mystery of creation. Even on the level of eminence theological language remains apophatic. It points correctly to the realities it deals with but is unable to express them (*laksyate na tû-'cyate: Taitt. Up.Bh.*, 2,2). Because our experience knows of no exact parallels of creation, our metaphysical thinking about it can never reach the level of experiential language. But "all metaphysics worthy of the name tends to transcend itself into the deep silence of mystical realization" (Pierre Scheuer).

University of Poona and De Nobili College

Poona, India

COMMENT

On Richard V. DeSmet, S.J.,
"Origin: Creation and Emanation"

HUGO MEYNELL

If there is a set of basic truths about the nature of things
to be sought out by the metaphysician, it is surely immensely
significant that these two metaphysical traditions of East and
West, the Hindu and the Christian, should be so largely in a-
greement with one another. I myself have often felt that the
so-called 'acosmism' of Shankhara was a good deal less incompatible with the Christian doctrine of creation than might at
first sight appear. After all, as Professor De Smet brings out, it
is Christian belief that, in comparison with the fullness of being
of God, the being of creatures is mere shadow. As he puts it,
'as participated being, the creature is non-being.' Cannot the
doctrine that Brahman is the one reality be taken as one very
forceful way of affirming the metaphysical uniqueness of God,
which no Christian would be inclined to deny?

I have no doubt of the importance, and indeed would be
inclined to assent to the truth, of Professor De Smet's main
contentions. But there remains a complementary task to the one
that he has performed, namely, to clarify how one can justify
the whole line of argument, at least as something more significant than an exercise in the history of ideas. One thing that a
philosopher reared against the background of analytical philosophy will find remarkable about this paper is its easy way with
the question of whether metaphysics, or at least the kind of
metaphysics discussed in the paper, is itself a valid enterprise. I
agree with Professor De Smet that in fact it is; but, unlike him,
I find that I have to fight every step of the way to justify such
a position.

What kind of arguments are there against the whole enterprise of doing metaphysics, or at least this kind of metaphysics;
and how might one counter them? Among contemporary analytic
philosophers, the hostility, as I see it, has two roots and takes
two forms, the first of which was more popular thirty years
ago, the second of which tends to be in the ascendant now. The
first attacks metaphysical propositions on the ground that they
fail to meet the empiricist criterion of meaningfulness and truth.
All meaningful propositions, which are not true by virtue of the
meanings of their terms, must be such that the course of experience would at least tend to show that they are true or false.
Metaphysics fails to meet the criterion, and so must be ruled

out as nonsensical. It has by now been very widely accepted that the criterion of meaningfulness laid down in the last sentence but one is not only difficult, but in the nature of the case, impossible to form adequately. This, however, has not led to any large-scale rehabilitation of metaphysics.

There is now another reason for its rejection. It is pointed out that language has normal contexts of use and application, in ordinary human interaction, and in special and determinate areas like those of scientific inquiry and religious devotion. Those very general questions about the nature of reality, and the rest of it, asked by the metaphysician, involve language 'gone on holiday', out of its normal place of work, and hence not to be taken as significant.

More recently, in the last decade or so, a third view has been gaining ground, which is frankly metaphysical in one sense, though it negates most of the propositions which were defended by the proponents of traditional metaphysics. Kant said that the three great questions of metaphysics were those of God, freedom and immortality; the new materialism of Smart, Armstrong and Quinton entails the denial of all three.

Here are three distinct positions, all maintained by philosophers influential in contemporary English-speaking philosophy, all hostile to traditional metaphysics. How can the defender of traditional metaphysics fight back?

To follow Professor De Smet, in distinguishing radically between the methods of metaphysics and those of science, at this point, would be to play into the hands of those who reject metaphysics. They would simply regard this as confirmation of the thesis that the sciences constitute a valid way of attaining knowledge of the world, metaphysics not. Thus, though by no means contradicting what Professor De Smet says about the matter, I would prefer to stress the similarity and continuity between the two types of inquiry. All knowledge, whether that of the scientist or the metaphysician or of anyone else, derives from that wonder about the nature of things alluded to by Aristotle. The scientist achieves the knowledge proper to his craft by propounding and testing hypotheses against evidence available in experience. Could one not say that the metaphysician achieves his knowledge, if any, by reflecting on the fact that the world is nothing other than what human beings can come to know in the way exemplified by the achievements of science? One can wonder about the things and facts of experience, and in time come by scientific knowledge; one can also wonder about the overall nature of a world which is such that one can thus come to know about it, and in time perhaps come by metaphysical knowledge. And this does not seem to be too far from the kind of thing which is actually done by traditional metaphysicians. Thomas Aquinas distinguishes sharply between essence and existence, between, as one might put it, the '*how* they are' and the '*that* they are' of things. Is this not precisely what is assumed in effect by the natural scientist who propounds various accounts of *how* things may be in his hypotheses, and determines by observation or experiment *that* one of the hypotheses is probably the case?

Let us consider once again our three grounds of hostility to traditional metaphysics. I remarked on the apparent failure of the empiricist criterion of meaning; the reason for this is worth summarizing. There is no coherent formulation of it which is not self-destructive. There is no experience which tends to verify or falsify the proposition that all meaningful contingent propositions are such that they tend to be verified or falsified in experience. But if *that* ground for the attack on traditional metaphysics can be stigmatized as self-destructive, the second one I mentioned can be reproached as arbitrary or obscurantist. Why should questions about the general nature of things *not* be asked? Does not the practice of science itself presuppose a certain answer to them? And is not the validity of moral, religious, and political viewpoints simply left hanging in the air unless there can be invoked some independent principles of rational criticism, which do not simply assume the truth of this or that moral, political or religious view *a priori*? At least radical empiricism, for all that its criteria of meaning break down, seems to have been right in its attempt to provide some overall view of the nature of truth and rationality; short of doing that there seems no escape from arbitrariness and dogmatism.

This last point is taken by the third view. Upholders of this view state or assume that there *are* overall principles of rational investigation which issue in a general account of the nature of things, in other words in a metaphysics, but that this metaphysics or general account of the nature of things is materialist and has atheism as a consequence. It is worth emphasizing that this view assumes the falsity of the other two, both that based on the empiricist criterion of meaning, and that based on the linguistic *status quo*. The view that there is a single more or less coherent body of thought called 'modern philosophy'which is able to articulate clear principles destructive of traditional metaphysics and of theism, for all that it is put about by some professional philosophers, is quite chimerical. There are, to be sure, many widely-shared prejudices; but that is another matter.

When confronted by this third position, the apologist for traditional metaphysics has old but effective arguments against materialism, brilliantly deployed by such thinkers as Berkeley and Hegel. According to the scientific materialist, there is a real world revealed by scientific theory of which the sensible world of everyday is a mere appearance. But the world which transcends sensation is every bit as much a mental construction of the scientific theorist as the world of sensation is conditioned by the organs of human perceivers. The traditional metaphysician will agree with the scientific materialist as to the reality of the world postulated by the scientific theorist, but he will be impressed with the force of the idealists' retort that it is a mental construction. The synthesis of the materialist thesis, and the idealist antithesis, seems to be that the world is indeed a mental construction, but not *our* mental constitution. This, of course, heads straight to theism.

Do we have any model for understanding the state of affairs of the universe as it appears to scientific investigation, namely, an intelligible state of affairs which *is* the case, but which does not *have* to be the case; which is, in the traditional jargon, contingent rather than necessary? It happens that we do, and it is in human agency. It is of the essence of human agency that one may conceive a range of states of affairs which are within one's power, and will that one among them be implemented. God is deemed to be that which is related to the whole contingent universe, in much the same way as the human subject is to his actions and products. Even if the soul or *atman* is not identical with God or *Brahman*, it is, as Christian and Hindu metaphysicians have both recognised, our best model for knowledge of God. What is, in fact, the case is only to be expected: systems of thought which purport to make nonsense of discourse about God effectively make nonsense of talk about human agency.

If it is God's will alone which determines which of the infinite range of possibilities is realized in the world, or whether any of the possibilities is realized at all, it may easily be seen that a doctrine of creation, as opposed to emanation, must follow. Any need postulated in God to create at all, or to create this world rather than another, is in effect a conflation of the doctrine of creation with a doctrine of emanation. Creation follows strictly the analogy of free human action; emanation that of natural process. Professor De Smet has shown us the clear and forceful way in which Shankhara articulated this distinction.

Professor De Smet has presented us with an impressive East-West metaphysical consensus; my part has been, so to say, to defend his flank, by attacking positions from which it may be inferred that all such metaphysics is unfounded. I have suggested that limitations of human inquiry to exclude metaphysics in principle are prone to be either self-destructive (radical empiricism) or arbitrary and obscurantist (the philosophy of ordinary language); and that the revived metaphysics of materialism overlooks the consequences of the fact that the human mind acquires knowledge in the way that it does. The path is left open for a general account of the nature of reality which can be fully explained only as due to an intelligent will which, to quote Thomas Aquinas, 'all call God.'

University of Calgary

    Calgary, Alberta, Canada

CHAPTER XI

HARMONY IN NATURE AND MAN

EWERT H. COUSINS

To open the exploration of my topic, I would like to anchor myself in a classic text which expresses in a quintessential fashion the relation between God and harmony in nature and man. I believe I can make no better choice than the last canto of Dante's *Divina Commedia*, for it captures in poetic form some of the most profound metaphysical and mystical insights into harmony. The *Commedia* is, in many respects, a *summa* of Western thought, integrating classical and medieval culture and foreshadowing the Renaissance. Although our cosmology has changed since the 14th century, Dante's insights penetrate to a universal level and illumine the issues of harmony as we encounter them today. In his journey through inferno, purgatorio and paradiso, Dante marvels at the harmonies of the Ptolemaic universe, the progress of history and the stages of the soul's ascent into God. And he anguishes over the lack of harmony in his own city of Florence, in the human community at large, in the crimes of individuals and in his own struggle for virtue. With the aid of his guides--Vergil, Beatrice and Bernard of Clairvaux--Dante comes progressively to understand the patterns of harmony that integrate love and justice, desire and will, life and death, multiplicity and unity, the divine and the human.

Finally in Canto xxxiii of the Paradiso, when Dante has reached the summit of his journey, he is given a vision of three modes of harmony at the very heart of reality. Here the multiplicity of created forms in the universe is reconciled with unity in the divine mind; divine opposites are reconciled within the divinity; man is reconciled with God and harmonized within himself and with the universe. In the first of these harmonies Dante sees reconciled the multiplicity of creation with unity and simultaneously creation reconciled with the Creator. When Dante gazes upon God's infinite goodness, he exclaims:

> O abounding grace, by which I dared to fix my look on the Eternal Light so long that I spent all my sight upon it! In its depths I saw that it contained, bound by love in one volume, that which is scattered in leaves through the universe, substances and accidents and their relations as it were fused together in such a way that what I tell of is a simple light. I think I saw the universal form of this complex, because in telling of it I feel my joy expand.[1]

Dante here echoes a long metaphysical tradition that sees the unity of all things in the divine mind. In the depth of the divinity he perceives the ultimate harmony of the universe: "the universal form of this complex." All the disharmonies he had encountered in his journey are resolved in a higher divine harmony such that creation appears as a book whose meaning is now clear, for he sees precisely how it expresses God.

In the divine light Dante is given a further vision, this time of the harmonies within the divinity:

> In the profound and clear ground of the lofty light appeared to me three circles of three colours and of the same extent, and the one seemed reflected by the other as rainbow by rainbow, and the third seemed fire breathed forth equally from the one and the other . . . O Light Eternal, that alone abidest in Thyself, alone knowest Thyself and knowing, lovest and smilest on Thyself![2]

For Dante, the Christian, this is a vision of the Trinity, in which the unity of the divine nature is harmonized with the diversity of persons. As we will see later, this vision reflects a more universal metaphysical tradition in which divine opposites are harmonized: the divine ground with divine dynamism, the divine being with divine knowledge, divine justice with divine love. This balance of opposites within the inner realm of the divinity is the basis for all harmony in the universe.

One would think that Dante, after having penetrated into the harmonies of the universe and the divinity, would have completed his journey. But there still remains another harmony to be grasped: namely, the relation of man to the divinity. While gazing upon the divine light, Dante sees that it takes on human form: as Dante says, "painted with our image."

> That circling which, thus begotten, appeared in Thee as reflected light, when my eyes dwelt on it for a time, seemed to me, within it and in its own color, painted with our likeness, for which my sight was wholly given to it. Like the geometer who sets all his mind to the squaring of the circle and for all his thinking does not discover the principle he needs, such was I at that strange sight. I wished to see how the image was fitted to the circle and how it has place there.[3]

Again Dante responds as a Christian, for the human form within the circling divine light is Christ, the God-man. However, this specifically Christian image reflects a larger metaphysical tradition that grounds the nature of man in his relation to the divinity. According to this tradition man is most in harmony with himself and the universe when he harmonizes himself at the depth of his being with God, who is his source, exemplar and goal. This is precisely how Dante concludes his *Commedia*. In wonder he "wished to see how the image was fitted to the circle," that is how man is harmonized with God. As he gazed, his mind was "smitten by a flash wherein came its wish"; the tensions within his own person were harmonized--those tensions of virtue and vice, of will and desire, so vividly depicted in the inferno and purgatorio. The *Commedia* closes with Dante's a-chievement of harmony within himself, with the universe and with God: "Now my desire and will, like a wheel that spins with even motion, were revolved by the Love that moves the sun and the other stars."[4]

With Dante's view of harmony as a background, I will explore the metaphysics of the harmony in nature and man in relation to God. I will touch the three types of harmony revealed in Dante's three visions at the close of the *Commedia*. However, I will not expound Dante's metaphysics but rather my own positions, for which I take full responsibility. On many essential points, I believe they agree with Dante and, as such, reflect major metaphysical currents in Western culture. There are influences from Plato, Aristotle, Plotinus, Augustine, Thomas, Bonaventure and Nicholas of Cusa; there are echoes from Renaissance philosophy and German idealism. Since my topic deals with cosmology, I will make specific references to the twentieth-century speculation of Whitehead and Teihard de Chardin. In this way my positions will reflect both classical and contemporary philosophy.

Like many of the thinkers who have influenced me, my metaphysical positions have been shaped by Christian belief, especially belief in the Trinity and the mediatorship of Christ. This will be reflected at times in my positions; however, on these points, I will attempt to focus towards universal metaphysical issues rather than towards the distinctive Christian belief. Although my metaphysical positions reflect Western philosophy, I will attempt in the latter part of my paper to reach out towards distinctive metaphysical traditions of Eastern culture.

The paper is organized by way of four theses. Each thesis and its development are designed to state a position and to offer some reasons, but will not attempt detailed or formal proofs. Since the topic is comprehensive--encompassing God, nature and man--I have chosen to deal comprehensively with it, rather than to draw out a specific point and explore this in depth and detail. However, there is an over-all unifying perspective: namely, exemplarism whereby harmonies in nature and man reflect God as their exemplar.

Thesis 1: A study of nature and man reveals patterns of harmony which in their deepest metaphysical components consist of a union of being, intelligibility and goodness. Both in individual beings and in the relation of beings to each other, this union can be seen as a coincidence of opposites.

If we examine individual beings, we can discern at their deepest ontological level the components of being, intelligibility and goodness. I am taking 'being' here not in a static sense of mere facticity of existence, by in a dynamic sense of the power of being. Each being has not only existence but the power to be what it can be. This power of being expresses itself in the form or intelligibility of the being. Correlative to the power of being, the intelligibility of being is also take in a dynamic sense; the intelligibility of the being is in a process of becoming. If the form is the adequate expression of its power of being, then the being possesses the goodness of internal proportion or harmony. The being is in harmony with itself. Of course, all beings possess this harmony to some extent, but some are more harmonious than others. In the case of man, whose power of being is open to extensive possibilities, there may be disharmony between his power of being and his self-expression of his possibilities. The components of power and intelligibility can be seen as opposites, that is, poles of being whose coincidence in an appropriate relationship produces harmony in the being.

If we proceed from an individual being to groups or clusters of beings, we can observe the same dynamic structure. Beings can be related harmoniously in many ways, not only internally, within themselves, but also externally in relation to other beings. In the realm of multiplicity, then, many combinations of order and harmony are possible. The power of being lodged in an individual being can coalesce with the power of another being and produce new patterns of intelligibility with concomitant goodness. Since the goodness in such patterns involves a proportion among the components, there is an aesthetic aspect to harmony. The patters of harmony that are observable in the universe are myriad and are studied extensively in mathematics, physics, chemistry, biology, sociology, ethics, history and the other disciplines. The long history of cosmologies--mythic, philosophical and scientific--gives witness to the desire of man to find larger patterns of order and harmony in the universe.

In a universe in process of becoming, with many patterns of harmony possible, the question of chance emerges. I hold that order is ontologically prior to chaos, harmony to disharmony;

hence order and harmony are not mere random emergences out of a sea of chaos or naked possibilities. Rather the power lodged in being is itself oriented to producing patterns of order and harmony. I am suggesting here an ultimate orientation in the universe such as is expressed in Whitehead's category of creativity.[5] Although the power of being is ultimately oriented to produce harmony, the possibilities of harmony are manifold. This is based on many factors, which include an internal spontaneity and capacity for novelty within the individual being, and a wide range of possibilities growing out of the interaction of many beings. Hence the process is open to a considerable range of randomness. Although I recognize a general thrust towards harmony in the universe, I wish to leave open the question of whether there is a single pattern of order for the universe as a whole, as is claimed by Teilhard de Chardin's evolutionary theory, or whether the process is open-ended, as claimed by Whitehead.[6]

Although I will deal with the problem of evil later, I wish to make an observation here. The goodness involved in harmony has many dimensions and can be viewed from many perspectives. What is harmonious for a being in one respect may be disharmonious in another. Although a certain food might be harmonious to one's appetite, it may be injurious to one's health. What is beneficial to one being in a harmonious relationship may be destructive to another in the same relationship. Our biological support system is a classic example of this discontinuity in harmonies. For example, higher forms of life must necessarily prey on lower forms for their biological nourishment and survival. A delicious meal is harmonious to the human, but destructive to the fish or steer that provided the main course. Alhough this is the case on the biological level, when we enter the human level, where persons are involved in complex relationships, the ideal of harmony here is the mutual enrichment of all persons in a harmonious relationship. This is the type of relationship which Teilhard de Chardin identifies as a union which differentiates,[7] a harmonious relationship in which the persons are mutually fulfilled. I believe that this is the highest form of harmony and can be seen as a dynamic coincidence of opposites of mutually affirming complementarity.

Thesis 2: These patterns of cosmic harmony are grounded in God as their cause, exemplar and goal. This manifests that the inner nature of God is constituted by a harmony of opposites, which is the ground and exemplar of harmonies in the universe.

The harmony in the universe must bve ontologically grounded in God. I base this assertion on several principles, each of which includes the other in some way: (1) the principle of causal dependence of contingent being on necessary being; (2) the principle of exemplarity, whereby finite perfections are expressions of the absolute perfections of God; (3) the principle of concretion or limitation, whereby God is the presupposition making possible the specification of perfection in finite form; and (4) the principle of finality whereby the orientation of beings toward their finite goals requires God as absolute good. I hold, therefore, that the cosmological approach to God is valid, in a generic way that would echo, for example, the Pseudo-Dionysius, Thomas, Bonaventure, Teilhard de Chardin and Whitehead. I am taking here the cosmological approach in a broader sense than a formal proof for God's existence, although I hold that such a proof is possible provided it be complemented by a psychological-epistemological and ontological approach. I do not wish to make the cosmological proof for God's existence the main focus of my paper, but rather to presuppose its generic validity and concentrate on the relation between the harmonies in the universe and God as their exemplary ground.

If God is required as the ground of cosmic harmonies, what kind of God is so required? What can we learn about the nature of God from the existence of harmonies in the universe? To assert that God is the exemplary ground of cosmic harmonies implies something about his very nature. He is by that fact primordial harmony, primordial order, primordial Logos. And as ground of harmony, he possesses harmony super-eminently; as ground of order, he possesses order super-eminently; as ground of intelligibility, he possesses intelligibility super-eminently. It is appropriate, then, to call his name Logos. As divine Logos, he possesses the perfections of harmony, order and intelligibility in an absolute way. He possesses these perfections not in part but in their fulness; and he possesses them not merely potentially, but actually. Thus he is pure, actualized Logos and not merely the potentiality of actualization, waiting upon the world to realize his actualization. In assigning to God pure actuality, I side with classical metaphysics in opposition to Whitehead.[8]

Consequently God is not the absence of Logos--merely the void, the abyss of being, the unactualized ground of all possibilities. Nor is he the negation of Logos--naked chaos, destructive, uncontrolled brute power. Although he is Logos, he is more than Logos. He is indeed the void, the abyss of being, the unactualized ground of all possibilities; and he is also power, but power which is creative, which out of the abyss of silence, comes to expression in Logos. I am here proposing a dipolar model of God, which is different from that of Whitehead and Hartshorne.[9] God is dipolar in himself not merely in relation to the world; he has a non-manifested pole and a manifested pole--both on the level of the divinity itself. These two poles are related according to a coincidence of opposites of mutually affirming complementarity. They are not in radical opposition, but mutually interpenetrate and affirm each other.[10]

Just as there is power, intelligibility and goodness in the harmony in the universe, so there is power, wisdom and goodness within the divinity. The poles of the divinity are harmoniously balanced: the non-manifested pole is balanced by the manifested pole. The power which brings the silence of the abyss to speech is balanced by its own adequate expression. The divine power of expression is boundless, and the actualized divine expression is equally boundless. The Logos is the adequate, harmonious expression of the primordial creative power. This means that within God there is a boundless harmony of opposites and hence the fulness of the goodness of harmony. In this way, not merely as Logos, but as dynamic process, God is the exemplaristic ground of all dynamic harmonies in the universe, as described in the previous thesis: whether these be the harmonies of power, intelligibility and goodness in individual beings or in clusters of beings.

The polarities in God which I have just described suggest the Christian theology of the Trinity, and reflect Dante's second vision of harmony, cited above. However, one need not see them as distinct differentiations within the inner life of God, namely, the persons of the Trinity, revealed to Christians through the life and work of Christ. The can also be seen as aspects of the divine nature: 'trinitarian principles' in Tillich's term, or 'appropriations' in the classicdal medieval theological tradition.[11] The metaphysical position which I am proposing here would place these divine polarities midway on a spectrum between the Christian Trinity and an emphatic affirmation of the divine simplicity which would see no ground for polarities within the divine life.

God is the fulness of harmony in two ways: in the Logos expresssion of the divine creative power and in the harmony of the dynamic expressive process. There is actualized, then, within God the fulness of dynamism, the fulness of self-diffusive expression, the fulness of harmony--and thus the fulness of actualized fecundity. This means that the divine fecundity is adequately actualized on the divine level--from all eternity to all eternity. God does not depend on the world in order to be dynamic, self-diffusive and actualized, as is the case in a standard interpretation of Hegel and in Whitehead's system. Although creation is indeed theophanic and the expression of the divinity in space and time, God does not need this external expression in order to be dynamic or actualized.

This is a crucial metaphysical issue, one which has been raised pointedly by Lovejoy in *The Great Chain of Being*.[12] How reconcile the fulness of God's perfection with the fulness of his self-diffusiveness? This is indeed an insurmountable problem if one requires the world for God's self-diffusion; for then creation becomes necessary and this world must be the best possible world, in which all possibilities are actualized. Such a view radically compromises God's transcendence and his freedom. If, however, as Lovejoy fails to take into account, the self-diffusion is seen not outside but inside the divinity, the problem is resolved.[13] The world is freed from bearing the impossible burden of actualizing the divine fecundity; and God is saved from collapsing into the world and having his boundless self-diffusiveness submerged in finite structures. Paradoxically it is the very transcendence of his self-expressiveness that makes authentic theophany possible. If God is transcendently dipolar in himself, the boundless harmony of his inner dynamic process makes possible all limited forms of harmony in the universe.

Thesis 3: Man achieves inner harmony by grounding himself in God as his source, exemplar and goal. This is also the ultimate root of his harmony with others and with the universe.

Following in the path of Dante, we have moved from the harmonies in the universe to God as their ground and exemplar. Like Dante we have then been drawn into the harmonies within the divinity--into the divine polarities which ultimately grounds the harmonies of the universe. And with Dante we now turn to search out our own image in God. Hopefully, we will see the divinity "painted with our likeness" and in this harmony of the divine and the human find the ultimate harmonizing of all inner and outer tensions so that like Dante we can be harmonized with "the Love that moves the sun and the other stars." For having been rooted in the power, intelligibility and goodness of God, we are harmonized within ourselves, with other men and with the universe.

Dante reaches this harmony only at the summit of his journey; he began in the terror of the dark forest where he had lost his way, and he proceeded through the horror of the inferno and up the purifying fountain of purgatorio. This implies that man begins in disharmony and must ascend to harmony: he must be transformed, rectified, re-oriented. In the metaphysical tradition that sees man as image of God, this means that man must turn again to that divine ground which is the root of his power, his meaning and his goodness. This implies a turning on man's part or a redeeming action from God--or a combination of the two.

Like all beings, man has the potential for harmony; but in a radical way this potential is thwarted and unrealized. He is immersed in the problem of evil, in finitude which limits his possibilities and in the very distortion of his power. Since he is finite, his power is fragile; his meager being is threatened by non-being; he is dizzied by an ontological vertigo. Yet while he stands on the brink of nothingness, he asserts his frail being in defiance and destructiveness. Instead of imaging his power in harmony, he produces disharmony and discord, chaos and meaninglessness; the proportion within his being is shattered and fragmented. This is the image of man that Vergil unveils to Dante as they journey through the inferno.

Man requires a metamorphosis, a radical re-centering by which his power is grounded in the divine power as his source, his form is grounded in the divine intelligibility as his exemplar and his goodness is grounded in the divine goodness as his goal. Although this grounding will reinstate harmony at the depths of his being and establish him in harmony with other men and with the universe, there still remain limits to the realization of this harmony. There is the diminishment of death that Teilhard has analyzed, and the limits to the realization of harmony that Whitehead has observed in a pluralistic universe. Although Teilhard optimistically saw increasing harmonies realized in time as evolution moves towards Omega, Whitehead saw that it was only in the consequent nature of God that harmonies could be realized beyond the perishing of the process.[14] Ultimately it is only in God that all limits of harmony are transcended; for he is the Harmony of harmonies--beyond all limit, beyond all perishing. Like Dante in his final vision, man can find his identity in God and can be drawn into that harmonizing "Love that moves the sun and the other stars."

Thesis 4: The principle of exemplarity can be extended into the non-manifested pole of the divinity, which will reveal a further level of harmony between the universe and God: between the non-being of finitude and the non-manifested pole of God. A clarification of this level can reveal a further harmony, by way of coincidence of opposites between Western and Eastern metaphysics.

It has been characteristic of a main thrust of Western metaphysics to see in the universe power, intelligibility and finality, and to see God as the ground of these components. This is the model of God and the universe I have explored above. It is possible, however, to plunge more deeply into the nature of God, exploring his non-manifested pole. We see here in his nonmanifested pole that he is the negation of the very components we have just affirmed: he is rest, not energy; silence, not speech; darkness, not light; non-being rather than being. However, these negations are of a distinctive type; they are not the absolute denial of their alternatives, but their opposite pole. The non-manifested pole of God is the rest out of which energy flows, the silence out of which speech emerges, the darkness out of which light shines, the non-being out of which being appears.

If God has a non-manifested pole, what is its significance for the universe? It has, I believe, great significance, which deserves more attention than it has been formally given in Western metaphysics. Does the non-being which interpenetrates the finite universe reflect exemplaristically the nonmanifested pole of God? I believe that it does, and as such is not so threatening as Western philosophers, especially existentialists, have at times surmised. For the non-being of finitude not merely negates the power and intelligibility of being but also participates in the positive reality of God's non-manifested pole.

Such a consideration calls for a re-examination of the doctrine of creation, whereby God makes the world out of nothing. What is this nothing? Is it merely the denial of the minimum reality of being? Or is it in some way God himself? In the exemplarism of the Logos pole of the divinity, one can claim that creatures exist virtually in God and even actually as divine ideas. In this sense we can say that creatures are made out of God, for they have a prior existence as archetypes in the divine mind. Since they have no prior external existence outside the divine mind, we can say that they are made also out of nothing. Thus creatures are made out of God and out of nothing. I would like to make a further suggestion here--that we reach a metaphysical point where we can make the following statement: Creatures are made out of the nothing which is God. That is out of the non-manifested pole of God which is prior even to the divine power and Logos. The very nothingness that surrounds creatures, in their externalized existence outside the divine mind, is itself ultimately rooted in God and the expression of his most profound dimension, his nonmanifested pole.

To see in the nothingness of creatures a reflection of the highest level of the divinity is to grasp an extraordinary coincidence of opposites. In the Logos traditions of Western thought matter stands at the lowest rung of the hierarchy of reality. Yet matter, as it approaches non-being, can reflect most penetratingly the loftiest pole of the divinity--what metaphysical mystics like the Pseudo-Dionysius and Meister Eckhart have called the nondifferentiated divinity and the Godhead above God.

These considerations suggest that Western metaphysicians might re-examine the Hindu notion of God as material cause of the universe and the Buddhist understanding of the relation of the phenomenal world to the Void. The coincidence of non-being in the universe and the non-manifested pole of the divinity might provide a meeting point for the West and the East--a point of harmony in metaphysics that would bring into a global context the harmonies that both cultures have explored in nature and man.[15]

Fordham University

New York

NOTES

1. Dante, *La Divina Commedia*, Paradiso, xxxiii, 82-93; English translation by John D. Sinclair, *The Divine Comedy of Dante Alighieri*, Vol. III *Paradiso* (New York: Oxford University Press, 1961), 483.

2. *Ibid.*, 115-120; 124-126.

3. *Ibid.*, 127-138.

4. *Ibid.*, 140-141;145.

5. Alfred North Whitehead, *Process and Reality* (New York: Macmillan, 1929), pp. 30-32.

6. Pierre Teilhard de Chardin, *The Phenomenon of Man* (New York: Harper and Row, 1965); Whitehead, *op. cit.*

7. Teilhard de Chardin, *op. cit.*, 260-268.

8. Cf. Whitehead, *op. cit.*, 519-533.

9. Cf. Whitehead, *loc. cit.*; Hartshorne, *The Divine Relativity* (New Haven: Yale University Press, 1948).

10. For a detailed study of this type of coincidence of opposites in Bonaventure cf. Ewert H. Cousins, "Bonaventure, the Coincidence of Opposites and Nicholas of Cusa," in *Studies Honoring Ignatius Charles Brady, Friar Minor, 1976* (St. Bonaventure, N.Y.: The Franciscan Institute, 1976), pp. 177-197; and *Bonaventure and the Coincidence of Opposites* (Chicago: Franciscan Herald Press).

11. Paul Tillich, *Systematic Theology*, Vol. I (Chicago: The University of Chicago Press, 1951), 250-252; Richard of St. Victor, *De tribus appropriatis personis in Trinitate* (*PL* 196, 991-94); Thomas Aquinas, *Summa theologiae*, I, q. 39, a. 8; Bonaventure, *Breviloquium*, p. 1, c. 6.

12. Arthur O. Lovejoy, *The Great Chain of Being* (New York: Harper and Row, 1960).

13. Cf. Ewert H. Cousins, "Fecundity and the Trinity: An

Appendix to Chapter Three of *The Great Chain of Being*," *Studies in Medieval Culture.*

14. Teilhard de Chardin, *op. cit.*; also *The Divine Milieu* (New York: Harper & Row, 1965); Whitehead, *op. cit.*, 519-533.

15. For a study of the non-manifested pole of the divinity in relation to world religions, cf. Raimundo Panikkar, *The Trinity and the Religious Experience of Man* (New York: Orbis, 1973); cf. a response to an earlier printing of Panikkar's position, Ewert H. Cousins, "The Trinity and World Religions," *Journal of Ecumenical Studies*, 7 (1970), 476-498.

COMMENT

On Ewert H. Cousins

"Harmony in Nature and Man"

JAN PLAT

In dealing with his very comprehensive topic Prof. Cousins has made a remarkable use of some basic ideas of a contemporary philosophy, commonly called process-philosophy and especially prominent in America through the metaphysical writings of A.N. Whitehead.

With the process-philosophers he takes being in the dynamic sense of power of being. Lodged in each individual being, this expresses itself in the form or intelligibility or logos of the same being. This dynamic process, wherein the form is produced by the power of being, is indicated as self-expression, or expression of its possibilities, as self-diffusion, and as inner creativity. The form is ever in a process of becoming, the being is a creative advance into novelty. If the form is the adequate expression of its power of being, then the being possesses the goodness of internal proportion or harmony. But how can we decide, if and to what extent in a given individual being, for instance in a bee, its form is an adequate expression of its individual power of being? Suppose this bee lacks a wing can we say that its form is in disharmony with its individual power of being. But how can we know that, since we know the power of being only from its expression?

From the paper I draw the conclusion that the dynamic process of self-expression and self-diffusion is going on, not only in each individual being of *this world*, but also in God's innermost nature. A dipolar model of God is proposed. The non-manifested pole designated as the void, the abyss of being and the unactualized ground of all possibilities; that is the loftiest pole and the highest level of divinity. The manifested pole is called also the Logos-pole. The paper speaks of a divine creative power, which comes out of the abyss of silence to expression in Logos. The non-manifested pole of God is the rest out of which energy flows, the silence out of which speech emerges, the darkness out of which light shines, and the *non-being* out of which being appears. Prof. Cousins emphatically distinguishes this dynamic process or coincidence of opposites, which plays within the inner life of God from all eternity to all eternity, from creation in the common sense of the word, the making of the world out of nothing by God. Creation in this latter sense is theophany; it is also a process of external self-expression of the divinity in space and time. By this distinction of internal from external self-expression Mr. Cousin opposes his dipolar model of God to that of Whitehead and Hartshorne. In their natural theologies these process philosophers think of God also as dipolar, not in Himself, but in relation to the world. They thereby introduce a pantheistic way of thinking about the relation God-world, more or less in the manner of Spinoza's theology (for Whitehead rather less than more). *Deus est omnium rerum causa immanens, non vero transiens" Ethica*, I, Pr. XVIII.

But does there remain any reason to posit two dynamic poles within God, when the relation God-world is thought of not in the pantheistic manner of Spinoza, Hegel, Whitehead and Harshorne, but in accordance with classical Western metaphysics, where pure actuality was assigned to God. For pure actuality seems to exclude any process of *actualization* within the divinie.

On one side Mr. Cousins is willing to apply Whitehead's category of creativity to God, he speaks of God as a dynamic process; on the other hand he wants to stress, that God does not depend *on the world* in order to be dynamic, self-diffusive and even actualized. Binding God to the creative process in the sense of process philosophy does require dipolarity in God himself, but where the Logos pole is unambiguously stated as the result of a process of actualization does not seem to harmonize with the classical natural theology doctrine of pure actuality and absolute simplicity.

I would not hold at all costs to that doctrine. The idea of God proposed by Prof. Cousins with its dynamic dipolarity seems more in accord with trinitarian theology and makes it possible to avoid a position whereby God is hardly conceivable as a really living being. But there are some difficulties.

Let me try to put it in an orderly way. (1) Prof. Cousins because of his sympathy with process philosophy wants to apply Whitehead's category of creativity on God. (2) This creativity entails dipolarity, a pole of divine creative power and a logos-pole, wherein the power-pole expresses itself. (3) In opposition to Whitehead he wants to posit this dynamic dipolarity in the inner life of the divinity itself. (4) The question is whether this dynamic dipolarity, the Logos-pole of which is an actualized one, is compatible with divine perfection, especially with pure actuality as assigned to God in classic natural theology. Put in another way, the question is whether dynamic dipolarity is a transcendental notion like the classical ones of being, one, true and good, or perhaps better by integrating three of them in the dynamic sense of power, truth and goodness? In late medieval terms: is dynamic dipolarity a *perfectio simpliciter simplex*? It is a much discussed epistemological question whether after the purification of our notions anything is left of their original content.

Prof. Cousines states that if God is transcendently dipolar in himself, the boundless harmony of his inner dynamic process makes possible all limited forms of harmony in the universe. But could limited forms of harmony in the universe not have their ground simply in God's ordering intellect?

Under Thesis 4 Prof. Cousins invites us to reexamine the doctrine of creation--taken here in its current sense as world-creation. He suggests a sense in which we would say: creatures are made out of God and out of nothing. I see no difficulty in the former, i.e., out of God, insofar as all creatures have an ideal preexistence in the exemplarism of the Logos-pole of the divinity. However, I have great difficulty in understanding, and even more difficulties in accepting the latter, i.e., out of a nothing which is also God, that is to say, out of the non-manifested pole of the divinity, the void or the abyss of silence. It seems to me that the nothingness of the non-manifested pole of God is of a quite other kind than the nothingness of the finite creatures or of their matter. How is one to conceive the latter nothingness as a participation or a reflection, may I say an image, of the lofty nothingness of the non-manifested pole?

Even after repeated reading of the development of the 4th thesis I am not confident that I have understood its intended meaning. Certainly Prof. Cousins must develop further the chain of thought, which has brought him to his bold suggestion.

CHAPTER XII

THE WORLD AS THEOPHANY

JEAN LADRIÈRE

In a general way the term 'theophany' can be taken as signifying 'manifestation of God.' But the notion of "manifestation" is itself quite complex, with many possible meanings according to the degree of immediacy (or, correlatively, of mediacy) that it connotes. The idea of 'theophany' indicates a sort of direct presence which excludes intermediaries, whether they be of the ontological order as in the case in which the world relates to God only through rather numerous hierarchial levels of beings, or of the inferential order as in the case in which the world supports reason in raising itself to the recognition of the existence of God and his attributes. Thus, the meaning of the term theophany may be expressed better by the term 'visibility' than by 'manifestation,' inasmuch as visibility stresses the immediacy of manifestation. The question to be asked then is in what measure and according to what modes does the world render God visible?

Thus stated, the question involves a certain number of ambiguities that one must begin by clearing up to the degree possible. First of all, in what sense shall we understand the term "world"? A preliminary definition might be nature, understood as the ensemble of beings which at least in principle are accessible to perception and which constitute the place in which human beings are rooted. It is in the whole of nature, understood as 'cosmos,' that the idea of theophany has its meaning. Understood from the point of view of human beings, nature is the place of one's existence and the field of one's action; from a more intrinsic perspective it can be considered as its own unfolding, possessing in itself the principles of its own activity. Certainly, it is always through an interpretation--which remains an act of the human spirit--that nature is understood in one or the other fashion, but it can be interpreted either as an autonomous field of production or as a simple component in human systems of action. Here we shall consider it from the first of these modes.

Nonetheless, not all ambiguity has been removed. At the present time there are two major approaches to nature. One is based directly upon perception, here the conceptual structure in which nature expresses itself does no more than extend the content of spontaneous experience. The other, on the contrary, is disconnected from immediate perception and expresses itself in the conceptual context of modern science which is largely dependent upon the possibilities of mathematical representation. In one sense the contrast is not as clear-cut as is often suggested, for from the moment of its conceptual articulation what has been experienced or observed is placed in perspective. In a certain way this impoverishes the multicolor and definitely varied content of what is given in direct contact, though it adds the organizational and clarifying contribution of the spirit.

In this regard the manner in which Greek philosophy for example developed the concept of nature is as distant from what is immediately perceived as are contemporary representations. What is especially characteristic of thought concerning nature, precisely as thought, is that it achieves a certain totality which is expressed by the concept "cosmos." This is of a totally different type than perceptual totalization which closes off what is visible at the ever-elusive and indetermined line of the horizon. It is on the level of cosmology that thought concerning nature attains its fullness; only there does it detach itself resolutely from appearance and boldly begin to exercise its distinctive power. This was as true of the cosmology of the *Timaeus*, which reconstructed in a prodigiously ingenious manner the system of the heavens on the basis of a mathematical theory of musical harmony, as it is of modern relativist cosmology which reconstructs the spatio-temporal structure of the ₍universe on the basis of certain very highly general hypothesis about the relations between matter and energy and between space and time.

It remains no less true that the images of the world corresponding to these conceptual constructions are profoundly different. The ancient vision is still relatively consonant with a spectacle of the heavens: the image of a sphere turning around a point tied to an observer is continuous with what the simple observation of the constellations might suggest. On the contrary the modern vision at this point is more abstract and in certain aspects counter-intuitive. But it has the triple advantage of suppressing the privilege of the observer, of considerably enlarging the dimensions of the universe, and especially of giving us an evolutionary representation which not only is static but which moreover is essentially asymetric. This presents us with a universe which in one sense continues the challenges itself and in another sense does not cease to construct itself.

Because it is relatively close to perception and consequently also to feelings, the first or ancient view, even in its most elaborate conceptual expressions, is more apt for sustaining a theophanic interpretation than is the modern vision, which is difficult to explain in a correct manner in intuitive terms inasmuch as it is essentially bound to formal speculation. Is it not true that a cosmic vision can reveal through feelings a transcendent presence? Does not such a revelation take place in admiration, fright, and enthusiasm before what is absolutely transcendent? On the other hand, as we shall try to show later, the theophanic aspect of the world is never a mere interpretative vision rather than a direct reading of what is perceived. Inasmuch as the ancient vision is a conceptual construct, it has no privileged position over the modern vision. Under certain conditions both are susceptible to a theophanic interpretation.

Indeed, from a certain point of view modern vision has characteristics which in this regard are more favorable, due especially to its developmental character as indicated above. In any case, our question must be taken in the present, for it is the modern vision of nature which occupies us. Thus we shall take the term "nature" in the sense of the cosmic whole as represented in modern science even though this be totally conjectural and provisional.

Beyond the concepts of ancient philosophy, one could naturally call upon mythological representations, whose theophanic character is so clear as to be, as it were, consubstantial with this type of interpretation of nature. Myth expresses itself in the language of symbols and seems therefore, of its very nature, to be apt for grasping the visible as a mode of divine presence. Symbols unite and separate; they bespeak at the same time both proximity and distance, immanence and otherness. Of their very structure they permit the spirit, through a term given in experience and thus familiar, to see a reality which in principle is not a matter of direct experience but inaccessible and hopelessly cut off. They enable one to grasp indirectly, through the real unifying connection in the very element that differentiates them, both the familiar term and the reality to which it points. It will be tempting therefore to assert that the theophanic vision of the world has its true place in the symbolic interpretation of nature, such as we find in the myth, and that one loses this to the very degree that one passes from the symbolic to the conceptual order.

Whereas the world appeared for Greek speculation to be penetrated by the divine, modern representation is radically alien to all transcendent interpretation. It has been sufficiently stressed that the scientific view of the world is, or has been, realized in opposition to metaphysics and the theologies. Its project consists essentially in explaining in an autonomous manner and by itself the forces of nature and the structures in terms of which it is organized. For modern science nature is radically self-productive.

Nonetheless it must recognized that mythic vision is profoundly ambiguous. Should one say that it interprets the world on the basis of the divine or that it construes the divine on the image of the world? Moreover, is it not the category of the "sacred" that must be used rather than the category of the "divine," at least if one associates the latter category with a notion of a reality which is both personal and transcendent? Symbols are equivocous; they include an irreplaceable power of suggestion but have their true significance only in a context which fixes its area of significance.

The symbolic language of myth functions differently than does the symbolic language of the great religions, for the context of myth is discourse that is in some way directly related to the sacred, and the symbols it uses are only apparently separated. The distance that it sets between the visible and reality that it intends to manifest is not that constitutive distance in which transcendence affirms itself and is made visible, but only a structural distance which is the condition of interpretation. One cannot disengage the signification without engaging the interpreter. In mythology the sacred figures precisely in an interpreting role; it is directly in terms of superior powers and events located beyond that nature as understood. This does not mean that it enables one to see another reality than oneself. The sacred, as a system of interpretative terms, is only a construction by means of which the world can be grasped as such, that is, through which nature can be seen as a whole. The true content of mythical discourse is then nature itself inasmuch as it is an autonomous power upon which man knows himself to be dependent and whose benevolence man can only invoke.

In order for nature really to take on theophanic power it must first be grasped in its own value, that is in categories which do not presuppose that which must be made manifest through them. When the signification is immediate there is no real manifestation, but only the functioning of a system of intelligibility appropriate to a certain type of language in which formal conceptualization as such is not yet available. On the contrary, it is at the moment of constitution of non-symbolic systems of interpretation, which do not refer, even on the simple level of modes of speech, to anything other than purely immanent factors of explanation, that the question of theophany can begin to be posed.

But our question involves a second ambiguity. When one asks if the world is able to make God visible in a certain manner, does one already employ a concept of God or does one depend on the world itself to teach us about God? In the first case the question becomes whether the world can be read as manifesting, at least as regards certain attributes, a God which is thought to have been grasped conceptually in another way, either by metaphysical speculation or by reflection upon a certain form of religious experience. This is a matter of asking about the eventual congruence, at least in some partial degree, between an itinerary towards God based upon nature and other itineraries, accessible in an independent manner, which the testimony of nature can at most enrich by its particularly concrete connotations. In the second case the question becomes one of asking if there is an admissible reading of the world which is capable, not only of recognizing the presence in nature of a God who is known in another manner, but of truly discovering the existence of a transcendent being and providing a sufficiently precise representation of that being. It is understood that in this second case it is necessary to examine whether this representation corresponds or not with the idea of God as it might be apprehended through religious experience or metaphysical speculation.

In order that the term "theophany" have full force it would seem necessary that the world be able by itself to provide positive indications of the existence and nature of God. It is not sufficient that it lend itself to an interpretation which discovers in it the presence of God such as could already be known by other routes. It must on its own account be able to attest to God in its own manner and make him known in an original and autonomous way.

This brings us to the examination of a third ambiguity involved in our question: in what sense must one understand the "visibility" which is connoted by the term "theophany"? Visibility, as we have seen, can be considered as a particularly strong form of manifestation, as a relatively direct mode of appearing, but this cannot be a matter of that immediate visibility which characterizes the directly perceptible aspects of nature. It is a matter of grasping a reality without any perception or immediate manner of grasping. This suggests the profoundly paradoxical character of the visibility we are treating, namely, that the idea of "theophany" evokes a mode of transparence which gives nature the power through its own appearance to make apparent the divine reality. This would be a manner of considering the world which in its very manifestation would manifest a transcendent otherness; the mission of the world would be precisely to manifest that transcendent. Thus, the term "visibility" would be taken in its most immediate sense.

Such a theophanic reading of the world would be entirely different from either type of speculative inference; (a) ascending from visible things towards their invisible source by the mediation of an idea of order or of causality, or (b) taking the point of view of the absolute, enabling us conceptually to assist in the deployment of visible reality from the absolute essence and internal necessity of its super-position. But in thus taking the term "visibility" in too lateral a sense do we not risk falling into the illusion of symbolic mythology or turning to a mystical interpretation, and thus missing what is proper to "theophany"? If, in fact, nature has a merely apparent consistency, and if an intensive look is able to discern under the veil of its multiple forms the very reality of the divine, then we are forced to chose. Either there is no real difference between nature and God and it must be concluded that the divine reality is only nature itself considered in terms of the majesty of its sovereign affirmation and the all-powerful character of its operations. Or nature is in effect only an immense and shimmering illusion which the spirit must penetrate in order to discover the only true reality, that is, the absolute. That is, either a naturalized god or a god withdrawn in the purity of his essence. Such a god would project outside of himself, not the reality of being, but an imponderable transparency which lacks any truth through which his essence might be hidden as much as divined.

On the other hand, mystical interpretation turns towards experience which primordially is not of nature, but of the divine as it is seized in the depth of one's soul. Only on the basis of such experience can visible reality be understood as revealing the presence of God. The interpretation proceeds here from a sense of the profound unity of being, from the universality of divine action, and from its penetration to the most intimate dimension of each fragment of reality. The mystical vision is a vision of things in God, not a vision of God through things. It grasps nature, not first in its reality, but as the particular manner of manifestation of the unicity and infinite expansiveness of the divine essence. It reunites in a simple interiorly unified glance what we ordinarily grasp only in indefinitely multiplied fragments.

Because it attains the Source of being in this unified manner, it does away with the itinerary which otherwise would begin by detaching itself from the sensible and move thereafter through an interior ascesis destined to break away from the "I" and all its attachments. It is not that nature is necessarily denounced as an illusion, but the radical character of the call to the soul to unite itself to the divine essence and to recognize there the presence of the entire universe demands a purification of the senses, of affectivity and of the spirit. For these suppose that one distance him/herself from all that is visible and return to the most intimate region of the soul where it grasps most immediately that Act which makes it to be.

But if we restore fully to nature its reality, consistency

and intrinsic significance, do we not thereby lose definitively the idea of "visibility"? Do we not fall thereby necessarily either into a kind of natural pantheism which interprets nature entirely in terms of itself as an entirely self-consistent reality, or into a type of metaphysics which appeals fundamentally to inference in order to move from nature to its source? It is here that the real issue lies. Is there a way to make the divine visible that will be neither simply an illusory transparence nor simply a contribution to the speculative process drawing its power merely from the force of reason and hence from principles that derive from the structure of the human spirit? A "theophany" of nature must take its position in relation to these two if it is to have meaning and a place. Is such a position conceivable?

A more attentive analysis of the notion of "manifestation," to which the notion of "visibility" belongs, should help to clarify the subject. Phenomenology provides an almost exemplary model of a process which provides the strongest speculative meaning to manifestation. It teaches us that the self-manifestation of reality is not the simple self-positing of an appearance which is exhausted in the evidence of what presents itself, nor is it simply the making present of "being there." Rather, it is articulated according to a complex structure in which what is already manifest returns at more and more profound levels of manifestation. As a result a full understanding of the most immediate appearance must lead inevitably to bringing into evidence the corresponding conceptual explicitation of the basis upon which appearance is produced. Such a movement of thought, which is essentially speculative to the measure that it develops an interpretation that gets to the foundations, is distinct from the process of inference in that it depends not upon principles of reasoning which permits passage from one proposition to another, but upon the movement of reality inasmuch as it is manifestation. In sum, it is the understanding of reality as manifestation and not as simple position which constitutes the first interpretive principle, and one might say the speculative premise, of all phenomenology.

On the basis of this understanding it becomes possible to see reality as deployment of itself and as movement towards its own self-appearance on the basis of the principles by which it is constituted, that is to say, on the basis of the ontological nucleus which enables it simultaneously to be what it is, to develop itself in all the various modes of its manifestation, and to be accessible to the radical search for understanding. This ontological nucleus could be called the essence, if this be understood as the first principle of self-deployment. But this essence is neither immediately apparent nor really separated from what is apparent; rather, it is the power in appearance which makes things appear--that stance from which a thing shows itself and has its effective content.

To read reality as manifestation then is not to read in a double register which superimposes upon the perception of appearance a deciphering of essence, but a single reading which proceeds from appearance towards essence. But if essence does present itself immediately and as such it is not possible to understand the whole of the manifest as the essence coming to light, descending from the region of principles towards that which simply presents itself to be seen as the result of a process. In contrast, the phenomenological unveiling is an ascent, beginning from what is manifest in appearance, and uncovering there both a completeness and a need. This draws the spirit towards an ever more adequate grasp up to a culminating moment at which that which is uncovered hands over the secret of its own appearing. At that moment the essence uncovers itself, though from the beginning at the very heart of appearance it had been present in a non-explicit manner calling the spirit to a task of interpretation equal to the full dimensions of its self-positing.

In sum, the phenomenological process redoes, in inverse direction, the immanent movement of reality. In ascending once again towards the essence it goes counter-current to the flow of manifestation, but it does so in order to understand more fundamentally how this flow itself takes place. It is truly a work of constitution, for in reconstituting in a somewhat retrospective fashion the deployment of the essence it makes evident how that deployment took place, how the essence achieved its visibility, and how consequently the visible is constituted in the full variety of its multiple articulations.

This process of unveiling, which is simultaneously both regressive and constitutive, is not at all arbitrary. It follows the indications contained in the very giving of that which presents itself to be seen. This is because the structure of this presentation involves an articulation of the moments which have in themselves both the positive character of the determinations which are asserted and a lack which reveals, as in a raw state, the already active presence of the following moment. By progressively explicitating what is thus announced in each determined affirmation, thought can bring out the complex of the conditions of appearance. This is what is meant by essence understood as the principle of its own manifestation and of the concatenation of its constitutive moments.

The structure of the gift is precisely manifestation; what is given makes itself be seen, but announces itself only according to its truth. Thus the essence also points back, through a succession of steps in which that which is made explicit becomes more and more true, to the essence in which what is immediate has the fullness of its signification. Essence then is not truly different from appearance; it is the truth of appearance because in a certain way it is the very reality of appearing. As principle of its deployment it is fundamentally nothing other than the total deployment of that which manifests itself, the mature manifestation of what presents itself to be seen. If there is question then of returning from appearance towards essence this is only to the degree in which there is required some thematizing explicatation for working out the reality of the deployment in all its fullness and with its constitutive structure. Hence manifestation is necessarily self-manifestation and the full comprehension of phenomena as such is without doubt a reconstruction of the movement of its phenomenalization. That movement does not take us outside of the phenomenon but enables us to penetrate more adequately and rigorously the structural conditions of phenomenalness, that is, that which constitutes a phenomena and even this determined phenomenon.

Thus, if nature can be theophany, this is not according to the structure of manifestation which moves back from the appearance to the essence. For the essence, understood in the sense of a phenomenological unfolding, does not possess that radical otherness which is constitutive of the structure of theophany. Thus, if we are to understand by "visibility" a form of manifestation, we cannot draw in any literal fashion upon the manner in which phenomenology understands manifestation. Nevertheless, in the phenomenological enterprise there is an indication which can prove useful, for it provides an example of a type of process which, on the basis of the manifest but without inference in any proper sense, goes beyond (without properly transcending) to the very constitution of the visibility. This process accompanies the very development of a phenomenon and is within the giving itself. It does not depend upon principles of understanding exterior to the phenomenon which might be applied to what is proposed in the appearance.

If there is a sense in which the world can be theophany that quality should be able to be understood by a process which uncovers the visibility of the divine in the very ways in which the world gives itself; it should extend in some manner from within the visibility of the world itself toward the visibility of the divine. Just as phenomenology moves from appearance to essence by clarifying the very structure of manifestation as this understands itself, so also a theophanic reading of nature should move towards recognition of the divine presence within it, following the indications contained in the very structure of the visibility of nature. It is necessary that this recognition give full value both to the dynamic reality of the presence of God in nature and to the radical otherness, that is to say, to the essentially transcendent character of the divine. Visibility, understood as an eminent form of manifestation, should therefore be both non-phenomenological and non-inferential. However, it can neither offer itself for direct vision nor be totally estranged from the visibility of the world. In order to become explicit it needs an original interpretation which extends the authentic comprehension of nature.

As such, however, an interpretation does not make something "visible". It is found in a discourse whose nature is to enable what is given to be comprehended; and makes more explicit meaning that is partially hidden. It applies semantic means as instruments which have interpretative force only to the degree in which, by virtue of their mutual relations and proper connotations, they are able to make an intelligible structure appear. In sum, in interpretation properly speaking what is interpreted borrows from the interpreting the power by which it reveals its meaning. Further, theophany is a certain form of interpretation; the world can be theophanic only with a view which enables it to appear as inhabited by a Presence which surpasses it. Visibility includes at the same time both manifestation and interpretation: from manifestation it retains the property of making apparent the very structure of the donation, and from interpretation it retains the property of penetrating even to the most hidden meaning. As manifestation it holds in infinite distance that which it renders manifest; and as interpretation it inserts the meaning that it uncovers within that which is concretely present. If God can become visible through the world, this must be both in the height which separates the world and in the quasi-immediate accessability of that which offers itself to the grasp of the spirit conceived in analogy to sensible perception. We might call this spiritual visibility.

Our question can be reformulated now with relative precision: is there a reading of nature according to modern understanding which can enable us to discover in it, after the mode of spiritual visibility, a Sovereignty through whose attributes we can recognize Him whom the highest traditions have called God? The spectacle of nature gives one the sense of an all-powerful benevolent Presence, which is at the same time both infinitely distant and infinitely proximate, eminently worthy of fear, of admiration and of confidence, and inviting both celebration and praise, songs of thanks and of jubilation. All this is sufficiently attested by innumerable witnesses; it is a very common experience for which the human soul is naturally prepared. Naturally, it is sometimes difficult to unscramble in that feeling what is a sacralization of the forces of nature, or sort of cosmic pantheism, from what is an authentic recognition of the divine. In any case we do not wish to look in that type of experience, because we are looking for a theophanic and an intellectually founded comprehension of nature. Clearly such a comprehension could not have the type of immediacy which pertains to evidences of the heart; inevitably moments of interpretation and even of different levels interpretation must intervene.

First of all, a theophanic reading of nature is possible only if in one way or another it is grasped as a totality. This does not mean that it must be understood as a kind of undifferentiated global mass or as the simple unity of absolute self-position: totalization by no means excludes structuring--quite the contrary. What modern science of nature makes it possible to grasp, particularly on the cosmological level, is that the cosmos in its unity can be represented only on the basis of a precise mode of structuring. In any case, only on the basis of particular conditions can the analysis finally move up to global configurations: totalization is achieved by beginning from the local, which confers upon it its efficacy.

We do not have an immediate apprehension of all, nor can we form an idea of the manner in which it is active on the most individual or particular levels of the universe. Nor do we have at present a truly unified science of nature: even in physics the effort to elaborate a unitary theory has thusfar failed. On the one hand, we do have some cosmological theories and it is especially on this level that one notes the effect of totalization. Also we have some theories on the constitution of matter on the elementary level which thusfar have not succeeded in establishing themselves on a truly unified basis. Between the two extremes we have a certain number of givens and some theories on the behavior and evolution of intermediate structures from atoms through molecules, stars and stellar systems to galaxies. For its part, biology opens up some very unifying perspectives regarding the fundamental phenomena of life, such as its molecular basis and the elementary mechanisms of synthesis, control and reproduction on which the diverse living forms are built in the infinite variety we experience.

On the level of the sciences of nature we already have a totalizing approach, though it is far from giving us a unified view of phenomena. It is only a sketch, but it is already sufficiently articulated to give some overall indications: a deepened and detailed study of the question should take account of *all* actually available global factors. On the one hand, even though when considered at short enough intervals it presents relatively stable configurations, nature is essentially processive. More exactly, it is constituted of the mutual development of two large and opposed types of processes. On the one hand, stand processes of degradation, the theoretical expression of which is entropy in closed systems. On the other hand, there are the processes of emergence which generate new and increasingly diversified and complex configurations whose theoretical expression is still being sought. The cosmological model of the indefinite expansion of space from an initial single reality presents an overall irreversible evolution of the universe in the sense of a growing global entropy. The corresponding image is that of progressive expansion beginning from a highly concentrated level of energy.

Living forms, by contrast, are a more striking and undoubtedly more elaborate example of the processes of organization and complexification. The local phenomenon of increasing organization is the counterpart of the global phenomenon of progressive expansion. It is as if the progressive dispersion of initial energy is compensated by the emergence of increasingly sophisticated, autonomous and effective forms. In fact this is probably the condition for progressive dispersion. The two phenomena are not located on the same level. The unfolding concerns only matter at its most fundamental and indifferent level, that of energy as a sort of general, pure and still unconfigured potency. Organization, in contrast, concerns the natural architectures in which what is determinative are the structural conditions, rather than their indispensible substrata of energy.

On the other hand the stability of forms, which is striking for our immediate perception, is only a relative stability of structure assured by a permanent flow of its constituent interactions. The living cell has an extremely elevated level of organization. It is constructed in such a manner as to assure the maintenance of its level and type of organization, but succeeds in doing so only by means of incessant, extraordinarily complex and delicately regulated activity. On this basis new syntheses continually compensate for the incessant degradations of its constituent elements. This is true with more or less elevated degrees of complexity at all levels of organization. Even what one calls "elementary particles" are not as the term suggests to the imagination, solid and resistant granules of matter occupying a certain space and exercising action upon other granules. Instead they are the more or less durable results of not yet clear processes, which in the final analysis themselves are undoubtedly only diverse modalities of mobilization of fundamental energy. As Eisenberg has suggested, this is a sort of zero level of what we call matter.

On the basis of these indications furnished by the first level of interpretation, which is that of the sciences in nature, a second interpretation can be developed--now on the level of speculative thought. Understood as process, nature is perpetually at work making itself or becoming in an astonishing multiplicity of its forms. What in the final analysis is dominant here is not the dispersion, but the development of organization which is at the same time differentiation, singularization and individuation. At all levels the relative stability is only a facade for incessant activity. As Whitehead has profoundly shown, nature is "passage": it can be understood as totality only in terms of becoming, and each moment of this becoming is a new emergence in which up to a certain point all is reproduced, but in which also new forms appear. Therefore there is at the same time both continuity and discontinuity. By means of that which has already been constituted novelty is able to produce itself, but every step of complexity constitutes a definitive step and an irreducible advance in contrast to what preceded it.

The emergence is the appearance of quality, of pure difference; it marks the passage from potentiality to actuality, from non-figured to figuration, from elementary to complex, from support to structure, from pure conditions of appearance to the effective autoproduction of that which appeared in its original singularity. There is a term, which once again is suggested by Whitehead, that attempts speculatively to characterize the status of a reality which thus presents itself as the emerging self-production of itself: it is the term "creativity." In the categorial Whiteheadian schema this is the category of the ultimate. It cannot be defined in itself, but whose sense is clarified through the whole system of categories in which it makes itself explicit. This indicates that here we attain an absolutely first characteristic. It is not properly speaking inferred from theoretical representations of modern science, but it is called for by that which they suggest: it is a matter of interpretation, but according to a hermeneutic which does no more than follow the internal movement of the manifestation. It reads nature according to the visible articulations in which it first produces itself, and upon which scientific interpretations are based.

Now a third level of interpretation opens up. To see nature as creativity is to see it as process, incessant emergence, continuous production of itself, perpetual novelty, a gushing forth, an inexhaustible energy, unfathomable possibility, an ever-renewed initiative, actualization, flow of being, generosity, diffusion of itself, and an unlimited expansion--in brief, as the action of giving or sharing. This suggests to us a new speculative step--a particularly dangerous but decisive moment in our development--which consists in moving from creativity as structural condition to creativity as original assertive act. According to this interpretation the creativity of nature, as sensed in the second interpretative moment, would appear only as the trace of an absolute initiative within what we are able to understand of the visible world. According to the indications of the idea of creativity, we can represent this as diffusion from a superabundance of being, as ever renewed communication of energy without limitation, and finally as gift without reserve. It passes beyond itself to constitute a real order with its own powers of subsistence, action and evolution in an internal flow from its own essence which surpasses all configuration.

The image which here comes most spontaneously to the mind is that of a Source or Spring. The idea of creativity sends us back to an inexhaustible superabundance, precontaining in itself, not as simple exemplars but as the original instituting power, all the possibilities of organization and figuration, and thus all the actual and potential variety of nature considered in in its full evolutionary exuberance. The image of the source helps us to attribute a place to that superabundance and to clarify the sense of the interpretation which is proposed. If creativity were considered as the last word of the reflection it would be conceived as coextensive with nature itself. But by definition, creativity represents that in nature which is always infinitely in excess in relation to that which has already shown itself; it is that which irresistibly draws nature forward beyond itself.

To identify creativity with nature would thus amount to either removing what is essential to the significance of creativity, by imagining it to be already in that which is actually constituted, or making of nature itself a power which radically surpasses the visible. In the first case, one falls short of what the emergentist vision of the world can legitimately suggest. In the second case, one absolutizes nature and makes it an ultimate instituting power--the source in a radical sense. But, the whole question lies just there. Should creativity be conceived as totally immanent to the forms which it generates and thus definitively as identical to nature itself, envisaged not only in its actual visibility but according to the total system of its possibilities? Or should it rather be conceived as attached to a source distinct from nature? Does it lead us to an originating reality which would be of the type of *natura naturans*, or towards a place which itself would be the origin of the origination?

It is interpretation that must decide this for all depends on the manner in which creativity itself is understood. If one understands it only as an invention of forms, as ever acting energy and as inexhaustible productivity, then one could be tempted to choose the sense of a *natura naturans*, not basically distinct from the *natura naturata*. This is the position of naturalistic pantheism. But if one is attentive to what this tells us of the generosity it contains, if one understands it as revealing the basic goodness of being and its benevolent proximity--as in an elusive smile which floats upon the world and each thing--then one is directed rather toward an interpretation which seeks to attach creativity to the initiating act, as is suggested by the image of source.

Further, if that act must be interpreted as the origin, not only of the originality of forms and of their multiple beauty, but also of all that renders the universe worthy of confidence, available and friendly, then it must be conceived as being of a personal nature for only in the experience of personal being do we find that such qualities can have their meaning and true basis. This leads us to trace creativity back to a personal source which is distinct from nature and surpasses any emergentist process that supports the world from the exalted heights of its own position. This source can be discerned in the very spectacle of the profusion of created forms, in the majesty of the universal rhythms, and in the "creative advance" which, is as it were, the very thrust of cosmic life. In the abundant profusion, gratuitousness and variety of worldly architectures, in the splendor of days and nights, in the lustre of beings and the conflictive harmony of the world, there is manifest something of its proper inexhaustible, super essential beauty, and especially of its generosity, mercy and tenderness.

This interpretation is not an inference. By a causal type of reasoning we have moved from creativity to a creative act, but only in order to propose an interpretative reading of creativity. This enables one to see reflected on the visible level an expansive act of infinite power of which the creativity of nature is but a finite counterpoint. It remains necessary to compare such an interpretation to metaphysical procedures depending upon critically based inferences and which are of the highest rational authority. This image of God which appears or can be worked out on the basis of certain attributes must also be compared with that which reflection based upon human action, especially strict action or religious experience, can reveal of God. In truth it is neither the power of interpretation based upon native or human action nor that of inference that really joins us to God who reveals himself. At the very least such steps can point toward that place in the field of human experience at which the religious experience which receives revelation can take place.

If there is question here of theophanie this is so to the degree that the interpretation is in some way directly concerned with nature that reveals itself. This introduces an essential discontinuity in the process of understanding and implies in addition an inevitable moment of decision. But, if it can enable us to come to the idea of some superabundant and benevolent Source of what is creative in the universe and thence of the universe itself, it must be noted that this gives us an idea of the Source only on the basis of creativity, which itself gets its sense from what our image of nature suggests. Thus, through the different interpretations which are proposed, from that a scientific vision to a personal Place that is the universal source of being, there is a certain shift of visibility. We move from what is immediately given on the level of experience and of intelligible constructs, which provides a first interpretation that is duly controlled according to the criteria of scientific method, towards what can be revealed only on the basis of interpretation.

In one sense the process merely reconstructs by successive steps the original deployment of that which is given, and on that basis it is close to a certain form of phenomenology. In another sense, however, precisely inasmuch as it is interpretative, it underlines at each stage the discontinuity introduced and the accompanying initiative of the spirit. On the one hand, there is the natural prolongation of an initial reading which assures the transfer of visibility. On the other hand, some transitions depend entirely upon the strength of the decisions on which they are based and which diminish the efficacy of the step. The notion of visibility is in mid-route between the two: between self-manifestation and interpretative transposition. Interpretation underlines a certain unbridgeable distance between the immediate and the ultimate evocation of the Source. Nonetheless, it provides a sort of visibility which is not intuitive, but has a closer analogy to perception than to conceptual order.

If the world can be considered as theophany, it is at the cost of an interpretation which inevitably eliminates the immediate. But through this interpretation a vision can be elaborated which learns to discover, along with the spectacle of the world, the personal presence which both inhabits and surpasses it. This is a second vision which is not apparent at first sight. But on the basis of the interpretative decisions which control its development there is to be found in this second vision the hidden sense of the world and of the creativity which supports it under the form of an expansive Generosity which invites confidence and celebration. Spiritual visibility has neither the evidence of feeling nor the rational force of that which is demonstrated. But it has a clarity which relates it to the concept and a concrete fullness which relates it to feeling. In it the distant becomes close without losing its distance, and the hidden is manifest without losing its mystery. It makes it possible to see even that which is directly visible while protecting the absolute difference of that which it makes available. It supposes an ascesis of spirit and consent to what is proposed.

For the one who agrees with the personalizing interpretation of creativity nature becomes, not simply the symbol, but the effective and continuous constitution outside of itself of the Act which pervades all. The intrinsic productivity of nature becomes, not only the sign, but the very reality of the appearance of the sovereign productivity by which it is supported above the abyss. In the immensity, profusion and glory of the world there shows through something of the height, inexhaustibility and brilliance of its origin. Nature becomes this transparent milieu not by abolishing itself, but by asserting itself in a massive affirmation of its proper essence. This allows to appear that light without duration to appear, whose presence and efficacy is attested by the secret pulse of life itself, where the mystery of its becoming and of its creative instauration is reaffirmed at each instant. The world as theophany is revelation as well as duration and concrete stuff; it is the continuing trace of an originating source whence all has its actuality and creativity.

The theophanic vision, pertains to the eyes of the soul. It is that which Thomas Traherne celebrated in his poem "La vision":

> To see the Fountain is a blessed thing;
> It is to see the King
> Of glory face to face. . . . "

Université Catholique de Louvain

Louvain-la-Neuve, Belgium

NOTES

1. Thomas Traherne, *Poèmes de la félicité*, trans. J. Wahl (Coll. Le don des langues; Paris: Editions du Seuil, 1951), p. 96.

CHAPTER XIII

ON THE REDUCTION OF TEMPORAL CATEGORIES WITHIN THE PROCESS OF DIVINE INTERVENTION

EVANGHELOS A. MOUTSOPOULOS

The human conception of the process of divine intervention cannot be static. It must take into consideration the dynamic image of the human creative process, in order to apply it to another process at a different level.

Augustine was right in observing that before time was created by divine decision, there was no "then," i.e., no past at all.[1] One should admit that, in general, the tripartite system of temporal categories: past, present, future, as conceived through analytical considerations of human consciousness, is not applicable to the divine conception of the process of becoming. Such a temporal analysis results from the inability of human consciousness to grasp the process in question in its totality.

Bergson has stated that an analytic approach to a process of this kind is required by the human mind, for it has no other way to grasp duration both as the framework and as the reality of becoming. In other words, Bergson insists that human mind is not theoretically, but practically oriented. It therefore splits the totality or whole of duration into a multitude of temporal parts, thereby dividing the world and minimizing the difficulties of its influence upon it.[2]

According to Bergson, the idea of divisible time has resulted from the application of the reality of divisible space to the reality of durational flow.[3] This provides a supplementary reason why the classical conception of the tripartite division of time into present, past and future has never been, and could never be, applicable to any scheme for the manner in which divine intelligence, as outside any temporal categorization, grasps reality.

Hence, the divine conception of becoming would be either that of duration or that of eternity. Spinoza develops a particular conception of duration related to eternity and opposed a general conception related to time.[4] As Spinoza influenced Bergson extensively, the above ideas of Bergson on the issue can be integrated into the classical form.

On the other hand, according to theological concepts, it is clear that, in every case, God chooses the appropriate moment to intervene in the becoming of Creation. There is a precise moment of intervention; it is understood as an act of creativity of--among other things--time itself. Besides, there is a moment chosen for redemption, which also is precise in its uniqueness. Finally, there is a moment which has been already chosen, but which remains still unknown to mankind--that of the last judgment. Such moments, which objectively express divine intentionality concerning man and the world, cannot be conceived according to the static classical model of the combined categories of past, present and future. They require an underlying dynamic model whose structure is based on the combination (or rather the opposition) of two categories, that of "not-yet" and that of "never-more."[5]

Within such a context the category of the "present" cannot be conceived as denoting any period of duration. Just as the classical temporal tripartite scheme is reduced to a dynamic bipartite scheme, the present itself is conceived, not as a period, but as a precise point with only an operational essence. It becomes a *minimum* and, at the same time, an *optimum*,[6] since it determines the "kairic" character of divine intervention. It is considered, however, as always having been present *in advance* or prospectively in the divine consciousness, which refers to it non-temporally, through its own intentionality.

This reduction of the system of temporal categories to a system of "kairic" categories is necessary in order to allow one to move from the level of human to the level of divine consciousness of becoming. This reduction aids in understanding the series of changes in the relations between God and the world, as well as between God and man, by enabling them to be seen as a series of landmarks which divide the entire process of divine interventions, not from a quantitative, but from a qualitative point of view. The prospective of divine intervention finds its best expression in the opposition of the "kairic" categories of "not-yet" and "never-more." Through these it is possible for human understanding to go beyond its traditional conception of time in order to reach and perhaps grasp the structure of the process by which the divine conception of becoming is realized --in both senses of that term--through divine intervention.

University of Athens

Athens, Greece

NOTES

1. *Confessions*, 11, 13.
2. Cf. E. Moutsopoulos, "La critique du platonisme chez Bergson," *Les Etudes Bergsoniennes*, IX (1970), 123-156.

3. Cf. *idem*, "From the *Stream of Consciousness* to the *Flow of Consciousness*: the Bergsonization of Pragmatism," *Athena* (1968), pp. 109-120.

4. Cf. *idem*, "Time in Spinoza's Work," *Scient. Annuary of the Faculty of Philosophy of the University of Athens* (1964), pp. 473-485.

5. Cf. *idem*, "Temporal and 'Kairic' Categories," *ibid.* (1962), pp. 412-436.

6. Cf. *ibid.*

COMMENT

On Evanghelos A. Moutsopoulos,
"Man and History"

F.P. HAGER

How can God in his eternal perfection, in the perfect eternity of his being, be responsible for man's history and be the cause of the temporal conditions of man's life? This has always been one of the main problems of philosophical theology as well as (in particular) of the philosophical reflexions on religious experience. Very closely linked with this problem is another one: How can man conceive this relation between the eternal God and man in his temporal reality, if man is essentially temporal not only in his practical life, but even in his understanding and feeling? A third problem would, so to speak, summarize the two problems mentioned before: How must divine conception of human temporality and history be defined and explained by man?

The problem of explaining the relations between God or divine reality in its eternity and man in his temporality, or more generally the world in its becoming, is important and complicated enough in the context of the classical metaphysical speculation founded by Plato and Aristotle before the background of ancient Greek philosophy. Here the greatest difficulty is to explain, how the perfectly untemporal and unchangeable reality of the divine can come together and can find a causal relation with the imperfect, changeable and deficient reality of the world of becoming, including several aspects of man's being. Is it by perfect form or essence, by intellectual power, by perfect unity or specifically by its eternity and stability, that God is able to be in a constant, eternal way the cause, condition and source of the world of becoming and the temporal reality of man? The most important problem here seems to be to find a bridge between the perfect and transcendent reality of the divine and the imperfect, ever changing process of becoming in man and world.

But the problem of the temporal or nontemporal relations between God and man becomes even more difficult and complicated with the revelation of the Old and New Testament. Here God is still perfect and eternal in his being, but he creates the world and with the world he creates time and temporality (as an essential character of the world). This first act of God has the feature of an intervention, but even more clearly this is the case for redemption and last judgment. They are decisions taken from the beginning but having consequences within the development of human history. With the redemption God becomes man and introduces himself into man's history without losing in any way his perfect eternity as God. Here in the act of incarnation and redemption, if anywhere, the categories of time and history get their importance and relevance. As a consequence of Christian and Jewish revelation, history[1] comes for the first time into a close metaphysical relation with the reality of the divine. History with the irreversibility of its events (in their chronological order) reaches a metaphysical importance, which it did not have for pagan Greek metaphysics. Therefore the problem becomes more and more important: How can God, the eternal creator of the world and master of history, conceive history in its temporality?

In this general context the paper of Professor Moutsopoulos is of special interest owing to the way he asks the fundamental questions and exposes the problem, as well as in virtue of the solution he gives for the problem in question. If I understand him correctly, he puts the problem as follows: God is eternal and he is the creator of the world, the redeemer and ultimate judge of man; his relation to man is characterized by a series of fundamental interventions, that is by creation, redemption, last judgment.[2] God is the creator of man and the master of man's history, and man's history as a whole is a dynamic process. God himself, in his responsibility for man's being and as the originator of man's history, must act dynamically; He cannot be conceived by man statically. For all these reasons (namely, first God's eternity and untemporality, second the nature of God's activity, his acting by interventions, and third the process of man's history and the development of his creativity conditioned and created by God) it is impossible to conceive God's relation to man in the traditional temporal categories of past, present and future. In dividing time into divisible parts, they are a result of the application of the reality of divisible space to the reality of durational flow.

How then can the relations between God and man be interpreted adequately? Obviously by viewing God's conception of the process of becoming in the mode of duration or eternity and with the "kairic" categories of the 'nevermore' and the 'not-yet'. This kind of understanding God's creative activity would, at the same time, account both for God's perfection as pointed out by the classical tradition of Greek and later metaphysics and for the interventional activity of God in choosing the right moment (*kairos*) for creation, redemption and last judgment, as testified by religious--especially Christian--faith.

What are the historical implications of this solution and what are its systematic problems? In identifying them I shall try to give a summary of what seem to me to be the most important points in need of discussion.

The first and fundamental historical implication of the solution offered by Professor Moutsopoulos is certainly that he presupposes the truth of what Christian and Jewish revelations and faith say about the relations between God and man. Undoubtedly, in the context of these religions God's relation to man is fundamentally marked and characterized by divine interventions such as creation, redemption, and last judgment. One should not forget, however, that other conceptions of the relations between God and man are possible which do not include the specific notion of divine intervention. Is the truth of Christian or Jewish revelation simply presupposed here, or are there special reasons for which Professor Moutsopoulos thinks that the conception of divine intervention in man's history is a particularly adequate formula to describe God's relations with man?[3]

A second historical implication of the solution under discussion is the theory of the *Kairos*, and of the kairic categories, of which Professor Moutsopoulos speaks. Obviously his special version of a theory of kairic categories, to which temporal categories must be reduced in order to understand God's conception of the becoming of the world and of man's history, has some relations to the ancient Greek notion of *Kairos* as distinguished both from *Aion* and from *Chronos*. It is well known that the notion of *Kairos* and to *Kai rion* has an important place in the ethical and political, if not in the metaphysical theories of Plato, Aristotle and the Stoics. This becomes even more important in the religious tradition founded by the New Testament and continuing till, for example, the theology of Paul Tillich and his circle in our century. The main relations and distinctions should be given close consideration.

Concerning the systematic problems of the general subject and of Professor Moutsopoulos' solution, I shall briefly enumerate, together with some commentaries and critiques, a series of questions, which should be discussed.

The very centre of Professor Moutsopoulos' paper on the relations between God, on the one hand, and man and history, on the other, is certainly his stressing of the interventional character of God's activity, which can be conceived by man only in kairic categories. So *Kairos* is the very bridge between God's perfection and the process of man's history. This raises first a number of questions concerning the nature or essence of the *Kairos*, in which God intervenes: Is *Kairos* the only medium between God's eternal perfection and man's temporality and evolution, between God and the reality of becoming? Is *Kairos* strictly transcendent in relation to time and temporal categories, and how can it then be a ruling moment in time (even being a minimum and an optimum within the process of becoming)? Is the kairic intervention of God reconciliable with his eternity and duration, is it even in some sense their expression and consequence, and if so, how can this be?

A further, second question of considerable importance seems to me to be, whether there is not behind the kairic interventions of God another necessary relation between God's eternity and man's temporality. That is, is there not a perfect model of time in God's eternity, so that time can be the image of eternity? Is this relation between the intelligible time in God as *paradeigma* of successive time and divisible time in the world and man's history and becoming not the necessary condition for the relations between God and man? Is divisible time a mere illusion of man's technical and practical ambitions,[5] or is it an aspect of the reality of becoming and at the same time an image of God's eternal perfection?

Professor Moutsopoulos speaks of a series of changes in the relations between God and the world and (with reference to revelation) it is sufficiently clear what he means by this. But what consequences does this series of changes have for God's being and the perfection of his being? Are these changes changes only in man's perspective, because man is subject to the process of becoming, or do these changes affect even God's substance as a perfect entity (or God's activity as that of a perfect first agent)?

In addition to that, let me focus on what seems a central question of this problem. Are there, besides the testimony of revelation, general reasons for human understanding and consciousness of a necessary and perfectly eternal being; of the thesis that time and temporality have a beginning and an end in eternity, and for the necessity of an intervening activity by God which man can conceive only in kairic categories? Whereas the classical metaphysical tradition gives several very convincing reasons for the necessary being of eternity,[6] it will certainly be more difficult to give natural reasons for the necessity of the kairic interventions of God, although we have heard some most brilliant arguments for this.

This question can be understood even more generally as a question on the relations between faith and reason: How can the principal dogmas of faith and revelation be justified from the standpoint of natural reason? Or should they first be simply accepted and then interpreted? This is, of course, not without importance and relevance when Professor Moutsopoulos quotes creation, redemption and last judgment as instances of the kairic interventional activity of God.

He mentions the kairic interventions of God as testified by

Jewish and Christian faith, and as explained by theological concepts. So far as these two religions are concerned, nobody could deny that these concepts have the greatest validity. But if the kairic activity of God is meant here to be decisive for man's life and history in a most general way, that is, for humanity as a whole and for people of every possible country, time and religious faith, then another question must be asked. How is the step made from the validity of these concepts on the kairic interventions of God, in their special religious context, to their absolute validity for mankind as a whole? How and by what argument or reason, can it be shown that these concepts are valuable truths, not only for these specific religions, but for the whole of humanity?

Last but not least, let me refer to the problem of the becoming God as a subject of discussion. Revelation hardly gives support to such a doctrine, and this conception is in contradiction too with the main assumptions of the classical metaphysical tradition from the Greeks down to the seventeenth and eighteenth centuries--Heraclitus with his divine Logos not excluded. On the other hand, the conception of a becoming God (even of a God attaining his own perfection by becoming himself in man) can be found in more than one prominent philosophy of our century, such as that of Bergson or of Scheler, not to omit the earlier conception of Hegel on the Absolute. I mention this problem here, because one might be tempted to suppose that the best explanation for the process of becoming in the world is the notion of a becoming God, who finds in man's history the fulfillment of his own perfection.

To conclude, it should be stressed that the theory of the kairic interventional activity of God is, of course, not the only way in which the relations between God and man's history can be interpreted and explained metaphysically. The speculative system of Hegel is only one of the most famous alternatives. It gives to the relation between God and man's history the utmost importance by seeing in man's history the fulfillment of the process of perfection for the Absolute. It has no need for kairic interventional activity, but interprets the process of the relations between God and man in a dialectical way, which has to provide for continuity and eternity in temporality. Yet here God's transcendence is in danger, and the self-perfection of the Infinite in the finite remains, in principle, a highly problematic thesis. Hence, let's turn our attention to the eternal God, who creates man and rules man's destiny by kairic intervention.

Universität Zürich

Zürich, Switzerland

NOTES

1. Moutsopoulos, in the discussion, made the distinction between a cyclic conception of history (a Greek conception, e.g., in Hesiod and Heraclitus) and a linear conception of history (the Jewish-Christian conception). In my view the cyclic conception of time in Greek metaphysical thought is not a conception of history, but a mythical conception of time and temporal process. What I mean in my commentary is only the linear conception of history as the irreversible succession of meaningful events in time. If Moutsopoulos in the discussion compared Hesiod with Plotinus he could do that only in comparing non-temporal relations (in Plotinus) with mythical time and not with history (in Hesiod).

2. In the discussion following the paper George McLean pointed out that we must make a clear distinction between God's interventions in a proper sense (as unique events in the Jewish or Christian conception of history, i.e., in a religious conception of history, which is concerned with the creation of the world, the passion and salvation of Christ, and the last judgment) and a more general notion of divine intervention (in the sense of every act of causation by the Absolute). In the discussion these were often confused with one another. In my commentary, I mean only the more narrow religious sense of intervention. Whereas only this "religious" intervention of God can be "kairic," the other conception of divine intervention comes close to the notion of continuous causation of the world and man's history by God (see Descartes' conception of a *creatio continua* as a series of interventions).

3. In the discussion, Moutopoulos has explained that the kairic interventional activity of God is a hypothesis he makes in his paper, and in that sense it is for his reflections only a point of departure. But for every Jewish and Christian believer the kairic interventions of creation, redemption and last judgment cannot be mere hypotheses. If we endeavour to give a consistent metaphysical theory of the kairic interventions of God, we must discuss them not so much as hypotheses, but as valid (or non-valid) affirmation on the objective nature and activity of God.

4. See Plato: *Parmenides*, 151e3-155d4, and my interpretation of this passage in F.P. Hager: *Der Geist and das Eine* (Bern und Stuttgart: Verlag Paul Haupt, 1970), pp. 142-149. For time as the (moving) image of eternity see Plato *Timaeus* 37c6-38b5.

5. This is obviously in some sense the view of Bergson. See H. Bergson: *L'Evolution cre atrice* (Paris: Alcan, 1925), pp. 295s and the interpretation of Moutsopoulos in "La critique du platonisme chez Bergson," *Les Etudes Bersoniennes*, IX (1970), pp.

152ss, part. 153.

6. What I mean here are not only explicit distinctions between time and eternity as, e.g., in Plotinus (*Enneads* III, 7), but all the well-known "proofs" for the existence of God, such as Anselm's ontological argument and Thomas' *quinque viae*. They all prove a perfectly eternal being above and beyond any temporality and process of development in time.

7. In the discussion (and later) a distinction has been made between sacred and secular history. Within the context of the former the kairic interventions of God would make sense; within the context of the latter, they would not. But this distinction is of no great help to our problem and from a religious point of view it is quite a meaningless distinction. God is, of course, the master of history in its totality including secular history. His interventional activity in creation, redemption and last judgment is understood as true for the whole of humanity and man's history, of which it is the beginning, the middle or centre and the end. The problem remains the same: to demonstrate by natural and general reasons that the truth of divine interventions, as testified by revelation, is of universal value.

PART IV

FREEDOM, THEOLOGY AND ETERNITY

CHAPTER XIV

EVOLUTION AND TELEOLOGY

EVANDRO AGAZZI

FUTURE AND DESTINY

One of the deepest differentiating elements which exists between the religious (and philosophical) context, on the one hand, and the scientific, on the other, is the fact that the concept of destiny is central to the religious way of thinking and is manageable inside the philosophical horizon, but has no place within the scientific discourse. As a matter of fact, one could even say that religion is in itself that complex of thoughts, beliefs, expectations, existential attitudes, personal commitments, and behaviour prescriptions which is concerned in the most direct way with the problem of the "destiny of Man" and which involves, indirectly, a general consideration of the "destiny of the world." The same kind of existential problems, when they are considered from the viewpoint of a more specific and technical intellectual analysis, become subject-matter for philosophy. Even if the words adopted are sometimes different, the most intrinsic meaning of the problems remains quite similar, e.g., when philosophers speak of the "sense" of life or try to make a philosophy of history. In science, on the contrary, it would sound very strange to speak of the "destiny of the universe"; the much more neutral expression of "future of the universe" is preferred, though nobody really explains the true semantic difference between these two ways of speaking. We shall begin, therefore, by sketching out very briefly this semantic difference.

In religion the idea of Destiny (which may well be written with a capital D) corresponds to the notion that God has put an intention or project in the world and included man in it. Stated differently, it corresponds to the notion that God has something comparable to a "Will." In this sense, nothing can happen without God willing it, and the whole development of cosmic and human events is nothing but the realization of this often inscrutable divine design. This is the destiny of world and man, so to speak, "in itself." For man, the notion of destiny has the additional meaning of something "toward which" he is directed but which, in various ways according to the different religions, also depends on his own will and manner of its application. To summarize, we could say that the religious idea of destiny expresses the most evolved conception of finality, that is, one which realizes the determined, conscious and almighty will of some Entity.

THE ELIMINATION OF FINAL CAUSES FROM SCIENCE

In philosophy, such a personalization of God is tendentially discarded, and even in the case of theistic philosophies God always appears under the aspect of a set of "predicates," rather than under the aspect of a "subject." It follows that, although it has been quite customary in the tradition of Western philosophy to conceive of God also as an Ultimate End, this came about as an application of a quite general and, so to speak, "non-theological" principle, the "principle of finality." This principle was purely ontological and independent of the different denominations it could receive. One has only to remember, e.g., the Aristotelian doctrine of the "four causes," including the "final cause," in order to understand the real basis on which finalism was introduced into philosophy proper. That this finalism applied to nature no less than to man is a very good indication of how distant it was from any religiously conceived idea of destiny.

In science, finally, even this depersonalized idea of finality found no permanent place. As a matter of fact, the consideration of "final causes" has been prohibited in science for some centuries. This was not because the investigation of the "causes," as such, was discarded; quite the contrary, from Newton to Ampère, to Helmholtz and practically to all the scientists until the end of the 19th century, the discovery of the causes is advocated as the proper goal of natural science. Only "final causes" were constantly ostracized and the fight against them has been perhaps most clearly emphasized during the long controversy opposing vitalism and mechanism in biology. The documentation and analysis of this conceptual attitude of modern science cannot, and need not, be encompassed within the limits of the present paper; it is already well-known and agreed upon. We intend, rather, to examine briefly the main reasons alleged for the intolerance in science of finalistic considerations.

When people speak frankly, they very often say that the overall important reason for not letting finalism enter into science is that it could somehow lead to involving in science the postulation of a Supreme Intelligence. They see such a possibility to be so dangerous to science that every methodological laxity which could precipitate this perspective must be opposed. It is easy to perceive in this position a flavour of the ancient polemics between science and religion and the expression of a kind of enmity toward any possible intermingling of religion in scientific discourse.

Kant's Attitude Toward Teleological Judgments

Other less aprioristic arguments are also to be found. One very serious argument is that finalistic or teleological judgment are typically without any proper cognitive status, as Kant has already clearly established. One readily recalls that Kant actually recognized that we feel strongly inclined to express teleological judgments about nature. Nevertheless, he introduced the distinction between the "determinant" and the "reflecting" judgment, endowing only the first with objective cognitive validity, and ascribing the teleological judgments to the second. One need only recall the *Critique of Judgment*, and especially its second part, in which this doctrine is developed. We can, therefore, consider the objections against the appropriateness of teleological reasonings about nature as being based essentially on epistemological reasons related in some way to the Kantian position, and, as such, as being of an intrinsically philosophical nature.

In addition, it is often claimed that the reference to any kind of finalism is contrary to "the spirit of scientific methodology," which is clearly recognizable by the adoption of well-determined "laws" accompanied by the specification of suitable "initial conditions." At variance with this spirit, all teleological patterns of reasoning necessarily involve a reference to some "final conditions." These are not empirically specifiable in most cases, and therefore do not provide material for the application of any rigorous lawlike reasoning.

The Mechanistic Paradigm of Science

These are among the most typical reasons presented against finalistic considerations in science. We shall evaluate them in reverse order, beginning with the "methodological question," of whether the teleological manner of thinking be at variance with the scientific mentality. It should be clear from the arguments alleged that all depends on a certain "model" or paradigm of scientific knowledge that is tacitly accepted as constituting *the* scientific approach itself, or as such. It is not difficult to recognize that such a paradigm has been provided by mechanics, i.e., by a particular science which, in turn, was imitated by many branches of physics. The question therefore immediately arises, whether the model of scientific discourse is rightly attributed nowadays to mechanics, especially inasmuch as it has become clear since the time of Mach that such a primacy of mechanics was merely an historical and not a theoretical privilege. The fact that mechanics was the first discipline to reach a considerable scientific rigor made it the natural basis of the subsequent developments in physics, but this could not possibly enable it to constitute the *conceptual* foundation of the whole of physics. We may now repeat with even greater reason that there is no plausible justification for imposing on scientific methodology as such the general criteria of mechanics and of those disciplines which accepted its (at least methodical) leadership. In other words, one would need to give a convincing *argument* that general laws plus initial conditions constitute the only model for a scientific treatment of every question. The simple indication of several instances in which the above criterion has been fruitful cannot substitute for this argument. In fact, today, as we shall see below, the most general requirements of a scientific explanation do not coincide with this excessively restricted model.

Coming now to the more specifically philosophical objection, for Kant mechanics was already playing the role of a paradigm, not only of science, but of satisfactory knowledge as such. A rather detailed analysis is needed to justify this claim; the author of the present paper has provided it elsewhere.[1] Here, let it suffice to point out how, e.g., in the Preface to the Second Edition of the *Critique of Pure Reason*, one finds explicit assumptions that mathematics and physics constitute the "examples" (in the sense of exemplar models) of that knowledge which deserves to be qualified as "science." In Kant's times, physics was practically nothing other than Newtonian mechanics. It follows that while Kant felt it necessary to give an a priori foundation to the most general theoretical principles which appeared to lie at the roots of Newtonian mechanics, he did not feel the same for other conceptual frameworks that did not play such a role. In consequence, he gave a full transcendental foundation to the cognitive cogency of the pattern of deterministic causality. In contrast, he considered finality to be rooted in another kind of a priori which had no cognitive value--being related to the "feeling of pleasure or displeasure" and not to "the legislative authority of understanding," to use the terminology of the third paragraph of the Introduction to the *Critique of Judgment*.

Kant claims to have derived his doctrines from a rigorous and uncommitted critical examination of "pure reason," in which no presuppositions of any kind should play a role. It is well known, however, that he could not actually rid himself of the accepted models of knowledge which dominated his time. What has been said here about Kant may be repeated for the subsequent century as well, especially if we consider the cultural environment of the scientists. Many of them were Kantian in a most serious sense (to mention only Helmholtz), and the mechanical worldview celebrated its major triumphs during the first half of the 19th century. It is no wonder then that the philosophical position regarding the cognitive untenability of finalistic judgments was reinforced during that historical period. Further evidence of this is found in the great effort displayed by several physicists to give an account, in terms of mechanical determinism, of irreversible thermodynamic processes and of "evolutionary" patterns at large.

FROM METAPHYSICAL TO SCIENTIFIC EXPLANATION

The less important objection is the one we could call "antitheistic" or "antimetaphysical," because it cannot really concern teleology in any special sense. Indeed, if one is concerned about not mixing metaphysics or religion with science (which is, generally speaking, the correct position), one should feel no more in danger with teleology than with deterministic causality: both can be either amplified in a metaempirical sense or used in a restrictive scientific sense. When Napoleon asked Laplace which place he had reserved for God in his cosmological picture, Laplace's answer was: "I had no need of this hypothesis." Not even Laplace's cosmology, based upon strict deterministic causality, made this answer a valid answer. For even within such a causality one still could ask the question about the First Cause, which gave rise to the rigid laws of mechanics and gave the world its 'initial conditions'. Laplace's reply simply expresses the fact that in science one is not concerned with problems related to the "ultimate reasons." But if this be true, one can equally well use the principle of finality without making reference to a Supreme Intelligence, and, in such a way, propose a finalistic cosmology, or more modestly give finalistic explanations of some particular domains of facts which appear to be fruitfully investigated from this viewpoint.

Our last statement leads us to the central point of the entire discussion, i.e. to the appreciation of the proper role that such principles as deterministic causality or finality can play in science. The ancient point of view was that one must look in science for the true causes of the observed phenomena. This already allowed the a priori removal of certain features from the realm of these "true" causes. Substantial forms, hidden qualities, and "final causes" used to be included on this black list. Especially in the first half of the 19th century, the admitted causes were very restricted in species, being practically confined to forces acting between material bodies, having the character of attractions or repulsions, directed along the straight lines joining these bodies, and having a magnitude dependent only on their mutual distances. Since the well-known crisis of "classical" physics, contemporary science has adopted quite a different methodical attitude: natural phenomena require an "explanation" and the concept of such an explanation is purely logical. In fact, a set of phenomena is considered to have been explained if one finds some general statements which, in addition to some particular ones, enabled one by means of a correct logical deduction to obtain the statements describing the phenomena involved. No particular requirements are postulated for the "general statements," which are currently called "hypotheses," even when they receive more qualifications and are labelled, according to their generality and explanatory power, "laws" or "principles." This is because the relation of "explanation" is a relation between sentences and disregards their ontological reference. There are, of course, additional refinements of this notion of scientific explanation, which add supplementary requirements to the minimal feature that an hypothesis provide the basis for the deduction of sentences describing phenomena. Such refinements remain ontologically uncommitted, as can easily be recognized by considering how many different positions are upheld, e.g., by physicists, about the ontological interpretation of their accepted theories. Conventionalism, phenomenalism, strict operationalism, realism and idealism are all to be found among these positions, but this does not affect the general agreement about the "explanatory power" of the theories involved.

If this is the general spirit and the mature awareness reached by contemporary scientific methodology, how could such ontological discrimination still be accepted as excluding teleological hypotheses from the domain of scientific explanation? As a matter of fact, if the adoption of one such hypothesis really enables the correct deduction of observational sentences and also can receive the other kind of methodical supports and refinements normally requested for the acceptance of an hypothesis in the empirical sciences, one cannot justify the refusal to take this kind of hypothesis into consideration. At this point, only a prejudice could form the basis of such a refusal.

DETERMINISM AND FINALISM

But prejudices of the said kind actually exist, and in the history of science we have already seen some reasons for their becoming so influential. One must say, on the other hand, that pure philosophy has its own responsibilities in this matter. We must not underestimate, e.g., the role played by the Cartesian ideal of applying a mathematical manner of reasoning to every question as a methodological "model" of all intellectual inquiry. This imposed a strict deductivistic feature upon all manner of rational enterprise. As one can easily see, the first paradigm of "determinism" is actually to be found here, namely, the most complete, detailed and "necessary" deduction of every particular aspect of reality. Mathematical determinism is actually the direct ancestor of physical determinism, and this did not happen by chance. As is well known, Descartes identified the essence of material bodies with extension and, as a consequence, the theory of extension (i.e. geometry) became equivalent with the theory of material bodies (i.e. with physics). In this way a metaphysical "mechanicism" was introduced, bearing in itself all the cogency, but also all the a priorism, of a mathematical theory. This enables one to understand also Spinoza's analogous position, which in a way was an even more rigorous application of a generalized reasoning *more geometrico* than that of Descartes. Here one can also find the most radical opposition to final causes. The Appendix to the First Book of the *Ethics* is the clearest example, and perhaps one of the most violent attacks against "final causes" in the whole history of philosophy. It is true that the finalism rejected here calls God's will into play for explaining accidental physical events, while, under the names of *conatus* or *inclinatio*, a kind of finality intrinsic to things is admitted by Descartes and Spinoza themselves. But it is also true that these polemics paved the way for the complete elimination of final causes by the philosophers and scientists of the Enlightenment.

We are not going to investigate these historical and more hidden responsibilities for slighting finalistic ways of thinking. Nevertheless, this philosophical tradition should be taken into serious account if one were to write the history of the "deterministic" worldview (and equal attention should be paid, for opposite reasons, to the strong vindication of the final causes which is to be found in such a deep and scientifically minded thinker as Leibnitz). What we want to note here is rather that, from a purely philosophical point of view, all this meant a drastic impoverishment of the notion of "cause" as it had been conceived throughout the philosophical tradition, starting at least with Aristotle. The original meaning of cause was actually a very rich one, expressing in a way the whole complex of things which are able to satisfy the intellectual exigencies of comprehension and explanation or, if one prefers, to satisfy the exigencies of the *logos*, as being different from the exigencies of the pure empirical ascertainment of facts. In this sense, to find the cause was equivalent to "give reason" for a fact or an entity; and that is why Aristotle could speak of several kinds of cause, one of which was precisely the "final cause." The deterministic tenet is a reduction of that complexity of meaning to the very restricted sense of the Aristotelian "efficient cause," i.e., of the cause that "produces the effect," so to speak, from behind. We are surely entitled to ask whether this elimination of the other meanings of cause were justified. The best way to answer this question seems to be to consider which aspects of reality could not properly be accounted for without some of the other causes.

From this point of view, it appears that the elimination of the final cause surely amounts to a mutilation of something actually present in our *cognitive* experience. Surely, there are many "purposive behaviors" around us. This is true at least at the level of the human community for which the indication of goals, intentions, and aims is a necessary requirement for rational explanation. In this sense we can say that we *know* that some actions or facts take place because of some purpose that is being finalistically presupposed. From this very fact, it should be clear that there exist at least some circumstances in which the teleological pattern of reasoning is adopted in a cognitive sense. But, once the principle of finality as such appears to be commonly adopted in human reasoning, there is no justification for prohibiting its use outside the domain of the "conscious behaviors."

No explicit or good reason is to be found in the long polemic against finalism, except the aprioristic tenet which "presupposes" that every event in the world, including so-called free decisions, is the offspring of a possibly very long and complicated chain of strictly deterministic conditionings. The "metaphysical" character of this claim can be tested even through the Popperian criterion of its unfalsifiability; indeed those who are unable to actually show this alleged chain simply make the excuse that this depends on the complexity of its different steps. In this sense, one can apply against the antifinalists the same argument Spinoza used against finalism in the already mentioned Appendix to the First Book of the *Ethics*. He says there, that the appeal to some divine design is usually made because one is unable to trace back the long chain of the predetermining conditions of an accidental fact to its proper origins; hence the divine will appears as a kind of substitute for our ignorance. One could repeat here something very similar, namely, the a priori "principle," that only deterministic explanations must be looked for, covers our actual ignorance of the alleged "initial conditions" and leads us to state that they must exist somewhere, even without any practical possibility of uncovering them. In this way, the statement has no less the character of a belief than the statement which involves God's will to explain accidental events.

DOMAIN OF APPLICATION OF TELEOLOGY

Once the rejection of teleology in itself has appeared as fully unjustified, one can begin to see how and where it might have its most significant applications. One must not go from one extreme to the other and replicate with the finalistic approach the same kind of exaggeration that took place with the deterministic one. In addition, one must not forget that much of the mistrust of finalistic considerations arose in the history of our culture as a consequence of the idle and superficial use of teleological explanations, which often appeared as a disreputable way of getting rid of complex problems without really explaining anything at all. The idea of teleology, in its most "neutral" sense, seems to be an appropriate kind of "categorization" when we are in the presence of facts or events which show a coordination of deterministic chains which: (i) is not necessitated by these chains themselves; and (ii) produces a "result" which is not able to be explained by following the dynamics of the singular chains involved, but only by taking into consideration the special coordination or "design" connecting them.

Needless to say, intentional human and, at least to some extent, animal behaviors manifest these characteristics. Teleological explanation is usually not contested in these cases, because the presence of some "design" or of orientation toward some goal is easily accounted for by the patent presence of the human or animal "designer.' People begin to become diffident when the same pattern of reasoning is adopted, e.g., in the case of physiological "functions." There, a coordination of processes leading to a certain goal is quite patent, but one seems to be afraid to be compelled to admit a "designer" if he admits the design. In any case, this fear is quite naive because on the same basis one should be afraid of admitting an "agent" if he admits the existence of an "acting force," or of admitting a "legislator" if he admits the existence of a natural "law." Anthropomorphism is not more likely to affect finalistic reasoning than it is to affect the more usual deterministic one; the same methodological attitude should be sufficient to prevent it in both cases.

Evolution and Teleology

The same can be said when we pass from the consideration of the functioning of living beings to much more complex perspectives such as the conception of biological evolution. The profound meaning of this intuition was to extend to the entire system of living nature the idea of dynamic development as realizing a certain "design" which thus far had been limited to individual living organisms. In this sense, one can say that the major conceptual element in evolutionary theory is the vindication of teleology in the face of the idolatry of mechanical determinism which dominated physics. As a consequence, all the effort spent on showing the compatibility of evolution with deterministic causality, and giving a non-finalistic interpretation of evolution itself, were in part superfluous and in part misleading. They were, and remain, superfluous, inasmuch as teleology does not express finality *against* deterministic chains of facts, but rather the finality *of* these chains, that is, the fact that these chains appear coordinated into a design which in itself does not follow from any one of them. They are misleading insofar as in the effort to eliminate the idea of teleology from evolution, they actually attempt to deprive it of its most challenging intellectual novelty. The proof of the intellectual poverty of such efforts is given by the fact that they are obliged to call "randomness" into play at those points at which the most delicate questions arise. In this way, one gets that balanced mixture of "random and necessity," as it is expressed in the title of a famous bestseller, which as such is an admission of failure. The deterministic explanation works well as long as the problem is that of describing how some mechanisms act when certain very exceptional circumstances are, hypothetically, realized; but no explanation is given for the origin of these circumstances. They are simply postulated as happening "by chance," which simply means "with no apparent reason"; not to give a reason, however, is tantamount to being "unable to explain." In this way one sees that explanations are provided about matters which do not need them, i.e., on the points where mechanical chains and routines are running their usual course, while we are left without an answer precisely at those points at which the alleged mechanical explanation should face its challenger. It would be much more sensible to speak of a "design," bringing the deterministic chains together at some strategic points, rather than to leave such "black boxes" in order only not to become involved with the idea of teleology.

In addition, one should notice that all the efforts towards a statistical mastering of evolution and change through mechanical determinism are effected by some serious drawbacks. Consider, e.g., in thermodynamics, all the reasonings which try to recover some kind of determinism by the use of states of equilibrium. The price to be paid for that is to conceive the process as proceeding toward a complete disorder, which implies the "oblivion" of the initial conditions, i.e., of one of the cardinal prerequisites for every mechanistic explanation (think of the Boltzmann's distribution function tending to Maxwell's curve). Moreover, the states of equilibrium are quite exceptional and the real problem is rather that of justifying stability outside them. On this point again, traditional tools, which try to trace back change to invariance, fall short of the goal.

Leaving these slightly technical considerations aside, we should note that in the case of evolution as well as in several other cases in which the idea of a "better" stage or of progress, i.e., of an "advancing" or "positive" modification, are implicit, the teleological pattern is already present by the simple fact that a value judgment is tacitly at work. As this value judgment is surely not of a "moral" kind, it must express some fitness or appropriateness with respect to some goal, or design, or pattern. All possible deterministic explanations can at best clarify how this goal is reached, but not why it is there. We repeat again that the issue in question here is only a "categorial" one. It does not imply as such any metaphysical reference; it can be handled through some scientific and even formal and mathematical treatment, as the examples of general systems theory or the mathematical theories of structures and their evolution have already begun to show.

CONCEPTUAL ADEQUACY AND LOGICAL SIMPLICITY

A last objection against the adoption of finalistic viewpoints in science is that the introduction of "designs" or the like is contrary to the methodological imperative of simplicity, to the "Occam's razor" criterion, which requires that the number of postulated theoretical entities in a scientific theory be restricted to the minimum. We gladly admit this methodological canon, but it raises the question of how one is to evaluate simplicity. If one considers the great number of *ad hoc* hypotheses or conjectures that are commonly advocated, e.g., for giving non-teleological explanations of biological events, and if we consider additionally their high complexity and unlikeness, we must say frankly that they are really very far from being "simple." Indeed, they are so complicated that only the fact of being intrinsically non-inconsistent allows them a non-zero probability of being true, and thus the possibility of having been realized sometimes "by chance." In other words, while the admission of teleological patterns makes the semantical basis of science more complex--inasmuch as it contains more independent notions, but simplifies its theoretical constructs--the adoption of the strict mechanistic viewpoint acts in exactly the opposite sense. Sometimes to accept a complication in one sector means an intrinsic simplicity of the whole. (Take the example of Relativity theory which, during its beginnings, had no clear experimental support, but was proposed by Einstein and accepted by many others because it introduced a great "simplification" in Mechanics. This was true, but was also made possible through a drastic "complication" in the geometry and the four-dimensional metric introduced for describing the universe.)

It should be quite clear by now that no serious objections can be raised from a scientific viewpoint against teleology. Even where they are alleged to be scientific, the objections are actually the expression of a metaphysical position. People who do not admit the existence of a creator of the world and believe in a strict materialistic cosmology try not to adopt in science any intellectual construction that might be somehow reminiscent of a creationist conception. But this also means that one who does not share such metaphysical antipathies need not feel bound to those epistemological mutilations. Moreover, if one accepts the metaphysical doctrine of a Creator of the world and of man, one has many reasons for not refusing the teleological way of thinking which, besides being scientifically unobjectionable, does not raise psychological difficulties. Let us repeat: such a manner of thinking is neither a consequence nor a support of a theistic or creationistic worldview, whose foundations must be looked for on explicit and sound metaphysical ground, for a strictly deterministic way of thinking is quite compatible both with a creationistic worldview and with the idea of a destiny of man and world. But, precisely because all this is true, there is no reason why one should not be able to resort to this theoretical tool. It is capable of enriching our perspectives and approaches in religion and philosophy, as well as in science, and of bringing them closer together. This would help in reaching that harmonized unity of our intellectual activities which is one of the most important present goals at this stage of civilization.

Universite de Fribourg

Fribourg, Switzerland

NOTE

1. Agazzi, "From Newton to Kant: The Impact of Physics on the Paradigm of Philosophy," in *Christian Theology in the Context of Scientific Revolution*, Communications of New York Symposium, July 1977, Methodios Fouyas, ed. (Athens, 1978); reprinted from *Abba Salama*, IX (1978), 52-76

COMMENT

On Evandro Agazzi

"Evolution and Teleology"

SUSANNE MANSION

There are so many important questions that could be discussed in Professor Agazzi's very interesting paper that it is necessary to chooose between them. I shall leave more or less aside the historical discussions--interesting as they may be--and concentrate on the theoretical content of the paper. I shall present in a different order, and perhaps in a slightly different light, some of the questions that seem to me particularly important and likely to lend themselves to a fruitful discussion.

1. It should be quite clear, first, that Prof. Agazzi's paper is mainly concerned with the use of teleology, or final causality, in science and not in philosophy or metaphysics. This being so, one could perhaps wonder what the impact of his demonstration is upon on the general theme, "Mam amd God." The answer is found in the very last sentences of his paper. On the one hand, says our author in his conclusion, people who reject all sorts of teleology in science do so under the influence of a metaphysical--or anti-metaphysical--prejudice: they are materialists and they instinctively shy away from anything that reminds them of a creationist conception of the universe, where an intelligence is responsible for the existence of the physical world. But, on the other hand, he goes on, for those who admit that the teleological way of thinking is "neither a consequence nor a support of a theistic or creationist worldview," there is no reason why they should not be able to resort to this theoretical tool (teleology) in science and for the benefit of science, as well as in religious thought and philosophy, with a view to an "harmonized unity of our intellectual activities," which is of course a major present goal.

It is thus important for a metaphysician to try to eradicate the prejudice against teleology from the mind of scientists and, though reintroducing final causality into science, to bring science, philosophy, and even religion, closer together.

We could perhaps first ask ourselves whether we agree with the author on all these points. A thorough discussion of them might lead to the much wider issue of the relationship between science and philosophy in general. It may be a good thing to realize that this problem is at the root of the matter, for only a clear idea of the mutual relations between science and philosophy shall we be able to appreciate the exact content of the concepts we use in each field, and the exact meaning of words employed commonly in science and philosophy, though with a different signification.

2. A second problem of great interest the notion of teleology itself, as applicable to science. Prof. Agazzi was careful to state that the idea of a final cause is not restricted to "intentional behaviour," that is to say, that no sort of consciousness is *needed* in order for a teleological process to exist and to be liable to a finalistic type of explanation. What is needed, in Prof. Agazzi's terms, is "a coordination of deterministic chains (of events) which (1) is not necessitated by these chains themselves; and (2) produces a "result" which cannot be explained by following the dynamics of the singular chains involved, but only by taking into consideration the special coordination or "design connecting them." Paraphrasing the last part of this sentence, we could call into play what the author says a few pages further down a propos of the problem of evolution. This "special coordination" or the "design" that connects several deterministic chains, or again the "result" that cannot be satisfactorily explained by the chains themselves is labelled in the case of evolution: "a better stage," "progress," or "an advancing or positive modification." Indeed, it seems to me almost impossible in a finalistic language to avoid using some such terms implying a *qualitative* appreciation of the final stage of the process. Who would think of talking of finality in a chain of events that lead to nothing remarkable in some respect or other? On the other hand, how to avoid using a teleological language--overtly or covertly--when describing biological processes for instance, whose "normal" outcome is beneficial for the living individual or for its species, and *because* it is thus beneficial?

All this amounts to saying that if we want to reintroduce final causality into scientific language--that is, if we want to do so without committing the sin of anthropomorphism--we shall have to find a *scientific* meaning to these vague words or phrases like "good," "beneficial," "positive," "marking a progress," etc. Is that possible? It is debatable, but in any case it seems to be a necessary condition for a justified use of teleology in science.

Let us go a little further into this matter. Prof. Agazzi rightly pointed out that the presence of a design and consequently the need for a finalistic explanation are easily admitted, nowadays at least, in the case of human and, to some extent, animal behaviour because of the patent existence of a designer in these cases. The time of radical behaviorism is over and one would not now find many people ready to do away with the category of consciousness or of the "psychic," since even the Freudian "unconscious" is of a psychic nature. But the problem is not there. According to Prof. Agazzi, it is much more to decide whether a teleological explanation may be considered as valid in the case where any form of consciousness is absent, as in physiological processes for instance or in the evolution of the living world. It is in the field of "natural" sciences that the Cartesian prejudice against finality is really strong, which is not surprising since Descartes tried to reduce life to a mere mechanism. It is plain then that what we need in order to react against the Cartesian dogma is the notion of a natural finality as contrasted with psychological (that is, intentional) finality. I would add even that we should be careful to banish here all metaphorical use of a psychological language and refuse to understand *natural* finality as a degraded form of what we experience in our own purposeful activity.

But then a double problem arises: have we got such a concept of a purely natural finality? And how are we going to define it in scientific, factual terms? The two questions are different, for a common sense notion of natural finality that could perhaps be used as a starting point for a philosophical reflection on the subject, is not precise enough to constitute a scientific tool of research.

3. Another major question, linked with the preceding one, is that of the relationship between finalistic and deterministic explanation. Prof. Agazzi certainly does not want to replace one type of explanation by the other, for the finality he is trying to vindicate is not established *against* determinism--however the latter may be conceived--but is said to be quite compatible with it. Nevertheless the exact sense in which finality and determinism agree is not so easy to perceive, nor is the precise point at which they hinge with one another.

To put the matter quite crudely. Supposing the deterministic chains to be uninterrupted (as Kant thought they must be), what *need* have we of a final cause? They seem quite sufficient to explain all that happens. If, on the other hand, there is a gap somewhere, what *right* have we to fill it by a finalistic explanation? The introduction of a design, the idea that something *must* happen' in order to account for its otherwise unexplained appearance, is exactly what Spinoza rightly could not bear. So we seem to be in a paradoxical situation. Teleology is acceptable in science only if it is, so to speak, inscribed in the facts that science investigates, but to be so inscribed seems to be equivalent to being a part of the deterministic chain, so that we apparently can find no place for final causes in science.

Something quite different is, of course, suggested by the paper we are examining. It is neither a simple, isolated fact nor a series of simple facts in our experience that call for a finalistic explanation, it is rather a *quality* in the facts themselves and in their concatenation, as we saw above. But if that be so, and if efficient and final causalities do not compete with one another, ought not we use a different language when talking about their respective effects, in order to mark the difference of level between these two types of causality?

Here are some examples of the related problem. Can the same event happen at random *and* by necessity? Can the same fact be the result of a necessary efficient cause *and* be produced *because* some end is pursued? Is it exactly the same fact or the same event we are describing in these very different ways? If so, how to explain that we admit of no exceptions to the physical laws whereas we readily accept that nature's purposes are not always fulfilled. The only way out of the first difficulty seems to be to admit that randomness is not *opposed* to necessity, but rather to what is obtained through the action of a final cause. So it is at the level of finality that we shall have to decide whether something happens at random or not, meaning in the first case that it has no need of a finalistic explanation, but just results from necessary, antecedent causes. We thus imply that the need for a teleological explanation arises when an additional meaning is detected in facts that would be satisfactorily accounted for by deterministic causes *in abstraction* from this additional meaning. A solution to the second problem I have mentioned should be looked for along the same lines. These and other questions of the same type will in any case have to be faced if we want to justify the use of final causality in science.

4. Turning now from science to philosophy, but still following Prof. Agazzi's hint at the end of his paper, we could ask ourselves what is the role of teleology in philosophy, and especially in metaphysics.

Everybody will agree that finality is a big subject for philosophical thinking. Not only because the philosopher is at home when he criticizes the concept of finality in its application at the scientific level, but because philosophy is the very Place for an investigation of all kinds of causality, an investigation which does not suffer from the self-imposed limitations of the scientific inquiry.

A comparison between different forms of teleology--between intentional and natural finality, for instance--would be quite appropriate. But I think that the use of the final cause in metaphysics, and particularly in the proof of the existence of God, is the problem that should interest us most here.

It should be quite clear from what Prof. Agazzi said that no conclusion of any kind can be drawn for or against the existence of a divine Organizer of the world from the application of finalistic reasoning in science. Whether such an Organizer exists or not is a strictly metaphysical question which must be investigated on a metaphysical basis. Nevertheless, it is certainly not out of place to ask ourselves here what we think of this celebrated proof, which Kant himself said should always be mentioned with respect.

In the form it takes in Aquinas' fifth way, for instance, it is no doubt meant to be a metaphysical proof, for it takes its start from a comprehensive view of the universe. Since it primarily relies on the ordering of the physical world, it presupposes that an authentic philosophy of nature is possible. This thesis was taken for granted at the time of St. Thomas, but can create serious problems at the present time when the scientific approach is regarded by many as the only valid mode of knowledge of the physical world.

If we accept the latter thesis (which is not my case), it seems that we shall have to decide whether some philosophical view of nature based on science would constitute a sufficient ground for such an argument. But then would not all the fears of the scientists materialize and would not such an argument be open to their above-mentioned objections?

A second delicate point is the passage from an order to an ordering Mind (Intelligence and Will). Are we entitled to posit such a Mind as the governing principle of the world taken *as a whole* when we do not think it necessary to suppose an intelligence to be present in even the most refined works of nature taken in particular, for instance, in the instinctive behaviour of animals?

These, to be sure, are only samples of the questions that could be asked in connection with the finalistic argument for God's existence and with the place of teleology in metaphysics.

University of Louvain

Louvain, Belgium

CHAPTER XV

ABSOLUTE BEING AND FREEDOM

R.J. NJOROGE

Observing some metaphysical and religious traditions, we note that they affirm the transcendence of the Absolute Being, which for the time being may be called 'God' with all the vagueness of the word. At the same time they affirm a certain independence of man, a kind of independence which is viewed as the basis for man's freedom in action. In such metaphysical and religious systems man is seen as accountable for what he does and can be an object of censure and even damnation, for he is viewed as intrinsically free. This position accords well with juridical systems which, operating on the assumption that man is free--except perhaps in cases of 'children' and 'abnormal' persons--maintain that man can therefore be punished for failure to obey societal prescriptions. This position also accords well with religious teachings which affirm that to a certain extent man's 'salvation' depends on the exercise of his free will. Furthermore, this position accords well with the common sense notion that persons can be blamed for what they do and honored for their freely chosen 'good works'.

This position, however, is faced with certain metaphysical problems pertaining to the nature of being. The problem is this: if we can talk of Absolute Being which is the source of all beings, how is it possible that man can bring about free choice which is a mode of being? How is this mode of being to be reconciled with the absoluteness of God, which subsumes within it all modes of being?

One way of handling this question is to affirm that even though there is this dilemma pertaining to how this mode of being can be independent, the intrinsic freedom of man has to be taken on faith, for revelation teaches the existence of such freedom. This position of faith has not, however, satisfied many minds which endeavour to grapple with this issue on the level of human reason unaided by 'revelation'. These minds, seeing that it is contradictory, on the level of human reason, to maintain the transcendence of the Absolute Being and a certain independence of man, have tended to argue that man is essentially an aspect, a manifestation, of the Absolute Being. The supposed freedom of man is then really a mistaken raising of our psychological awareness of freedom to the metaphysical level. They argue that we think we are absolutely free, in the metaphysical sense, because we are conscious of our freedom on the psychological plane. They continue to argue that the fact that we 'feel free' is not a sufficient reason for maintaining that we are free in a deeper, metaphysical sense.

These minds, endeavouring to overcome the contradiction mentioned above, opt for some sort of pantheism, such as that of Spinoza, whereby man, viewed as a totality, is seen as a manifestation of God. Other systems, such as that of Hegel, see the Absolute as that which is expressed in Nature and the Human Spirit, and as a result it becomes impossible to affirm human freedom. Determinism thus replaces freedom.

It should be noted also that the path towards determinism is not merely via the conception of the Absolute Being. Indeed there is a scientific path that leads to determinism. This scientific path views human actions to be products of causal factors that form a series. These causal factors can be biological, social or environmental imperceptibly they condition human action; though on the psychological level this appears unconditioned, is nevertheless determined.

This paper aims at the following:

1. To show that whether a man takes the libertarian or the deterministic position he undergoes a certain psychological and moral exigency which, as it were, ensures that he adheres to certain values. There is a sense in which we can assert that the determinist and libertarian positions merge or converge in the area of value and the supposed irresponsibility emanating from determinism is seen to be non-existent.

2. To show that even though there is this convergence of the two positions in the area of value there is a sense in which, we could say, metaphysical positions (and in this case libertarianism and determinism), determine or affect the values we hold, and especially our views of the human person.

3. To show that the adherent of the 'free will' position 'contemplates' or 'explains' the world, including the human reality, in a manner that is different from the way the determinist 'contemplates' the world.

The fundamental aim of this paper is to endeavour to use the notions of freedom and determinism as the springboard for discussions pertaining to metaphysics and value or 'ethics', that is, a starting point for reflections on the relationship between metaphysics and those prescriptions which guide men all over the world. I believe that in a world, such as ours, where there are multiplicities of metaphysical and religious beliefs, it is imperative to consider seriously this relationship so that we may get an insight into the possibilities of our common survival, which is possible to the extent that there is agreement on certain basic values.

PSYCHOLOGICAL AND MORAL EXIGENCY

Considering the biological and psychological constitution of man we note that man has a certain 'facticity' (to use an 'existentialist' term) which, as it were, determines him to seek what he judges to be necessary, such as the value of survival, etc. This facticity, considered as operative in human activity, is what I am calling 'psychological and moral exigency'. It appears that man obeys this facticity whether he is a libertarian or a determinist; thus in a certain sense the libertarian and the deterministic positions can be reconciled.

This reconciliation is possible precisely because the two positions are held by men who, in virtue of their being men sharing in a common humanity, are naturally endowed with tendencies or dynamisms which tend towards similar values, such as the conquest of the vagaries of the environment, and thus are able to continue in existence. Both the determinist and the libertarian are endowed with drives, needs, etc., which constitute compelling demands arising from their human nature and which call for the allegiance of both. There are, then, biological, social and moral demands built in the human personality with different degrees of intensity in diverse personalities.

Now, in the light of these compelling demands which are constitutive of the human personality it appears absurd to assume that determinism of necessity leads to succumbing to circumstances, to irresponsibility and even despair. Such an assumption is absurd becaise it overlooks the fundamental point that man, apart from being a person who holds metaphysical and religious beliefs about the universe, is also psychologically and morally constituted. In a word, man is not only a metaphysician; he is also a psychological and moral being. As a moral being, for instance, man pursues the 'call' of duty which in a certain sense supersedes libertarian and deterministic positions. The moral demand of duty arises in both the libertarian and the determinist at certain crucial moments of life.

In the area of value, then, we can bring together both the libertarian and the determinist. Indeed we can cite many cases in which both, as it were, converge. For instance, both may, irrespective of their metaphysical positions, condemn acts of wanton cruelty of human beings and both may strongly believe in the intrinsic worth of the human person. It is worth noting that the libertarian position and the deterministic standpoint are analogous to the views of the theist and the 'humanist'. In this connection, Ian T. Ramsey in *Freedom and Immortality* points out that Bertrand Russell, a non-theist or simply 'a humanist', presented with wanton cruelty feels obliged "to oppose it; he discerns a Duty to eradicate it,"[1] a moral standpoint which may, mistakenly, be assumed to be the monopoly of the theist. A. J. Ayer, the British logical positivist, discussing the same point, states that "if cruelty is absolutely wrong, it would still be wrong even if Christians would say *per impossible*, the superior being did not condemn it."[2] The fundamental point we want to make here is that just as a theist and a non-theist can agree on certain values, irrespective of their religious and metaphysical beliefs, so too can a libertarian and a determinist uphold similar values irrespective of their contradictory metaphysical positions.

We can then affirm that there is sufficient evidence to hold that there is moral exigency as a constitutive principle in the human personality, an exigency which defies, in a measure, metaphysical standpoints. True, this moral exigency may be different among different men depending on their biological, social and moral experiences. The 'sense of obligation', for instance, is a pertinent factor. In this connection, R. M. Hare in *The Language of Morals* rightly points our that "it is a *fact* that we have this feeling of obligation--different people in different degrees, and with different contents."[3] To overlook this point is, in my view, to gloss over the fact that while man upholds metaphysical and religious beliefs he is at the same time morally constituted. The feelings of obligation are found in various human situations and climes, whether we talk of the people of Asia, Europe or Africa, and they, as Hare notes rightly, "are reinforced by all those factors which psychologists have listed; and the total result is what is generally called a feeling of obligation."[4]

The total thrust of these considerations is to point out that the supposed ills that stem from the metaphysical doctrine of determinism are not logically entailed in giving allegiance to that doctrine, though prima facie, it appears to compromise or inhibit pursuit of values which may be dear to us. The determinist does, like all of us, pragmatically seek those goods which, arising from his biological, psychological and moral nature, are seen or rather are 'compulsively seen' as necessary for life.

Thus, there appears to be another 'law of being' which, operating as a form of dynamism within the human personality, as it were compels the human person to seek certain values. To the metaphysician of the immanentist bent of mind, this compelling law is really the expression in the human person of the Absolute Being. To a person of positivistic bent of mind, this law is merely a tendency or propensity of the human being whose reason for existence is the fact that it is there!

EFFECT OF METAPHYSICAL POSITIONS OF VALUE

We have pointed out that, given man's facticity which is characterized by a variety of dynamisms, value can be said to be capable of superseding metaphysical positions; in this case value can be said to be capable of superseding deterministic and libertarian positions.

However, a certain qualification is now necessary. For although, in a sense, metaphysical positions can be superseded by value there is meaning in affirming that metaphysical positions do, in their turn, dispose us to take certain value positions towards the human being or simply 'person'. The point in question is implied by Louis Arnaud Reid in *Philosophy and Education* where ie asserts (in connection with education):

> Our metaphysical assumptions (of one sort or another) will affect many practical things we do in education. To take one example only, *punishment*. If we punish, *why* do we? On a purely determinist or 'conditioning' view, we ought to punish only in order to alter, by conditioning, a child's behavior in the *future*. To punish him for what he *has* done would be irrational and could only be a kind of revenge. The poor child was conditioned to do what he did. On the other hand, if one thinks of a child as having some measure of freedom to choose to do or not to do, we can consistently regard him as responsible for what he did. Here, *if* punishment is ever justifiable, it is justifiable for quite a different reason, that he responsibly did wrong."[5] (The emphasis is Reid's.)

It would appear that underlying the determinist's imposition of punishment, in this example, is the assumption that the poor child is a product of causal factors. This attitude of the determinist might tend towards leniency arising out of sympathy for the sorry state of the child. On the other hand, the libertarian might tend to be astringent towards the child for he sees him as a person who has the freedom to act differently. The determinist is eager to change the causal factors so that they may be consonant with the value he wants to inculcate in the child, while the free will adherent tends to overlook these causal factors and view the culprit as responsible for his actions, that is, as the sole factor in his activity.

This rather banal example is meant to vindicate the position that the metaphysical doctrines of libertarianism and determinism tend to have their corresponding value positions with regard to, say, the human person and that these doctrines in a measure differently determine the way we behave towards others. To the extent that our mode of behavior towards others constitutes a value, these metaphysical doctrines can be said to have their corresponding expression of this value. A court judge of a deterministic turn of mind might tend to consider a criminal as a person who needs therapy rather than punishment. Indeed this possibility is not far-fetched given the fact that in various juridical systems the views of clinical psychologists and probation officers are sought by judges prior to passing sentences. Two factors justify punishment within the deterministic view, namely, the determinist's belief in the possibility that the person can be changed and his belief in, or allegiance to, value in accordance with the moral exigency we have discussed.

THE CONTEMPLATIVE DIMENSION

It should be noted that we began discussing the libertarian and deterministic positions by considering the points of their convergence. Then it was noted that the conception of this convergence calls for qualification; in this connection it was noted that even though two positions can sometimes converge in upholding similar values there is a sense in which the two doctrines differently 'color' some of the values we hold especially towards the human person. Thus our discussion of the two positions has moved from points of convergence toward certain points of divergence. Now we shall continue discussing further points of divergence that can be discerned in the two metaphysical positions. This further divergence pertains to what I call "the contemplative dimension."

The adjective 'contemplative' is formed from a verb which means in this context "to consider or think studiously; to ponder; meditate."[6] The determinist and the libertarian consider or ponder reality differently. The reality that is pertinent to this discussion is first and foremost human activity. Now, while the determinist and the libertarian may perform similar actions as a result of psychological and moral exigency, they tend to view these similar actions differently. They tend to 'explain' their activities differently, though they may describe them in similar terms. There is a great difference between 'explanation' and 'description' and it is imperative to bring out the difference between these two terms for they are apropos to our understanding of the difference between determinism and libertarianism via-a-vis the contemplative dimension.

Description answers the question 'what?'; explanation answers the question 'why?'. The 'what' is revealed through some sort of observation which shows the characteristics, e.g. colors, extension, relations, etc. Description is, therefore, immediate, close to sense experience and, understood broadly, pertains to a greater part of the physical and social sciences. These sciences, which are descriptive in the broad sense of the term, have their peculiar methods of testing or, if you like, verification through sense experience.

Explanation, on the other hand, has, in the sense I am to use it here, the tendency to transcend the immediate; it moves towards greater and greater generality. Often statements characteristic of explanation are not testable in the scientific sense of the term. This element of being untestable is characteristic of many statements found in transcendent metaphysics and theology, disciplines whose statements are pre-eminently explanatory. Explanation accords well with the metaphysical and theological demand for understanding. Of course, it should be noted that many hypotheses of the physical and social sciences are explanatory, but the ultimate basis of their validity is their verification in 'sense' experience. In contrast, those of metaphysics do not have to be 'verified' in this scientific sense--e.g., such statements as 'God is the cause of the world'.

The contemplative dimension of the libertarian and deterministic positions is characterized by explanation, at least. We shall first consider the 'free will' position, then proceed to the position of determinism with regard to their explanatory aspects. In considering their explanatory aspects I hope, at the same time, to show that each has more than one version.

The Libertarian Position.

I have been using, and will continue to use, the term 'libertarian' in the sense whereby it applies to all those who subscribe to the doctrine of 'free will'. Within libertarianism, however, there are a number of versions of the doctrine; some are psychological while others are metaphysical and religious. We shall first consider 'psychological libertarianism'.

The psychological libertarian considers situations when he performs actions without compulsion. Seeing that there is no, say, person, animal or thing which compels him to act he considers himself to be free in his activity. For instance, philosopher Ian Ramsey maintains that 'free will' is revealed in "a moment of decision"[7] when we act without the influence of what he calls "external pressures," that is, when our decision has our "personal backing."[8] In Ramsey's view free will is revealed when an action is performed "with due deliberation,"[9] that is, when man is conscious of himself as the 'I' that performs an act as opposed to moments when man performs an act purely as a matter of habit or routine. In Ramsey's view when a person performs an action conscious of himself as the agent that performs the act he exercises 'decisive activity'. At that moment something special occurs, and that something is, in effect, the consciousness of oneself as the 'I' which freely performs the action.[10]

Note that the action itself can be described in empirical terms but these empirical terms, do not reveal the decisive element. This means that purely scientific descriptions or accounts have no access to this element which is at the foundation of the exercise of 'freedom' in this sense. There is, therefore, something transcendent about a free act understood according to psychological libertarianism:

> The claim for free will is, then, that in a moment of decision there is disclosed the 'transcendent' character of a man's personality. It is in making such a decision that he realizes he is not limited to the objective behavior he displays to a scientific observer.[11]

In this account of psychological libertarianism it is man himself who knows when he acts 'freely' and when he does not; it is man himself who knows when he gives 'personal backing' to what he does. When a person performs an act under duress there is absence of this 'personal backing'. But this absence is not accessible to scientific description; it is known only to the agent.

In a nutshell, to be free or to have a free will, according to psychological libertarianism, is to be able to perform an act conscious of oneself as the agent who gives 'personal backing' to the act.

The other version of libertarianism uses a different language of freedom. It is metaphysical and religious and is characteristic of positions similar to that of Thomas Aquinas whereby the human will is considered not to be necessitated to pursue any finite object. In this version of libertarianism the human will is considered to be free with regard to any object which is not the "Absolute Good," God. To Aquinas, "the will does not desire of necessity whatever it desires,"[12] but "the will of the man who sees God in His essence of necessity adheres to God, just as now we desire of necessity to be happy."[13]

It is evident that when a psychological libertarian speaks of the free will and when the Thomist does the same, both attach different meanings to the idea of 'free will'. To be free in psychological libertarianism is to be able *to perform* actions with deliberation and without external pressures, whereas to be free in the Thomistic sense is to be *disposed* in such a way that one is not necessitated to choose anything which is not the Absolute Good.

Thomistic libertarianism must further be distinguished from another free will doctrine which, while accepting the proposition that only the Absolute Good can necessitate the will to adhere to it, rejects the belief that the Absolute Good exists. This type of libertarianism has the concept of the Absolute Good as the end sought by the will, but repudiates the view that there is in reality such an Absolute. Thus this sort of libertarianism, which may be consonant with atheism, has some sort of grasp of the Absolute as a concept, but not the Absolute as that which exists. It maintains that it is invalid to move from the concept of the Absolute to the affirmation of the existence of such an Absolute.

This position is reminiscent of Kant's criticism of the ontological proof of the existence of God (Absolute). It should be recalled that to Kant when we say 'God is' or 'There is a God' we do not add any new predicate to the conception of God but merely affirm the existence of the subject with all its predicates--we posit the object in relation to our concept, and the content of both is the same; Kant affirms that "there is no addition made to the conception, which expresses merely the possibility of the object by our cogitating the object--in the expression 'it is'--as absolutely given or existing."[14] The fault in the ontological argument, according to Kant, is that the 'ens rationis' is given 'real existence' or extra-mental existence instead of remaining on the level of pure mental existence. The libertarian who repudiates the existence of the Absolute subscribes, in a measure, to the Kantian position; he accepts only the possibility of conceiving the Absolute.

Another libertarian position is the view of William of Ockham to whom the will is so absolutely free that "even in the direct presence of the divine essence, God Himself, it is possible for the human will not to will this most perfect good. The freedom or indetermination of the human will is unalloyed; so much so that the human will is not naturally determined or necessitated by anything whatsoever."[15] This position of Ockham is, except for its 'God-talk', akin to the view of existentialism of the Sartrean sort whereby man is 'condemned to be free'.

The Position of Determinism

Certain criticisms levelled against determinism gloss over the fundamental standpoint of this position. Contrary to the view of the critics, a determinist does not deny the existence of our consciousness of freedom as a psychological state. Like the psychological libertarian, the determinist has the psychological awareness of choosing 'freely'; he is aware of Ramsey's 'decisive activity' mentioned above. He considers various alternatives for choice and 'catches' himself carrying out the process of deliberation and giving personal backing to what he does. Thus on the level of consciousness he considers himself to be 'free' on many occasions when there are no obvious external forces compelling him to act. The question that arises at this juncture is: how does the determinist differ from the psychological libertarian?

The answer to this question lies in the way the determinist 'explains' his consciousness of freedom in the psychological order. In explaining the phenomenon of his consciousness of freedom he says as it were: "the fact that we feel free, the fact that we are conscious of freedom does not nullify that there is a factor which necessitates us to act in the way we act. This factor which necessitates us to act in certain ways does not appear in consciousness, but it is nevertheless there as a determinant of our activity."

The factor in question is viewed differently depending on whether a person takes the scientific or a metaphysical path in upholding determinism. The person who upholds determinism through the scientific path will be referred to here as a 'scientific determinist' without implying that his position is unmetaphysical. The person who upholds determinism through the metaphysical path will be referred to here as a 'metaphysical determinist'.

The scientific determinist sees any human action at any particular time to be a product of causal factors which form a series, and these factors may, in his view, have biological, social, environmental origin. However, to such a determinist these factors do not appear in consciousness at the moment of acting, but they are nevertheless operative and influence our activity. Thus the scientific determinist differs from the psychological libertarian not with regard to consciousness of freedom, but rather in the *explanation* of that consciousness. To the psychological libertarian the fundamental factor in action (free) is the free activity of the 'I', while to the scientific determinist the fundamental factor(s) is the causal element.

The metaphysical determinist, on the other hand and like the scientific determinist, recognizes the existence of a factor that determines our activity. Like the scientific determinist he maintains that this factor does not appear in consciousness. The way this factor is viewed depends on the metaphysical determinist's conception of the nature of reality. Some determinists, taking a position akin to Spinozism, view human action as the expression of the Divine Reality; both in the modal and substantial sense, whatever is, 'part' of the Absolute. Hegelianism also lends itself to this interpretation, for the Absolute expresses itself in Nature and in the human Spirit. Again, what is fundamental here is not the rejection of the consciousness of our freedom, but rather the contention that underlying our activities there is another factor, in this case the Absolute, which is operative albeit unperceived by one's consciousness.

Thus a determinist, whether scientific or metaphysical, can in one logical tone of voice say we are free and in another logical tone of voice say that we are not free. The former logical tone of voice pertains to our consciousness of freedom, while the latter refers to freedom understood metaphysically.

The determinist can also meet the Thomist, Ockhamist and existentialist objections. With regard to the Thomist position, the determinist may employ a conditional and affirm: "if the will is free with regard to all that is finite, then this freedom is itself determined, and if the ontological structure of man is such that it is necessitated to seek nothing but the Absolute Good then this structure is really determined." To the Ockhamist and the existentialist the determinist may have this to say: "if it were the case that man is not necessitated to seek anything, even the Absolute Good, then this non-necessitation is a form of determination of the human being."

The foregoing considerations constitute attempts to show that while the libertarian and the determinist may have similar experiences on the level of consciousness they differ in the explanatory and contemplative dimension. To the determinist all that has happened, all that happens, and all that will happen is contemplated as necessary; this fact applies to all human activity whether past, present and future. To the scientific determinist the ultimate principle of all that has occurred, occurs and will occur is the causal law of nature, to the metaphysical determinist the past, present and future of human action and other entities, is the expression of the Absolute Being. Thus to the determinist all human striving, all value, all conflicts in the world, all what we call 'good' and 'bad', etc., are subsumed under one ultimate principle, namely, the Absolute for the metaphysical determinist, and necessary laws of nature for the scientific determinist. To the metaphysical determinist, the 'freedom' which we experience in the psychological order is a manifestation of the Absolute, God.

To the libertarian there is an element of indeterminateness in the 'free' human action, though there are different versions of the way this indeterminateness is conceived, as we saw in our consideration of the psychological, Thomist, Ockhamist and existentialist forms of libertarianism. While some libertarians introduce the notion of the Absolute Good in their discussion of the indeterminateness of the will, some do not indulge in this contemplation of the Absolute. Where the Absolute is contemplated by both the determinist and the libertarian the role of this Absolute is conceived differently with regard to its relationship to the human will. The total effect of these considerations is that the contemplative dimension of the two positions is different.

CONCLUSION

As a result of the foregoing treatment of libertarianism and determinism, the two philosophical viewpoints which appear to be unavoidable in discussion of freedom, we can assert: (a) on the one hand, there is a sense in which value can supersede metaphysical positions, (b) on the other hand there is a sense in which metaphysical positions can determine the way we justify value and, to a certain extent, can dispose us to cherish certain values, apart from determining our contemplation of the world and our own human experience.

Finally, the paper raises the vital question of the relationship between metaphysical/religious beliefs and value, a question which is urgent at a time when man needs to understand his condition as a prerequisite for reconstructing a better world for human life.

Kenyatta University College

Nairobi, Kenya

NOTES

1. Ian T. Ramsey, *Freedom and Immortality* (London: SCM Press Ltd., 1960), p. 44.
2. *Ibid.* Quotation by Ramsey taken from Letter to *The Observer*, Oct. 13, 1957.
3. R.M. Hare, *The Language of Morals* (London: Oxford University Press, 1952), p. 165.
4. *Ibid.* See also to J. C. Flugel, *Man, Morals and Society*, especially Chapter 3.
5. Louis Arnaud Reid, *Philosophy and Education* (London: Heinemann, 1962), p. 28.
6. Webster's *New Collegiate Dictionary* (Springfield: G. & C. Merrian Co., 1961), p. 179.
7. Ian T. Ramsey, *Op. Cit.*, p. 26.
8. *Ibid.*, p. 22.
9. *Ibid.*, p. 24.
10. *Ibid.*
11. Ibid. p. 26.

12. Thomas Aquinas, *Summa Theologiae*, I, 82, 1.

13. *Ibid.*

14. Immanuel Kant, *Critique of Pure Reason*, trans. by J.M.D. Meiklejohn (New York: Dutton, 1969), p. 346.

15. Arthur P. Monahan, *On the Confines of Two Worlds* (Antigonish, Nova Scotia: St. Francis Xavier University Press, 1964), p. 153.

CHAPTER XVI

FREEDOM AND OMNIPOTENCE: LOVE AND FREEDOM

FREDERICK SONTAG

In the present age, the contrast between 'freedom' and 'omnipotence' is, I believe, the proper setting to use for a discussion of the nature of God. Most classical Western theologies give 'omnipotence' and 'power' primary treatment in discussing God's attributes. In this case freedom becomes a derivative notion, which is then developed so as not to compromise the prior decision to preserve, at all costs, God's control of the world's development. We all know that, with Hegel, process was introduced into God's nature as essential, and much discussion in our century has centered on ways to view God as limited. For some, the only way to save the notion of God in modern times is to abandon omnipotence.

Insofar as this metaphysical tendency stems from a growing desire to make freedom the primary divine attribute, this movement seems to me to be both correct and unavoidable as we approach the 21st century. In almost every area we can name, whether social, political or economic, the press in our century has been to gain freedom and independence of control. There is no reason that, as philosophers, our thinking about God should be exempt from this pressure. In fact, it is likely that our theologies will be irrelevant unless we think about God with the notions of liberty, freedom and contingency as our first consideration.

However, for religious and theological purposes, much is lost if God's omnipotence is surrendered too quickly. No matter what the tradition, our belief in any religious promise of deliverance or salvation depends upon our conviction that the God behind these offers does indeed have the power for fulfillment. As we note in every struggle for freedom, individual liberty is opened up. But in this dispersion of power, it becomes more difficult to maintain social and political control over the forces we have let loose. Parts of today's world slip into chaos because the unrestrained demand for freedom and self determination without infringement refuses all discipline.

In approaching this core metaphysical and human problem, I want to suggest that 'love' provides a way to interpret 'freedom' which enables it to stop short of personal and social disintegration. This also allows God's 'omnipotence' to be interpreted in a new way so that control is maintained, but without the wholesale determination of every event. Like every critical term with which philosophy deals, 'freedom' has no single meaning. Our problem is always to find a way to approach it so that it will give us the meaning we seek from it. Likewise, 'love' is important in human life, but often it is unsuccessful and the cause of pain, because we forget the varieties of meaning it has in its raw state.

By way of introduction to the issues before us, let us begin with a brief glance at Aristotle and Thomas Aquinas. Aristotle has left us two concepts which continue to be formative in our thinking about metaphysical principles. First, that necessity characterizes what is good; and, second, that thought forms the essence of what is divine. "The first mover, then exists of necessity; and in so far as it exists by necessity, its mode of being is good and it is in this sense a first principle" (1072 b 10).[1] When Aristotle tells us this, we know he excludes change. Not being capable of being otherwise is what is best. Matter and potency are also excluded from the ideal state. What is most divine and precious should not change.

It is true that love enters into the life of Aristotle's unmoved mover, but only because the final cause produces motion by being loved vs. all other things which move by being moved (1072 b 3). The key fact for our consideration is that no internal motion is involved in such affection. Love happens *to* the first principle and is not characteristic *of* its nature. "The object of desire and the object of thought move in this way; they move without being moved" (1072 a 23). As we know, actuality is always metaphysically primary and regulative for Aristotle. It defines what 'good' means, and it forms God's substance.

God, of course, has life, but for Aristotle it is "the actuality of thought" that is life (1072 b 26). However, in contrast to human reasoning, we are dealing with thought of a special kind: The nature of divine thought "thinks of that which is most divine and precious, and it does not change; for change would be change for the worse, and thus would be already a movement" (1074 b 25). Love happens to such as God. If his love went out to other things, it would subject him to change. "It must be of itself that divine thought thinks . . . and its thinking is a thinking on thinking" (1074 b 34). The divine thought and its object are the same, but wherever love is felt, we know this cannot be the case.

Aristotle's metaphysical advantage, of course, is that the omnipotence of his God cannot be challenged. It would be wrong to say that his unmoved mover is not 'free'. If we did, Aristotle would protest that its freedom is protected by placing it above the damaging touch of change. It is not threatened by these passions which are the seeds of destruction. Aristotle's God has the freedom of Spinoza's Substance, that of being cause of itself and of being dependent on nothing other than itself. Such certainty is a form of freedom vs. dependency, for Plato must have taught Aristotle that to 'love' always involves a lack and the confession of a need. What Aristotle has done is to take omnipotence and define his preferred sense of freedom in that light, as countless others still do today.

Perhaps we can see the core of the problem with which this approach to freedom leaves us when we examine Thomas Aquinas' discussion of 'love' as a divine attribute. Aristotle could exclude love from his first principle and avoid problems by doing so. As a Christian, Aquinas is plagued by being forced to account for love as a part of the divine nature. Thomas' metaphysical principles still side with Aristotle. His God, however, has more similarities to Plato's world maker, which perhaps accounts for the fact that the early church fathers found neo-Platonism such a congenial setting for their doctrine. Can the compromise which Aquinas reached provide us with a clue of how to reshape a metaphysical base more attune to different notions of freedom today? And in doing this, can we let "love lead the way"?

When Thomas Aquinas considers the divine attributes,[2] it is instructive to note which attributes he treats and the order in which he lists them. After the question of the existence of God, 'simplicity' heads his list in characterizing God. Since love is never simple, we know love cannot determine Thomas' thinking about God in any major way. In fact, we can be sure love will be for him a derivative concept. Freedom cannot enter in as such, except as 'immutability' specifies what freedom is allowed to be. Unity, infinity, and eternity follow next in order. 'Will' Thomas treats later under ethical considerations, as he will do also with the passions. They are not constitutive of God's substance.

Since body is denied to God (Pt. I, Q. 3, Art. 1), emotions such as love are too physically connected to be very high in consideration. Matter cannot exist in God. Saying this preserves an Aristotelian immutability, but it produces complications where God's relationship to the world is concerned, because his divinity so unlike what we experience. Accidents are excluded too, and Thomas cites Aristotle in saying "The first cause rules all things without commingling with them" (Pt. I, Q. 3, Art. 8). Love and freedom, of course, always lead us to greater involvement with others, and even at times to dependency. When Thomas speaks of God's perfection, he cites 'actuality' first, following Aristotle's lead (Pt. I, Q. 4, Art. 2). A creature may be like

God, but God is not like a creature (Pt. I, Q. 4, Art. 3). The relationship is asymmetrical, which tells us that it is not modeled on love.

Goodness again is defined in terms of actuality, and God is immutable because he need add nothing to himself (Pt. I, Q. 9, Art. 1). There is no succession in God's eternity, and this follows from his immutability, which again proves to be the dominating concept (Pt. I, Q. 10, Art. 2). We can apply names substantially to God's essence, but in himself he is one in reality. He is only multiple in the way our ideas apprehend him (Pt. I, Q. 13, Art. 4). When Thomas tells us that, in God, will follows on his intellect, we know freedom cannot be given a very wide berth (Pt. I, Q. 19, Art. 1). God's will is entirely unchangeable, which alters radically any notion of will as we experience it in ourselves. The divine will is not absolutely necessary, but it is necessary by supposition (Pt. I, Q. 19, Art. 7) and so still not subject to change.

Thomas does not devote a great deal of attention to love, although he wants to assert that in God there is love. However, the crucial point to note is that "He loves without passion" (Pt. I, Q. 20, Art. 1). Thomas knows passion would introduce composition into God, and unity led the list of Thomas' divine perfections. Thomas does quote Dionysius and then asserts that by love God is placed outside himself (Pt. I, Q. 20, Art. 2), but he does not develop this interesting suggestion. If he did, it might revolutionize his thinking about God. God is said to love all things insofar as they are good, which if true, severely restricts us in attributing compassion to God. In Thomas' eyes mercy is not an affective passion. (Pt. I, Q. 21, Art. 3).

The providence of God reaches even to individual selves. However, since every exercise of free will must be subject to divine providence (Pt. I, Q. 22, Art. 2), we know that freedom is again restricted in order to protect omnipotence. Thomas does not want to impose necessity on all things. Some events will happen 'from contingency', but they still have been foreseen as happening. There is no distinction between what flows from free will and what is from predestination. God operates through secondary causes as well as directly, so that which flows from free will is also of predestination. The necessity is the same, although the distance and connection of the event to God can vary.

God also falls under some controls, for power is subject to wisdom. God could do things other than he has done, as discussed today in terms of possible worlds, but "the power to do them does not come from His will, but from His nature" (Pt. I, Q. 25, Art. 5,). God's will and freedom do not determine his nature; for Thomas, God's nature determines his will and also what can be called free. The universe could not be better, given God's nature; we do live in the best of all possible worlds, as Leibniz thought. But this is really because Thomas is convinced that his necessary and fully actual God is the best of all possible Gods. Here lies the crucial issue and the key to our accomplishing any reform in God.

If the will and the intellect are not diverse in God, which Thomas says is true (Pt. I, Q. 27, Art. 3), no change in our notion of freedom and love is possible. Aristotle has formed his God on the model of thought, and this may be his crucial mistake. Then, attributes of perfected thought will control our definition of the nature of man and God. If, on the other hand, will is distinct from the intellect, though thought remains a part of God, it need not control every decision. What price do we pay if we reject the model of thought and begin to think about God by using love and freedom? We cannot have it both ways. The choice Aristotle forces on us is right. Omnipotence cannot reign supreme if our will is subject to the contingencies of love. If we begin with will, is there any advantage in a God who voluntarily restricts the omnipotence his power would allow him to exercise if divinity chose? Does self restriction involve any ultimate loss of power--for power obviously is curtailed for the moment? The answer depends on where we rank love as a metaphysical principle. If, like Plato, we treat love as able to reveal the structure of Being, the essence of Being cannot be all, or even primarily, mental. Volition and affection hold a central, if not a controlling, position. Aristotle's unmoved mover is the thinking man's God. That is, if you use thought as your sole clue, then completion, omnipotence, form, necessity and actuality tend to take the ascendance in discussing God. It is not so much that thought must always exhibit these qualities, as it is that thought requires the lead of affection if it is to be any different from Aristotle's model.

Love, of course, is changeable, and therefore it can be destructive. We know that, where God is concerned, we have reason to shy from attributing such qualities to God. From this we learn the lack of necessity that governs the way we must think about God. In fact, the centuries of disagreement over God's nature, or even his existence, in itself testifies to the lack of dominance of necessity in what is divine. If it were not so, thought should long ago have reached a conclusion that reflects the necessity found in the object known. This finality in philosophy has been suggested but never achieved, all of which tells us that today we should try a less rigid model for God. If we do, we gain a better explanation of human uncertainty where God is concerned.

Kierkegaard, of course, was convinced of an inescapable uncertainty in man's relation to God. Yet strangely he held to a classically necessary God whose nature then made human faith into a paradox. Using love as one key to our understanding of Being, even purified love as it exists in God makes uncertainty a reasonable human response. Love sometimes tries to dominate and to control; all love in the world does not avoid using necessity as its model. As Plato says, desire continues because we want to possess the object of our love not just for the moment but eternally. Love can be just as stern, and actually much more irrational, a model than thought.

This is why we must couple freedom with love in order to use it as a key for understanding God. Thomas places goodness higher in God than will. Thus choice becomes a form of necessity because it is controlled from above. We should take freedom as the highest attribute but say that love must not follow impulse--which the quality that has caused metaphysicians and theologians to reject it. Instead freedom is the goal that love is bound to in God, and such freedom is what men also should seek to bind their passions. When love as an affection accepts freedom, it uses intensity and passion to open alternatives rather than to close them off. It becomes a liberating not a binding force. It accepts contingency and no longer needs necessity to maintain either equilibrium or control.

Saying this may give us a picture of God's action and our desire which we might like to hold, but what evidence is there that God is like this? In the first place, we must put some weight on what we judge to be the suitability of a metaphysical scheme or theological framework to an age. That is, we do not need to adopt Hegel's view that there is a metaphysical view corresponding to each historical period. But we do witness a loose fit of metaphysical principles to an age. Views once powerful tend to wane, although sometimes later they return to power in men's minds. This lack of linear progress indicates that no metaphysical proposal can hope to be final, although some may be more fruitful than others for a period. The "death of God" in theology may have come about because a picture of God built on omnipotence will today lead few to any vital Being. We may have to postulate, as well, that God alters the dominant tendency in the divine nature in various human eras. Certainly such a picture of God offers a better explanation of why human belief in God is subject to such vicissitudes. Otherwise, all men should in their thought relate to an omnipotent God of pure actuality in the same way. In fact, thought about God has never achieved that stability. But if emotion does play a heavy role in the change of hunan attitudes toward God, should this indicate a powerful emotional base in God too?

With 'freedom' as our controlling idea (vs. necessity for Aristotle), we better understand why God might voluntarily have restricted his omnipotence. As many theologians have thought, installing predestination is open to a divine power and is a simpler path. The only problem with settling for this superior intellectual neatness is that it fits more the world God considered but rejected in creation than it does the world of contingency we ourselves experience. As our human quest for freedom continues to explode in the late 20th century, it becomes even more clear that Descartes' God-of-clarity-and-distinctness is a dream. Such a deity is not very close to reality as it was created and as we deal with it--even in natural science.

The Gods of all metaphysicians are possible. We must select the one most likely to have created the world as we experience it. Of course, in the dawn of the modern world, the God of Thomas Aquinas did fit the hope to complete at last the intellectual task with precision and finality in theory. But now that dream of early modern science lies broken around us. It is time to search for God in new images. We need not go so far as to surrender omnipotence, that classical holy grail of theologians. For the God who can experience love in himself and willingly set aside his power in order to allow freedom and thus accept contingency into the divine nature--this is still a God fully capable of control. The issue is how and when God chooses to exercise it and how he goes about making these determinative decisions.

POSTSCRIPT

Jorge Luis Borges, the Argentinean poet-story teller, builds his graphic images on an intricate metaphysical base. Attracted by metaphysics, but accepting no system as true, he makes a game of the mind out of all of them. Human thought endlessly makes its way through concatenations of causes and affects without ever exhausting infinity. Metaphysics is a branch of the literature of fantasy--and yet it is no less true for that fact. Borges stories use mystery and employ surprise effects to achieve that sacred astonishment at the universe which is the origin of all true religion and metaphysics. The world is a book and the book is a world. Both are labyrinthine[3] and enclose enigmas designed to be understood and participated in by man.

One of Borges more famous stories, "The Library of Babel" (pp. 51-48), describes the universe on the model of the library. The reader (author) wanders in it in search of a book and discovers the formless and chaotic nature of almost all the books.

"For every sensible line of straightforward statement, there are leagues of senseless cacophonies, verbal jumbles and incoherences" (p. 53). The Library contains all books, but the happiness of realizing that all secrets are at hand to be disclosed is offset by realizing that "the possibility of man's finding his Vindication can be computed as zero" (p. 55). At one time it was hoped that a clarification of humanity's basic mysteries might be found, but this inordinate hope was followed by an excessive depression. "The Library is unlimited and cyclical" (p. 58). The human species may be extinguished, but the Library will endure: "illuminated, solitary, infinite, perfectly motionless, useless, incorruptible, secret" (*Ibid.*).

Borges once reports: I come from a dizzy land where the lottery is the basis of reality ("The Lottery in Babylon," p. 30). I want to suggest that the God of Borges' world might be one who could fit the 21st Century. In "The Secret Miracle", Borges recounts a dream in which a man reports to the librarian at the Clementine Library that he is looking for God; the librarian's reply is: "God is one of the letters on one of the pages of one of the four hundred thousand volumes of the Clementine" (p. 92). The name is written down and thus theoretically could be found: the odds against the final finding are just high, and the wandering among the volumes is immense. In a story on "The Theologians" (p. 119-126) Borges reminds us that "in questions of theology there is no novelty without risk" (p. 119), and Kafka, Kierkegaard, Nietzsche and Katzantzakis certainly testify to the willingness of theologians to take risks in recent times.

If this is what the quest is like, however, it must reflect something of the nature of that which is sought. God must enjoy labyrinths and be the author of labyrinth and odyssey. A god, Borges reflects, "ought to utter a single word and in that word absolute fullness" ("The God's Script," p. 171). We just do not possess that word, nor do we know for sure that it has been spoken. Borges explains the origins of our words and our urge to write: "This imminence of a revelation which does not occur is, perhaps, the aesthetic phenomenon" ("The Wall and the Books", p. 188). We write metaphysics to capture what we probably cannot capture and yet which, we are convinced, is in theory there to be captured. A God who would design such a labyrinthine world and put speaking creatures in it must certainly prize freedom above all else, in himself as well as in us. Yet, in the natural order we seem to experience a freedom tempered by love, since control and order are possible for us from time to time. Freedom need not lead to license and self-destruction. But we realize that necessity and emotionlessness have been abandoned in favor of controlled risk, by God in the decisive moment of creation and now by us.

Pomona College

Pomona California

NOTES

1. Aristotle: *Metaphysics* in *The Works of Aristotle*, Vol. VIII, trans. W.D. Ross. (Oxford: Clarendon Press, 1948). All references are to this edition.

2. *Summa Theologica*, Vol. I, trans. Dominican Fathers, (New York: Benziger Bros., 1947). All references are to this edition.

3. *Labyrinths: Selected Stories and Other Writings*, ed. Yates and Irby (New York: New Directions Publishing Corp., 1964). All page references are to this edition.

COMMENT

On Professor Sontag's
"God of Love and Freedom"

THOMAS A. FAY

In his text Professor Sontag remarks ". . . this is really because Thomas is convinced that his necessary and fully actual God is the best of all possible Gods. *Here lies the crucial issue and the key to our accomplishing any reform in God*" (p. 7, my emphasis). Further, he notes "We should take freedom as the highest attribute but say that love must not follow impulse, which is the quality that has caused metaphysicians and theologians to reject it" (p. 9) According to Professor Sontag then the crucial issue concerns whether God is fully actual, the *actus purus* of the Scholastics, the best of all possible Gods or not. He further suggests that the way to accomplish the reforms which he feels are necessary in our thinking about God is by making freedom the highest attribute, under the direction of love.

This, it seems to me, poses several difficulties. The first of these concerns the nature of God. If God isn't fully actual--isn't "the best of all possible Gods," to use Professor Sontag's expression--what is he? Are we to return to the anthropomorphic models of primitive religions in which God is seen as endowed with passions such as anger, vengeance, vindictiveness, and so on? Sontag at least implies this, since on p. 6, he seems to take St. Thomas to task for not getting passions into the divine nature, and his citation of St. Thomas, *Sum. Theol.*, q. 20, a. 1, "He (God) loves without passion" appears to be a criticism of him. The same problem appears on p. 5 with regards to the emotions, such as love, (though for St. Thomas love is not an emotion at all, but rather the first act of the intellectual appetite, the will), matter and accidents. It would seem from a reading of this section that Sontag would prefer to have matter, emotions, accidents, mutability and a certain weakness (as the opposite of omnipotence, which he rejects, e.g., pp. 1, 4, 7, 10) in the divine essence.

But then we are left with the very large problem of just what kind of a God that would be. Would it really be a God at all? What is meant in using the term God? If it is merely a revised and enlarged version of a human being, why do people need one at all, as they seem to from the evidence of the universality of the concept? Isn't Professor Sontag's view really a rather naive anthropomorphism?

Further, he notes on p. 5, "love and freedom, of course,

always lead us to greater involvement with others and even at times to dependency . . . . A creature may be like God, but God is not like a creature. The relationship is asymmetrical . . . ." Sontag finds this notion of St. Thomas unacceptable. But I wonder if Professor Sontag has considered sufficiently the alternative. If he wishes to implicate God in man's affairs in the way he seems to suggest, that is, as he remarks on p. 5, "love and freedom, of course, always lead us to greater involvement with others, and even at times to dependency . . . ," then it would seem that he is going to purchase this at a very high price indeed. He must sacrifice the very attribute in God which he holds to be highest, freedom, since he has now made God dependent on the world and to that extent not free.

It was precisely this type of difficulty that St. Thomas clearly saw and successfully avoided. If God is to be God at all, he surely must be free, as Professor Sontag has quite correctly insisted. The problem with his position, it seems to me, is that he winds up by losing the very freedom he seeks to vindicate. St. Thomas saw this difficulty and therefore insisted that the relationship between God and creatures be asymmetrical, that is, a real relationship of existential dependence when viewed from the human's side, but not when viewed from God's. This did not entail sacrificing God's presence to man, since God is present in man and the world by his essence, presence and power (Sum. Theol. I, q. 8, a. 3). Nor was this merely a cold, impersonal presence but involved intimacy, and thus on this point of God's presence to man Thomas quotes the well known saying of Augustine: *"Tu autem eras interior intimo meo . . . ."* Thus Thomas was able to preserve both the divine freedom and also the intimacy of God's presence to man, in his doctrine of immanence and transcendence.

Certainly if one restricts one's considerations to metaphysics only this does not have the richness that one would find in St. Thomas' theology. Thus in taking up the question of love (*Sum. Theol.* II-II, q. 23, a. 1) the first point which Thomas examines concerning man's relationship to God is whether or not God and man might properly be called *friends.* The answer, to be sure, is in the affirmative and God's relationship to man is spoken of as a *"quaedam amicitia,"* that is a relationship of friendship. In order to understand adequately what St. Thomas has in mind here, one must remember all the things that Aristotle had said about friendship in Books VIII and IX of the *Ethics,* for example, "the friend is another self," since this was the intellectual background from which Thomas was writing. So it would seem that St. Thomas' teaching on immanence and transcendence still affords one with a very rich source, from which to address these problems; it is perhaps not so sterile, jejune and unrewarding as Sontag finds it.

Further, I would question whether Professor Sontag is correct in his assertion on pp. 4-5 that, ". . . we know love cannot determine Thomas' thinking about God in any major way." As a matter of fact when treating of our knowledge of God in the *Sum. Theol.*, I, q. 13, Thomas arrives at the conclusion in article 11 that the name *qui est*, he who is, is the most proper name of God. This is a strictly metaphysical position, defining God's nature in terms of Being, and one, I am sure, that Professor Sontag would find quite cold and unappealing. However, it is interesting to note that, having established this metaphysical point in one brief article, when St. Thomas takes up the question of the love of God "De amore Dei," I, q. 20, he devotes a complete question to it; and further when he moves into the area of Christian theology, I, q. 37, the whole of this question is devoted to "the Name of the Holy Spirit, which is Love." But how could it be otherwise since St. Thomas was, after all, first and foremost a Christian. Certainly no less for him than for any other Christian must the Johannine statement be true, "*Deus est caritas*," God is love.

This further suggests the total unacceptability of Sontag's statement on p. 4, ". . . Aquinas is *plagued* by being forced to account for love as a part of the divine nature" (my emphasis). To assert that St. Thomas was plagued by being forced to account for love as a part of the divine nature would be to say that Thomas' theology was merely a veneer adventitiously applied *ab extra*, whereas the exact opposite is true. His theology is an organic whole. Sontag's treatment here further suggests that he has forgotten the title of the works he is quoting, viz. *Summa Theologica*. The works must be seen as a whole, and that whole is a theological whole, not merely a metaphysical one. Therefore one does not adequately interpret the first twenty-six questions, the *De Deo Uno*, if one places them in an hermetically sealed vacuum. They are rather a *potential part* of Thomas' theology, using the term "potential part" in its strict Thomistic sense. Therefore, if one wishes the fullest and most adequate knowledge of God, one ought not to stop at the *De Deo Uno*, which is merely a propaedeutic, but to go on to core of the *Summa*.

This also suggests a further difficulty with Sontag's paper. In replacing omnipotence by freedom and love, Sontag desires, as he tells us, for example, on pp. 1, 9, and 10, a metaphysical framework which will be relevant (p. 1) for the age. But, it may be asked, whether this is the correct approach? Or does this seemingly laudable intention of making metaphysics relevant to the age mask a failure of nerve? Isn't it true that a metaphysician ought to pursue the truth with perfect confidence that the truth is never irrelevant, and that the metaphysician ought not to dance to the latest tune which the age pipes? A long time ago, Plato remarked, and Thomas quotes him frequently enough, "*magis amicus veritati,*" I should rather be a friend to truth than men.

This of course is not to say that metaphysics is unrelated to the age in which it finds itself. Rather, the relationship between metaphysics and the culture of an age is a symbiotic one. Thus, it is true that metaphysics reflects the thinking of the age. But in addition to this, and this is crucially important, it ought to provide the conceptual framework for the newly developing future culture which, hopefully, will lead to a richer, fuller, more human existence. In order to do this, of course, it cannot merely passively accept and reflect the prevailing quotidian values uncritically and seek to redo itself in order to achieve acceptance by the age in which it finds itself. Rather, it is precisely its task to examine the metaphysical roots of the culture and to point out its inadequacies. Thus, instead of making freedom the paradigm so that metaphysics can be made meaningful to our contemporaries, one ought really to do just the opposite and show precisely how making freedom the paradigm has led to the cataclysmic results mentioned by Professor Sontag in his paper, especially on p. 2 where he quite rightly notes, "But in this disposing of power it becomes more difficult to maintain social and political control over the forces we have let loose. Parts of today's world slip into chaos because the unrestrained demand for freedom and self determination without infringement refuses all discipline."

Professor Sontag thinks that love will provide an adequate way to forestall this slippage. But how will the love which he proposes be able to do this since his position seems to come very close to blind voluntarism, the Nietzschean "Will to Will." This contention seems to be justified since on p. 7, for example, he states that the primacy of thought is to be rejected and that thought, "need not control every decision." What is decision-making, deprived of thought, but blind irrationalism? This is a difficulty which has not escaped Sontag's notice. As he notes on p. 9, "Love can be just as stern, and actually much more irrational, a model than thought." He suggests that this difficulty can be overcome if we couple love with freedom, but the argument seems to be circular. That is, in the beginning of the paper we were assured that the drive to unrestrained freedom and lawlessness, which so characterizes the world in which we live, would be held in check by love. At the conclusion of the paper, when Sontag notes that love can at times be most irrational, he attempts to cope with this problem by taking refuge in freedom. It seems then that the argument is perfectly circular, and that we are back where we started--with an ungrounded metaphysics.

St. John's University

New York, New York

CHAPTER XVII

PHILOSOPHY, RELIGION AND THE COMING WORLD CIVILIZATION

LEROY S. ROUNER

The fundamental contemporary human problem is one of community: namely, shall we learn to live in relation to Nature, each other, and God in such a way that we allow for diversity, and yet find common goals to keep us from destroying one another? This question has been the dark shadow behind our conversations, from Santiniketan (*Man and Society*[1]), to New York (*Man and God*[2]), to Jerusalem. Our specific question today is the implications for man and society of our "divine goal." Immediately we are aware of diversity.

As Jews, Christians, Muslims, Buddhists, Hindus, Marxists, and many others, we call God by numerous names, understand God in various ways, and find ourselves generally at odds with one another on questions of the reality of God and the meaning of God for our experience. Nor are these only inter-religious conflicts. They are also intra-religious. Some Christians are closer to some Hindus than they are to other Christians in their notion of God, for example. We need to explore common beliefs which will not deny the integrity and distinctiveness of our special commitments, but will make us conscious of a common, human religious bond. By way of introduction, however, a word first about how the human community in which we all participate is threatened by the limited communities which claim our most intimate, fierce and tenacious loyalties.

In 'traditional' societies communities are bound together by natural symbols, the most important of which are blood, region, language, class or caste, and religion. Succeeding generations are identified primarily through familial blood lines, but a sense of place, a mother tongue, a social role and reverence for the gods of one's tribe are also given 'in one's blood.' This profound yearning of like for like, galvanized by our instinctive fear of the stranger, continues to fashion the deepest human bonds. Traditional communities, however, can be inclusive only by also being exclusive. Alienation is inevitable in traditional societies, since the sub-communities of a traditional culture are ineluctably at odds with one another. Further, traditional communities have limited geographic range; they are characteristically localized and therefore ill-equipped for modern society, with its wide ranging communications technology and its individualism.

In Asia, Africa and Latin America, colonialism used scientific technology and military force to superimpose administrative coherence on large 'nations' which were fraught with communal conflict and, indeed, lacked strong common motivation for national unity. Anti-colonialism provided negative motivation but left newly independent nations without a sense of common identity. In India, for example, regional, linguistic, caste and religious loyalties are still strong and it is not yet clear what it means for both Kashmiris and Tamils to identify themselves as 'Indians.' It is clear, however, that the survival of the nation depends on discovering such a bond. The collapse of Pakistan into two nations bears eloquent witness to the difficulty of overcoming radical cultural differences. Within Western nations like the U.S., the recent rise of 'ethnicity' and the search for 'roots' has emphasized the power of traditional or 'tribal' community. But the West cannot forget that the power of 'tribalism' can be demonic. The outburst of cultural tribalism in Germany-- an 'Aryanism' of Blood and Soil--turned Gentile Christians to slaughtering their Jewish neighbors.

So the problem of community is a national one in the first instance. Most dangerously, however, it is global. Here the conflict is not so much between traditional communities as it is among large complexes of power, grouped under the leadership of certain large, industrialized nation states. The primal commitments underlying these larger struggles tend to be expressed ideologically and abstractly--'the West' defends 'freedom,' while 'the Soviets' defend 'socialism,' for example. On a crude level, this aspect of the international conflict also pits 'religious' societies against 'atheist' societies. On a deeper level, however, the conflict illustrates the radical danger to a 'global village' in which the ultimate commitments of large groups are at odds. Each prepares to destroy the other in defense of their own beliefs about the meaning of life and the way to live out that meaning. What the coming world civilization requires is some common commitment to the human community itself as an ultimate value, and I know no term strong enough to imply the spiritual force necessary to make that work except the word 'religious.' As a result, our conversations together seem to me to have the greatest practical importance. Some may regard a meeting of metaphysicians discussing humankind and God as fiddling while Rome burns. To my mind, ours is a fundamental issue of world survival.

II

Religion is a divisive element in traditional culture. When Gods are tribal powers, social conflicts are fraught with religious meaning because tribal gods are also in conflict. As polytheism gives way to monotheism in the history of religions there is a theoretical sense--implied in the term monotheism--that God is the Lord of all being, and not simply a tribal power. The great world religious traditions still had different names for God, however, and different notions of God's sovereignty over human kind. When these traditions came in contact with one another, they tended to revert to a tribal notion of God as militant defender of the ways and purposes of a particular people in conflict with an alien group. The literature of the Christian crusades against the Muslims in the medieval period, for example, is replete with illustrations of this reversion to theological 'tribalism.'

Metaphysical reflection will not prevent further reversions to tribalism among the world's great religions. What it can do is to analyze fundamental notions of God among monotheistic religions, and promote greater understanding by showing that certain groups of religions have certain fundamental views in common, and that each group genuinely needs something which the other has to offer. The metaphysical element in religion has come in for considerable criticism. The 'God of the Philosophers' has been regarded as abstract and compared unfavorably to the more concrete, vivid and immediate God known to a particular tradition, such as 'the God of Abraham, Isaac and Jacob.' In our present situation, however, the abstract problem of unity has taken on existential urgency. The common human sense of the presence of God was never as abstract as its detractors made it seem and the scriptural theologies of the various positive religions cannot do justice to this religious dimension of human experience. Only metaphysical reflection can deal fully and directly with this issue, and that is no small contribution to the coming world civilization. To have a notion of common religious ground is no longer a matter of idle speculation   but of common survival.

Many of our disagreements about the nature of God can be classified into two primary modes of relationship between God and the world. One mode is *emanationism*: God causing the world through a spontaneous overflowing, as it were, of God's own being. The other mode is *creationism*: God causing the world through consciously acting on something other than God's own being. The occidental traditions of Judaism, Christianity and Islam follow a 'creationist' mode of God's relation to the world. The oriental traditions of what we call loosely 'Hinduism' and 'Buddhism' follow an 'emanationist' mode. There is overlap, of course. Neo-Platonism and Gnosticism in the Western tradition are 'emanationist' in their cosmologies, and Ramanuja's *Visistadvaita* represents 'creationism' within the Hindu tradition. Fur-

ther, the typology offers only limited help in understanding a
tradition like Confucianism in the East or Marxism in the West.
What the typology does do, however, is to outline certain presuppositions of those cultures dominated by these religious traditions. The metaphysical presuppositions of any culture are, I
believe, most vividly expressed in that culture's religious mythology. As with traditional societies of old, there are certain attitudes of mind and spirit which are 'in the blood' of a cultural
tradition, whether a particular individual happens to be a 'believer' in its dominant religious tradition or not.

The emanationist view of God's relation to the world is
expressed vividly in the Hindu tradition of *Advaita Vedanta.*
Here the world evolves from God's *lila* or sport, the unconscious
exuberance of a dancing God at play. In this mode God does not
intend a world other than Himself. The world evolves uninten-
tionally from the very substance of God. There is no metaphysical duality at the heart of things as a result. 'Otherness' in
our experience is a mistake of perception in a world of *maya*,
and our spiritual task is to prepare for the moment of realization when that perception will be righted. The endless volumes
of wild tales in the *Mahabharata*; the profusion of temple carv-
ings at Khajuraho depicting every aspect of life; the intellectual
speculation in the Upanishads on cosmic rhythms of endless
aeons winding up and winding down and winding up again--the
point of this astoundingly rich aesthetic is to give the individual
all the time in the world to explore the disappointing truth that
time in the world holds no answer to life's fundamental problem.
That problem is evil, and anything that moves--like time--can
hurt you. The peace which passes all understanding comes only
through *moksha*, release to a realm beyond time, where Being,
Intelligence and Bliss combine, and nothing ever happens.

This emanationist model of God's relation to the world
characterizes what I shall call the Great Story of the East. It
has three important characteristics: its religion is mystical, its
ethics are stoic, and its cosmology is emanationist. It offers a
perfect solution to the metaphysical problem of evil, which I
take to be its primary purpose. Since the primary real is solely
the reality of God, evil has no ontological status. This solution
complicates the historical problem of evil, however, since--as
the Roman Stoics also discovered--there are very few people
with stamina adequate to the heroic disciplines which alone can
give one an experience of the non-reality of evil.

The creationist view of God's relation to the world is
vividly expressed in the creation stories in the Biblical book of
Genesis. In this tradition the world is a conscious and intentional creation of a God at work, and is fashioned from a nothing

of something which is not God-substance. The world is different from God. It is God's artifact, and bears the mark of his handiwork, as his creatures bear in themselves the *imago dei*, but God in his essential deity is other than humankind and the created order. As a result, there is a certain metaphysical duality at the heart of the created order in the Great Story of the West. The experience of 'otherness' is therefore a valid perception of how things are intended to be. In a creationist model there can be no theoretical solution to the metaphysical problem of evil, but there is a working solution to the problem of evil in history. Through prophets, a Messiah, even the incarnate presence of God's own Son, time becomes a vehicle of fulfilling the original intention of God's purpose in creation. As a result of God's work in history, the lost good of a Garden paradise is re-capturable in the promised good of a Kingdom which is not beyond time but is the fulfillment of time itself.

The Great Story of the West has three important characteristics: its religion is historical; its ethics are rooted in faith; and its cosmology is creationist. For emanationism, the world is essentially God, except that it does not appear that way in our experience. 'Realization' of Truth cannot derive from historical experience, given the power of *maya*, so it is discontinuous with that experience when it comes, i.e., it is a mystery. For all the naturalism and rich aestheticism of 'Hinduism,' spiritual fulfillment is not to be found in relationship to that which is other; it is to be found in the identification of one's deepest inwardness with the power of Being Itself. That inwardness is also Intelligence (because it is the truth about reality) and Bliss (because it is Stillness) and hence beyond the source of suffering (which is diversity/movement). The philosophy of life implied in an emanationist view of God's relation to the world is not so much 'other-worldly' or 'un-historical' as is sometimes claimed by Western critics since, from the perspective of a strict materialism, all religious views are somewhat 'other-worldly' and 'un historical.' The critical distinction is that creationism, given its initial metaphysical dualism, finds spiritual fulfillment in relationship to that which is other. Therefore, while time and history are ultimately transformed in creationist myths of fulfillment (e.g., the Christian notion of the Kingdom of God), the mode of being-in-relation, which characterizes the experience of time and history, is not negated.

The concrete expression of this aspect of creationist philosophy of life is the type of courage with which it faces historical evil, i.e., 'faith.' In its generalized sense, the distinction between stoic courage and the courage of faith is that faith is sustained by relationship to a source of courage 'within' the historical process and 'outside' the self. Stoic courage is sustained by 'the Real' but reality is not 'outside' selfhood, since there is no ultimate dualism. Because of the 'otherness' of God, and God's activity in the historic process, creationism finds courage possible, even after having exhausted the inner resources of selfhood. Even when faith has nothing to show for itself inwardly, it still provides 'the substance of things hoped for,' and 'the evidence of things not seen.' Given its muddy metaphysics, the problem for the courage of 'faith' is that it may be trusting in something that is not true. Stoic courage is 'true' enough, given its tidier metaphysic. The problem for the lonely individualism of Stoic courage is that it may be inadequate to the 'slings and arrows of outrageous fortune'.

III

There is little question, I think, but that those cultures whose religious base is 'creationist' are better equipped to relate their religious values and practices to the problem of historical change. My own tradition is Protestant Christianity; a bright star in its crown is its continuing conversation with changing currents of thought in the ostensibly antagonistic technological culture of the West. But those cultures whose metaphysical base is emanationist are clearly better equipped to relate their religious values and practices to the experience of life's coherence. By identifying the depth of one's own being with the ground of Being itself, emanationism provides a 'spiritual' sense of the unity of life with life. The abundance of animal fables in Hindu literature, and the significance of holy mountains and sacred rivers for Hindu piety, illustrate the sense in which the three fundamental realities of self, nature and society flow into one another in an emanationist culture. It is also true that, while few achieve that total tranquility of spirit which is the gift of *moksha*, there is 'in the blood' of an emanationist culture an acceptance of time's fateful vagaries which contrasts sharply with the anxiety about time characteristic of creationist cultures, especially in the modern West.

It is easy for an emanationist culture to speak of the essential unity of all peoples, since it presupposes the essential unity of all things. The difficulty is to make that sense of community effective in a concrete historical situation where social differences are confronted. For example, the Aurobindo Ashram in Pondicherry, India, has established a city inclusive of people from all over the world, as a model for the coming world civilization. The ideology of this venture is characteristic of neo-Hinduism at its best. The community has only a tiny handful of Muslims in residence, however, and it is, of course, the conflict between Hindus and Muslims which presents India with its most fundamental social problem.

Creationism's capacity to deal with concrete historical change is tied to its tendency toward religious exclusivism, which is marked in Islam and Judaism as well as Christianity. Emanationism's capacity to comprehend the fundamental coherence of life is tied to its tendency to mystical transcendentalism. Creationism becomes more comprehensive, and emanationism more concrete, through historic interaction in which the common human awareness of the reality of God provides a basis for adaptation of one another's perspective.

Two illustrations: The neo-Hindu movement in India from Ram Mohun Roy to Sri Aurobindo represents the gradual incorporation of ethical/historical concern into a previously transcendental spirituality. The work of the Ramakrishna Mission is a result. In metaphysics, Radhakrishnan's re-interpretation of the classical doctrine of *maya* is an example of transcendental spirituality being turned in the direction of social concern and historical relevance. In the West the modern experiment with dualism, stemming from Descartes' division of reality into two radically different kinds, has run its course. In the physical sciences the new motion of a 'thing' derived from quantum theory relegates some Newtonian notions of 'substance' to the realm of maya. The ecological crisis gives new relevance to the emanationist perception that selfhood, nature and society flow into one another and are interdependent. Process thought and 'panentheism' search out a new metaphysical coherence in the philosophy of religion. The growing influence of Hinduism and Buddhism on Western religions, and the development of an interreligious perspective within Christian thought (Hocking, Maquarrie, Wilfred Cantwell Smith, Ninian Smart, John Hick, Raimundo Panikkar) give 'ecumenicity' a more holistic meaning.

IV

A world civilization requires a binding religious ingredient. Its tangible form will be a perception of common values and beliefs not unlike the 'civil religion' which provides a basis for loyalty in a pluralistic society like the United States. Do we not all trust a God of love and justice who cares for all His creatures? Do we not all value care for one another as a great human virtue? Do we not all sense a need to make sacrifices that the human family may endure? Etc. To be effective, it must have the same ontological givenness which traditional communities find centered in their blood bond. Humankind itself is the blood community of a world culture. What was once a fond abstraction, entrancing social dreamers, is now the only realistic hope for the future. Blood, after all, is only a symbol. Biological blood types cross racial lines. Historical necessity promotes a sense of human blood identity, born of the hard geopolitical fact that we must all hang together or we will all hang separately.

Meanwhile, the great religions continue their conversation with one another. On the metaphysical level, a crucial question is the possibility of rapproachment between creationist and emanationist views. There is perhaps more common ground than the typology initially suggests. For example: What is the substantial difference between Sankara's notion of the *atman* and Augustine's notion of the *imago dei*? Here a major thinker from one tradition is very close indeed to a major thinker from the other. On an existential level, a critical conversation concerns the meaning of death. Emanationism seems to be in love with death. I see no experiential difference between emanationist notions of *moksha* and the naturalistic conception of death. Creationism seems to be afraid of death. It is the 'sting of death" which creationist religion seeks to overcome. Yet today occidental theologies show little interest in an after- life; and oriental views are increasingly focussed on a religious philosophy of life. Perhaps death is neither metaphysically as promising nor experientially as threatening as our two families of religious cosmologies have led us to believe.

In the Great Conversation which modern communications makes inescapable, certain common loyalties will have to be developed if we are to survive as a race. These need not be made up out of whole cloth. They would not serve us adequately if they were. Certain notions of love and loyalty are already present, none deeper than the growing sense of identity with one's own human kind. Beyond that we need not fear that one of the great religions will swallow others up. We are all in the process of re-conceiving our own deepest insight as a result of being thrown together with those who only recently were alien to us, and therefore to be feared and fought. We need adapt only as we are persuaded, in concerns both metaphysical and existential, that friends from another tradition have helped us discover useful and compelling truth. For the present, the only commitment we can ask of one another is serious participation in the conversation.

Boston University

Boston, Massachusetts

NOTES

1. George F. McLean, ed., *Man and Nature* (Oxford: Calcut-

ta and London, 1978).

2. George F. McLean and Hugo Meynell, eds., *Person and Society* (Washington: International Society for Metaphysics and The University Press of America, 1987).

COMMENT

On Leroy S. Rouner

"Philosophy, Religion and the Coming World Civilization"

JOSEPH NYASANI

Prof. Rouner's paper holds out the hope for genuine future human co-existence and has earnestly attempted to grope for the root cause of the present international predicament brought about by the paradox of religion. The paradox, if it be attributed to religion, has so estranged the international community out of all proportions as to recommend a re-assessment of religion. Indeed, in trying to cultivate his own tribal or national image or in trying to assert his own identity within a given geographical area, one finds oneself rubbing shoulders with one's fellow man. In the process, one easily surrenders to the blind forces of egocentrism, parochialism and base nationalism.

As each society prepares to destroy the other in defense of its own beliefs about the meaning of life and the way to live out that meaning, it may be asked whether religion or religious convictions provide the basis for divisive tendencies among the peoples of the world. Now, Prof. Rouner answers this question in the affirmative, and he does so with respect to traditional societies. "Religion is a divisive element in traditional culture. Gods are tribal powers. Social conflicts are fraught with religious meaning because tribal gods are also in conflict."

Prof. Rouner might already have proved the point conclusively through empirical evidence available to him in his observations of the cultural/religious behavior of the societies he calls traditional. However, there will be those who might disagree with his attribution of conflicts to religion in traditional societies. In my view, the attribution is temerarious and too generalized.

In the traditional society such as the one that mine has been, it is difficult to say that wars have been fought because of religion or because one, two or more tribal gods were at loggerheads with one another. Religious/cultural ties do galvanize the people in their aspirations to assert themselves, but only insofar as their political existence is threatened. But in such an eventuality, the sense of religious belonging serves only as a moral booster and not as the cause of conflict.

Moreover, it is hardly conceivable that a tribal god would advise war since tribal gods never have direct dealings with the living, but only through the mediation of the departed ancestors of those living members. It is the departed members that inspire any contemplated course of action in the society to which they belonged. Almost certainly the departed will advise war not so much for religious self-preservation as for political survival. In the situation where political survival is threatened the ancestors (or the manes) may advise war as the only alternative for ensuing that vital existential continuity of communion with living members. Even this assertion may not apply for the whole African people because of the varied practices and multiplicity of beliefs that distinguish them

I do not contest the fact that certain societies--and not necessarily traditional ones--can be impelled by religious sentiments and other related affiliations to go to war merely to defend their brand of belief. In fact, this has been the case in the Western countries. We all know of such holy wars as the Crusades and of the motives behind their prosecuting; wars of this nature have not been uncommon in history. But those who waged them with so much religious fanaticism and fervor did so as a result of an aberrant consciousness that failed to grasp the true values and meaning of human existence. Perhaps it is fair to say that Prof. Rouner has not adequately addressed himself to the misconception of these values and conditions of amicable human co-existence. In my view, he should have dwelt more in detail on these vital exigencies, rather than engaging in what could be regarded as an over simplification of the cause and remedy of the human predicament.

Some of the conditions that Prof. Rouner's paper might have looked into are those that underlie and spell out the purpose, meaning and sanctity of human dignity and the common destiny of man. Some are implied in his paper, but are not given the kind of consideration they deserve. Who doubts that there are regimes today that are suppressing and oppressing large sections of humanity not because they are out to defend religion, but because they have elected to follow a different criterion of human dignity? They have, so to speak, pulled themselves away from the right sense of human behavior and have preferred to defy every rule of human co-existence; they even use religion as a tool to affirm what they judge to be another conception of human dignity.

Prof. Rouner sees those cultures whose metaphysical base is emanationist as better equipped to relate their religious values and practices to the experience of life's coherence. But in any society that is neither creationist nor emanationist people are equally equipped with a spiritual sense of unity of life. They see themselves as forming one large community with the departed ancestors who intervene for them in times of hardship. This is a matter, not so much of religion, as of an ontological or, if you like, existential necessity and order.

Even progressive universalization of religious visions from tribal and totemic views to worldviews is not enough to bring about mutual respect and love. If anything, this must be achieved through harmonization of religious views and a genuine reappraisal of the social conditions that have contributed to the differences that are now dividing peoples of the earth along cultural, social and color lines. I would like to feel with Prof. McLean that universal peace as unity of order is unrealizable without a commitment to a genuine notion of charity. But a religiously founded notion need not serve as the basis for this even, though it might curb naturally egocentric impulses. Only after mankind has understood the meaning of human existence and human dignity, possibly through a worldwide crusade to restore the common values that have been sacrificed through aberrational tendencies of self-esteem, can I see religion playing a really meaningful role of stabilizing and sustaining the new order to which we aspire.

University of Nairobi

Nairobi, Kenya

CHAPTER XVIII

TIME AND ETERNITY

J. N. FINDLAY

This paper is entitled 'Time and Eternity' which suggests that there is something called 'Eternity' which is a very much better thing than Time. This at once raises the question: What is wrong with Time? We know what Time is, in the sense of being able to talk adequately about it, saying that this lasted a long time and that a very short time, that this happened at an earlier time than that, or that this was the case in past times but will not be the case in future times. And we have clocks and chronometers and documents and methods of dating, by which distance in time or length of time can be more or less precisely measured. And even the researches of Einstein do not forbid us to talk in terms of local time. Why then, when all such talk works so admirably and so verifiably, should we wish to bring in something else called 'Eternity', which is either merely an indefinitely long time, and so not at all interesting philosophically, or something else in which there is no earlier or later, no past and no future, and no long drawn out process of development or persistence, but only what is wholly other than time, and of which we have not had the slightest experience and can form not the most indefinite conception? It is surely a curious situation when we, who are essentially creatures of Time in all our learning and doing, and whose language and thought are finely adjusted to every nuance of temporality, should suddenly behave as if we were strayed visitors from Eternity, unable to understand how anything can become or change or last, or is not all there at once in some immutable, total concurrence.

I raise these points because in 1941 I attempted to carry out a project of Wittgenstein's, and to show how all the so-called problems of Time arose out of a strange misunderstanding of the flexible ways of our language, so that we asked questions which could not be answered simply because they violated logical grammar. The concept of the Now or the Present is in ordinary usage infinitely flexible: it can be stretched to cover a decade or a century, or narrowed down to cover what is over in a flash. We are therefore inclined to extend it till it covers the whole history of the universe, or to narrow it down till it becomes a mere limit, no sooner arrived at than departed from, and in which it is not significant to posit either a state or a change. In the latter case we have then the problem of constituting Time out of such momentary nothings, which are even *qua* nothings not there all together, or alternatively of wondering how anything can happen, if, before it happens, something else must first happen, and before that again something else, and so on ad infinitum. We have in short all the difficulties with which Augustine and Zeno plagued the ancients, and to which we may now add the difficulties with which McTaggart has worried the moderns, asking how the same event can be future, present and past, when it must be these incompatible things at different successive times, and these times in their turn must be future, present and past at different times, and so on ad infinitum.

To all these celebrated difficulties the line that I took up was plain: that they arose out of imposing a wrong exactness and a wrong generality on the flexible ways of our speech. Augustine and Zeno perplexed us since we failed to see that the present, though never of zero or infinite length, could be just as long or as short as we liked to make it, and McTaggart confused us since we failed to see that there were two distinct ways of talking about events and states, one which remained invariant wherever one was stationed in history, and one which changed according as one changed one's historical position, and that there was nothing self-contradictory in either form of speech but only in the attempt to combine them.

This type of linguistic solution, like Kant's phenomenalistic solutions of the Antinomies, gave me great satisfaction at the time. I soon saw, however, that the tendency of our speech to move in contrary directions was nothing contingent or arbitrary, but pointed to deep stresses within experience and in the reality which appears in experience. The experienced real involves, as Kant saw, both a permanence of form which maintains itself continuously whatever may flow through it, and which never breaks up into disjoined elements, and a disjunction of contents so absolute that none of them, however short-lived, can ever coexist with any other. All is at once continuous and yet always fragmented, an unbroken passing of phases into phases, which are yet wholly sundered and incapable of passing into one another. And if one asks whether the Now is vanishing or eternal, both answers are appropriate: its contents vanish incontinently, but it itself seems to endure. All this mysteriousness of flux was given classical expression in Husserl's 1906 *Lectures on the Phenomenology of the Inner Time-Consciousness* where there is an enduring form of phenomenological givenness in which new contents steadily slip from an 'originary' point of freshness, through a spectrum of growing staleness in which new contents steadily overlay them, until at length such overlaid staleness reaches a maximum, and they then take their place in the indefinitely extended, ordered past. What is remarkable in these descriptions is their astonishing mixture of preservation with supersession, of retention of content with continuous change of relative position. In a sense they bear witness to the marriage of time with timelessness even in the briefest experience of a flux which never ceases, and of an ordered map which emerges from the flux. And flux and map are not mutually independent but wholly parasitic upon one another: the time map is what is woven on the spindle of the flux, and the flux would not be a flux apart from the map that it weaves.

It may be thought that all this is merely psychological, and that the physicists with their Space-Time have quite done away with it. The experienced successiveness of time-states has in fact been held by some, e.g., Grunbaum, to be no more than a case of the secondary qualities: we see one after the other what are physically, in Space-Time, not in this manner successive. The modes of succession are not, however, at all like the secondary qualities, for they modify, not the content of states, but the manner of their being. Without necessary change in content, states pass from being about to be to being what now is, and from being what now is, to being what has been. It would be as absurd to treat being about to be, or having been as a case of quality or characters, as to do the same in the case of possibility or probability. A possible or probable shower of rain is not a shower of rain with a curious added determination: it is not really a shower of rain at all, but the possibility or the probability of one. In the same way a future or a past conflagration is not a very peculiar sort of conflagration: it is not really a conflagration at all, but only the aboutness-to-be or the having-beenness of one. One of the basic obscurities of passage is in fact the differing modality of its regions, a difference which does not obtain in the case of space. It is clear, further, that no relation of events as earlier and later can give them anything beyond a mere simulacrum of futurity, presentness and pastness. For what is only relatively future in the sense of coming after a given event may not be future *simpliciter*, if that event lies in the past, and what is only past in a similar relative sense need not be past simpliciter if it is only past relatively to some future event. The modalities of presentness, pastness and futurity are therefore neither qualitative nor relational determinations of anything in the world: they are modal differences, differences in the character of assertion or being the case, not in that of any content asserted or which is the case. If our experiences require expression in modal terms, there is no reason why events in nature should not also require it.

I do not think that modern physical theory has done anything to alter the modal character of futurity, presentness and pastness, nor to make them merely psychological or subjective. What it has done is to make them pertain to individual histories or so-called world-lines, the life of a given particle or traveling charge, the life of a co-location of particles forming a relatively stationary aggregate, the life of an organic aggregate with its informing psyche. On each such world-line there will be one and only one changing point of presentness, and the variously and varyingly distant having-beennesses of states no longer actual, and the variously and varyingly distant about-to-beennesses of states--possibly alternative--which are not as yet actual. What is peculiar to the modern physical picture is simply that the points of presentness on differing world-lines which are not intersecting fall apart, and that there is not a single uniform way of correlating them. They are not relative to some arbitrarily chosen event in a world-line, but to that world-line as a whole. They are the present, the past and the possible futures of this particle or this aggregate or this organism or this psyche, and not of the universe as a whole. The philosopher who comes off best in this strange situation is undoubtedly Leibniz: the universe is irremediably monadic. The only difference is that the influence which harmonizes and connects all the world-lines is not God, nor any featureless, inert medium, but that living, active interchange called Light, whose strange preeminence it is always so to regulate the distances and the speeds of all that it connects, that it always surpasses them in speed in precisely the same immutable though finite extent. The universe we live in is very strange. In the time of Newton its contents were thought to defer to those two great invisibles, absolute Space and Time: now they defer to the most visible of all phenomena, Light, offspring of Heaven first-born. If you will permit me to be irreverent, I find the cosmos in which we live very much like some small German principality, where everyone defers absolutely to the sovereign. *Was je geschieht, muss Durchlaucht immer die schnellste sein*: whatever happens, Highness must always be the fastest. What has happened in all this is that the unchanging, map-like aspect of Time has merely assumed a spatio-temporal rather than a purely temporal character: the lines on the map are still lines of flux and becoming which have in some way been frozen into timelessness.

Since I have introduced the physicists, I must also say a brief word about one of their further phantasies, that the 'Arrow of Time' is not anything categorial and invariant, but somehow connected with the Law of Entropy or increasing confusion, which declares that causal lines are always radiating forth from centres in every possible direction, and losing themselves in a variety of effects which never are bent back to the centre from which they spring, nor able to reconstitute its unity. The world is like a pond where a falling stone creates a series of ripples which fade out and are lost as they proceed to the pond's edge, but which never spontaneously arise and converge upon the centre, leading to the emergence from the water of the disturbing stone. On the other hand there are physicists who hold that for long periods entropy may be reversed, and that energy will then not disperse itself in widely radiating effects, but gather itself together in great, central accumulations. The fact that physicists canvass both of these possibilities shows that they really do not identify Time's Arrow with increasing entropy, since they conceive of it as operating in either direction.

If I now had the time, I should try to spell out the exciting phenomenology in which world-lines independently converged towards definite Predetermined outcomes of which there might be many advance indications. It would be a conspiratorial and a teleological rather than a causal world, and would be handed over to fate and predestination as regards the future, while conjecture, inference and wishful faking would be possible only in regard to the past. Our causal language would have to be revised or given a new slant, since it would be future events that would determine the present and the past rather than the other way round. I once conducted a competition in the journal *Analysis* in the 'fifties in which many young philosophers discussed the possibility of a world in which everything happened in reverse: one hardbitten analyst held that such reversal, if total, would make no difference at all. I do not myself think that this view was correct, though certainly nothing precisely like our memory or our anticipation or our practical choices could exist in such a reversed world. I am inclined to think that, despite the authority of Plato, no such reversed world is really thinkable. It does not make sense to conceive of events as hurrying on to fully predestined futures, while obliteration and vagueness infect everything that is past. Nor is teleology possible in a world which cannot build upon what has been so far realized.

It does not therefore make sense to conceive of the past as anything but wholly determinate and incapable of being affected by what happens afterwards, whereas it does make sense to conceive of the future as always involving alternatives, which may be decided one way or another by a unique form of causation analogous to choice. This form of causation may sometimes decide on the less probable alternative, and it is by such decisions that reversals in entropy may be explained. All world-lines will then have perfectly definite pasts but also definite possibilities of future branching, in which the less probable alternative will sometimes be followed. Whatever happens will be fully explained: spontaneity is a form of causality, not of chance.

What arises out of all this is, however, the basic problem of temporality: the emergence of something like a fixed, constant map out of a sheer flux In which constancy is not to be found. It remains hard to understand how, despite all the performances of clocks and other mechanical or intuitive modes of measurement, something whose whole being seems to consist in a flux, in which nothing exists together, should also be inseparable from ordinal and metric properties, which surely imply togetherness if anything does. It is even harder to conceive the matter when we reflect that time is nothing clearly conceivable apart from its contents, and that it is therefore in a sense perpetually being generated, and given body and meaning by those acts of decision or quasi-decision through which alternatives receive the *cachet* of actuality. All this is hard to conceive, but only a problem as long as we let it be one. Problems arise in philosophy only when we try to fit notions suited to one sort of situation to situations which require others, our problem being merely an obscure way of feeling a notional misfit. What we have to do in such situations is simply to turn our problem into our explanation, our difficulty into the essence of what is under examination. Time is accordingly nothing but a content-laden flux in which an orderly map of what has been is continuously growing out of the alternativity of what may be about to be. It is given as a package, in which constant form and variable content, open futurity and closed pastness, sheer flux and an ordered, metric deposit, belong inseparably together.

Kant with superb insight makes Time have three basic sides: it involves permanence, it involves succession and it involves coexistence. And since it is nothing apart from the content which fills it, its permanence must be a permanence of content as well as of form, which makes it a history of developing things and substances, always with some limitation of nature which sets bounds to their changes. Its succession must further involve the regularity or near-regularity with which the states lead one to another and are causally connected, whereas its coexistences involve the continuous impact of one causal line on another, and a reverse impact from the latter, so that it becomes a history of interacting things. Where Kant's insight failed him was in failing to see that an orderly, objective world need not be one dominated throughout by strict Newtonian determinism, but one capable of containing those free exercises of spontaneity which he felt forced to relegate to the noumenal sphere. Of course he failed to divine that, where there is no direct interlacing of causal lines, there can also be no plain

sense given to precise simultaneity, so that the variable alignment of events taught in the Special Theory of Relativity becomes readily conceivable. But Kant's recognition of the supreme
role of Light in being phenomenal nature together (see Kr.d.r.V.,
A 213)--a recognition also to be found in Hegel--went some way
in the direction of the later alignment of our whole Space-Time
metric about Light's critical velocity.

I have gone some distance towards integrating the times of
various world lines, among which the phenomenological times of
conscious beings are comprehended, with the unified Space-Time
map believed in by modern physics. Where, however, is the place
for Eternity in this strange monadological picture, where we
have rather an indefinite number of interlacing times than a
single Eternity in which all are transcended? The Eternity towards which I am tending is not, however, the mere negation of
temporality. It is not the timelessness of the truth that seven
added to five will make twelve, or that being white is compatible with being warm, or that being green covers a wider range
of possibility than being coral-pink. Eternity so spoken of is
irrelevant to Time, whereas the Eternity I am in quest of is
something that can in some manner be superimposed upon temporal matters, that can be predicated of the being of individuals
which arise, last, change and pass away in time, that can be
predicated of what they do and undergo at various points in
their history, and that can even be predicated in some higher-order fashion of the very time-modalities of their doing and
undergoing. It must in some sense be an eternal matter of fact
or truth that Buddha *is* receiving enlightenment or that Christ *is*
dying on the Cross--Meister Eckhart somewhere stresses the
truth of the latter--and it must in some sense be an eternal
matter of fact or truth that such an enlightenment or such a
passion occurred many, many centuries ago. It is clear that we
are in some manner able to give sense to a being the case,
which does not side-step or ignore, but brackets without altering the facts of development in time, that we can in some sense
conceive even temporal matters under a certain species of Eternity, as Spinoza first taught us to do and say. How can we
explain this understanding of even a higher-order modality which
can be superimposed upon, without destroying, the ordinary
time-modalities, but which also utterly transcends any form of
direct ostension or illustration?

I would reply that we understand it in that it represents a
limit towards which we are reaching out in all our conscious
endeavors, and a limit, moreover, that is necessary to the understanding of those endeavors as also to their very existence.
For it is wrong to identify the meaningful with the ostensible or

the illustrable: by the very act of gesturing in a certain direction, where nothing can be illustrated or shown, we can sometimes very precisely indicate just what we mean. For all memory involves an attempted transcendence of time and passage: it is part of the idea of memory, if not of its achieved actuality, that the most insignificant event in one's past is in some sense still there just as it was when it happened, and that it could be relived, in all its unfulfilled incompleteness, just as it then was. And all anticipation, despite its present alternativity, looks forward to a situation in which alternativity will vanish, and the sea-fight tomorrow become (or not become) an accomplished reality. If we could but hasten the passage of events, as they would be for an experience which advanced more slowly, and so embraced more in a single present than we do, we might very well be able, without foreknowledge, to see tomorrow's sea-fight as part of the same occasion as today. The notion of an experience in which all time, without loss of order, and without precise anticipation of later stages in earlier ones, can be compressed into a single luminous instant, is a notion towards which we are constantly tending. We know obscurely, and if only by analogy, what sort of state it would be. Such partial transcendence of temporality need not be confined to conscious beings: we need not follow Augustine in this ploy. Unconscious beings may be influenced by the whole of their past in a manner not grounded in present traces, and may decide for one alternative rather than another in a manner analogous to our choices. And we may see, as was said before, a remarkable naturalization of Eternity in the physical phenomenon of Light. For the photons-which bind the universe together, everything, without loss of order, will collapse into something like instantaneousness.

Obviously, too, the constant striving towards time-transcendence in the thought of metaphysicians and logicians, however much we may often deplore its superficiality, bears witness to their partial understanding of something that they cannot hope to illustrate. The arguments of Parmenides and McTaggart may be invalid, but what they seek to establish may at some level be significant and true. The objections of logicians to changing truth-values, or to an unsettled alternativity which, they hold, would violate the Law of Excluded Middle, may be ill-taken, but their feeling for the timelessness of truth and being springs from a sound intellectual heart. The modern elaboration of tense-logic by Arthur Prior, whom I am proud to remember as one of my pupils, has shown that such a logic demands difficult decisions, but that it can be developed without contradiction in a number of alternative ways. The Law of Excluded Middle raises no difficulty, since we need not identify the non-futurity of p with the futurity of not-p: the former may extend to the as yet unsettled status which is excluded by the latter. Either it will be the case that p or it is not the case that it will be the case that p, but the latter alternative does not entail that it will be the case that not-p. By and large, however, Prior has not persuaded the main body of logicians that tense-logic, any more than modal or intentional logic, represents a necessary and valuable extension of logic, and this refusal to take time seriously in logic, though in some ways deeply contemptible, yet bears witness to an obscure understanding and taste for the Eternal.

What emerges from all this? That there is nothing self-contradictory about Time unless it is made to stand wholly on its own legs. It points ineluctably to something beyond and more than itself, in which its distances and order will remain, but in which its vanishing will itself vanish. To understand the nature of Eternity, we must conceive of Being, of course quite figuratively, as having both a periphery and a centre, and as having lines that connect its periphery continuously with its centre. On the periphery lie all the objects that we call things in space, and states follow one another in time, and the characters of things and states often differ sharply from one another. I shall not say that everything on the periphery is wholly clear and definite and separate, for here too things pass into one another insensibly and have ill-defined contours. And here too everything grows into other things, or helps to make them thus or thus, and everything is in a sense everywhere since it makes some difference to everything else. But by and large it is possible to refer to definite, separate individuals, and make definite statements about them, and in some respects keep them out of the press of other things and of their contrasting characters. This is the field to which the common logic as well adjusted, though there is nothing in Logic is such to limit it to matters such as this.

There are, however, many zones of experience which are not part of this outer periphery of the world, and it is in these that the hard clarity and separateness of this outer region are gradually overcome. These are the regions of imagery, of imaginal and symbolic thought, and of the thought, even more notably, that is neither imaginal nor symbolic. There are also the regions of felt impulsions and stirrings which do not issue in peripheral behaviour. Peripheralist thinkers try to moor all these phenomena to the periphery by conceiving of them as perfectly mirrored in neural changes, and at some future date capable of being read off from such. Alternatively they seek their mirror in hypothetical peripheral behaviour that suitable circumstances might evoke.

I do not believe in either of these peripheralist ruses. The most simple association by analogy often operates with analogies too novel and too highly generic to be comprised even in the repertoire of the versatile, highly practiced neurones, and the jungle of hypothetical behaviour is better illuminated by what we inwardly think and want rather than the other way round. In the higher zones of experience there is further a great leaping about among free universals, and an exploration of their intrinsic connections, and there is also that sympathetic entry into the experiences of others which can never literally be our own. And in connection with this latter form of transcendence, there is further an emergence of goals and values that are interpersonal, and which represent what everyone can and must seek for everyone. In these higher zones, too, there will be an increasing transcendence of Space and Time, the most remote things becoming for us as things present, so that some act of imperial cruelty reported with all the remorseless compassion of Tacitus becomes as much a present anguish as an atrocity recently perpetrated.

I do not believe that the spectrum ends there, but that it can be continued in states of meditative concentration even within the limits of this present life. To me it seems ontologically likely that there are states of what I may call liberated experience where the profitable and necessary link of the psyche with its peripheral body will become a reminiscence, where the separateness and compulsiveness of data stemming from bodily sensitivity will be attenuated, and above everything will gradually assume a more dreamlike yet intellectually lucid character, penetrated with meanings and values and interpersonal understandings, which will in the end lose their last links with sensibility, and will become those purely intellectual intuitions sometimes hesitantly spoken of by Kant. Then we shall live in the true environment of Minds and Ideas, and not in the contingent confusion of their dispersed instances, though preserving all such distinctions as are to be found in the latter. At the apex of this progression I conceive that we shall advance to a unity which, while preserving all the order and distances of temporal progression will none the less dispense with the piecemeal, fragmented, developmental character of Time. We shall in short enter Eternity, of which perfection Time is the ever imperfect image. This Eternity will be that of the perfectly Enlightened or Divine Reason, in which we and our histories will be accorded such place as fits the degree to which we become pervious to it, or rather to the extent to which it has made us pervious to itself.

I wish here particularly to express my conceptual debt to Spinoza, who, more than any other, put Time back into Eternity, instead of leaving it to languish in some illusory place outside. There is probably a temporal survival of at least some part of our thinking, conscious life after the dissolution of our bodies, possibly a repeated descent of the same life into a series of bodies, as Plato, Buddha and other wise persons have taught us. But surely in the end we shall wish to be taken up into the Divine Reason, and to live with it out of Time, as pieces of history that are none the less eternally living, and lit up, like the stained glass of York and Bourges, by the unutterable, intellectual Light of Heaven. I fear that this paper has degenerated into a sermon; I cannot profess to have fully understood all the above, but its continuous coherence with what I do understand makes me sure that it is mainly true.

Boston University

Boston, Mass.

COMMENT

On John Findlay,

"Time and Eternity"

KENNETH L. SCHMITZ

During a recent visit to the Old City of Jerusalem, descending the steps to the Church of the Dormition of Mary, I met Professor Findlay ascending them. When I asked him what was going on inside the church, he replied: "There is incense, many lamps and much singing. It is all very multitudinous." I quite mistook his meaning to be that of Hegel's in the *Phenomenology* which expresses both the necessity of devotion in the development of religious consciousness and his own personal distaste for religious ritual, the murmur of voices without a single thought. I learned later, however, that Professor Findlay had a much more neo-Platonic meaning in mind, and that he considered the Armenian service to be a genuine plenitude, a super-abundance, multitudinous indeed!

It was with this latter sense of multitudinosity that I put down the paper after my first reading. I had the impression of a quiet flow of thoughts, at points attaining a majesty, animated with a deep fervour in keeping with its theme, and by no means contrary to reason, for reason has its quiet passion too. At the end of the paper Professor Findlay fears that he has given us a sermon. I think that he has named the correct genus, but that what he has given us is not a sermon, least of all a degenerate one. We certainly have not been preached at. What he has given us is a *hymn*, indeed a hymn of praise, a *confessio* in the original sense of the word: a philosophical prose hymn that is not an ordinary argument, but that nevertheless is not without argument.

In an earlier article[1] Professor Findlay had maintained a firm and seemingly unparadoxical position: There is nothing wrong with the concept of time and with its language. It is plain and adequate and becomes a perplexity only when we expect too much precision and generality from it. We are essentially temporal beings. The language of time is familiar to us and quite sufficient for our everyday concerns and ordinary expressions. There seems to be neither need nor justification for the intrusion of the concept of eternity, especially if it is taken as timeless. We have enough problems without also taking up the stance of a stranger to time, perplexed by the movement in this world. Initally satisfied with this "resolution," or exorcism, he soon came to a new appreciation of the question of time and eternity. This new appreciation is the first turning-point in the account given in this paper.

You will have noticed that nothing really changes in the new statement of the problem: All the familiarity of temporal language remains and the difficulties or conundrums of time re-emerge from their brief exile. What is new is the question now asked, and it is: What stress is at work in our language and in our experience to drive us in contrary directions, i.e., towards plain sensible speech about ordinary time, on the one hand, yet towards the paradoxes and conundrums concerning time, on the other? The shift does not occur by adding or taking away the elements of the problem, but in the approach to it. Indeed, the paper does not move so much by a strictly formal argument as it does by making available to us what I have called a *kaleidoscopic* shift in which the elements which have been there all along are exhibited in new ways. This kind of shift is a key to the dynamic of the paper. It occurs once more at an important juncture of the paper, and discloses itself gradually as rooted in the very conceptions that underly the paper.

The first kaleidoscopic shift, then, is as follows: If we adopt plain speech about familiar time as the *sole* standard (the position of the 1941 article), then eternity-talk becomes foolish, arbitrary and fruitless. On the other hand, if we go on and ask *why* there are such paradoxes in time-talk, we begin to restore the balance between eternity and time, and thereby open up the possibility of legitimizing talk about eternity. The shift makes possible a fresh look at the features of time. They fall into three groups: First, there are the *moments* of time (past, present and future) and their linguistic equivalents, the *tenses*. Second, there are the *modalities* of time: possibility, actuality and necessity. Third, there are the *factors* of time: permanence, succession and co-existence. These features disclose a unique dynamic constitution and are quite enough to warn us that time is not a *substantial* thing, nor are its features the states or qualities of things.

Nevertheless, time is not simply *formal*. A too exclusively mathematical conception of time may conceive it as a frozen quasi-spatial map, or may take time to be simply a correlation of points on a line, the distance between those called "early" and those called "late." The burden of much of the paper is to exhibit the trans-formal character of time. Moreover, the key to the movement towards a conception of eternity is to be found also in those features that show time to be a unique form of duration.

A first trans-formal feature of temporal duration is manifest in *permanence*, a permanence that is neither simply that of the content nor of the form, but is the interplay of time and its content. The "now" is both evanescent and yet ever-present, and out of an endless flux there emerges an ordered map in which events take up their status in an ordered past. Any account that reduces time to the mere succession of points, one earlier than another, misses the trans-formal nature of time and the duration discernible in it. But *succession* also exhibits this trans-formal character. For the permanence of things in time and their causal lines is the basis of the irreversibility in their succession. (And here we are treated to a sort of *verkehrte Welt*). An additional trans-formal element is to be found in the interaction and ac-tual co-existence of various lines of successive causation, an actual simultaneity that is the condition for there being a uni-verse. The modalities of time also exhibit the character of dura-tion, since they exhibit the manner in which things come about and are. It is here, too, that we find genuine alternativity, i.e. a future that lies open to real alternatives, in which the less probable will sometimes be realized.

Such are the lines to the "solution" of the problem of time as Professor Findlay presents them in his paper. Or rather, the lines show that the problem of time is not a problem at all. The so-called problem arises only if we isolate the features of time and pit them against each other. Thus, if we take time to be sheer flux, we then wonder how a definite order can arise from it. Or again, if we take eternity to be sheer timelessness, we then ask how it can be related to time in any way. The true "solution" is to avoid creating such unnecessary problems, and to take the whole package as it is given to us in and through a phenomenological description.

This "solution" is very like the first formulation of the problem, and is another kaleidoscopic shift. All elements remain the same, but a new integral approach is taken towards them. The advantage of such a solution to the nature of time is that eternity is also already present, and this prepares for the third kaleidoscopic shift in which an approach through the trans-for-mal features of temporal duration will yield the conception of eternity. For eternity is not something other than time, as if were added to time. It is, we are told, the duration that is dis-cernible in time, a duration made available to us and unified by a sort of kaleidoscopic shift.

In this shift (which has been underway almost from the beginning of the paper) a new theme announces itself.[2] It is the shift from temporal to eternal duration. It rests, if I have un-derstood it, upon a fresh and vigorous reworking of Husserl's time analysis in which pastness and futurity penetrate the pre-sent to constitute the flowing *now*. This range of past-present-future can be extended flexibly so that a certain order of events remains within the integrated unity of the *now*. This may well be what is meant by "bracketing without altering," though I must confess that at this point the waters of Siloe begin to flow rather too fast for my weak eyes and they become somewhat clouded by the rapid passage of the waters. What is intended, however, seems clear enough to me in its general lines: What can be taken in ordinary light to be dispersed and fragmentary can be seen in the light of eternity to be internally unified. A higher order of duration can be "superimposed" upon temporal matters. Not only do the very moments of time converge upon one another (the metaphor of compression is used), but certain eternal "matters of fact," such as the great acts of religious founders, are held to burst the bounds of confinement to one or another temporal moment and to be *actually true* for all moments. "In some sense,"--but how are we to take this sense?

We are told that the higher order modality of duration which we call eternity represents a limit towards which we reach out by necessity in all of our conscious endeavours--in memory, in thought, in metaphysics and in logic. In this reaching we achieve partial transcendence of the ordinary flow of time. Yet this pointing towards something beyond itself and more than itself is necessary if time is to be coherent in its own terms. This pointing beyond is indicated in certain "zones of experience" that ought not to be neglected by the philosophers, such as regions of imagery, symbolism, the free play of thoughts, meditative concentration, and experience so liberated that sensibility will itself become a reminiscence. We will have reached that eternity which is with us all along and to which Plato's realm of Ideas and Spinoza's free man give witness. Its name, it seems to me is *durational unity*.

To summarize: I find two principal moments in the paper. First, the exhibition of the durational features of time that carries time beyond a merely formal conception. Second, the gathering of the features of time into a higher-order modality, that eternity which is characterized by the nondispersal, by the convergence and intrinsic unity of the distinctive features of time.

What I should like to hear more of may be put as three points concerning Professor Findlay's conception of eternity. First, if order and distance remain in eternity, what *kind* of unity does it exhibit? Does not the durational element of eternity come to settle in the end upon simultaneity and co-existence? (But then, that seems to be a truncated temporality, the very abstractness that eternity was meant to forestall.) Or does a conception of plenitude come finally into play? But then, how?

Through the convergence of the durational elements themselves? Or through critical events and figures in time, such as Christ or Buddha? Second, the closing page shows a reversal. It turns out that it is not, after all, we who have gained access to this ever-present eternity, but eternity itself which "has made us pervious to itself." What are the grounds for this reversal? Is it the need for a unity which prevents the dispersal of temporal duration? And does the concept of plenitude play a role in this reversal? (But of course, it could not be a concept in any ordinary sense, but would have to be an actual, if ideal, plenitude, after the manner perhaps of a Platonic form?) But what kaleidoscopic shift might disclose the grounds for this reversal? Finally, the flexibility of the *now* is meant to show how an order of differentiated events can remain in their difference and yet be included within a single enduring *now*,--thus, *now* can be an era, a movement, a century. How are we to discriminate between purely formal and subjective limitations, such as an hour or a century, on the one hand, and the non-arbitrary order and duration of events that demand to be gathered into a unity of time that is neither formal, subjective nor arbitrary?

For myself, I would look for more transcendence in the conception of eternity, but the strength of this "kaleidoscopic" conception of eternity is that it presents eternity that has been there all the time. There is no doubt that this omnipresence is an indispensable and important aspect of eternity when duration is conceived under the aegis of unity.

Trinity College

    University of Toronto

NOTES

1. "Time: A Treatment of Some Puzzles" (1941), reprinted in *Language, Mind and Value: Philosophical Essays* (London: George Allen and Unwin, 1963), pp. 39-56.

2. It is taken up also in *The Discipline of the Cave* (Gifford Lectures, 1964-65; London: George Allen and Unwin, 1966), and in *Ascent to the Absolute* (London: George Allen and Unwin, 1970).

ON PHILOSOPHICAL ECUMENISM
A DIALOGUE*

R.M. MARTIN

Crede mihi, miseris coelestia numina parcunt;
Nec semper laesos, et sine fine, premunt.

R.M.M. Good day, Herr F. It is good to see you again after our meeting in Jerusalem.

F. Good day. That was a most interesting meeting, wasn't it? What a fascinating city, Jerusalem, and a perfect place for a philosophical meeting. A city of the ages, of all seasons, of all shades of opinions, the most ecumenical of all earthly cities and at the same time a *civitas Dei.*

M. Yes, and I suppose if philosophical divergences are to be brought into the open, it should be there of all places. I am glad to see you now, for I know you are an admirer of Professor Findlay, and are fond of quoting from his writings. Much of what he said in Jerusalem concerning my paper,[1] you know, seemed to me--and indeed to others too--somewhat distorted and not quite cogent.

F. I am sorry if you feel that way. Sometimes he does exaggerate a bit publically, you know. He thinks it helps to create an effect and to get people to listen.

M. Yes, but it can also seriously mislead. In any case, I would like to ask you some questions as to what his views really are, for you of course know them much better than I. To begin with, I would be interested in knowing more clearly just why he laments what he calls 'formal logic' to the extent he seems to, and on every possible occasion seems to derogate its role in philosophy.

F. He has great respect for formal logic and some of its achievements. What he laments is "tailoring what is [philosophically] worth saying to the limited resources and the artificial rigors of an arbitrarily exact scheme of diction." He applauds "tailoring logic to what is worth saying."[2]

M. I think we have no problem as to what is "worth saying," as he puts it. I, like him, have the profoundest respect for the great philosophic classics, and I want none of them expunged, not even those with which I might not personally agree. The study of the history, the *exact* and highly detailed study of its history, has always seemed to me one of the two chief pillars--the other is logic itself--of philosophical study. Everything important that has been said is eminently worth saying, even though much of it we would now wish to reject. The really important views, I suppose, are those that have either persisted or at least reappeared from age to age, perhaps in almost unrecognizable garb.

F. The difficulty is that formal logic is so narrow. It condones as valid forms of inference only those so childish and simple that no one ever fails to keep to them, and neglects the really difficult and important forms of inference, which we really wish to know about and which might be really helpful in our philosophical work.

M. There is truth to what you say. Peirce, you know, said something similar years back. Much depends of course on how widely logic is construed. My fear is that you are construing it too narrowly, and fail to take account of some important recent advances. Logic, like the sciences, is subject to continual growth and development, you know. It never really had the dogmatic slumber often attributed to it, although of course there have been periods during which not much progress was made.

F. You may be right, but Professor Findlay means by 'formal logic' what is ordinarily meant in the English-speaking world.

M. So much depends on whom one talks to, and when. A decade ago there was perhaps some agreement, at Oxford, say, about what formal logic is. But the climate has changed and 'formal logic' is now construed there much more broadly, now that they have a real logician, Dana Scott, in their midst. As a friend of mine put it, now at Oxford there is a real logician for the first time since the period of Duns Scotus and Ockham. Logic an exact *science*, you know. I worry, you see, about your speaking of logic as something being "tailored," in the fashion presumably of a suit of clothes. You tailor it this way or that as fashion or taste dictates. But this is not at all what one does in logic, any more than in physics or biology. It is not *we* who make logic; it is rather that logic is made for us, tailored for us, if you like, by the Supreme Tailor of all. You and Findlay speak of logic as having only "limited resources" and of "the artificial rigors of an arbitrarily exact scheme of diction." Here again, these epithets seem to me rather askew. There is nothing arbitrary about the logical scheme when properly understood, and its resources are by no means limited--any more than any science is limited--especially when newer developments are taken into account. In any case, they are much less limited than you seem to suggest.

F. What Professor Findlay means is that logic should exhibit "true neutrality." It [p. 288] "ought to be such that it allows us to think and talk as unitively or as disjunctively as our empirical and rational insights warrant. It should not evince a prejudiced preference for an extensionalism geared to a pluralism of sheerly individual objects, herded at best into sets or classes by synsemantic functions which can themselves never be independently talked of. The purely descriptive gossip of ordinary life--"This house is to the left of that', 'All the houses in the street are painted white'--fits creakingly into this pattern, but even in ordinary talk our adverbs, our conditionals, our attitudinal expressions, etc., fail to fit it, and the whole of science and philosophy, including the philosophy of those who formulate such gossip, cannot be stated in it."

M. Well, a good deal has been said here, the gist of which I can agree with. The *way* in which it is said, however, seems to me unfortunate. And on almost every point, it seems to me, grievous blunders are being made. In the first place, I have been urging for years the neutrality of logic. Ryle did so also, you will recall, in his views of logic as "subject-matter" neutral. Also Carnap, Godel, Heinrich Scholz, Fred Fitch, and others. Indeed, there is an honorable history of this view, going back to Aristotle. Just *de facto* logic does exhibit true neutrality, in just Findlay's sense, I think. He speaks of a "prejudiced preference for an extensionalism," forgetting apparently all the work on non-extensional logics going back to Frege, as well as all the recent effort expended attempting to formulate them on a firm extensional basis. And why is the preference for extensionalism "prejudiced"? Findlay neglects to note that extensionalism is a view firmly based on certain desirable principles, including so-called principles of extensionality, that are so fundamental, basic, and well-entrenched (historically even) that one does not wish to give them up lightly. Well, this is not the occasion to present a full-fledged defense of extensionalism, but only to point out that the most casual glance at the history of logic, especially recent work, would be enough to convince anyone that the view is not the result of a mere "prejudiced preference."

F. But there is so much that you simply cannot do just on the basis of extensions. You must allow for intentionality in the senses of Brentano or Husserl, and accommodate all manner of intentional discourse.

M. Yes, this is true. But much depends on how intentions are handled logically. It was mentioned that extensionalism is firmly "geared to a pluralism of sheerly individual objects, herded at best into sets or classes by synsemantic functions which can themselves never be independently talked of." Now this seems to me clearly in error. Many purely extensional set theories are at hand in which sets or classes are the only entities admitted.[3] Some logicians prefer such theories, in which there is no reference to the contaminate world of "things" in any way whatsoever. And if you don't like set theories, then there is my 'homogeneous' logic at hand, in one interpretation of it, in which there are only classes and no individuals.[4] A humble thing perhaps, but mine own. Thus extensionalism is by no means geared to a pluralism of "individuals," nor need it be such that sets or classes are not able to be spoken of in them independently. There is still more to say against what you said a moment back. The view that "our adverbs, our conditionals, our attitudinal expressions, etc.," cannot be handled within an extensional logic is also thoroughly mistaken. Please let me call attention to a good deal of recent work in which just this is being done.[5] Of course these matters are not easy, but progress is being made. Some of the work on adverbs, for example, harks back to Reichenbach; that on attitudinals, to Ajdukiewicz. The analysis of conditionals is still highly controversial. But it seems to me premature surely to suggest that the handling of these cannot be made to fit the ordinary kind of logic. You say also that "the whole of science and philosophy [just think what a staggering totality this is!] . . . cannot be stated" in an extensionalist framework. Can you name an intensionalist one in which it can be? Are you not making here an almost preposterous demand?

F. No, I am not demanding too much, nor is Professor Findlay. "One cannot get far in science or philosophy without making intensions (spelled with an *s*), rather than extensions, one's primary theme of reference, and it is further important that they should represent genuine and deep affinities, not superficial alignments dependent on chance usage or the misguided ingenuity of some logic-chopper."

M. I think you are right in this contention in essentials, and I can agree with you while firmly remaining an extensionalist. The whole matter depends on how intensions are introduced and handled. But you speak of intensions *ex cathedra*, and seem to disregard all the painstaking work that has gone into the attempts to formulate an exact theory of them during the last hundred years. Is all this being dismissed under the grand rubric of "logic-chopping?" If so, just think of the great logicians being dismissed in this way: Frege, Peirce, Russell, Carnap, Church, Tarski, to name only a few. You speak as though these men had never written, and as though you had nothing to learn from them. And you pay no attention to more recent work in which the theory of intensions is put on a more secure logical footing. These great authors do now after all belong to history and their ideas are of contemporary interest only in so far as they can be reformulated so as to meet present standards of rigor, to be of relevance to contemporary structural and transformational linguistics, to be of use in handling problems in the philosophy of science, including the social and humane sciences, and the like. Of course, I would wish to add here aesthetics and systematic theology, but not many of my logical *confreres* would go along with me in this.

F. What Professor Findlay has in mind is the sort of thing Aristotle did when "he followed his purely formal *Prior Analytics* by the *Posterior Analytics*, which emphasized that the scientific, as opposed to the dialectical syllogism, must always employ genuine universals as middle terms, universals which *Nous* has picked out, and which are the explanatory essences of the matters on hand."

M. I have this sort of thing in mind also. Let us word it in more contemporary terms. The narrow formal logic of quantification theory with non-logical constants is to be supplemented with the calculus of individuals, with an event logic, with logical syntax, semantics, and systematic pragmatics. And of course notions of probability must be brought in also, the various ones clearly distinguished from one another and then suitably interrelated. Here as elsewhere *Distinguer pour mieux unir* is the guiding principle. Incidentally, it is very important also to provide for probability sentences in intensioned contexts. This is a problem most theories of probability have almost completely neglected.[6]

F. Well, suppose we were to grant you that there have been gains in the theory of intensions of which Findlay has not taken account sufficiently. Still, "one [p. 219] . . . cannot hope to get far in philosophy, or in the humane or social sciences, without making intentions (spelled with a *t*) one's prime objective of reference, and so recognizing as illuminating and informative, and not merely 'opaque', occurrences to which the true-false antithesis is irrelevant, and which, in such occurrences need not have the logical relation[s] that they otherwise would have. For it is unfortunately often as possible to believe in the false as the true, and to see logical connections which are not present, while failing to see connections which in independent contexts would be there. The formalist, like the moral rigorist, hates the probabilism of intentional discourse, for while intentionality involves intelligence, and intelligence will open our eyes to logical connections, it is also a matter of degree, and its exercise therefore a matter of probability. The extensionalist and the rigorist accordingly seek to excise from philosophy and the humane sciences most of what is worth discussing in them."

M. Are you not forgetting here that intentions (with a 't') are a special kind of intension (with an 's') and thus that the logical techniques capable of handling the latter can handle the former also? Much of the motivation for seeking a logic of intensions has been to be able to handle "opaque" contexts of sentences concerning believing, knowing, surmising, enjoying, and the like. There is no doubt but that there are now ways of handling such sentences that are adequate for making the distinctions you are asking for here, in particular to distinguish between the truth and falsity of what is believed, known, or whatever, and distinguishing all these from the truth or falsity of the full sentences stating that belief, knowing, or whatever, i.e., stating that so and so believes, knows, or whatever, such and such. A theory that could not do this would surely not be acceptable. And all such sentences, including those believed, known, and so on, can be "illuminating or informative" quite irrespective of their truth or falsity. What a person does not believe, for example, may be quite as illuminative of his character as what he does. It seems to me that you are quite wrong, however, if you say that the formalist "hates the probabilism of intentional discourse." On the contrary, it is just he who has contributed most to our understanding of the workings of probabilism, which can then be applied to intentional discourse quite as much as to any other. Sentences believed can be themselves probabilistic, as well as the full sentences stating the believing. Of course there are immense difficulties here in being sure of just what notion or notions of probability we are using, of which are the most suitable, of how they are interrelated, and so on. Surely you cannot really think that such eminent writers as vonMises, Reichenbach, Lord Keynes, Sir Harold Jeffries, Carnap, and deFinetti have "excised from philosophy and the humane sciences most of what is worth discussing in them." It is rather that their contributions are paving the way for the techniques by which such matters may be more reliably discussed than heretofore. Again, I am not saying that there are not difficulties here, but rather that there has been real progress you seem to refuse to admit.

F. But you are neglecting the really important things. "There are [p. 283] other interests than the desire to . . . accord with the exclusions demanded by logic. There is above all the interest in achieving a certain luminous perspicuity and simplicity of vision, and an overriding of the randomly diverse and independent, which is also the inspiration of science. Einstein would never have got far if he had rejected the thesis of the unsurpassable, yet finite velocity of light, or the conception of a universe finite yet unbounded. In the same way an idealism like Berkeley's, Fichte's or Husserl's, courageously rejects the intuitive thesis of the independence of physical objects from the subject who perceives them or otherwise intends them, and makes them all no more than a very special sort of intentional object, with their own unique manner of constitution."

M. I see no reason why the exclusions demanded by logic--sloppy formulation and invalid reasoning--rule out "luminous perspicuity" and "simplicity of vision" in either science or philosophy. On the contrary they are quite essential to both. As concerns Berkeley's idealism, you will perhaps recall my little paper of some years back, "On the Berkeley-Russell Theory of Proper Names," which tried to provide a suitable logical basis for it.[7] Just recently an eminent Berkeley scholar said to me that this paper had helped him very much over the years. I was glad to be told this, never having been quite sure whether that paper had really hit its mark or not as regards Berkeley. Russell too, you know, strove valiantly with this problem, and it has always seemed to me that Findlay has not paid enough attention to the relevant chapters in *An Inquiry into Meaning and Truth*. English philosophers of his generation have tended, I think, to condemn Russell for his more popular writings, and have failed to give him credit for his real achievements. The best of Bertie, don't forget, is very good indeed.

F. But Findlay has in mind something more, "of framing concepts that . . . [he calls] 'iridescent', in that they involve a systematic shift through several antilogistic positions, conceiving things in terms of the shift rather than the single vision. . . . An iridescent concept is . . . one that manages genuinely to reconcile different members of an antilogism, so that one manages to understand how, in their mutual tension, they are nonetheless complementary 'sides' of the same situation. It is here all-important that we should distinguish a spurious iridescence in which no genuine concept emerges . . . to the case where the philosopher, by a judicious use of language, really pushes us over the borderline, so that we are really able to see how positions we took to be irreconcilable, really fit in with one another. Such an insight of course modifies the positions in question, since there can be no greater modification than one which changes irreconcilables into reconcilables, but such a modification in a sense also preserves what it modifies, since its sense depends on the original exclusion which it in turn transcends. The concept of iridescence is, in short, itself a case of iridescence, since it preserves in its sense the exclusiveness that it also excludes."

M. Well, the whole point of the reconciliation is, I suppose, that what is at first contradiction is so modified as no longer to be one. A "spurious" iridescence is one for which such reconciliation cannot be given. I like the phrase 'by a judicious use of language', which is no doubt supposed to include the elimination of ambiguity, of any apparent contradiction, and so on. Perhaps too, as Findlay suggests, the notion of iridescence is itself iridescent, although probably one has to move into a metalanguage to say this, so that we need also a notion of *metairidescence*. It is also interesting that only *concepts* are iridescent, not things, according to this account. This raises of course the very different problem as to how concepts are to be handled in any exact way, once we get beyond the level of common talk and vague historical jargon.[8]

F. Findlay's plea is "for the re-introduction of a logic of aspects." Iridescent concepts contain many aspects. Consider an example from Aristotle. "There are few expressions more frequently used by Aristotle than the adverbial form n, Latin *qua*, English 'as', or 'in so far as'. Thus a line can be considered *as* the boundary of one region and also of another, and while *as* bounding one region it may be concave, *as* bounding the other it will be convex. The convex and the concave are not only different but opposed aspects, and yet we understand perfectly how they complete one another, and are in fact the same line differently regarded. In the same way a thing may be one thing *qua* constituent stuff and another *qua* organized unity, and again we see just how these aspects fit together and complete one another. . . . Again Aristotle readily conceives that a given motion or state may be at once an action for *A* and an undergoing for *B*." There are many other examples of similar kind. "Aristotle in these teachings is not merely conflating disparate functions without showing how they can belong together: he is challenging us, not always with perfect success, to grasp their necessary mutual completion in the same way in which the simpler geometrical structures are to be found in the more complex ones."

M. I am glad you explicitly bring up the word 'qua', the logic of which has only quite recently, I think, been formulated. Frege seems to have been the first to have sensed what this is, in essentials anyhow, in his notion of the *Art des Gegebenseins*.[9] One and the same entity may be taken under different *Arten des Gegebenseins*, the totality of which perhaps may be regarded as the *Sinn* or sense of the name of that entity.[10] Of course it is difficult to be sure of precisely how Frege here should be interpreted, but this comment is not an unreasonable way of construing the *Sinne*. It seems to me that what you want as a "logic of aspects" can be fully handled in terms of the *Art des Gegebenseins*. To carry this out in detail, of course, we must go way beyond Frege and bring in all manner of delicate logical matters that have been clarified since his day.

F. Well, if that is the case, all to the good.

M. Of course there are many technical refinements to be made in all that I have said, but we need not go into them here. Let us stick only to the essentials. Bearing all that we have been saying in mind, I would like now to ask you about some of the things Findlay said at Jerusalem in criticizing my paper. He began, you will recall, by expressing due respect for the achievements of modern logic, and he said right at the start that he thought that some of the historically great metaphysical views do permit of a logical reconstruction in modern terms. He mentioned Proclus, St. Thomas, and Christian Wolff as typical philosophers whose views he thought could very likely be given such a reconstruction. He failed to point out, however, that this has never been done. Not even the first steps have been taken in reconstructing these views in any adequate fashion--except for Father Salamucha's pioneering work on the *ex motu* argument in St. Thomas mentioned in my paper. He doubted, however, whether this kind of thing is worth doing. But if not, then I have difficulty in seeing how his respect for logic is any more than lip-service. It is quite clear from his comments in Jerusalem that he was not taking into account the material I have drawn attention to above. He did not mention, incidentally, Salamucha's work, which is generally regarded as a landmark in the history of this sort of thing.

F. He does not object if you want to play silly games with symbols, but you can never express more in them than you can express in our ordinary language. This is one of the things he said, you will recall.

M. Yes, I recall very vividly his saying this, and it seems to me a pity that he did. I agree with Findlay, in having the highest respect for our ordinary language. My respect here is probably even greater than his, for I have been making a real effort recently in studying logical forms for various kinds of ordinary sentences and the transformations taking us from the forms to the sentences and back again.[11] No one can do very much of this sort of work without realizing how incredibly complicated our natural language is, and how within it in a few short words we can, almost miraculously, be able to say so much. The further we look into the complex structure of language, the greater our respect for it. The business of the logical analysis of language, as I see it, is not to compete with it, to "regiment" it, or anything of the kind, but to analyze it and to attempt to formulate the rules governing sentence construction in terms of certain basic linguistic particles. Of course it should do a good deal more also, but at least this much. The work here is not dissimilar to that of any scientist confronted with the complex data he wishes to study. The important thing in the logic of a language is not what we express, but *how* we express it. Perhaps every sentence in a natural language can be "represented", in a logical form--many linguists think this and carry out their professional work in accord with it. They study the sentences of a natural language by means of their forms, and the sentences then *mean* whatever their forms do. The point of seeking the forms is not to express *more* than can be done in ordinary language, but to be able to say it better, in a logically responsible way, to say it unambiguously, to say it in the light of the whole, incredibly complex structure that the whole of language exhibits. And so on. Findlay's comment seems to me based on a total lack of interest in, and respect for, all the progress that has been made in structural and transformational linguistics during the past century or so.

F. Perhaps he does not care about all this new "smart aleck" pseudoscience. In any case, he did call it that at Jerusalem, you will remember. His disparagement of logic is concerned primarily with its use in philosophy.

M. Yes. But, as it goes in the theory of logical form for sentences of a natural language, so it goes with the sentences of a metaphysical system. The attempt to subject the system to a logical reformulation helps us tremendously to come to understand better what that system really is, and what is said within it. There is an enormous literature on this subject. You will recall the splendid things Frege has to say about it, and Russell of course, and Whitehead, and Woodger the biologist, and Nelson Goodman, to mention only a few. It seems to me that Findlay has failed to understand the important role logical reconstruction must play in metaphysics, taken either historically or systematically. I for one welcome the increased minding of one's *p's* and *q's* in the detailed study of specific texts from Plato, for example, on the part of younger scholars. There is no doubt but that the future will see a great deal more of this in the study of all the historically great philosophers.

F. Even if one were to succeed to some extent with some philosophers, Findlay said, you remember, there are others for whom it cannot be done. He was thinking especially of Plotinus and Hegel.

M. Yes, I recall that he objected violently to my suggestions concerning Plotinus. He especially objected to the principle, **Pr6** in my paper, that

$$\vdash (x)(\sim x = \text{One} \supset \text{One Emx}),$$

that the One emanates into everything other than itself. He objected that the principle is no "clearer" than the ordinary English statement. He called it in fact 'meaningless gibberish', but I do him the courtesy of not thinking that he meant this to be taken very seriously. The statement is no more gibberish than the natural-language original. Making the statement in this exact logical way helps us to understand the vocabulary of the reconstructed Plotinic language as a whole, to see how sentences are formed out of that vocabulary, to understand the definitions of the theory, and the basic principles of it. He seemed to think that the sole merit claimed for my statement of this principle is that it is "clearer" than its original. Well, it is surely as clear anyhow. But everything done with symbols can be done more cumbrously without them, so there is not much point in complaining about the use of symbols. The important role of this formula, aɴd of the others, is to make explicit and concise the salient fundamental principles of the system. His objections to **Pr6** are akin to those who object to the famous formula *110.643 in *Principia Mathematica*. Why go through all this rigamorole of symbolization, they ask, merely to prove what we already know, that $1 + 1 = 2$? Clearly such an objection is beside the point and rests upon a misunderstanding of the aims of the whole enterprise.

F. But you brought in mathematical set-theory. For this Findlay has no use whatsoever; he thinks it a lowly subject, almost beneath contempt. Also it is quite foreign to Plotinus, who emphasizes the *instantiability* of the intelligible, and this has nothing to do with your new-fangled sets.

M. Yes, I recall that he expressed contempt for set theory. Again, I am not sure how seriously he intended this. Much of the history of mathematics of the last 150 years is intimately concerned with sets and their interrelations. Unless one can provide a viable alternative, if one excises sets from mathematics he will not have much left. Now of course it is true that sets in the modern sense play no role in Plotinus. But many regard them as the modern prototype of the intelligibles, the *eide*. This view was well said some years ago by Paul Bernays, you will remember. Please recall that part of the aim of my paper was to bring Plotinus up to date and to try to show that his great vision is in harmony with modern mathematics and science. The use of set theory is not the only way to do this, of course; I chose it because it is the most widely accepted way of providing foundations for mathematics and the one *prima facie* closest to Plotinus. And of course I was not concerned literally with just Plotinus, but rather with Plotinus in modern garb. All of its historically great metaphysical views should, in my opinion, at some point be viewed systematically in the light of modern knowledge, as well of course as viewed historically in terms of their own time. Now as to instantiability. My reading of Plotinus is that the world of objects, of nature, is really a part of the cosmos, and hence that for him objects do really exist, albeit in a kind of inferior way. If I mistake not, this is the view of Hilary Armstrong and of John Anton, two of our finest Plotinus scholars. Thus we can say that object x is an instance of *eidos y*, both objects and *eide* being values for variables. If Findlay wishes to allow only *eide* and to regard objects as *eide* "thisified, thatified, or thotified," as he puts it, he has quite a job on his hands to formulate just what he means. Thisification presumably involves a kind of ostention, or a notion somewhat akin perhaps to *haecceity*. I do not believe that he has anywhere formulated the logic needed to govern such notions in the necessary detail and in accord with present-day standards of rigor.

F. Perhaps not, I recall also that he thought that what you said about Em, the converse of the relation Em of emanation, was preposterous. You claim that by means of it we can handle the notion of the "return to the One," of the aspiration of the *Eide* and of the *Psyche* to return to the purity of the One. A great deal more is involved in the theory of the return than can be gotten out of this very narrow relation.

M. But please recall accurately what I said, that the "Plotinic theology is implicit in the theory concerning Em and Em as regards the One." Of course additional *meaning postulates* in Carnap's sense must be added concerning Em not provable from the postulates concerning Em. Also further primitive notions may be needed with postulates interrelating their designata with Em. In all this, however, Em is clearly the fundamental notion.

F. But your handling of Plotinus leaves out completely the "dialectical" character of his thought, Findlay said, the tentative, visionary groping after fundamental truth, even if it should lead to contradiction. This you will never be able to supply within your exclusivist, formalist, extensionalist framework.

M. I am glad you mention this, for that is one very important point we neglected a few moments back in speaking of iridescent concepts. Everything said about them is now relevant to our discussion of Plotinus. Findlay insists that we distinguish between cases of "spurious" iridescence and real iridescence, cases of the latter enabling us "to see how positions we took to be irreconcilable really fit in with one another." Now surely most of the iridescent concepts he finds in Plotinus are real and not spurious. But here is something we neglected above. Perhaps we should say that cases of spurious iridescence belong to what

Reichenbach, you recall, dubbed 'the context of discovery', whereas cases of real iridescence belong to the context of justification or of assertion. Contradictory aspects are useful for discovery, for the dialectical or visionary entertaining of one possible hypothesis after another, some of them perhaps contradictory. But in the final reconciliation, these various aspects are harmonized satisfactorily within an all-embracing vision formulated in terms exclusively of mutually consistent *Arten des Gegebenseins.*

F. Well, even if you were to succeed to some extent, there is Hegel, whom your methods cannot possibly touch. You made some ridiculous comments about Hegel, in your talk about manifestation and embodiment, Findlay thought.

M. Please recall that I made no claims about Hegel whatsoever in my Jerusalem paper. I merely took the liberty of borrowing two of his terms in attempting to bridge the seeming gap between absolute monistic idealism and our modern scientific knowledge. However, I am challenged by this point about Hegel. Others have told me essentially the same thing, in particular Errol Harris. It is a matter I would like to inquire into. I cannot, in my heart of hearts, think that Hegel cannot be approached *logistice*, to use Wilfrid Sellar's word, in some appropriate fashion. No doubt to do so will be difficult, but I for one would like to see what could be done here. So far as I am aware, no competent logician has attempted the task, so it seems to me a bit premature to say that it cannot possibly succeed. In any case, Findlay has no respectable *proof* that it can't. We should never contend *a priori* in advance that something ing cannot be done. This is to block the road of inquiry, one of the worst methodological sins, according to Peirce.

F. In spite of what you say, Findlay deplores the superficiality of most of what logicians do. In his paper on "Time and Eternity," presented at the Jerusalem conference, you will remember, he had deplored "the objections of logicians [p. 10] to changing truth-values, or to an unsettled alternativity which . . . would violate the Law of Excluded Middle." In fact, logicians have refused "to take time seriously," and "though in some ways deeply contemptible," this does "bear witness to an obscure understanding and taste for the Eternal." All your logic is of no help in trying to do what he was trying to do in that paper. He is (pp. 8-9) "in quest of . . . something that can in some manner be superimposed upon temporal matters, that can be predicated in some higher-order fashion of the very time-modalities of their doing and undergoing. It must in some sense be an eternal matter of fact that Buddha is *possibly about* [italics added] to receive enlightenment or Christ to die upon the Cross; it must also be in some sense an eternal matter of fact or truth that Buddha *is* receiving enlightenment or that Christ *is* dying on the Cross . . . and it must in some sense be an eternal matter of fact that such an enlightenment or such a passing occurred many, many centuries ago. It is clear that we are in some manner able to give sense to a being-the-case which does not side-step or ignore, but brackets without altering the facts of development in time, that we can in some sense conceive even temporal matters under a certain species of Eternity, as Spinoza first taught us to do and say. How can we explain this understanding of even a higher-order modality which can be superimposed upon, without destroying, the ordinary time-modalities, but which also utterly transcends any form of direct ostension or illustration"?

M. I find these comments, and in fact Findlay's whole paper, fascinating, but he is really playing right into my hands unwittingly. His talk of Eternity fits in beautifully with the logician's tense of timelessness, of which Frege and Peirce were perhaps the first to call attention to. But they did not connect this "time" with Eternity in the almost theological sense in which Findlay speaks of it. Please let me comment on his points one by one. I think it quite wrong to say that logicians do not take time seriously. Peirce and Frege were perhaps the first explicitly to introduce variables for times and to quantify over them. They both did this by assuming first that sentences can be formed tenselessly. The tense of timelessness is prior to the introduction of specific deictic expressions for the handling of the ordinary tenses. And to this of course a good deal of additional material concerning actions, their completion, and so on, must be added to handle the aspectual character of verbs. Once all this is done, there is no difficulty about the law of excluded middle, at least in the form

$$`(x)(t)Fxt \vee \sim Fxt)`,$$

that for all x and all time t, either Fxt or not. What Findlay is in quest of seems to me precisely what logicians are eager to provide him with. In the tense of timelessness, the very tense of the law just stated, properties can be predicated of individuals at different stages of their careers. And if the resources of event logic are available, predication may be made of what they *do* and *undergo*, and of the times or events of these doings and undergoings. In the tense of timelessness, it may be said that Buddha at a certain time is possibly about to receive enlightenment, that at a slightly later time he is receiving enlightenment, and that time is now several centuries back. In no way do any of these statements side-step or ignore the facts of development. All this is logical commonplace if suitable expressions for times or events are introduced and characterized by appropriate meaning postulates. It remains of course to connect this with Eternity, with the vision of the cosmos *sub specie aeternitatis*. I think I have done this, to some extent anyhow, in my paper and in the previous papers therein referred to. Starting with Whitehead's primordial valuations, you will recall, stated of course tenselessly but embracing all time and becoming in their scope, I worked back to the great discussion of God's nature in St. Thomas. And lo and behold, much of that takes on a new clarity --and magnificence, be it said--if viewed in somewhat Whiteheadian terms. Of course one must go way beyond Whitehead to do this. One must distinguish various kinds of "valuations," and one particular way of doing this leads one directly to St. Thomas' "five signs of will." (I have not mentioned Boethius, nor does Findlay, but we should not neglect him in this context.) In a similar vein all discourse about Eternity in the literature of Absolute Idealism can, I think, be handled, stripped of course of purely literary embellishments. The purely literary is something we must all seek to avoid in philosophy, as Whitehead used to emphasize. To be able to write too well is a kind of philosophical curse: one tends to let pretty words and phrases take the place of depth of thought. Too much musical talent is a kind of curse too, for the performer, ease of achievement taking the place of depth of mastery of the several styles.

F. Perhaps your philosophical views are closer to mine than I had thought. The "metaphysical age into which we seem to be moving," Findlay has said, will be more ecumenical than that of "the bright, brittle, fragmented thinking of the age which is passing."[12] He believes that there are "several modes of thought-approach" and that three of these anyhow "represent essential sides of philosophy, which we must try to practice conjointly." These are what he calls "the austerely analytical, the speculatively systematic, and the iridescent or dialectical." If what you have said is viable, then of course logic, in the broad sense in which you speak of it, has much to contribute to all three approaches.

M. Yes, I think so. But allow me to strengthen Findlay's pleas somewhat. I would urge that we should practice these three approaches not just conjointly but *cooperatively.* It is a pity we all work in so fragmented a fashion when there is so much we can learn from one another. I think it a pity also that Findlay has used his high eminence to vituperate against logic, rather than to have called attention to its value. If he had done this latter, philosophers would perhaps have been more encourraged to undergo the hard labor of mastering logic and of keeping up with newer developments of relevance, so that we could all get ahead more readily with the job to be done. And whatever one individual's views may be, let me recall Whitehead's prophesy--one of my favorite quotes--made many years back. "We must return to my first love, Symbolic Logic," he said. "When in the distant future the subject has expanded, so as to examine patterns depending on connections other than those of space, quantity, and number--when this expansion has occurred, I suggest that Symbolic Logic, the symbolic examination of pattern with the use of [bound] variables, will become the foundation of aesthetics. From that stage it will proceed to conquer ethics and theology."[13]

F. What an extraordinary statement. I have no doubt but that Whitehead is a great philosopher, so I suppose we should take this statement seriously.

M. Yes, I think we should, and Findlay should too. There is much we can learn from so seminal and original a mind as Whitehead's. Findlay has some very interesting metaphysical views of his own, you know, and they are much too important to be allowed to languish about in merely metaphysical terms. They should be formulated in accord with contemporary technical standards, it seems to me. Well, do not let me detain you any longer. It has been a pleasure talking with you, and I hope we shall be able to chat again on another occasion, more deeply and more cooperatively.

F. I, too. Good day.

NOTES

*This dialogue was written by Richard Martin after an intensive interchange with John Findlay on these topics at the ISM Conference on: "The Person and God," held in Jerusalem. The dialogue appeared as Chapter VIII in R.M. Martin, *Primordiality, Science, and Value* (Albany: State University of New York Press, 1980).

1. "On Some Theological Languages," which was presented at the meeting of the International Society for Metaphysics in Jerusalem, Aug. 18-22, 1977; see above.

2. J.N. Findlay, "Ordinary, Revisionary, and Dialectical Strategies in Philosophy."

3. See, for example, the works of von Newmann, Bernays, and Godel, to mention only a few.

4. "A Homogeneous System for Formal Logic."

5. See especially *Events, Reference, and Logical Form* and *Semiotics and Linguistic Structure*.

6. See especially "On the Language Causal Talk: Scriven and Suppes," in *Pragmatics, Truth, and Language.*

7. *Philosophy and Phenomenological Research*, 13 (1952), 221-231.

8. Cf. *Events, Reference, and Logical Form*, pp. 15 ff.

9. See especially "On Sense and Reference," second paragraph, and n. 8 of the *Begriffsschrift*, or *loc. cit.*

10. See "A Reading of Frege on Sense and Designation," in *Pragmatics, Truth, and Language.*

11. See "Some Protolinguistic Transformations," in *Pragmatics, Truth, and Language.*

12. "Ordinary, Revisionary, and Dialectical Strategies . . . " p. 275.

13. In *Essays in Science and Philosophy* (London: Rider, 1948), p. 99.

INDEX